# Cyberformalism

# Cyberformalism

## Histories of Linguistic Forms in the Digital Archive

Daniel Shore

JOHNS HOPKINS UNIVERSITY PRESS   BALTIMORE

Johns Hopkins University Press

2715 North Charles Street

Baltimore, Maryland 21218-4363

www.press.jhu.edu

*Library of Congress Cataloging-in-Publication Data*

Names: Shore, Daniel, 1980– author.

Title: Cyberformalism : histories of linguistic forms in the digital
    archive / Daniel Shore

Description: Baltimore, Maryland : Johns Hopkins University Press, 2018. |
    Includes bibliographical references and index.

Identifiers: LCCN 2017039610 | ISBN 9781421425504 (hardcover : alk. paper) |
    ISBN 1421425505 (hardcover : alk. paper) | ISBN 9781421425511 (electronic) |
    ISBN 1421425513 (electronic)

Subjects: LCSH: Grammar, Comparative and general—Syntax—Data processing. |
    Semantics (Philosophy)—Data processing. | Historical linguistics.

Classification: LCC P291 .S466 2018 | DDC 415.0285—dc23

    LC record available at https://lccn.loc.gov/2017039610

A catalog record for this book is available from the British Library.

*Special discounts are available for bulk purchases of this book. For more information, please
contact Special Sales at 410-516-6936 or specialsales@press.jhu.edu.*

Johns Hopkins University Press uses environmentally friendly book materials,
including recycled text paper that is composed of at least 30 percent post-consumer
waste, whenever possible.

We fill pre-existing forms and when we fill them we change them and are changed.

Frank Bidart, "Borges and I"

# Contents

# Preface

## *Fighting Words*

Scholars of the humanities love words. We work in, on, and with the written word; practice what Friedrich Nietzsche termed "connoisseurship of the *word*"; are wordsmiths or wish to be; labor over documents composed, as Hamlet archly puts it, of "words, words, words"; debate the meaning of what the New Critics called "the words on the page"; and study worlds made of words, accessing things, *res*, insofar as they are captured in and constituted by words, *verba*.[1] The expression of this love has often proceeded under the name of *philology*, from the Greek *philo + logos* (love of words).[2] The humanities have periodically sought to return to the well-spring of philology to revitalize their methods of inquiry and replenish their disciplinary authority, especially in an era increasingly indifferent or overtly hostile to humanistic inquiry.[3] The philologist, or lover of words, studies not only the meaning of a word but also its origins and development, the history of its use, its predecessors and successors, and its relations both to concepts and to other words. In the stories told by philologically inclined humanists, words take the part of protagonists. "A word may become a sort of solid entity," writes William Empson, "thought of as like a person."[4] Philology seeks to recover the vitality and intricacy of words that have been dulled with overuse or scuppered by disuse. If, as Emerson writes, "language is fossil poetry" and the "etymologist finds the deadest word to have been once a brilliant picture," then philologists are the paleontologists of language, unearthing and reconstructing what Honoré de Balzac called "the life and adventures of a word."[5]

Though *philología* is old—the noun first appears in Plato, and Eratosthenes of Cyrene seems to have been the first to assume the title of philologist, in the third century BCE[6]—its advanced age has not dulled its ardor for words. Scholars continue to write not only entries in glossaries and encyclopedias but books and essays under banners like "historical semantics," "cultural semantics," and "critical semantics."[7] Unlike lexicographers, who study words in order to compile general or specialized dictionaries, humanists of all stripes bestow love disproportionately on "loaded words,"

"words that count," and "words that matter."[8] They unpack "the structure of complex words" and debate the meaning of "keywords" and "keywords in our time," words that promise, under analysis, to unlock a culture's most closely held secrets.[9] They study the way we interpret and fashion our identities in the terms provided by "inherited vocabularies."[10] Unsurprisingly, the "vocabulary of psychoanalysis" receives more philological care than that of pop psychology, "Shakespeare's words" more than Shackerly Marmion's, "Milton's words" more than William Davenant's.[11] Scholars spin narratives of cultural conflict and change out of a precious few words ("five words," say)[12] and sometimes devote entire books to the history and analysis of a single, pivotal word.[13] Samuel Johnson's self-deprecating definition of the lexicographer, the student of words, as a "harmless drudge" aside, they know that words are key to understanding our collective life.[14] The impact and value of a scholar's work is partly a function of his or her ability to select the words and corresponding concepts that, when rescued from neglect, reveal themselves as vital to our deepest concerns.[15] Not all research in the humanities so obviously orbits words, but rare indeed is the book or article that does not engage in etymology, *Begriffsgeschichte* (the history of concepts), the history of ideas, or some kind of informal historical word study.[16] What T. S. Eliot said of the Anglican preacher Lancelot Andrews is still true as well of the finest humanities scholarship: it "takes a word and derives a world from it."[17]

As a scholar trained in the study of early modern literature and the humanist rhetorical tradition, I too am a lover of words. I love their fossil poetry, their curious and contingent careers, their startling metamorphoses. I love that the word *academia* emerges from an olive grove and that the word *tragedy* rides in on a goat.[18] Like the poet and scholar Sarah Howe, I delight in knowing "the spiraling path from Γένεσις to genetics" and in sharing this knowledge with students and sometimes (to their occasional annoyance) friends.[19] Words can be beautiful and powerful: beautiful in their shape on the page, feel on the tongue, and sound when spoken; powerful in their ability to bear witness, name or conceal truths, and carve up the world. To meet a beautiful and powerful word is to want to know its past, its family, where it has traveled, and what it has suffered.

Yet humanist philology's long romance with words has grown too comfortable, too stiflingly monogamous. Philology needs to have a deliberate falling out with words—a conscious uncoupling or trial separation—so

that it can engage in a period of linguistic promiscuity. Rather than needing a "return" to philology of the kind proposed by Paul de Man or Edward
Said, we need to send philology in search of other paramours, other signs
on which to lavish its affections. Humanists have for too long worked with
a conception of the linguistic sign unnecessarily limited solely to words
and, less frequently, fixed sequences of words. There is more to the history
of language than is dreamt of in our etymologies. Linguistic creativity is
not the selection and combination of individual words into a sequence. Semantics does not live by words alone. In addition to regarding words as
what Roland Greene calls "semantic integers,"[20] as the basic building blocks
of expression and meaning, humanities scholars need to practice the trick
(second nature to linguists and logicians) of seeing words as temporary
and replaceable values of abstract variables.[21] A more promiscuous philology will need to learn to look not only at words but through them, with a
deliberate indifference, to the categories they occupy.

Changing how we regard words is the first step in bringing into view
the *linguistic forms*—the variously abstract, complex, and idiomatic sign
units, composed at least in part of lexically unfilled categories (or blanks,
slots, or variables)—that are the topic of this book. Consider, as a preliminary example, the sentence in the previous paragraph "Semantics does not
live by words alone," which instantiates a form, *[noun] does not live by
[noun] alone*, abstracted from a well-known biblical passage, "Man does not
live by bread alone."[22] We have a great deal to learn from even apparently trivial forms of this kind. My argument about linguistic forms is
threefold:

First, these forms have consequential social, intellectual, and literary
histories that are irreducible to the histories of individual words or concepts. For this reason, they deserve attention from a wide array of humanities scholars as well as from linguists. Linguistic forms form us, shaping
not only our utterances but also the way we live together, make choices,
understand the world, and style ourselves, and they do this all the more
profoundly because they have only seldom risen to the level of explicit attention, analysis, or criticism. They do conceptual work without naming
concepts. They encode and enact our most fundamental assumptions on a
level less visible, because more abstract, than the words that fill them and
thereby partially conceal them from view. We speak of choosing our words
carefully, and if a particular word offends us, we can sometimes cut it off,

excising it from our vocabulary. Yet the most pervasive and general linguistic forms are unavoidable, nonoptional, if we wish to say anything at all. They are engines of thought, vehicles of cultural memory, knots of conceptual relations, nooses of ideology. They perform fundamental social and cognitive work. No less than words or sequences of words, they are part of what the poet and critic Donald Davie called "the eventfulness of language," constitutive of the manifold pleasures of poetry and prose.[23] They serve shifting personal, practical, intellectual, aesthetic, reformist, and subversive aims. The career of a linguistic form, like that of a keyword, has much to teach us about who we are and, if I may put it this way, how we got ourselves into this mess. The import of linguistic forms is captured superbly by the lines of the Frank Bidart poem "Borges and I" that serve as this book's epigraph: "We fill pre-existing forms and when we fill them we change them and are changed."[24]

Second, it is only now becoming feasible to recover and retell the long, rich, and consequential histories of linguistic forms, thanks to the development of massive, digital, searchable full-text archives and advanced search engines capable of matching abstract patterns as well as the keywords and fixed phrases indexed by print finding tools. The *cyber-* of my title, a prefix that will doubtless strike some as outmoded or even archaic, is from the Greek *kubernetes* (pilot, steersman). It was first used to denote self-governing feedback systems and later came to refer broadly to the technological extension and modification of human capacities.[25] Cyberformalism is a prosthetic formalism, what Donna Haraway calls a "cyborg semiology."[26] By formulating searches of varying complexity, the cyberformalist pilots digital search engines through thousands or millions of texts to retrieve tens, hundreds, or thousands of matching utterances. This is not a matter of replacing John Henry with the steam shovel, but of conducting inquiries for which pick and shovel are ill suited. It is the *cyber-* that allows this book's *formalism* to operate as a fully historicist mode of inquiry. Shrewd use of existing digital search capacities can expand the range of linguistic forms susceptible to inquiry, and the development of new search capacities has the potential to expand that range further still. I would not have been able to write this book using the archives and search tools available ten years ago. My hope is that its methods will seem rudimentary (or, preferably, fundamental) ten years from now.

Third, the significance of an utterance's linguistic form is not intrinsic, evident in itself, its correlation to content, or its homology to social structures or cultural processes, but is instead conventional and diacritical, emerging only in its differential relation to other forms. When Franco Moretti writes that "theories of form are usually blind to history, and historical work blind to form," he is speaking primarily of generic form, yet this double, oscillating blindness is all the more thorough at the level of the sentence or phrase.[27] Just as one cannot plausibly claim to understand novelistic form on the basis of having read a single Jane Austen novel, so too is it misguided to seek to grasp the significance of an utterance's form in isolation. In his essay "The Return to Philology," Paul de Man writes that literary analysis begins with "the bafflement that . . . singular turns of tone, phrase, and figure produce."[28] Yet the appropriately baffled philologist cannot simply intuit the "singularity" of an utterance but must ascertain it through comparison. Linguistic creativity and innovation are, as "romantic" theorists of language from K. W. F. Schlegel to Noam Chomsky have quite rightly claimed, ordinary and everyday occurrences.[29] Language users regularly speak and write sentences never witnessed in the history of the world. Yet there is no wholly singular or originary utterance, no utterance that does not participate in or alter received forms, since every utterance is also a repetition and transformation of other, previous utterances and must be studied and understood as such. An extreme version of contextualism holds that, as the linguist James R. Hurford formulates it, "full understanding of a sentence, to the extent that this is ever attainable, requires knowledge of the whole corpus of prior texts which this sentence echoes or transforms."[30] While searchable digital archives, for reasons I explore, can never deliver us this idealized "full understanding," they can help us to discern the conventions governing a form by allowing us to situate it in the system of differences from which it gains its meaning. We understand the linguistic form of an utterance when we

1. grasp its symbolic character, construing its meaning and use (interpretation);
2. create new utterances that share the same form (production);
3. describe its parts, their relation to the whole, and the signifying relation of parts and whole to discursive function (analysis);

4. model the language faculty, or grammar, by which it was generated (reconstruction); and

5. recover its past and situate it in the wider context of its use (history).

Each type of understanding can apparently exist prior to and independently of subsequent types; that is, we can comprehend the form of an utterance without being able to reproduce it in new utterances, reproduce it without being able to analyze it, analyze it without being able to reconstruct the capacity that generated it, and perform all of these operations without historical awareness of how past speakers and writers used it. Yet historical awareness is not merely an inessential surface layer sitting atop deeper, independent foundations. I aim to show that recovering the history of a linguistic form has the potential to revise our understanding of its meaning and use, our criteria for how to produce new utterances with the same form, our analysis of the form's part-whole relations and their functions, and even our reconstruction of the capacity by which particular utterances were generated.

Though I want readers to accept these claims, this book is concerned with more than winning assent for a set of propositions. As a work of methodology, it aims as well to have an effect on the practice of fellow humanities scholars, persuading them that they too should abstract from individual words and the concepts they signify to study the social, cultural, and intellectual histories of linguistic forms; employ and improve on the methods of discovery, interpretation, and explanation that are tested in the case studies that follow; and take up existing digital search tools and build new ones in the service of an increasingly promiscuous philology.

A humanities that adopts the methods and aims of this book will look somewhat different from the humanities that we have now. In addition to our already extensive etymologies of words, it will produce myriad histories of forms, collectively establishing a body of facts of the kind "In the early part of the seventeenth century, English preachers began to speak about imitating Christ in the conditional rather than the indicative mood, enjoining their listeners to do what Jesus *would do* rather than what he did," or "Blaise Pascal reworked the classical counsel to *act as if* into a technology for producing belief in God," or "*Paradise Lost* made depictive adjectives into a marker of the English grand style," or "Humanist grammar schools diffused *Was it for this* and the sentences it initiated across two and a half centuries of English literature." We will first make and then speak about these facts in much the same way we once made and now speak about other facts of literary, linguistic, cultural, and intellectual history. Like the first attestations of the lexicographers, facts about the history of linguistic forms will be subject to contestation and revision. Like other kinds of cultural and historical facts, they will prove significant only when situated in broader explanatory narratives. Scholars will offer conflicting descriptions of the provenance, diffusion, and cultural consequences of linguistic forms and debate the relative merits of these accounts. In addition to decoding the form of an utterance as meaning (interpretation), describing and analyzing it as a pattern on the page or in performance (formalism), or treating it as a recipe for mental events in time (reader response), scholars will study a form's history as it manifests in and is changed by use. Even when studying the intricacies of syntax, formalists will be thoroughly historicist. Roland Barthes notably said that "a little formalism turns one away from History, but . . . a lot brings one back to it."[31] Searchable digital archives provide the material conditions for a lot of formalism, making possible the analysis of linguistic form not as an escape from history (as with much New Criticism) or as a step in the reconstruction of the bio-universal, culturally invariable principles of language competency (as with Chomskyan generative grammar) but as a fully historicist mode of inquiry. Instead of describing and interpreting linguistic forms in isolation, formalists will study them by comparing their various instantiations within and across periods.

Historicists, for their part, have nothing to lose but their lexical chains. They will be positioned to exercise the kind of analytical attention to grammar and syntax usually left to formalist critics and, increasingly, to linguists. Some number of them may prove willing to abstract from words to the categories they occupy. Instead of treating every text as a very complicated ransom note, composed by pasting together words and phrases cut from other texts, they will treat every text as a very complicated Mad Lib, in which the blanks as well as the words are inherited from previous texts. In addition to the relations that link words and world, *les mots et les choses*, they will attend to the social, cultural, and cognitive work that linguistic forms do in the world. And when existing search tools cannot retrieve the forms humanities scholars deem worthy of study, they will learn the requisite linguistic and programming skills, or partner with computational linguists and computer scientists, to build new search tools that can.

The first two chapters of this book are methodological. Chapter 1 defines *linguistic form*, argues that abstract forms warrant inclusion in the family of linguistic sign units, describes the processes by which they come to have a history, and surveys the obstacles—technical, practical, and intellectual—that have so far made them practically invisible to humanistic inquiry. Chapter 2 argues for search, no less than the quantitative and computational methods currently dominant in the digital humanities, as an epistemologically valid and intellectually valuable tool for engaging with increasingly massive digital archives. It describes the advanced search tools, as well as the attendant skills, requisite for the philological study of linguistic forms.

The opening chapters on methodology are followed by four case studies, each of which narrates the long *curriculum vitae* of a single linguistic form. Chapter 3 tracks a fixed phrase, *Was it for this*. Composed of four function words, it opened the 1798 version of William Wordsworth's epic poem *The Prelude*. Over the past four decades prominent romanticists have proposed a dozen possible sources for the phrase, including Pope, Milton, Shenstone, Harington, and Virgil as Wordsworth's originals. Yet the digital archive allows us to discover not ten or twenty but more than a thousand new uses of the phrase between Henry Howard, Earl of Surrey's translation of Virgil's "quod hoc . . . erat" into English in 1557 and the publication of *The Prelude* in 1850. Understanding the wide diffusion of *Was it for this* requires that we look beyond the phrase itself and its constituent words to the dramatic, temporal, and affective elements of the linguistic form that the phrase imparted to the sentences it initiated. It also asks us to challenge the reductionist assumptions that underlie many of influence study's basic concepts.

Chapter 4 charts the history of *act as if*—or, more precisely, command or counsel with the form *[verb] as if [sentence]*—across two millennia, from the writings of Seneca and Saint Paul to Dale Carnegie and the present-day self-help industry. I show that philosophers like Blaise Pascal, Immanuel Kant, and William James and a multitude of less prominent writers inherited, transformed, and handed this form down to their successors in a long and innovative intellectual tradition. The rise of *act as if* as a means of fashioning one's actions and even, following Pascal, one's most fundamental beliefs is, I argue, both a product of and a reaction against what the philosopher Charles Taylor describes as "a secular age." The linguistic form *[verb] as if [sentence]* is employed as a supplement to faith in an age for which religious belief is increasingly one viable option among many.

Chapter 5 traces the history of the counterfactual conditional in the discourse of *imitatio Christi*. Over the course of the seventeenth century, English preachers and theologians increasingly wrote about imitating Christ in a new way, challenging Christians to do not as Christ did but rather as he would do. They used the conditional (*would do*) to bridge the historical gap between seventeenth-century Protestants and their Redeemer. The shift in mood encouraged the faithful to perform Christlike actions that Christ never performed even as it freed them from the obligation to perform all, or even any, of Christ's actions. This previously unnoticed modal shift, I argue, constitutes a watershed event in the history of the discourse of *imitatio Christi*. The effects of this event can be seen in the popular religious literature of the nineteenth century as well as in the current proliferation of merchandise bearing the question "What Would Jesus Do?"

The fourth and final case study investigates a telltale marker of Milton's style, his use of depictive adjectives. Unlike the forms studied in the first three case studies, depictive adjectives have no fixed lexical content: *He drove **drunk**, I played **injured**,* and Milton's "The great Creator from his work returned / **Magnificent**"[32] all participate in this form even though they share no words in common. In contrast both to the twentieth-century scholarship that followed Erich Auerbach in narrating the history of style as the development of Cicero's *genera dicendi* (the levels, registers, or types of style) and to the statistical metrics of recent computational stylistics, this chapter proposes a history of style that, looking back to Seneca as its sponsor, unfolds through the imitation of markers. Studying the history of a marker such as the depictive allows us to understand the style of an author or a work not as a set of metrics or the instantiation of a genus but as a composite of manifold historical trajectories.

My selection of these case studies rather than others merits explanation. I have chosen cases that illustrate the diversity of linguistic forms and have arranged them in order of increasing abstraction: from a fixed phrase, *Was it for this*, that imparts a form to the sentences it initiates; through a partially unfilled phrasal template *[verb] as if [sentence]*; through a form defined by grammatical (specifically modal) categories rather than a fixed syntactic configuration or word order; to an entirely abstract form, the depictive adjective, which is made up solely of categories without any lexical content whatsoever. Not incidentally, the technical difficulty of finding these forms increases with each chapter. Tracing *Was it for this* requires searching widely used digital archives with only the most basic technical know-how, whereas studying a wholly abstract form like the depictive exceeds the capacities of even the most advanced existing corpus query and natural language processing tools.

I have also strategically chosen to trace linguistic forms that illuminate and revise some of the core concepts and narratives of the humanities. Each case study uses a comparative historical approach to the form of utterances to enrich and rework a basic concept of literary study: influence, fiction, imitation, and style, respectively. In developing an explanation for a form's history, each study also reassesses a major historical metanarrative: literary influence as a succession of strong precursors, secularization as the decline of faith, modernity as the rise of historical consciousness, the history of style as the dialectical synthesis of high and low *genera dicendi*. I hope to show that the histories of linguistic forms provide a fresh vantage from which to rework even these well-handled and oft-disputed metanarratives. Conversely, these studies suggest that linguistic forms have the peculiar and contingent careers they do for complex cultural and historical reasons that humanists (rather than, say, linguists or cognitive scientists) are best prepared to study and understand.

Finally, my selection of forms for study is inescapably dependent on my expertise and limitations as a scholar, which would be pointless to conceal even if it were possible to do so. I have deliberately chosen to study forms that underwent substantial developments in the historical period in which I was trained, the early modern period, though not necessarily in my discipline, English literature. Each study identifies a form that changed dramatically in the sixteenth and seventeenth centuries and explores the causes of that change and its effects even up to the present day. Only with a base camp set up in my field of expertise have I dared to pursue linguistic forms across the varied landscapes of the *longue durée*. Where my small Latin and less Greek, French, Italian, and German have permitted, I have sought to show how the careers of linguistic forms traverse boundaries of nation and language as well as period, genre, and discourse.

The book concludes with two shorter, speculative chapters. Rather than tracing the history of an individual linguistic form, chapter 7 sketches out how the forms possessed by a single writer—Shakespeare no less—might be gathered and systematized into an encyclopedic work of reference. It proposes that forms, along with words, compose a *constructicon*, a structured repertoire of combinatory symbolic units of various degrees of abstraction. Where chapter 7 imagines a complete work of reference, a closed repertoire, chapter 8 attends to the limits of cyberformalist inquiry as a positive, empirical, philological project. Taking up a single, exemplary utterance, Nietzsche's "Gott ist todt" (God is dead), it suggests that studying the history of linguistic forms, even as it seeks to establish philological facts, simultaneously expands the scope of indeterminacy and resurrects many of the questions that, in twentieth-century theory, arose from the structuralist account of the nature of the linguistic sign.

Writing this book has involved a peculiar challenge that I like to call "the embarrassment of method." Humanities disciplines (and doubtless my own discipline of literary studies in particular) value the kind of erudition that seems to emerge fully formed, like Athena from the head of Zeus. Initiation into these disciplines involves learning to present the fruits of one's intellectual labors without a tactless and distracting account of the labors themselves. No one becomes well read without much reading, yet a special kind of admiration is reserved for those scholars who, on the page and in person, have most convincingly drawn a veil over the process by which they have achieved mastery of their subject matter. I suppose this is why I once heard it said admiringly of my outlandishly learned graduate adviser that "no one ever saw him read."

If even being seen reading can puncture the veil of scholarly *sprezzatura*, how much more embarrassing is it to divulge the role of something so gauche as a search engine in the production of knowledge? Unveiling is not necessary or desirable in all cases. Once the card catalog had been established as standard research equipment, it was pointless pedantry to inform readers that books on the topic "kingship" were located by looking in the "Ki" drawer of the catalog. Yet it is especially critical to preserve and make public one's research methods in moments of transition, when those methods can no longer be taken for granted as basic elements of professional know-how and especially when the effects of new research tools on the very shape of our knowledge are still undetermined. Young scholars seeking entry into humanities disciplines are invariably under pressure to imitate their predecessors, which has often involved recoding the results of their digital searches as printed texts in order to recode method as erudition. I am less concerned with any supposed moral costs of this recoding than with its stifling effect on disciplinary self-awareness. When disciplinary norms push scholars to conceal the changing means of knowledge production, they make us less able to reflect on those means thoughtfully, to see their limitations or the new possibilities they offer. One of the salutary effects of recent work in the digital humanities has been to make it acceptable for scholars to acknowledge their use of, and reliance on, digital tools with a directness that might have been deemed indecorous even a decade ago. Opening our research methods to view also dispels the misguided notion that humanities inquiry has ever been a-prosthetic, independent of technology. As book historians like Ann Blair have brilliantly demonstrated, erudition has always been the product of an array of tools for finding, digesting, storing, and accessing knowledge.[33]

Though this book is a work of argumentation rather than a how-to manual, it nevertheless endeavors, when possible, to divulge its methods of investigation, including the search tools and search strings I used to locate textual evidence for the philological narratives retold in its pages. Where methodological opacity or a residue of apparent erudition remains, I ask the generous reader to attribute it to the embarrassment of method.

# Acknowledgments

Like all books, this one depends on the work of others to a degree that its author cannot fully fathom. Some of this work is technical as well as intellectual. The corpus linguists Mark Davies (byu.corpus.edu) and Andrew Hardie (cqpweb.lancs.ac.uk) have built research tools that can do things I only dimly dreamed of as a graduate student. May humanists have the wherewithal to use well what they have made. I thank Chris Curtis for working with me on a machine learning classifier and helping me to see its potential for literary research. I have been grateful for the encouragement and advice of a number of brilliant linguists: Adele Goldberg, William Croft, Paul Hopper, and especially Michael Israel, who shaped my thinking at crucial junctures and whose expertise has saved me from many though doubtless not all errors of linguistic analysis.

Throughout the research and writing of this book I have benefited from the camaraderie, insight, and criticism of many people: my terrific colleagues at Georgetown University, among them Caetlin Benson-Allott, Ashley Cohen, Nathan Hensley, Brian Hochman, Sarah McNamer, Patrick O'Malley, Ricardo Ortiz, Cóilín Parsons, Sam Pinto, Nicole Rizzuto, Jason Rosenblatt, Henry Schwarz, and Duncan Wu; the community of early modern scholars, including Jeff Dolven, Steve Fallon, Tobias Gregory, Matthew Harrison, Jonathan Hope, Jonathan Lamb, David Loewenstein, Joe Loewenstein, Tom Luxon, Lynne Magnusson, Jeff Miller, Martin Mueller, Gerard Passanante, Gail Paster, Joanna Picciotto, John Rogers, Nigel Smith, Paul Stevens, Chris Warren, and Michael Witmore; the digital humanists Richard So, Ted Underwood, and Scott Weingart; and graduate school friends and mentors Edward Baring, Angus Burgin, Steph Burt, Stephen Greenblatt, Steve Hequembourg, Jacob Jost, Barbara Lewalski, Julie Orlemanski, Leah Price, and Gordon Teskey. Matthew McAdam, of Johns Hopkins University Press, helped to shape the book at an early stage, and the external reviewers for the press offered constructive advice, almost all of which I gladly accepted. Joanne Allen, my copy editor, showed exemplary patience and saved me from more pratfalls than I care to admit. I am indebted to

Aaron Winslow for his work on preparing the index. I express especial gratitude to Carolyn for fit conversation; she always seems to listen, ask, probe, suggest, and encourage in just the right proportions.

Institutions as well as individuals aided the writing of this book. An American Council of Learned Societies Fellowship, a joint Folger Shakespeare Library and Andrew W. Mellon Fellowship, a Georgetown Junior Faculty Fellowship, and smaller research grants from Georgetown University and Grinnell College together gave me sufficient time to write. The Folger Shakespeare Library's Early Modern Digital Agendas Seminar in 2013, funded by the National Endowment for the Humanities, introduced me to essential tools, techniques, and interlocutors. I have benefited from the opportunity to share parts of the argument in seminars at the Universities of Chicago, Maryland, Virginia, and Washington; at the Folger Shakespeare and Newberry Libraries; at Carnegie Mellon, Dartmouth, DePaul, Drew, Harvard, Ludwig Maximilians, Princeton, Rutgers, and Yale Universities.

Versions of some chapters have been published in other venues, and I am grateful to be able to share them here. Most of chapter 3 appeared in *Modern Philology* 113.3 (2016): 398–421, © 2016 The University of Chicago; an earlier version of chapter 5 appeared in *Critical Inquiry* 37 (Autumn 2010), © 2010 The University of Chicago; a longer version of chapter 7 first appeared in *Shakespeare Quarterly* 66.2 (Summer 2015): 113–36, © 2105 The Folger Shakespeare Library.

This book relies on digital archives that are the product of the combined labor—much of it unrecognized, painstaking, and poorly remunerated—of a huge number of librarians, archivists, bibliographic photographers, typists, transcriptionists, graduate student assistants, and technicians. I dedicate the book to them.

# METHODS

# 1

## Linguistic Forms

### Language beyond the Lexicon

Imagine that two centuries from now scholars of literature and culture still exist, and you are a twenty-third-century scholar of that period of English and American cultural history that strangely described itself as "late modernity." Reading through the messy, recondite, and frequently toxic mix of printed books and periodicals, Internet blogs, social media feeds, and corporate-sponsored advertorials that compose your archive, you come upon the following sentence: *Wednesday is the new Friday*. As a fluent speaker of twenty-third-century English who is relatively comfortable with earlier stages of the language, you know all of the words in this sentence. You also understand its basic structure, the use of the copula *is* to predicate the complement of the subject and of the adjective *new* to modify *Friday*. Though you sense that there is something about this sentence you don't quite grasp, you decode it successfully enough that you can move on to the sentences that follow, your eyes passing over it without pause.

Yet in the course of your research you begin to come across other, similar sentences: "Red is the new black," "*Orange Is the New Black*," "Forty is the new thirty," "Donuts are the new cupcakes," "Sitting is the new smoking," and others. After reading just a few of these sentences, you begin, consciously or not, to understand that they share more than the fixed sequence of words *the new* or a general predicative structure. Rather, each utterance participates in the form *X [be] the new Y*, which signifies the supersession of noun *Y* by noun *X* selected from a common semantic category (days of the week, colors, ages, drinks, desserts, animals that belong to the emperor, etc.). In learning this form, you come to know, on the one hand, its morphological and syntactic structure, the complex relations between its prefabricated (*the new*) and variable (*X, Y, be*) parts, and, on the other hand, the functional role it plays in discourse, its communicative use. Though you never hear instances of the form spoken, you gather that it is used with a playful or ironic intonation in a range of relatively informal registers, genres, and situations. Your knowledge entails, among other things, being able to distinguish instantiations of this form from other, similar utterances, such as *Rob Manfred is the new Commissioner of Baseball*, that indicate the assumption of a role by a person. It also involves the ability to fill the form's variables appropriately to produce new or at least unwitnessed sentences like *Corporate republics are the new capitalist democracies* or *Biochips are the new microchips*. Filling *X* and *Y* requires knowing that the variables are mutually dependent rather than free: the noun you choose for *X* will constrain the appropriate choices for *Y*, and vice versa. Your research also turns up a small number of linguistically inventive instances of the form, including "Weird Is the New Cool" and "Quiet Is the New Loud," that extend the *X* and *Y* variables to accommodate adjectives in place of and functioning as nouns. If you are an inventive or playful user of language, perhaps you think to extend the variables still further to include elaborate noun phrases or even entire subordinate sentences, creating recursive utterances as complex as *Weird is the new cool is the new red is the new black.*

Since you are a student of culture, your curiosity does not stop once you've learned to comprehend the structure and function of *X [be] the new Y* and produce inventive instances of it. You also begin to develop a broader account of the role it played in the culture of late modernity. It is no accident, your research suggests, that the form first arose in the discourse of the fashion industry (with *black* or *navy* as the prototypical value of *Y*), since its various instantiations analogically extend to other spheres of life the cyclical temporality of fashion, in which one season's color, cut, cloth, or stitching is invariably displaced by the next season's.[1] Familiar as you are with the deep anxiety late moderns felt about the dizzying pace of technological, scientific, and historical change, you suppose that the form was for them a means of not only describing the relentless displacement of outmoded or obsolete ways of living but giving this process a comfortingly ironic expression, turning anxiety into verbal play through hyperbole (Friday, after all, remains Friday even as Wednesday assumes its mantle). The form appealed in part because it leaves the relevant semantic class shared by *X* and *Y* unspecified, requiring the interpreter to infer or invent it. In the case of *Coffee is the new wine*, an informed interpreter might judge that coffee supersedes wine not simply as a beverage but as the exemplary beverage of bourgeois connoisseurship and expense, though the sentence itself makes no mention of these features. The form offered to writers and speakers, listeners and readers alike the opportunity to deploy highly specific and timely cultural knowledge—to display their social savvy and evident (if facile) verbal ingenuity.

The previous paragraphs adopt an estranged perspective on what I take to be a bit of linguistic knowledge, knowledge I suspect many, though perhaps not all, of this book's twenty-first-century readers already share, whether they realize it or not. Though *X [be] the new Y* is widespread among early present-day speakers of English, we might be tempted to dismiss it as an inconsequential linguistic and cultural epiphenomenon, no less ephemeral and no more important than the trends it is used to spot. Yet I offer it only as an introductory example of a larger category of linguistic entities that will require humanists to revise nothing less than their conception of the linguistic sign. Before the recent and ongoing efforts to escape the prison house of language that have been characterized as a "turn against the linguistic turn," humanists were dedicated if restless citizens of the empire of the sign.[2] Ferdinand de Saussure's account of the sign as an arbitrary union of signifier and signified allowed scholars across humanities disciplines to step back from the interpretation of texts to interrogate the collective, conventional systems of differences that make meaning possible. As the signifying system par excellence, language became the model for understanding how every medium of communication, every domain of culture, every kind of human identity is constructed. Semiotics did not merely hold out the promise, as Saussure proposed in his 1916 lecture course, of a "general science" of systems of meaning; it also allowed scholars, in the mode of critique, to reveal the contingency of those systems and disclose their internal contradictions.[3] Any anthology or history of twentieth-century literary and cultural theory that includes the semiotics of Roland Barthes and Julia Kristeva; the structuralisms of Roman Jakobson in linguistics, Claude Lévi-Strauss in anthropology, Jacques Lacan in psychoanalysis, and Louis Althusser in Marxist theory; the archaeology and genealogy of Michel Foucault, the deconstruction of Jacques Derrida, the poststructuralist feminisms of Hélène Cixous and Luce Irigaray and Judith Butler; the deconstructive race studies of Henry Louis Gates Jr. and bell hooks, the cultural studies of Stuart Hall and Dick Hebdige, and the postcolonial critiques of Gayatri Spivak and Homi Bhabha—the litany could go on—will necessarily tell a complicated story about the changes wrought in and by the structure of the sign.[4]

This story has been skillfully told before and will doubtless be told again, and it is not my purpose to rehearse it here.[5] I wish instead to suggest that the successors of Saussure (no less than those of Charles Peirce and Edmund Husserl) have worked and continue to work with a regrettably limited conception of the linguistic sign that includes only the most concrete and (phonetically or graphically) manifest signifying units: words or fixed sequences of words.[6] In the lectures of Saussure, who began his career as an Indo-European etymologist, the "linguistic sign" is a "two-sided psychological entity," a "link . . . between a concept and a sound pattern" (66). Thus *arbor* is "the word by which Latin designates the concept 'tree,'" and *s-ö-r* the "French sequence of sounds" that "signal" the "idea of 'sister'" (67). As an illustration of the arbitrariness of the sign, Saussure observes that "the signification 'ox' has as its signal *b-ö-f* on one side of the frontier [between France and Germany], but *o-k-s* (*Ochs*) on the other side" (67–68).[7] Signs, in his theory, are "concrete entities"; they are explicitly "not abstractions but real objects" (101). Jacques Derrida famously deconstructs Saussure's "phonocentrism"—the metaphysical priority of speech over writing—yet even as he inverts this priority, putting writing before speech, grapheme or "trace" before phoneme, he conserves the concrete exteriority of the sign, the sign as a sensible "mark."[8] He inhabits, in order to deconstruct, the house that Saussure built out of words. In spite of careful attention to idioms, tropes, and figures of speech, Derrida's writings employ a conception of the conventional linguistic sign that remains circumscribed to words, most notably the "founding concept-words of ontology."[9]

This chapter aims to wake humanists from their lexicodogmatic slumbers. It argues for expanding the conception of the sign beyond words to include the variously abstract, complex, idiomatic and productive symbolic units that I call *linguistic forms*.[10] I raise *linguistic form* as a cover term under which to shelter a large family of abstract signs that—though so far left out in the cold by scholars of literature, history, and culture—has since the late 1980s been studied with great care by a growing cadre of cognitive and constructional linguists.[11] These linguists refer to members of this family with a rather intimidating array of technical terms: *lexically open*, *partially filled*, and *unfilled constructions*; *grammatical, syntactic, formal, abstract,* and *schematic constructions*; *schemata* (the plural of *schema*) or *constructional schemata*; *formal, variable,* and *constructional idioms*; *syntactic patterns, phrasal patterns, phrasal templates,* and even *snowclones,* the cliché phrasal templates of which *X [be] the new Y* is a prime example.[12] Such abstract sign units are of special interest to linguists because of their (highly controversial) role in the human language faculty, but I bring them to the notice of humanists primarily so that we can explore their long, rich, and manifold histories and their social, cultural, and intellectual (as well as linguistic) consequences. In the midst of the humanities' turn against the linguistic turn, I hope that enlarging the empire of the sign might prompt scholars to give the linguistic another turn.

### Abstract Signs

Like traditional Saussurean signs (*tree, sister, ox*), linguistic forms are conventional, Janus-faced pairings of signifier and signified. Yet unlike the utterances people actually speak and write in a natural language, they are composed at least partly of open or unfilled categories (blanks, slots, variables) that can be filled in a variety of ways. Contra Saussure's insistence on signs as concrete entities, words (as Derrida has shown most powerfully) are necessarily also abstract or ideal, which is why we can say that the spoken *s-ö-r*, the manuscript *soeur*, and the printed *soeur* are all, despite their differences, instances of the same word. By contrast, linguistic forms are at least partially abstracted *from* words. They accommodate multiple distinct utterances, and they make a semantic and pragmatic contribution to the utterances they accommodate. They are to varying degrees idiomatic; their meanings are not wholly derived from the words and categories that compose them. No less than words, they assume their roles as signs in relation to other signs in a system of differences; they are inherently symbolic, never semantically or pragmatically "pure" or autonomous.[13] We learn linguistic forms as integral units, either by abstracting constituents from individual utterances or by generalizing over multiple utterances.

The unfilled variables in linguistic forms can stand in for syntactic, grammatical, phonetic, pragmatic, and semantic categories such that they can be specified by basically the entire universe of linguistic, conceptual, and pragmatic criteria. Pragmatically speaking, the *N* of *If Eskimos have N words for snow* will be an ordinal number large enough (four, seven, dozens, a hundred) to make a tendentious point about the interdependence of language and culture.[14] Limericks are composed of templates for which the categories are primarily phonetic; the *X* and *Y* of *There once was a man from X / Who kept all his cash in a Y* must rhyme.[15] Some variables are based on an identifiable prototype or best example in relation to which other instantiations are understood as variations.[16] Sentences like *I feel therefore I am*, *I shop therefore I am*, and *I drink therefore I am* participate in the form *I [Verb] therefore I am*, based on the English translation of René Descartes's renowned *cogito*, "I think therefore I am." More often than not, variables stand in for a complicated mix of overlapping criteria. The *X* of *In space, no one can hear you X*, the prototype of which appeared on posters advertising the 1979 film *Aliens*, is standardly a nonfinite verb or verb phrase, *scream* but not *screamed* or *screams*; the present participle, *screaming*, would be a departure from the category even though it is grammatically acceptable. Because it is subordinate to the main verb, *hear*, the *X* variable is constrained by semantic as well as syntactic criteria, accommodating verbs denoting actions that produce sound (*laugh, applaud, slurp*). Someone who fills the form with a nonsonic verb (*steal, blog, philosophize*) has either misunderstood its usual semantics or chosen to disrupt it.[17] As Donald Davidson notes, "There is no word or construction that cannot be converted to a new use by an ingenious or ignorant speaker."[18]

The snowclones of the previous paragraph are only the most fixed, concrete, prefabricated, idiomatic, cliché, and—in our present Internet meme culture—conspicuous of linguistic forms. Utterances participate in a hierarchy of increasingly abstract forms. *[Subject] [Predicate]* is more abstract that *[Subject] is [Complement]*, which is in turn more abstract than *God is dead*. Formality is a question not of metaphysical opposition but of relative categorical abstraction.[19] Linguistic forms are formal relative to the constituents that fill them, and they can be unevenly abstract, a mixture of fixed words and unfilled categories. Not all linguistic forms specify a fixed configuration of words and variables. They can be defined as well by simple grammatical categories such as tense, mood, voice, aspect, case, and so on. Though their syntax differs, *What would Jesus do?* and *Would Aristotle say this?* are both interrogative, counterfactual conditional questions about the actions of persons. By substituting different words in the open slots, one can ask new questions that share this form, questions like *How would Jesus do this?* and *Wouldn't Virgil have written it this way?* These utterances all include the word *would*, but linguistic forms need not share fixed lexical elements; they can function as conventional sign units with any overt phonetic or graphemic marks. *He faxed his mom a letter* and *She kicked the goalie the ball* both instantiate the form—a fully schematized construction—that linguists call the *ditransitive* and notate as *Subj V Obj$_1$ Obj$_2$*.[20] Though *We got robbed* and *Dogs must be carried on the elevator* have no words in common, both utterances participate in the passive (they are both passive constructions). Unlike phrasal templates, forms characterized by grammatical categories rather than fixed words or syntactic configurations do not lend themselves to a sequential notation of words and variables.[21]

Linguistic forms are not merely abstract descriptions of utterances or of the similarities between utterances.[22] They play a productive role in language. Every form can be filled with various constituents to produce some number of distinct utterances. A form with a single variable, like *I X therefore I am*, can accommodate as many utterances as there are nouns that can fill *X*. The number of possible utterances that instantiate a form grows geometrically with each additional abstract category.[23] And when a form accommodates recursion (the embedding of forms within forms, like Russian nesting dolls), it can accommodate an infinite number of discrete utterances.[24] Gertrude Stein's "Rose is a rose is a rose is a rose" is a well-known example of an utterance whose form (*X is a Y*, for which *Y = X is a Y* and *X = rose*) could extend indefinitely through recursion, as well as accommodate other noun values for *X* in place of *rose*.[25] The productivity of a form is not just a result of its variability; it is also a result of its limitations. In selecting a particular form as a scaffold for utterances, we accept constraints on what we can utter—on which words, phrases, or embedded forms we can choose to fill its empty categories. Linguistic forms narrow and partially specify the infinite range of things it is possible to say so that we can say something finite, this rather than that, which is to say anything at all.

We speak and write in forms that are not of our own making, forms that are the work of earlier tongues and hands. From other speakers and writers we inherit more than words or even the fixed, frozen, or fossilized sequences of words that philologists have studied under names like *gnomē, sententiae, commonplaces, adages, proverbs, mottos, sayings, saws, aphorisms,* and *maxims* (in an older dispensation) and *clichés, catchphrases, slogans, phrasemes, listemes, collocations, syntagms, strings, conventional multiword expressions*, and *n-grams* (in the new).[26] The linguistic past also bequeaths to us a huge repertoire of forms of various degrees of complexity and abstraction, waiting to be filled anew. All we hear when we listen to speech is one sound after another, and all we see when we read is one character or mark next to another, yet without conscious notice or apparent effort we nevertheless grasp utterances as instantiations of abstract and complexly structured forms. Studying a form is therefore partly a matter of defamiliarizing and making explicit the linguistic knowledge that writers and speakers already implicitly possess and use whenever they write or speak. Yet as a mode of historical inquiry, cyberformalism is also concerned to recover knowledge, at once linguistic and cultural, of forms that have passed from our memories and are preserved only in the inorganic memory of written documents. To study the history of linguistic forms is to reveal how our utterances are dependent on the collective creation we call language for far more than words and sequences of words.[27]

Though we inherit forms, we are not merely the passive hosts upon which they feed and breed before spreading to others. Linguistic forms are sites of creativity. We fill them with new constituents to produce utterances never witnessed before. Conversely, we make fixed utterances opportunities for combinatorial invention by abstracting some or all of their parts to allow for substitution, turning them into emergent forms, as when Hamlet (bratty child that he is) templates his mother's entreaties and spits them back at her:

QUEEN
    Hamlet, thou hast thy father much offended.
HAMLET
    Mother, you have my father much offended.
QUEEN
    Come, come, you answer with an idle tongue.
HAMLET
    Go, go, you question with a wicked tongue.[28]

Filling a form in a new or innovative way may revise it for those who come after us.[29] Just as an innovative novel may alter the possibilities of the genre, so too may an innovative utterance alter the possibilities of a linguistic form. Through use we change usage. We put forms to fresh purposes, import them into different discourses and contexts and speech genres, translate them from one language to another, and confer new meanings and associations on them. We alter the constraints on a form's categories by filling them in ways that analogically stretch and violate their conditions of inclusion. And we reconfigure forms by combining them with others to produce hybrid offspring that subsequently take on distinct and productive lives of their own. The resulting process is a dialectical oscillation between abstract form and instantiated utterance that can sometimes look a bit like the children's game Telephone: *God is everliving* might be emptied to the form *God is [Adjective]*, filled as *God is dead*, emptied to *God [Verb Phrase]*, filled as *God became man*, emptied to *[Noun] became [Noun]*, filled as *Man became God*, and the constituents recombined with a distinct form, *[Noun] is the new [Noun]*, to produce *Man is the new God*, and so on, forever and ever without end.

In this made-up sequence, linguistic forms appear as the creatures of a moment, ephemeral abstractions that live only long enough to provide a bridge between utterances in an endless, mercurial sequence of transformations.[30] Yet some forms (including those to which the case studies in this book are devoted) achieve a high degree of stability, not only between people within a particular linguistic community but across long stretches of history, acquiring layers of significance and producing myriad utterances over decades, centuries, or even millennia. The conventionalization, standardization, stabilization, and diffusion of such forms are no less in need of explanation than their change, variation, and desuetude. Like generic forms or verse forms, linguistic forms are historically contingent entities rather than unchanging Platonic essences. The law Derrida articulated for genre holds true for them as well: an utterance participates in a linguistic form without belonging to it.[31] Every utterance is in excess of the forms it instantiates, and every form, conversely, is by virtue of its abstractness in excess of its instantiation in any utterance. This double excess provides the continuity necessary for us to identify *a* form, a conventionalized unit distinct from others, and the discontinuity necessary for us to speak coherently about how a form changes, becoming other than itself, over time.

### Scales of History

Linguistic forms are woven into human life, culture, and history at every scale. As Ronald Langacker puts it, they are "sociocultural skills . . . well-rehearsed patterns" that shape our interactions with others.[32] Even the most abstract forms, those composed solely of grammatical categories, play important parts in our most intimate relationships. One of the fictional interviewees in David Foster Wallace's short-story collection *Interviews with Hideous Men* confesses: "I have a history, a pattern so to speak, of, for instance, coming on very fast and hard in the beginning of a relationship and pursuing very hard and very intensely and wooing very intensely and being head over heels in love right from the start, of saying I Love You very early on in the relationship, of starting to talk future-tense right from the outset."[33]

The symptoms of the hideous man's pathology are, by his own account, not just psychic and emotional but linguistic; his "pattern" of symptoms includes inappropriate uses of verb tense as well as unruly desires. He marks the shift into the future tense, like the utterance of the utterly derivative but nevertheless charged "I Love You," as a momentous romantic event. Because it is something that one starts to do at a particular point in a relationship, one may start to do it too soon, "very early on," which suggests that there is a range of socially appropriate times to do it, none of which, presumably, are "right from the outset." The sequence of tenses exists in conformity to or violation of a schedule of traditional expectations about the proper expression of desire. The hideous man does not say what he talks *about* in the future tense—the grammatical category can accommodate a potentially infinite number of distinct utterances, though we can of course imagine an array of likely or appropriate possibilities. What is at issue is neither a particular proposition nor a particular choice of words (even words like *will*, *going to*, or *shall*), but rather the introduction of the future tense itself as a significant event in the unfolding of a romantic relationship. Though the future tense is a grammatical category without a fixed phonetic or graphemic mark, it is nevertheless a *sign*, a bearer of conventionally established meaning serving a conventionally established function within the context of the relationship. Its advent, Foster Wallace's character supposes, carries with it evident emotional and interpersonal risk: by projecting a relationship forward in time, it precipitously raises the question of whether the relationship has a future.

It is tempting to diagnose the hideous man's unusual cognizance of the way his verb tenses deviate from the normative schedule as a part of his crippling pathology. Most people, it is safe to say, do not mark, remark, or remember their language use so closely. You might realistically be expected to recall a first "I love you," but not your beloved's first use of the passive or the conditional. Yet even when you do not take conscious notice of the advent of a grammatical category like the future tense as an event, it may still register in your body—the sweat of your palms, the flush of your skin, the pounding of your heart. And even when such events and the longer histories they compose escape conscious notice, they are often partially preserved, represented and refracted in the boxes of love letters stuffed under the bed, in the anecdotes divulged to friends, and in the romantic stories retold in novels and poems and on stages and screens.

The grammatical category of the future tense has a history in virtually every relationship, one that might progress from introduction, through dispersion and regularization, to extinction or displacement. In the normative schedule at once rigorously observed and inevitably violated by the hideous man, the impassioned future of *When will I see you again?* might give way to the quotidian future of *I'm going to pick up milk on the way home* before being finally extinguished in the desolate past of *You were the love of my life*. As it accumulates a curriculum vitae over the course of a relationship, the significance of the future tense changes. It means something different on a fiftieth anniversary than on a first date or a one-night stand. It acquires a layered history of shifting discursive functions that are at once specific to the history of the relationship and parasitic on larger social norms and expectations. As with the protagonist of any good philological story, the life of the future tense is inescapably combinatory, unfolding not in isolation but in transformative encounters with interrogatives and statements and imperatives and conditionals; with the first, second, and third persons; singular and plural; regarding a vast array of topics; in promises and threats, prayers and hypotheses, speculations and prognostications; in idioms fixed and variable. The absence of the future tense—its total or partial taboo, its conscious or unconscious omission from the collected utterances of a relationship, with the implication that the relationship has, can, or should have no future—may be no less significant, may indeed be more momentous, than its regular deployment and presence.[34]

The histories of linguistic forms play out on scales much larger and longer than that of personal relationships. Consider the Preamble of the United States Constitution:

> We, the People of the United States, in Order to form a more perfect Union, establish Justice, insure domestic Tranquility, provide for the common defence,

promote the general Welfare, and secure the Blessings of Liberty to ourselves and our Posterity, do ordain and establish this Constitution for the United States of America.

Politicians and activists from Abraham Lincoln and Susan B. Anthony to Barbara Jordan and Barack Obama have mined this sentence for the building blocks of their oratory and the foundations of their political philosophy, seizing especially on its resonant opening phrases: "We, the people," and "a more perfect Union." Yet the linguistic form of the Constitution's opening sentence, like the words that fill it, has also had a far-reaching afterlife. At issue is nothing so singular as tense. Abstract from the resonant words and phrases and we are left with a phrasal template that can be notated as *We, [Appositive Noun Phrase], [Purpose Clause], [Performative Verb Phrase]*.

The constitutional law scholar Akhil Reed Amar observes that "like the phrases 'I do' in an exchange of wedding vows and 'I accept' in a contract, the Preamble's words actually performed the very thing they described."[35] The sentence does not merely portray an act of constitution; it *constitutes*, as the emphatic auxiliary verb "do" makes especially clear. "We . . . establish" does not describe a completed event in the past but at once describes and performs an open-ended act in the present. The force of "the People" lies not merely in the concept to which it refers but in the fact that it appears as (in apposition to) a first-person-plural subject, "We," rather than a third-person-plural *they*. Where *they the people* points to an other, "We, the People" names a corporate self, a self that incorporates some people while inevitably excluding others. Garrett Epps calls this an "act of ventriloquism," since the Constitution was in fact written in secret by "some fifty-five men, distinguished in the new nation by their wealth and prominence, meeting in the Pennsylvania State House in Philadelphia between May 25 and September 17, 1787."[36] "The People" ventriloquized by the first-person plural names no preexisting citizenry. As Michael Warner writes, "Our society's representational policy rests on a recognition of the abstract and definitionally nonempirical character of the people."[37] Even now, more than two centuries after it was written, the first-person-plural "We" simultaneously calls into existence "the People of the United States" and enlists them in the acts of ordaining and establishing.[38]

The order of the Preamble's categories is also consequential. Its main verbs ("ordain and establish") do not directly follow the first-person-plural subject. They are postponed by an extended purpose clause, "in Order to . . . ," that designates in advance the reasons for which ordaining and establishing are performed. Like the document they initiate, the actions at once named and performed by these verbs are means to explicitly collective ends, in light of which they must be understood and interpreted. The Preamble does not simply juxtapose the first-person plural, purpose clause, and performatives in a sequence; it fuses them into a single, integral, complexly structured utterance. A collective act that, for the sake of a shared aim, we continuously perform together: this is not simply what the Preamble means, but what, in its very form, it is and does.

Analysis of this kind is necessary to understanding the significance and consequence of the Preamble, but it is not sufficient. The establishment of the sentence's linguistic form is a historical event whose significance can only be fully grasped as part of a longer history. The Constitution was written to replace the Articles of Confederation, which had been ratified in 1781, and its form, no less than its choice of words and phrases, differentiates it from that earlier document, which begins with a salutation:

> To all to whom these Presents shall come, we, the undersigned Delegates of the States affixed to our Names send greeting.
>
> Whereas the Delegates of the United States of America in Congress assembled did on the fifteenth day of November in the year of our Lord One Thousand Seven Hundred and Seventy seven, and in the Second Year of the Independence of America agree to certain articles of Confederation and perpetual Union between the States of Newhampshire, Massachusetts-bay. . . .

Unlike the initial "We" of the 1789 Constitution, the "we" of this opening sentence is not incorporative; it includes only "the undersigned Delegates of the States," a named and enumerated set of men that the following sentence recasts in the third person as "the Delegates." When the states are subsequently invoked, they too are named and enumerated as a *they*, not a *we*.

Instead of performing an indefinitely ongoing act of constitution, the second sentence merely reports a past act, "the Delegates . . . assembled did . . . agree," carried out on a specified date, 15 November 1777. The opening lines express no purpose or aim for the sake of which this past act of agreement took place. A purpose clause appears only in, and specifically for, article 4:

The better to secure and perpetuate mutual friendship and intercourse among the people of the different states in this union, the free inhabitants of each of these states . . . shall be entitled to all privileges and immunities of free citizens in the several states.

Here, as in the remainder of the document, "the people" are addressed only in the third person, as the grammatical object (direct or indirect) of various acts, never as a corporate subject capable of speaking, acting, or enacting. "The people" never assume the role of an agential *we* that extends across the borders of the several states. The Articles of Confederation exhibits in the form of its sentences what Amar calls the "hallmark[s] of a multilateral treaty regime based on the sovereignty of each state."[39] When the Committee on Style gathered separately to draft the Constitution's Preamble for consideration by the Convention at large, they took care to replace the linguistic form as well as the propositional content of the Articles.

The form of the Constitution's opening sentence has its prehistory in the form of other sentences. But the US Constitution makes it into a sign unit, an integral whole, that has its own long afterlife. When the members of the South African Parliament drafted their own constitution in 1996, they had the American Constitution, among others, before them as a model. The South African document begins with the familiar first-person plural and appositive ("We, the people of South Africa") but then diverges strikingly from its American model:

We, the people of South Africa,
Recognize the injustices of our past;
Honour those who suffered for justice and freedom in our land;
Respect those who have worked to build and develop our country; and
Believe that South Africa belongs to all who live in it, united in our diversity.
We therefore, through our freely elected representatives, adopt this Constitution as the supreme law of the Republic so as to
Heal the divisions of the past and establish a society based on democratic values, social justice and fundamental human rights;

Lay the foundations for a democratic and open society in which government is based on the will of the people and every citizen is equally protected by law;

Improve the quality of life of all citizens and free the potential of each person; and

Build a united and democratic South Africa able to take its rightful place as a sovereign state in the family of nations.[40]

In addition to reconfiguring the order of its American template, reversing the performative verb phrase and the purpose clause ("We . . . adopt . . . so as to"), the South African Constitution inserts four main performative verbs in the first sentence: "Recognize . . . Honour . . . Respect . . . Believe." Where the US Constitution, as E. L. Doctorow wrote, "is syntactically futuristic: it prescribes what is to come,"[41] the South African Constitution defers the articulation of a shared future so that it can first acknowledge the injustices of the recent past, "our past." (In the American context, the Declaration of Independence, rather than the Constitution, had recognized the wrong done *to* the nation; official recognition of the wrong done *by* the nation would await future documents like the Gettysburg Address and the Emancipation Proclamation.) As a law scholar who helped to draft South Africa's interim constitution of 1993 observes, the 1996 document's turn to the past "is intended to be cathartic."[42] The initial sentence acknowledges a past stained by apartheid (a word that appears nowhere in the document) so that the subsequent sentence can pivot toward a more just, equal, and open vision of the future. When the postponed purpose clause, "so as to," finally appears, its first item, to "Heal the divisions of the past," ensures that retrospection is built even into the document's prospective aims. The 1996 South African Constitution adopts and revises the linguistic form of the US Constitution's Preamble to meet the distinctive pressures of a national history already in progress, a history bearing the deep wounds of racial injustice.

The brief narrative I have presented here is necessarily only a fragment of a much broader history. A full study of linguistic forms in preambular sentences would need to examine a wider array of official documents, showing, for example, how the US Constitution differentiated itself from the Articles of Confederation as well as from the Declaration of Independence and how it drew and combined elements of its linguistic form from the Mayflower Compact of 1620 and the Massachusetts Constitution of 1780. It would need to compare the state constitutions drafted and enacted prior to 1789 as well as the royal charters for the colonies. Likewise, fully understanding the linguistic form of the South African Constitution would require comparing it not only to the US Constitution but also to the country's own 1908 Constitution and the 1993 interim constitution it superseded, as well as the myriad other national constitutions drafted between 1789 and 1996. Carried out by a linguistically attentive legal scholar, such a study could also take into consideration the linguistic forms standardly used in contracts, charters, and compacts more broadly.

Every constitution is a succession of utterances instantiating various, overlapping linguistic forms at various levels of abstraction. But individual linguistic forms also have coherent and significant histories that stretch across the archive of constitutional documents. With some time and care, one could trace the appearance of a form's elements, their fusion, reconfiguration, displacement, and dispersion. One could also study the way a form has accommodated various constituting subjects ("We, the people," "We the undersigned Delegates," "We . . . the people of Massachusetts," "We . . . the loyal subjects of our dread Sovereign Lord King James") performing various acts ("establishing," "ordaining," "constituting," "agreeing," "adopting," "prohibiting") for diverse purposes (to "form," "provide," "promote," "secure," "ensure"). The instantiations and reconfigurations of these categories, no less than of the words that fill them, are a vital, consequential, and neglected part of the hugely complex stories of how people become *a people*, how a people identifies itself as *a we*, and how that we constitutes itself as *a nation*.

### Bags of Words

The history of preambular linguistic forms unfolds among an indefinite number of persons over a period of centuries. Yet it is still possible to specify in advance a relatively well-defined collection of constitutions, charters, and contracts that make up and preserve this history. That is to say, a scholar seeking to chart the history of the form *We, [Appositive Noun Phrase], [Purpose Clause], [Performative Verb Phrase]* will have little trouble figuring out which official documents, and even parts of documents, to consult. Yet because linguistic forms manifest at the level of individual utterances, they rarely remain confined to an easily identifiable or delimited set of documents. They are highly mobile, moving fluidly between topics, discourses, registers, genres, disciplines, nations, and even languages.[43] Their peregrinations extend from everyday speech to newspaper copy, formal legal documents, and the most rarified works of literary art. Since a form can accommodate various constituents, its history need not play out in a single section or subject heading of the library stacks. Generally speaking, the more abstract a form is, the more diffuse its instantiations will be.

Virtually every conceivable discourse makes use of linguistic forms as abstract and semantically general as Noam Chomsky's notation of predicative form, *NP VP*, which is simply the form of judgment or assertion, of saying something about something. The histories of more concrete forms may likewise be preserved in dispersed collections of documents much larger than any human being can read in a lifetime, in which any document may include only a single, consequential instantiation on any chance page. A scholar cannot reasonably hope to intuit in advance where—on what pages, in what documents, in what section of the library—an instantiation of a form will appear. The major obstacle to studying the history of a linguistic form, then, is finding its instantiations. In the following chapter, I explore how large digital archives and advanced search tools make it feasible to study the genesis, diffusion, variation, and cultural significance of forms across the vast sweep of the textual past. In the absence of these tools, it is no wonder that humanities scholars have been slow to study the histories of linguistic forms. Working in an age of print, they were in the position of Psyche confronted with the incessant labor of sorting asunder an intermixed pile of seeds—before the arrival of an army of helpful ants.

Searchable digital archives alone will not lead us to the study of linguistic forms. Since its rise in the late sixties and seventies, cultural studies has been pervasively (though not totally) lexicocentric, centered on words. Raymond Williams established the investigation of "keywords," words "of capital importance," as a primary occupation of cultural studies, writing that "changes in their use . . . bear witness to changes in the characteristic ways of thinking about our common life: about our social, political and economic institutions; about the purposes which these institutions are designed to embody; and about the relations to these institutions and purposes of our activities in learning, education and the arts."[44] In pursuit of the sign, structuralists and semioticians developed sophisticated procedures for identifying words, detaching them from utterances, and relocating them in a semantic field—the metaphorical equivalent of the physical space in which Claude Lévi-Strauss famously arranged his numbered index cards in "The Structural Study of Myth."[45] Deconstruction reconceived of the semantic field as an elusive economy of differential relations rather than a manifest structure of binary oppositions—speech/writing, presence/absence, male/female, nature/culture, and so on—but continued to populate it solely with words.[46] The intellectual historian Martin Jay offers a post-structuralist account of the semantic field when he writes that "words . . . do their work . . . by positioning themselves in shifting force fields with other words, creating unexpected constellations of counterconcepts and antonyms as well as a spectrum of more or less proximate synonyms."[47] Recent digital humanists speak of the semantic field as a "latent" or "hidden" structure to be extracted from deep within large aggregates of texts, whereas Lévi-Strauss had characterized it as "a higher order" or "a higher level" (431) floating above the text, but the altitude hardly matters: in either case reconstructing this field requires isolating word-signs from the abstractly structured and categorized utterances of which they are a part.[48] When words are the lone heroes of conceptual history, linguistic forms serve only as the unchanging scenery against which their intrepid narratives unfold.[49]

It would be a mistake to chalk the lexicocentrism of the humanities, digital and print alike, up to the influence of Raymond Williams, or the Saussurean conception of the sign, or indeed any recent critical method, tendency, or exemplar. Rather, scholars appear, by the evidence of their practice and sometimes by explicit assertion as well, to have labored under a view of language that John 1:1 conveniently dates back even to before divine creation: "In the beginning was the Word." Roland Greene begins his recent book on critical semantics with an exceptionally bald declaration of Johannine faith: "Stubborn and imperishable, words precede everything. Before literature represents, philosophy argues, or history records, there are words—protagonist words, complex words, keywords, and, not least, everyday words."[50] Words (like "the Word") precede the disciplines of philosophy or history, but do they really precede language or utterance, much less "everything"? Annabel Patterson (no stranger to the technicalities of syntax) likewise describes words as the *prima materia*, or first matter, of language, since "'language,' of course, means primarily *words*, the choice of words and their arrangements in units of sense and communication."[51] In her description, writing or speaking is a matter of selecting individual words from a lexicon and arranging them into larger "units of sense." The intellectual historian Daniel T. Rodgers, in his book subtitled *Keywords in American Politics since Independence*, writes that words "inspire, persuade, enrage, mobilize. With words minds are changed, votes acquired, enemies labeled, alliances secured, unpopular programs made palatable, the status quo suddenly unveiled as unjust and intolerable. Through words, coalitions are made. . . . Words make mass actions possible. Through words some of the most potent forces of modern politics are wheeled into motion. . . . They are the stuff that holds political movements and political coalitions together."[52] Rodgers credits words with a creative and transformative power just short of the divine *Logos* itself, through which all things were made (John 1:3). Though Hamlet articulates a similarly lexicocentric view of language when he describes the matter of his reading as "words, words, words" (*Hamlet* 2.2.210), he intends to be deliberately obfuscatory rather than informative.

What gets lost in the synecdoche whereby words are made to stand in for language as a whole?[53] Consider the simplified builder's language that Ludwig Wittgenstein imagines at the beginning of *Philosophical Investigations*, a language with a lexicon of only four words: *block*, *pillar*, *slab*, and *beam*.[54] Rather than indexing the world in the manner of a picture or diagram, these words, when translated into English, are used to mean something like *Bring me a slab!* or *Put that beam there!* Wittgenstein observes, however, that we have no more reason to treat *Slab!* in this imagined language as a "degenerate sentence" (*degenerierten Satz*) than to treat the English *Bring me a slab!* as a "*lengthening*" of the sentence 'Slab!'"[55] Though they speak only individual words, the builders have a grammar as well as a lexicon, albeit a grammar comprising a single linguistic form composed of a single blank category. *Block*, *pillar*, *slab*, and *beam* are used, in Wittgenstein's language game, not as nouns in a dictionary, the stand-alone names of things, but as imperatives, expressions of desire and commands enjoining action. They are all uttered as instances of what we might call *imperative nouns*, nouns used as commands.[56] The utterance *Slab!* is composed of not one but two sign units, the concrete word *slab* and the abstract imperative noun form *X!*, which is simple (it comprises a single category or blank) and wholly abstracted from lexical content (its only constituent is a variable). It signifies *Give me X!*, a meaning it gains from its role in what Wittgenstein calls the builders' "form of life." In English, the imperative noun *X!* can be more appropriately filled by some nouns or noun phrases than by others: thing nouns like *water* or simple noun phrases like *the big one* rather than more complex noun phrases like *working for the weekend* or *the way you look tonight*. Complicated conventions regulate what the form can accommodate and the situations in which it can be used. Imperative nouns will in many situations be so ambiguous, so difficult to disambiguate from other forms, such as the ostensive noun (*Bear!* meaning *There's a bear!* rather than *Give me that bear!*), as to be useless. In polite company, imperative nouns are generally verboten to anyone over the age of three. For adults they are perhaps best reserved for military drills or emergencies, when they can be accompanied by exaggerated hand gestures.

The imperative noun, like the nouns that fill it, has a history. Just as assiduous parents can keep a record of baby's words, from the first burbled phonemes to a full-blown adult vocabulary, so too could we record the history of a person's noun use from the nursery room (*ma!*) to the operating chamber (*scalpel!*) to the death bed (*light!*).[57] By the same token, we could conceivably explore how the use of the imperative noun has changed over long stretches of historical time, in various genres and discourses. Expanding the category of the sign to include the imperative noun requires that we revise John 1:1 along Wittgensteinian lines to posit the co-primordiality of words and linguistic forms: "In the beginning were words in the forms of their use"—a weak foundation for theology, no doubt, but a better starting place for philological inquiry.

Though digitized texts and digital tools make it increasingly feasible to study linguistic forms, the overwhelming effect of digital research methods to date has been a kind of hyperlexicalism, an intensification of the humanities' monogamous love of words.[58] Recent generations of scholars have come of age in an era of keyword searches, which, when coupled with massive archives, make it relatively easy to study etymologies with broader evidence and greater specificity than the entries in the *Oxford English Dictionary* and even to reconstruct shifting constellations of words over extended historical periods.[59] Statistically sophisticated methods of textual analysis, such as content analysis, topic modeling, semantic cohort analysis, and vector semantics, have similarly fixated on words as the units of measurement.[60] With a customary apology for the strategic crudeness of the method, scholars decompose texts into "bags of words," ignoring the syntax of utterances in order to count and calculate the relative frequency and co-occurrence of words or lemmas (the dictionary forms of words).[61] Even digital scholarship invested in grammar and syntax, pragmatics and rhetoric, has tended to measure words as proxies for these things, albeit "small" function words such as *the* or *a*, *thee* or *thou*, *who* or *which*, or *would* or *should* rather than lexically rich content words.[62] To study linguistic forms is to study precisely the aspects of language—order, structure, abstraction, categorization, syntax, part-whole relations, as well as the conceptual and logical relations they signify—that the "bag of words" approach dominant in the digital humanities discards.

Whether or not a Johannine faith in the exclusive primacy of the word dwells in the hearts of humanities scholars, it lives in their practice. Not only has it narrowed historical and philological inquiry, it has also shackled critique, which within the element of language has generally operated as an analysis of what Richard Rorty calls our "common" or "inherited" or even "final" vocabularies.[63] Since Derrida, the critique of vocabularies has worked predominantly by deconstructing opposed, binary terms, whether by inverting their hierarchy, showing their dependence on each other, or restoring to view an excluded or hidden third term. Eve Sedgwick offers an exemplary statement of this procedure in her *Epistemology of the Closet*, a book that aims to

> demonstrate that categories presented in a culture as symmetrical binary oppositions—heterosexual/homosexual, in this case—actually subsist in a more unsettled and dynamic tacit relation according to which, first, term B is not symmetrical with but subordinated to term A; but, second, the ontologically valorized term A actually depends for its meaning on the simultaneous submission and exclusion of term B; hence, third, the question of priority between the supposed central and the supposed marginal category of each dyad is irresolvably unstable, an instability caused by the fact that term B is constituted as at once internal and external to term A.[64]

I have no wish to diminish the importance, validity, or intellectual force of this procedure. Yet a critique of binary terms, however compelling, passes over the ideological workings of the forms those terms fill. Consider the following utterances:

> And it's oh! for the days when Men were Men.[65]

> . . . when America was America, when people pulled together and made no bones about it.[66]

> . . . when America was America; when there was a West; when a man could start with a capital of one hundred and fifty dollars borrowed money and make good.[67]

> . . . in early days, when women *were* men's mates, when women were women and not just ladies.[68]

> Dogs today are not what they used to be. . . . There was a time when dogs were dogs.[69]

> . . . a day when poetry was poetry, as to children cake is cake, whatever its shortcomings.[70]

The expression of nostalgic desire, the reactionary construction of history, the idealization of the past, and the implication of present decline—these are functions of the tautologous form $X$ *[Past Tense Copula]* $X$, not of any of the words (*men, America, women, dogs, poetry*) that have filled or might yet fill the form's categories.[71] These functions will be left unanalyzed, unchallenged, and undisturbed by a deconstructive critique of binary terms, an "imminent critique" of "basic vocabulary," or any other analysis that remains at the level of lexicon.[72] Tautologous forms need to be read against the grain in their own right, as Langston Hughes does in one of his best-known poems:

> Let America be America again.
> Let it be the dream it used to be.
> Let it be the pioneer on the plain
> Seeking a home where he himself is free.
>
> (America never was America to me.)[73]

In the movement from the initial, hortatory "Let America be America again" to the parenthetical aside "America never was America to me," the poem challenges both the received concept of America and also the nostalgic, idealizing function of tautologous form, which announces its category twice, first as empirical designation (what now goes by the name of $X$), then as ideal ($X$ as it ought to be). This form performs its work by inserting temporal difference into apparent self-identity, displacing $X = X$ with $X$ *was* $X$, implying that $X$ *is no longer* $X$ and, consequently, that now $X \neq X$. The opening line of Hughes's poem likewise implies that America is not equal to itself. Yet it splits the self-identity of America in two, distributing it to an exhorted future ("Let . . . be") as well as a purported past ("again"). The parenthetical aside of the fifth line heightens this non-self-identity to outright negation, rejecting the location of the ideal in the past ("never was") while leaving open the possibility of establishing it in the future. The poem later collapses the two terms of the tautology into a single, future declarative: "America will be!" Hughes does not simply employ tautologous form, he contests and reconfigures the form's use, negating its nostalgic function while recuperating the emotional force of nostalgia as hope.

It is a testament to the power of Hughes's reworking of tautologous form that candidates in two twenty-first-century presidential elections (John Kerry, Rick Santorum) have appropriated his poem's opening line for their campaign slogans—though perhaps this only shows that linguistic forms are not to be won over once and for all but are ever disputed property.[74] What Reinhart Koselleck writes of "basic concepts" is true as well of the linguistic forms in which we speak and write: they are "always both controversial and contested."[75] If cultural critique wishes to contest the ideologies that linguistic forms serve, it must learn to identify these forms, understand their workings, and study their histories.

Clearing away an unnecessarily narrow conception of the linguistic sign will not on its own open the floodgates of philological inquiry or linguistic critique. Practical and technical as well as theoretical obstacles have dammed the historical study of linguistic forms. Words are seductive objects of inquiry and analysis in part because they are so convenient. They are discrete. Since the demise of *scriptio continua*, writers have used spaces to mark where written words begin and end, making it relatively easy for both readers and computers to individuate them. As Hugh Kenner writes, "'Words' are blocks delimited by spaces. So we can count them."[76] For quantitative digital humanities work, words count because computers can count them reliably. As W. V. O. Quine remarked, "Words and their inscriptions" are "tangible objects of the size so popular in the marketplace," exchanged even between those working with different conceptual schemes.[77] For most practical purposes, scholars can speak not just of *a* word but of multiple forms of the *same* word.[78] As visible marks, written words can be manipulated much as other kinds of marks are. Depending on the medium, we can write, move, replace, and rewrite them, erase, blot, or cross them out and present them "under erasure." Words also obligingly wear their own nametags. This makes it easy to talk about them. We switch from using a word to mentioning it—calling it by name, so to speak—by writing it in italics, putting it between quotation marks, or changing our tone of voice. This sentence both uses and mentions the word *word*. The tools for studying words are abundant. In addition to what Raymond Williams called "the extraordinary advantage of the great Oxford *Dictionary*," there are specialized dictionaries and thesauruses and translation dictionaries and etymological dictionaries and phonetic dictionaries and slang dictionaries and even dictionaries of dictionaries, produced by scholars over two and a half millennia.[79] We also have a well-developed set of words for describing relations between words: not just synonyms and antonyms but also, in highly structured lexical databases like Wordnet, hypernyms, hyponyms, holonyms, coordinates, and collocates.[80] Many centuries of scholarship have made the study of words as close as the humanities gets to what Thomas Kuhn called a "normal science."[81]

Linguistic forms lack nearly all of these conveniences. Where words are discrete, linguistic forms overlap and nest inside one another. All but the simplest utterances instantiate multiple forms, which occupy the same graphic or phonic space, as it were, at differing levels of abstraction. No marks on a page offer sure guides to where forms begin and end. Some are as short as a single word (*Slab!*), others as long as the story that separates *Once upon a time* from *and they lived happily ever after*. Since they include abstract categories, forms are partly or wholly covert, withdrawn from view. We see or hear the word *Slab!* and must infer from context and convention that it is an imperative noun. Though we use and learn forms without apparent effort, analyzing them requires the often difficult work of conscious abstraction. If identifying a word is like pulling a loose brick from a wall, identifying a form is like extricating a filament from a spider's web. Because forms are not composed entirely of manifest marks, they are harder to manipulate. Crossing out a word does not thereby cross out the category that it fills; to the contrary, it may bring that category to our notice. Where words wear their own nametags, linguistic forms are naturally anonymous, making it challenging to speak about them. Referring to phrasal templates like *X [be] the new Y* is straightforward enough, since they comprise a fixed configuration of words and blanks. More abstract forms—those emptied of most or all phonetic or graphemic content, those without a specified word order—call for the kinds of technical vocabularies or abstruse formal notations for which humanities scholars have historically had little patience.[82]

While Johannine scholarship can build on two millennia of concerted lexicographical research, inquiry into the cultural history of linguistic forms must draw on a motley assortment of partial predecessors and methodological analogues. Many of these receive further notice in the pages to come, but one should be given particular recognition here: the tradition of humanist rhetoric, running from the rhetorical manuals of ancient Greece and Rome through the troposchematological tracts of the early modern period to the *Toposforschung* of E. R. Curtius and his disciples.[83] Of specific relevance is the rhetorical tradition's longstanding effort to taxonomize syntactic schemes (from the Greek σχῆμα, sometimes translated into English as "figures of construction"). Yet classical rhetoricians and their humanist successors only understood schemes to pick out a small subset of utterances, those that artfully deviate from normal word arrangement. As Quintilian writes, *figura*, including schemes, are limited to naming "that which is poetically or rhetorically altered from the simple and obvious method of expression."[84] Schemes have little or no purchase on ostensibly normal, ordinary, or artless speech patterns, and it is far from obvious that they even begin to name the full range of possible deviations. They also tend to be maximally abstract, made up solely of open categories, whereas linguistic forms can also specify uneven mixes of open categories and prefabricated expressions. And though rhetoricians like Henry Peacham and George Puttenham associated some schemes with particular meanings, situations, or functions, the rhetorical tradition at large treated them not as inherently symbolic, learned pairings of signifier and signified but as ornaments, decorations added to the meaning of ordinary language. The study of linguistic forms might be understood as an effort to enlarge the scope of rhetorical schemes to include artless as well as artful speech, norm as well as deviation, partially as well as fully abstract forms, signification as well as configuration.[85]

### Between Lexicon and Grammar

Linguists have long divided the kingdom of language, drawing a border between *lexicon*, a mental inventory of words and their meanings, and *grammar*, a system of rules for combining words into structured utterances. Noam Chomsky's linguistic theory, from early transformational generative grammar to the current Minimalist Program, has widened the separation between lexicon and grammar still further. Grammar, for Chomsky, is an elegant, universal, biologically determined, innate, a priori formal and computational system of general principles that operates independently of semantics and pragmatics, meaning and discursive function. The thesis of the autonomy of grammar, which he proposed in his groundbreaking 1957 work, *Syntactic Structures*, isolates grammar as well from use, practice, culture, and history.[86] The messiness, idiosyncrasy, contingency, and re-dundancy of culture and history are exiled to the lexicon, leaving the un-contaminated domain of grammar computationally optimal, economical, and even, in the regulative ideal of Minimalism, "perfect."[87] In this division of the kingdom, grammar is ruled by systems theorists, mathematicians, logicians, computer and cognitive scientists, biologists, and psychologists. Humanists, as students of culture and meaning, are confined solely to the lexicon. I take the continuing lexicocentrism of cultural studies—especially its focus, across disciplines, on the study of keywords—as a kind of de facto consent to this division of the kingdom. That is, even when they have explicitly rejected the universalism, essentialism, and nativism of Chomsky's theories of language, humanists have in practice accepted the autonomy of grammar.

The philosopher Donald Davidson provided an accurate survey of the divided kingdom of language when he wrote that the "systematic knowl-edge or competence of the speaker or interpreter" must include "the seman-tic role of each of a finite number of words or phrases" and "the semantic consequences of a finite number of modes of composition."[88] By their very nature, linguistic forms upset this division of the kingdom. They are dual citizens of lexicon and grammar, at once semantic and syntactic. Like the words of a "finite vocabulary," they are meaning-bearing signs possessing a "distinct semantic role." As with words, we learn them by making general-izations based on our experience of what others have said and written. Yet linguistic forms are also, in Davidson's terms, "modes of composition." Es-pecially when used in combination, forms allow us to construct complex utterances according to constraints that are often highly culturally spe-cific. To use a form, it is necessary to learn its discursive functions along with its combinatory potential, how its categories may be filled to produce various utterances.

So far as I can tell, no linguist denies the ability of speakers to learn and produce new utterances by filling forms like *X [be] the new Y* or *when X [Past Tense Copula] X*. (I trust that by this point you, dear reader, could produce new instances of each of these forms.) Yet the discipline of linguistics is deeply split on the issue of what role these forms play in the human lan-guage faculty. For Chomsky and the followers of his current Minimalist Program, they are part of the "periphery" of our linguistic competence, "his-torical residues" and cultural idiosyncrasies that are to be "eliminated" by the proper formulation of the principles that constitute grammar's pan-

human, biologically determined "core."[89] In the cognitive and constructional approaches to language that have grown increasingly influential in
the last two decades, by contrast, linguistic forms are constitutive of human
language capacity. Our linguistic knowledge is nothing other than a structured repertoire or network of sign units stretching from fixed morphemes
and words, through relatively concrete and idiomatic forms like *X [be] the
new Y*, to forms as abstract, pervasive, and semantically general as simple
predication, *[Subject][Predicate]*. In this view, there is no need to posit a universal grammar of the kind envisioned by Chomsky, since a speaker in pos-
session of this repertoire has all the linguistic knowledge he or she needs to
perform the combinatory work of assembling signs into the theoretically
infinite possible utterances of human language.[90]

Though my sympathies lie with the cognitive and constructional linguists, I offer here no direct contribution to this debate, which in any case
would require adopting the highly specific evidence, methods, and modes of
argumentation of the discipline of linguistics itself. To paraphrase Francis
Bacon, this book does not aim to make windows into men's *faculté de langage*.
It proposes no mechanism for identifying or generating all and only the
well-formed utterances of a language. Nor does it seek, as historical linguists
do, to characterize general processes of language change, processes like
grammaticalization, lexicalization, pragmaticalization, and discoursiza-
tion. It has no special concern for the diachronic phenomena (such as
changes in verb conjugation, the loss of the English second-person informal
pronoun of address *thou*, shifts in the use of personal and impersonal relative pronouns, and so on) that have typically occupied historical linguists.[91]
Studying the career of a linguistic form, as I practice it in the following
pages, is on a continuum with the narratological study of generic form. It is
less like reconstructing an algorithmic system of general grammatical rules
than it is like getting to know one's way around the conventions of a literary genre: learning to identify its parts, including which parts are fixed or
obligatory and which are variable; surveying the range of constituents it
accommodates; discerning its functions within larger discourses; situating
it in broader social and cultural milieus; attending to changes in its constraints as a result of use over time; identifying its relation to and difference from other genres as part of a larger differential system; and so on.[92]

The studies that follow borrow the tools of corpus and computational
linguistics to study linguistic forms insofar as they are consequential for

literary, intellectual, and cultural history. Their claims are founded on the evidentiary basis of the textual past, especially insofar as that past has been digitized and made available as searchable full texts. The histories I develop in the case studies make a range of historical truth claims: that a linguistic form, under a particular description, had a real historical existence (i.e., that it is not merely notional, imagined, or stipulated); that it was instantiated in particular written utterances; that it played a role in generating these utterances; that it acquired specific meanings and discursive functions through use; that these meanings and functions changed over time; and that these changes warrant cultural and historical rather than merely logical, psychological, or even linguistic explanation. These claims stand or fall on the plausibility of the narratives I develop and, more immediately, on the persuasiveness of my analyses of individual texts and utterances. As historical, philological claims, they may of course be challenged, either by offering a more persuasive reinterpretation of the evidence I present or by assembling a more comprehensive evidentiary basis, ideally with the help of more inclusive archives and more advanced search tools. I invite other scholars to do so.

When philology returns home, as it surely must, to the words and lexical concepts that have long been the primary objects of its desire, its passion and feel for them will be all the deeper and more perceptive for its liaisons with linguistic forms. In addition to the familiar structuralist and poststructuralist procedures of locating a word in a differential semantic field populated solely by other words, the philologist will also understand a word as a constituent of many forms, a filler of many blanks, a value of many variables. The contextualist dictum of the linguist John Rupert Firth, "You shall know a word by the company it keeps," has underwritten much work in computational linguistics and, more recently, in the digital humanities.[93] Yet Firth's dictum remains inadequate so long as it is taken to refer only to the "company" of other words; to it we must add a second dictum: "You shall know a word by the forms it fills."

2

**Search**

**The Many**

Allow me to propose a rough schematization of the last seventy-five years of literary scholarship. New Criticism was the study of *the singular*. Its key concern was the formal unity and integrity of the literary work as a cultural artifact, a well-wrought urn that it submitted to modes of attention and analysis typically referred to as close reading. New Historicism (among other varieties of cultural studies and historicisms) was the study of *the few*, even when practiced by its most virtuosic and obscenely erudite proponents. For this reason its analysis proceeded through juxtaposition and synecdoche, moving from exemplary or anecdotal parts, by way of representation, to social, cultural, and political wholes.[1] Massive and growing digital archives confront literary study with *the many*—too many to read in the manner of the New Critic or the New Historicist.[2] For this reason the study of the many as practiced under the banner of the digital humanities has been more or less synonymous with measurement, quantitative analysis, and statistical characterization.[3] How are we to understand the many except by counting it?

This book practices a qualitative approach to the many that seeks to generate philological knowledge from the results returned by search engines.[4] Where quantitative digital methods rely on the ability of computers to count and classify familiar and automatically identifiable objects (chiefly words), cyberformalist reading is made possible by the abstract pattern matching, filtering, and sorting functions of digital search tools, which slice the many into tranches thin enough to read and study without resorting to enumeration. Instead of sequentially scanning the thousands of sentences on the pages bound in a single book, the cyberformalist scans and studies the thousands of analogous sentences scattered throughout an archive and retrieved by well-wrought search strings.

Cyberformalist inquiry shares with quantitative methods the project of bringing some facet of the otherwise incomprehensible many within range of understanding, interpretation, and narrative. Yet unlike Franco Moretti's "distant reading," Stephen Ramsay's "algorithmic criticism," Michael Witmore and Jonathan Hope's "iterative criticism," or the quantitative methods of stylistics, it is emphatically close, attentive to the form, use, aesthetics, and cultural context of individual utterances, albeit utterances plucked from the unreadable many.[5] Instead of seeking to measure the haystack with greater precision, it aims to find and study new kinds of needles in it, sifting digital archives to bring a discrete subset of "the universe of speech acts," as Julie Orlemanski puts it, "to the point of experience."[6] Where distant reading displaces the text in favor of the "artificial constructs" that Moretti proposes as a "new object of study" (whether a graph, map, tree, table, or network visualization),[7] cyberformalism's approach to the many preserves a minimal link between the potentially pleasurable practice of direct textual reading and humanistic knowledge, which explains why this book, in comparison with many digital humanities publications, is so visually spare. Because it studies the many while remaining unapologetically loyal to the singular textual instance, it cuts against the dominant desire in the digital humanities for what Marshall McLuhan termed *allatonceness*, the ability to comprehend and characterize textual history in an ever larger, summative vision.[8]

In one sense, of course, the comparative methods of cyberformalism are as old as literacy itself. Scholars have always performed some version of what Peter Stallybrass has called "discontinuous reading," moving between texts to note differences and similarities.[9] But growing digital archives make it possible to compare texts on a previously unavailable scale and according to a more diverse, abstract, and complex range of criteria. This chapter offers a defense of and a manifesto for search as an instrument of qualitative digital inquiry. It begins by showing how humanists' accounts of search have been limited by inherited assumptions. Then it proposes that search makes it possible to find, study, and tell significant narratives about an expanded range of linguistic objects, including (though not limited to) the neglected sign units that I call linguistic forms. Finally, it argues that making full and responsible use of search tools requires that we collectively develop new disciplinary skills and methods: specifically, humanists will need to learn how to employ search languages, read search results, and perhaps most challenging, understand the nature of the archives in and through which we are searching.

### In Defense of Search

More than a decade into the twenty-first century, it may seem strange to devote a chapter to a defense of search. After all, by the end of the 1980s DOS-based text analysis programs like Word-Cruncher and TACT could already generate instant search results from local documents on a home computer, and Internet users have been searching the web using words and phrase queries since the launch of AltaVista in 1995.[10] At present a humanities scholar can no more plead ignorance of Google Books than he or she can of the *Oxford English Dictionary*. Haven't search tools been part of humanistic research for some time now, often with less than remarkable consequences? Are we not already weary of reading articles constructed, more or less transparently, around the results of a few keyword searches? Why devote attention to a tool that is at best a labor-saving device and at worst a way of circumventing the intensive study that leads to genuine understanding?

As these questions suggest, search has found no shortage of discontents, even as it has become an indispensable part of humanistic research, not to mention daily life in a networked society. The most unabashed critics proclaim that Google is making us "shallow," "stupid," or "dumb," but more scholarly treatments tend to express their discontent with search on behalf of either an authentic print past or a computationally advanced future.[11] Jonathan Culler worries about the fate of close reading in "an age where new electronic resources make it possible to do literary research without reading at all: find all the instances of the words *beg* and *beggar* in novels by two different authors and write up your conclusions."[12] Gayatri Spivak likewise opposes digital research in the name of a pastoral vision of what scholars "used to do."

> With electronic information control, it is as if there were unmediated knowledge. . . . So-called research projects. . . . are really only tabulating many different kinds of responses to simple questions. You can have the effect of

research very quickly without the effort of research. And nothing is accidental anymore because the connections are all already made for you. For an aesthetic education, it is better to do as we often used to do, to wander in library stacks, because you would see things that you hadn't thought about before. Or if there are no libraries, no dictionaries even, teach the mind to work out rather than develop consuming habits for the exigent cellphone. . . . The unexpected, the something that will have happened as a result of what we're doing, this thing that can't be caught by even the most insistent and imaginative of programming, that which is unprogrammable, that's what we have lost, haven't we?[13]

In this narrative of decline, active reading practices, which "teach the mind to work out," give way to mere consumption; research gives way to ersatz "research"; learnedness is manufactured without learning. Spivak joins Culler in regarding "electronic information control" as an evasion of reading and thinking. As the passive collection of "responses to simple questions," it is at once too easy, "without the effort," and overly directed, purposive, lacking in the instructive aimlessness and fruitful wandering of earlier methods of inquiry. Enthralled by the myth of unmediated knowledge, in which "the connections are already made for you," digital research obliterates the precious serendipity of scholarly inquiry, its potential to uncover "the unexpected" by way of the "accidental." Worse still, the digital dystopia is here and now, having already displaced what "we often used to do." The aesthetic education that once flourished in the soil of earlier print technologies ("library stacks") and grew even in those technologies' absence ("no libraries, no dictionaries even") is bound to wither in a hostile digital environment. An early modernist like myself is inclined to hear in these objections the echo of early Renaissance humanists who worried that new printed works of reference—dictionaries, encyclopedias, florilegia, and commonplace books—would degrade classical learning by making it too common and easy to acquire.[14]

Perhaps surprisingly, digital humanists have tended to join the pastoralists in regarding search with a mix of criticism, suspicion, and dismissal, albeit in the name of more sophisticated quantitative methods. A critique of the insufficiency and bias of search has arguably become the founding gesture of the quantitative digital humanities. As instances of this gesture I could cite Matthew Jockers's insistence that we "go beyond search"—a tool for "looking for, or noting, random 'things'" that is doomed to "support an argument" already in place—in order to engage in data mining, "the literary equivalent of open-pit mining or hydraulicking";[15] or Alan Liu's more measured observation that "no sooner does one come to depend on online searching than it becomes intuitive that one also needs advanced digital humanities tools and resources to practice scholarship in the age of Google Books";[16] or Stephen Ramsay's nicely turned version of the same claim: "Seek and you shall find. Unfortunately, you probably will not find much else";[17] or a host of others, but perhaps the most sophisticated version of this founding gesture is performed by Ted Underwood: "Search is a form of data mining, but a strangely focused form that only shows you what you already know to expect. . . . Our guesses about search terms may well project contemporary associations and occlude unfamiliar patterns of thought."[18] Like Spivak, Underwood worries that search "may well" reproduce your biases, telling you "what you already know" and protecting you from the "unfamiliar." Where Spivak looks nostalgically back to the authenticity of print tools, Underwood advocates for data mining techniques that use Bayesian statistics (especially topic modeling, a statistical technique that sorts words into groups based on the frequency of their appearance together) as "alternatives to search based on a more self-conscious, philosophically rigorous account of interpretation."[19] Search, in this view, is less a debased successor to wandering through the library stacks than an unwitting and undertheorized "form of data mining."

Although the media theorist Lisa Gitelman is concerned to assess the effects of our changing research methods rather than champion quantitative methods, she too warns that "online searching is bound to diminish the prestige of finding things": "Finding instances online—no matter its dwindling prestige—may be narrowing what counts as instance. Researchers specify search terms and search strings, whereas programmers devise what are called *keyword-in-context* and *term extraction analyses*. . . . Instances are increasingly constructed according to diction, in other words. they are found as instances because they have certain words or groups of words in them or indexing them."[20] In this prognosis, search is capable only of locating more and more instances of an increasingly narrow range of entities ("certain words or groups of words") of correspondingly less and less scholarly value.

Search's discontents, pastoral and digital alike, point out real intellectual and disciplinary risks, yet their criticisms are not specific to digital search tools but are instead conditioned and constrained by earlier technologies of the text. Culler, Jockers, Underwood, and Gitelman consider using search tools only to study "keywords," "terms," or "certain words or groups of words" and the "themes" or "topics" for which they stand. Culler's example keywords are *beg* and *beggar*; Jockers's, *whale* and *God*; Underwood's, *blush* and *shame*. Alphabetically arranged print reference works have long allowed researchers to locate precisely these objects of study.[21] The keyword is not a child of the digital age, even if it has achieved a new level of preeminence in it.[22] When Gitelman warns of online search narrowing our focus to diction, she could just as well be speaking of concordances, lexicons, etymological dictionaries, *Wörterbücher* (wordbooks), *Sprachschätzen* (phrase treasuries), and other products of what nineteenth-century Germans called *Wortphilologie* (word philology). The fault of narrowing inquiry to diction lies not, as Gitelman proposes, in our search tools but in ourselves, in the research practices and working assumptions we've inherited from centuries of print-based humanities research. We should not be surprised that digital search tools teach us what we already know when we use them to seek out what we have already long sought. Seek something different and you shall find something different.

Spivak, for her part, is not wrong to prefer the library stacks to the search box (on most days I share her preference), but she is wrong to treat digital inquiry as the fallen descendant of a technologically uncontaminated past; to do so is to misrecognize earlier technologies of the text no less than new ones. By naturalizing the library stacks as the authentic home of an aesthetic education, she effaces the way that education was (and still is) structured and limited by the spatial organization of the library and of printed cataloging systems. The Library of Congress Classification system, used in US research libraries, orders books together on shelves by subject headings, so that the research events Michael Witmore calls "encouragable accidents" are governed by the "structured adjacency" of volumes according to these headings rather than other productive structures of adjacency.[23] A researcher who starts in English literature (PR) will only arrive at Indo-Iranian languages and literatures (PK) by "accident" if he or she first wanders past Romance literatures (PQ), the "General" category of literature (PN), Hyperborean, Native American, artificial languages (PM), and so on. Search tools upset the monopoly that subject-heading schemes have long held over the structure of serendipitous discovery, creating new adjacencies on the basis of various, mutable organizational schemes and principles. How little faith one must have in Serendipity to suppose that a few programmers could do her in!

Like search's discontents, I do not doubt that scholars have used and continue to use digital search engines in narrowing, naïve, projective, biased, haphazard, lazy, unedifying, opaque, and unreflective ways, just as they have the print finding tools that have provided the techno-material foundations of humanistic research for virtually the whole of its modern history. As the youngest offspring of Mercury and Philology, digital search is in need of further discipline and guidance if it is to join its print ancestors as a fully respectable tool of scholarly research. That search requires further discipline does not mean that it is either a debased successor to more authentic print finding tools or an epistemologically stunted precursor to quantitative methods. It is capable of far more than simply reproducing our biases and of far less than delivering unmediated knowledge freed from the exercise of thought. Instead of regarding search as the most basic or minimal means of accessing the archival many, we should see it as a locus of digital and humanistic innovation, a potentially powerful aid to research that can, with sufficient creativity and rigor, allow us to study the history of entities for which there have been no print finding schemes.[24] Jockers's claim that "we are proficient at electronic search" is true only of the very simplest kinds of searches.[25] The difficulty of electronic search scales up with the complexity and elusiveness of the entities sought, without evident upper bound.[26] In many cases, the advanced search tools needed to expand the domain of philological inquiry have already been built by corpus linguists for the analysis of language variation and change;[27] we should take up these tools and repurpose them for cultural and historical inquiry. In other cases, humanists who wish to study a broader ecology of linguistic entities and patterns will need to take a hand in building new search capacities that make use of natural language processing (NLP) and machine learning. In all cases, realizing the potential of search for humanities inquiry will require the full expertise, intrepidness, creativity, rigor, and methodological self-reflectiveness of humanities scholars no less than the talents of programmers, corpus and computational linguists, librarians, and statisticians.

### Drinking Contests

In the past twenty years there have been enormous increases in the size of digital archives. But there have been relatively few substantive changes in the way humanists search archives of any size. We have not asked search tools to do much more than the traditional tasks of finding works, words, and phrases. For the great majority of scholars, search engines offer little more than a glorified index, card catalog, or concordance. But this limitation lies in inherited assumptions, not in search technology.

An anecdote from the distant past helps to bring more expansive possibilities of search into focus. The *Deipnosophistae* (Banquet of the learned philosophers), by the third-century grammarian and rhetorician Athenaeus of Naucratis, tells of how ancient scholars used philological party games to hone their abilities:

> One recited a verse, and another had to go on with the next. One quoted a sentence, and a sentence from some other poet expressing the same idea had to be produced. Verses of such and such a number of syllables were demanded, or the leaders of the Greeks and of the Trojans had to be enumerated, or cities in Asia and Europe beginning with the same letter to be named in turn. They had to remember lines of Homer which begin and end with the same letter, or the first and last syllable taken together must yield a name or an implement or a food. The winner gained a garland, but anyone who blundered had brine poured in his drink and had to drain the whole cup at a draught.[28]

Though the drinking contest makes for a fanciful anecdote, it demonstrates how an earlier moment in the practice of philology identified, categorized, and retrieved language according to patterns and criteria so various, by modern standards, as to seem capricious or arbitrary. In addition to being a trial of what Ann Blair calls "the storage medium with the longest history"[29]—the human memory—the contest was also an exercise in virtuosic recall. The challenges listed by Athenaeus imply, rather than exhaust, the sheer variety of possible ways contestants could organize and consult the verses and *sententiae* (brief moral sayings) in their mental storehouse. For the contestants, mnemotechnic mastery entails the ability to access this storehouse according to elaborate and overlapping metrical, phonetic, and grammatical as well as lexical and semantic criteria.

Any modern reckless enough to compete in such a contest would end up drinking a great deal of salty beer. Alphabetically arranged works of print reference, built with immense collective labor over the last five centuries, do little to supplement the deficiencies of modern, literate memories. A massive work of German philology such as Jakob Werner's *Lateinische Sprich-*

*wörter und Sinnsprüche des Mittelalters* may contain all the *sententiae* to meet the various philological challenges, but it lacks the apparatus to consult them as required.[30] The more than twenty-three million cataloged books in the Library of Congress would stand mute and unresponsive before the demand that they yield their sentences according to the ever-changing criteria of the drinking game.

Armed with digital search tools that make full use of existing technologies, by contrast, one could meet many, though not all, of Athenaeus's challenges. A search that uses an abstract pattern-matching language like Regular Expressions (to which I'll return) could run through all of Homer and Greek drama to identify lines that begin and end with the same letter. The regular expression ^[Ss].*[Ss][\.!\?;,]?$, for example, would match a line from an Attic comedy, "Sophos estin ho pherōn tapo tēs tuchēs kalōs" (Wise is he who bears what fate sends nobly), which begins and ends with an *s* (or rather the Greek sigma).[31] By cross-referencing words against a resource like the CMU Pronouncing Dictionary, one could identify lines comprising a set number of syllables or pattern of stressed and unstressed syllables.[32] The Named Entity Recognizers (NER) that come as standard parts of natural language processing software can automatically identify and extract person and place names from texts (though with various degrees of success; one wonders how NER would fare on the catalog of ships in the *Iliad*). With a scripting language like Perl or Python it would be straightforward enough to combine into a single word the first and last syllables of all the lines in an archive and run the results against lists of extracted names, or instruments, or foods. Only the challenge of producing another sentence that expresses "the same idea" would, in spite of recent advances in semantic search methods, obviously exceed the capabilities of existing technologies. And advanced search tools could conceivably retrieve matches not just from Homer, or Greek drama, or the handful of Greek and Latin poets memorized by a single scholar but from all the documents stored in the *Thesaurus Linguae Latinae* and the *Thesaurus Linguae Graecae*, or, for that matter, any available archive of digital full texts.

What objects of knowledge scholars study depends in no small part on what objects they can find. Every advance in our finding capacities expands the domain of things we can locate, access, sort, read, and make sense of through analysis and historical narrative.[33] Yet just because it is possible to search for a growing range of entities does not mean that it is worth doing so. Outside of a philological drinking game, it is hard to imagine why anyone might wish to investigate all the lines of Homer whose first and last syllables conjoined name a food. Broader notions of salience and value will necessarily guide and determine the search capacities we employ and the entities we use them to find and study. Which entities had real historical existence and meaning for the actors that spoke and wrote them? Which ones had literary, social, cultural, and intellectual significance? No less crucially, which ones will submit to our finite powers of understanding? If we do not wish to follow Lev Manovich in abandoning intelligible narrative for the unordered, infinitely reorderable, listlike structure of the database, then we will need to devote our efforts to objects of study about which we might tell stories of meaning and consequence.[34] Because this book seeks to establish the meaning and consequence of linguistic forms, the remainder of this chapter focuses on the search tools and methods that make it possible to discover and produce philological narratives about them.

### Search Languages

Published in 1992, five years before the invention of Google Search, Neal Stephenson's postcyberpunk novel *Snow Crash* imagines search as a matter of conversing with a virtual "Librarian," a "daemon" that, though capable of moving "through the nearly infinite stacks of information" in cyberspace "with the agility of a spider dancing across a vast web of cross-references," nevertheless appears in the ostensibly reassuring figure of a "pleasant, fiftyish, silver-haired, bearded man . . . wearing a v-neck sweater."[35] You ask, the Librarian answers. Outside science fiction, searching for anything more complicated than a word or fixed phrase is never so simple or intuitive. Retrieving linguistic forms requires learning specialized pattern-matching languages of varying degrees of complexity.[36]

Most fundamentally, these languages allow search engines to retrieve variability within fixity. For example, surrounding a search string with quotation marks instructs Google Books to retrieve a fixed sequence of words rather than the co-occurrence of keywords in a document. It also forces the search to match the *stop words*—most often small words like *the* and *of*—that are generally ignored in keyword searches and text mining. Including stop words brings into view what Daniel Rosenberg has vividly termed the "lowlands of language," grammatical elements that do not denote a particular concept but nevertheless play an active and indispensable role in the construction of meaning and discursive function.[37] An asterisk (sometimes called a wildcard or Kleene star) inserted into a fixed string matches any word. Wildcards are blunt but effective blanks. A search for *"It's * all the way down"* returns utterances in which the wildcard matches words for animals like *turtles, tortoises,* and *elephants* and, in more recent texts, words for abstract concepts such as *politics, culture, language, narrative, representation, contingency, constructions, objects,* and *networks* as well. Regular Expressions (regex), the pattern-matching language used in virtually all digital text processing, employs an extended vocabulary of symbols (*+.?|[](){}\) to specify variability with greater precision than a single wildcard does. If Google Books accepted regex, the string *((i|I)t's|(i|I)t is|(i|I)t was) \w{0,3} all the way down* would retrieve instances of the form missed by the more rigid search string above.[38]

Search languages become even more powerful when they access texts annotated with linguistic metadata such as part-of-speech (POS) tags. While linguists have tagged some small corpora for part of speech by hand, they generally run large corpora through automated POS taggers that, with training, can tag 96–97 percent of words accurately, though that percentage decreases for texts with nonstandard spelling or syntax.[39] POS tags make it possible to search for general lexical categories like nouns, verbs, and adjectives, as well as, in many cases, more granular subcategories like count nouns, modal auxiliaries, or superlative adjectives. You can search a tagged corpus for Hamlet's phrase "outrageous fortune"[40] or for all attributive adjectives that modify *fortune* (*[adjective] fortune*) or all nouns modified by *outrageous* (*outrageous [noun]*). POS-tagged texts are also standardly lemmatized, which makes it possible to retrieve the various inflectional forms of a word by searching for its lemma, or dictionary form. A search for the lemma of *go* will return instances of *go* but also of *goes, going, gone,* and even *went*.

Early POS tagged corpora, like the Brown Corpus of Standard American English, the Helsinki Corpus of English Texts, and the British National Corpus, were carefully constructed for the purposes of linguists. They aimed to represent the linguistic usage of a particular period or periods by sampling sentences or short passages from a large number of texts selected from a balanced set of genres and discourses. But their relatively small size (the Brown Corpus is roughly one million words) and eclectic mix of document types (sometimes including speech transcripts), as well as the difficulty of tracking samples back to full documents for contextual reading, means that they are of limited use for cultural and historical (as opposed to linguistic) research. Only recently have corpus linguists begun to tag large collections of full-text historical documents, like the forty-four thousand–odd full texts of the Early English Books Online Text Creation Partnership (EEBO-TCP), and make them publicly available for advanced searching. Because many of the leading POS taggers are free and/or open source and the computational cost of tagging is low, few obstacles now prevent scholars from tagging and searching increasingly large document collections on their own computers.

POS-tagged corpora are annotated at the level of individual words but provide no information about the structure of sentences or the relations between words. Automated sentence parsers, which are also standard parts of natural language processing software, perform the far more complicated and error-prone task of enriching digital texts with syntactic annotations. Here is the epigrammatic opening line of Zora Neale Hurston's *Their Eyes Were Watching God*, tagged for parts of speech:

Ships/NNS at/IN a/DT distance/NN have/VBP every/DT man/NN 's/POS wish/NN on/IN board/NN ./.

And here it is parsed and formatted for phrase structure by the Stanford Parser:

```
(ROOT
 (S
  (NP
   (NP (NNS Ships))
   (PP (IN at)
    (NP (DT a) (NN distance))))
  (VP (VBP have)
   (NP
    (NP
     (NP (DT every) (NN man) (POS 's))
     (NN wish))
    (PP (IN on)
     (NP (NN board)))))
  (. .)))[41]
```

With a fully parsed corpus it is possible to search not only for categories of words but for phrasal categories as well: not just nouns and verbs but also noun phrases and verb phrases, not just adjectives but also adjectives that are constituents of verb phrases.[42] A still further level of *dependency parsing* involves identifying functional relationships between the words in a sentence. Where POS tagging labels Hurston's "wish" as a noun, and phrase structure parsing categorizes it as a constituent of the noun phrase "every man's wish," dependency parsing labels it as the direct object of the verb "have" and identifies "man's" as its possessive modifier. Compared with POS tagging, parsing is in a relatively early stage of development. It is computationally expensive and adds a burdensome amount of metadata to texts. The best parsers are relatively good at determining the structure of standard journalistic prose, since they were trained on the human-annotated sentences of the *Wall Street Journal* in the Penn Treebank, but they have significantly higher error rates when parsing complex, unusual, or "literary" syntax. Searching or otherwise manipulating parsed text demands significant linguistic and technical expertise. I suppose that parsing is less likely than POS tagging to be widely used in humanities inquiry in the near future.

POS tags and regular expressions are most formidable in combination. Here is one of the many search strings I used in researching my third case study on *imitatio Christi*:

> ((jesus|lord|savior|christ) (*){0,10} (would|wold|wolde|vvould|vvold|vvolde) (not)?
> (have)? _V*|(would|wold|wolde|vvould|vvold|vvolde) (*){0,10} (jesus|lord|savior|
> christ) (not)? (have)? _V*).

The POS tag _V* retrieves all verbs; ? indicates optional elements, elements that can be present or absent; *{0,10} allows the specified words or phrases to be separated by up to ten unspecified words; | matches one of multiple alternatives (either *jesus* or *lord* or *savior* or *christ*). The search string will match all of the following sentences: *What would Jesus do? Our glorious and blessed savior wolde act even so. Would Christ have said this? Our lord wold not have performed the like.* Altering even one element of the string—substituting a _VD* for each _V* in order to retrieve only forms of the verb *to do*, or reducing the upper bound of unspecified words separating specified phrases from ten to five, or adding further spellings of *would*—will retrieve a different set of results.

Scholars used to plugging a few keywords into Google might be deterred by the time and effort needed to learn an artificial language, but they should not be. Pattern-matching languages offer precise ways of describing humanists' objects of study. And it is not necessary to master regular expressions or POS tagsets all at once. They can be learned piecemeal, in the process of research, as a particular line of inquiry demands, and there is no shortage of helpful guides and tutorials.[43] Though search languages may seem unfamiliar, they are continuous with longstanding humanistic traditions: POS tagsets are little more than abbreviations of the grammatical taxonomies that for centuries grammar-school students across Europe began to memorize as early as the age of three and that current students are perhaps more likely to encounter in the course of studying an ancient or second modern language. POS tagsets differ from longstanding taxonomies mainly in that they are machine actionable: in addition to naming the lexical category a word occupies, they allow a computer to retrieve all words that participate in the same category. Search strings composed in part or wholly of POS tags or abstract symbols are a strategic mix of what we already know and openness to what we do not yet know. No escape from the hermeneutic circle here; only the possibility of entering it in a newly productive way.[44] When we formulate a search string, we necessarily posit an initial, "projective" preunderstanding of a linguistic form, but we also submit that preunderstanding to revision in the encounter with the results that it retrieves.

### Reading Results

*Results* is a misleading term for the list of hits produced by a search, misleading because it is premature. Even with fluency in regex and POS tagsets, searching for linguistic forms is a messy and iterative interaction between human and machine, one deserving of Andrew Pickering's term *the mangle*.[45] Initial results often do little more than teach you how to formulate subsequent strings.[46] Rare is the string that retrieves all and only instances of a linguistic form. Information science uses two measures to assess the success of a search: *recall*, the fraction of true hits returned by a search; and *precision*, the fraction of false hits excluded by a search. Maximum recall means that a search returns no false negatives; maximum precision means that a search avoids all false positives. Recall and precision exist in tension: casting a wide net will catch unwanted prey, while aiming narrowly risks letting the quarry get away. But because search "results" are merely the starting point for the work of a human reader (rather than the basis for further computation), recall will generally take priority over precision, inclusion of true hits over exclusion of false hits, at least within the limits imposed by the patience of the reader. I am willing to read through one or two but not ten thousand snippets of text in search of fifty true instances of a form. Perfect precision may be undesirable for a further reason. Linguistic forms are diacritical signs defined by their difference from other forms. False positives make evident a form's differentia by placing it alongside other, neighboring forms, thereby forcing us to sharpen our criteria in order to explain (at least to ourselves and potentially to others) why we have judged them false.

Search results are indexical; they point us to other documents. In their indexical role, they are prosthetic aids to the scholarly technique that John Guillory calls *scanning*, in which the "reader might ignore the continuous meaning of a text, deferring comprehension until some textual signal brings the scanning process to a temporary halt and initiates a more intensive reading."[47] The results lists of Google Books, Hathi Trust, Gallica, and most other large archives of full text and/or page images are designed to serve a primarily indexical function, offering some configuration of bibliographic information (title, author, date) and short text snippet to aid the researcher in deciding where to halt scanning and initiate close attention.

Yet search results are more than lists of pointers. They are also revealing texts in their own right, texts that reward reading and analysis.[48] As texts, they fragment, select, aggregate, and order snippets of anterior documents in an archive to disclose patterns, regularities, disjunctions, gaps, and trends not evident in any individual source document. Humanists have traditionally treated search results exclusively as indexes, leaving analysis of results lists as texts in themselves to corpus linguists, who have designed a range of interfaces to make such texts maximally revealing. The most common of these is the keyword-in-context (KWIC) list. Here is a truncated KWIC list generated from the Corpus of Historical American English (COHA, four hundred million words sampled from 115,000 texts, 1810–2009) using the Brigham Young University Corpus Interface, designed by Mark Davies:

| | | |
|---:|:---|:---|
| Running a | keyword | search on this site |
| a | keyword | search that hunts down |
| | Keyword | searching simplifies finding the art |
| | Keyword | system cumbersome. |
| just close their eyes and think a | keyword | to get a menu in their head. |
| the | keyword | used to decode scrambled data |
| The | keyword | was presently discovered—"Race." |
| to me the | keyword | was "dehydrated." |
| Sure enough, the | keyword | yielded a directory of names[49] |

KWIC lists of this kind are built for scanning speed and efficiency. The repeated keyword *keyword* forms a central, inflexible spine down which the eye travels, remarking differences in the contextual ribs splayed out to the left and right. The list above is ordered alphabetically by the word immediately to the right of the keyword, but the BYU interface can sort, filter, and categorize by a variety of other criteria (date, genre, other words to left and right) to make visible other patterns, trends, and regularities. Bibliographic and generic information, if it appears at all, is abbreviated. Though it is possible to click on a result to see further surrounding context, the COHA corpus does not link to full texts; the questions corpus linguists ask rarely require reading, say, Kant's entire first critique or a novel by Elizabeth Linton, as I did to write the case studies in this book.

KWIC lists are designed to aid the study of lexical items, but when using POS tags and wildcard symbols to search for more abstract linguistic patterns it no longer makes sense for us to speak of keywords in context. Consider the following snippets, retrieved from the COHA corpus with the string [at*] [j*], [j*] [n*]:

a soft, fragrant June
a simple, substantial meal
The tall, Egyptian towers
a soft, happy confusion
the weary, unwashed females
the proud, impolitic Quixoticism
the entwined, silent couples

These utterances include no invariant word or phrase and certainly no key-word, participating instead in a sequence of abstract categories: [Article] [Adjective], [Adjective] [Noun]. Results like these are best conceived in terms of a central distinction of structuralist linguistics. Roman Jakobson fol-lowed Saussure in distinguishing between two kinds of linguistic rela-tions, which he mapped onto orthogonal axes. Speaking or writing involves combining on the horizontal, or *syntagmatic*, axis the words selected from a vertical, or *paradigmatic*, axis of possible alternatives. Every word is related both to the words that come before and after in the syntagm and to the associated words in the paradigm that could substitute for it. Whereas syntagms, in the terms Jakobson borrows from Saussure, are manifest "*in presentia*," visible on the page or audible in the vibrations of the air, the words in a paradigm are connected only "*in absentia* as members of a vir-tual mnemonic series."[50]

The results of keyword and phrase searches show how a fixed syntagm has been assembled into other, longer syntagms. The results of an abstract search, by contrast, show how the blanks specified by POS tags and symbols have been filled, matching the virtuality of paradigms with actual, historical syntagms. No matter how abstract the search string, the results are always concrete strings of words. Here is a small tranche of the results retrieved from CQPweb with the string {give} * the lie in EEBO-TCP texts published between 1500 and 1700:

gives the lie
give him the lie
giving me the lie
give tradition the lie
give Machiavell the lie
give scholars the lie
give Virgil the lie
gave them the lie
give Christ the lie
given himself the lie
gives Scripture the lie

By factoring out invariant elements, we can rewrite these results to make the vertical and horizontal axes still more obvious:

| Paradigm | Paradigm |  |
|---|---|---|
|  | himself |  |
|  | them |  |
| giving | me |  |
| gives | him |  |
| **Syntagm** give |  | the lie |
| gave | scholars |  |
| given | Machiavell |  |
|  | Virgil |  |
|  | Christ |  |
|  | Scripture |  |

As even these few results (11 out of 316) illustrate, this variable idiom exhibited a distinct polysemy in early modern England. To *give the lie* was, on the one hand, to slight someone's honor by accusing him (or far less frequently her) of mendacity, often as a preliminary to a duel.[51] But the idiom also signified an action that calls into question the very foundations of a system of belief, here named metonymically by Scripture, Christ, Virgil, Machiavelli, scholars, and so on. A loss of face, an assault on an ideology—only the latter meaning persists in ordinary use today.

In Jakobson's account, paradigms are arranged in succession, one after another, like the wheels on a slot machine.[52] But search results show that paradigms also nest recursively inside one another. The linguistic form retrieved by *{give} * the lie* comprises two internal paradigms—the first populated solely by the inflections of *give*, the second by the recipient of the lie—but the form is also, at the same time, an idiomatic unit selected from a virtual paradigm of other units, other forms that could have been chosen, filled, and grafted onto a longer syntagm instead. All but the very simplest of utterances contain paradigms within paradigms, wheels within wheels. The results of an abstract search string make visible both the combination of a linguistic form, as a unit of selection in its own right, with a variety of other forms and the various filling of the form's internal paradigms (blanks, categories, variables) with further selected units.

Another way to say that an abstract search transforms absent or virtual paradigms into a sequence of present syntagms is to say that it "projects the principle of equivalence from the axis of selection onto the axis of combination." This projection is what Jakobson terms the *poetic function* of language.[53] Search results exemplify the poetic function more reliably and more obviously than most poems, which might explain why people collect and share Google's autocomplete suggestions (predictions about a search string based on other users' searches) as "Google poems":

> sit silently
> sit silently doing nothing
> sit silently and watch the world
> sit silently and watch
>
> the funeral is
> the funeral is about to begin
> the funeral is for the living[54]

Gerard Manley Hopkins wrote that "the artificial part of poetry, perhaps we shall be right to say all artifice, reduces itself to the principle of parallelism. The structure of poetry is that of continuous parallelism."[55] If Google autocomplete produces the equivalents of epigrams or haikus, then the full results of an abstract search might yield an epic of thousands of lines structured by Hopkins's "principle of parallelism" (when order is specified) or Jakobson's more general "principle of equivalence" (when order is underspecified). Like Virgil's *Aeneid* or John Milton's *Paradise Lost*, the epic texts generated by search are, in C. S. Lewis's term, distinctly "secondary": they come after and index (point back to) the anterior texts of which they are composed.[56] Like centos, the patchwork poems created by fragmenting and rearranging the epics of Homer and Virgil, search results interrupt the linear structure of existing texts and assemble the resulting fragments into a new poem (a "made thing") that reveals the nature and history of a linguistic form in and through the variety of its instantiations.[57] Even the longest "epic" retrieved by an abstract search is but a single, fragmentary but potentially legible stanza of what Percy Shelley called "that great poem, which all poets, like the co-operating thoughts of one great mind, have built up since the beginning of the world."[58]

### Close and Hyper-Reading

As with actual epics, the results produced by an abstract search are revealing only to those who have eyes to see them. Humanities scholars have not always valued or welcomed the modes of attention requisite for transforming results lists into philological narrative. Some have fretted that forgoing the continuous, linear reading associated with the printed book will lead to what Sean Latham, following Myron Tuman, calls "frenetic reading," in which "harried and information-driven readers" skim lightly over the "density and linearity of the book," unaware of the depths of meaning it contains.[59] In the most sustained and careful attempt to understand the cognitive consequences of digital media, Katherine Hayles distinguishes between traditional *close reading*, which "correlates with deep attention, the cognitive mode traditionally associated with the humanities that prefers a single information stream, focuses on a single cultural object, for a relatively long time, and has a high tolerance for boredom," and *hyper-reading*, a term she borrows from James Sosnoski:

> Hyper-reading, which includes skimming, scanning, fragmenting, and juxtaposing texts, is a strategic response to an information-intensive environment, aiming to conserve attention by quickly identifying relevant information, so that only relatively few portions of a given text are actually read. . . . Hyper-reading correlates, I suggest, with hyper-attention, a cognitive mode that has a low threshold for boredom, alternates flexibly between different information streams, and prefers a high level of stimulation.[60]

*Hyper-attention* nicely names the mode of attention particular to digital search results, and Hayles points to empirical research suggesting that cognition occurs differently in front of the shifting texts on a screen than it does in front of the fixed text on a printed page. Yet the opposed categories of *close* and *hyper* reading, *deep* and *hyper* attention, while heuristically useful, nevertheless conceal significant continuities, continuities that cyberformalism seeks to exploit.

Because she uses *close reading* as the generic name for the absorptive, linear reading associated with printed books—what we once might simply have called *reading*—Hayles silently passes over the practices developed by many generations of formalist and historicist critics alike for whom close reading already entailed a kind of hyper-attention. In the hands of formalist close readers, the literary text (preeminently the lyric poem) is a mesh of overlapping patterns and links. The point of "reading in slow motion," as Reuben Brower described it, is not simply to "attend very closely to the words, their uses, and their meanings"; it is also to tease out a word's "connections with other words and meanings."[61] Literal deceleration (slow) and metaphorical proximity (close) permit the mind to skip forward and back to other parts of the text, noting complex, nonlinear associations and unpacking the plurality of possibilities folded into the single, sensuous literary object. This mode of reading was not the invention of New Critics but had long been part of humanist pedagogy. In the first chapter of the *Biographia Literaria* (1817), Samuel Taylor Coleridge recalls how his schoolmaster, the Reverend James Bowyer, would say that in "truly great poets . . . there is a reason assignable, not only for every word, but for the position of every word; and I well remember that, availing himself of the synonymes to the Homer of Didymus, he made us attempt to show, with regard to each, why it would not have answered the same purpose; and wherein consisted the peculiar fitness of the word in the original text."[62]

Guided by the principle of sufficient textual reason, the humanist reader learned to see each word ghosted by the synonymous words that could have been written in its place. If a poem under the scrutiny of formalist close reading is a complex pattern of internal links, then historicists open those links outward with such force that it becomes difficult to tell where Hayles's "single cultural object" ends and something else— context, culture, a world—begins. For the historicist, analyzing a text is partly a matter of discerning how it is made out of other texts. Though historicists and formalists alike might hesitate to describe a Shakespeare sonnet as an "information intensive environment" made up of "different information streams," their reading practices nevertheless belie its characterization as a "single information stream."

The distinction between *close* and *hyper* collapses from the other side as well. The reading of search results may at first appear to be *echt hyperreading*, since it involves the "skimming, scanning, fragmenting, and juxtaposing" of hundreds or thousands of texts. Yet if my own experience is any guide, such reading can lead to its own kind of "deep attention," engendering something between a meditative state (with the linguistic form serving as a repeated mantra) and aesthetic absorption (with successive instantiations serving as variations on a given theme). Repetition heightens sensitivity to the fullest range of differences: differences in constituents, context, use, meaning, affect, speaker, genre, and so on. The focus on a "single cultural object," the well-wrought urn of the New Critic, is indeed gone, but a newly constructed object, the sorted and filtered multiplicity of a form's instantiations, takes its place.

Quantitative digital humanities scholars often describe their research as "nonconsumptive," meaning that they "do not read, understand, or enjoy" the books they measure and statistically characterize.[63] Cyberformalist inquiry is decidedly consumptive: what Francis Bacon wrote in his *Essays*—"Some bookes are to bee tasted, others to bee swallowed, and some fewe to bee chewed and digested"[64]—still applies, though admittedly the ratio of consumption tips toward tasting. A Baconian nutritional pyramid updated for the study of linguistic forms might include some thousand books of which we sample only snippets in the results list, a hundred others of which we ingest a short excerpt, and, for the capstone, some few that we assimilate in full. As with all philological research, reading search results involves the cognitively demanding task of deciding when to stop and enjoy a proper meal. Maurice Lee is doubtless right that "given the vast and often arbitrary connections generated by searchable electronic archives, targeted research can unearth historical anecdotes to support seemingly any interpretive hypothesis."[65] Working in vast collections of searchable digital documents will require humanities disciplines to develop practices, norms, and evidentiary standards for distinguishing the genuinely significant connections from myriad arbitrary ones. But I also suppose, following Lee, that this decision will invariably involve aesthetic judgments, judgments of taste irreducible to explicit rules, preestablished methods, or quantitative measures.[66] The goal of tasting is not simply to pick out representative examples but rather to identify texts that are *articulate* in a double sense: as the joints (articulations) where the history of a form diverges from its previous course and as perspicuous expressions (articulations) of the causes of divergence. With or without digital search tools, the texts that a scholar identifies as articulate and therefore chooses to chew and digest will unavoidably shape the kinds of stories she will tell. Turning search results into philological narrative demands all the interpretive and analytical skills—all the cultural knowledge and practiced judgment—that humanists spend their careers cultivating. Not one jot or tittle of a scholar's training passes from use.

Though cyberformalism does not abrogate close reading, it does alter close reading's traditional modality. Close readers in the humanist tradition have long evaluated the words in a text by comparing them with other possible or conceivable words, often with the help of a reference work, in Coleridge's case "the synonyms to the Homer of Didymus." Cyberformalist inquiry shifts comparison from bare possibility to historical actuality, putting the word in relation to other words in an archive that have in fact filled the same form, served as values of the same variables. By moving from the possible to the actual, the cyberformalist seeks to ascertain what Foucault calls the "law of rarity": "*Everything* is never said; in relation to what might have been stated in a natural language (*langue*), in relation to the unlimited combination of linguistic elements, statements (however numerous they may be) are always in deficit."[67] In relation to the combinatorial "*everything*" that is "never said," any discourse will be a "distribution of gaps, voids, absences, limits, divisions," a comparative "poverty" rather than an unconditioned "plenitude."[68] Only a sliver of the multiple (and in cases of recursion, infinite) ways that a linguistic form could acceptably be filled will appear in an archive of any size. Advanced search capacities allow us to study the distribution of a form's instantiations in relation not to a notional plenitude in which everything is said but to its distribution in other periods, archives, genres, nations, and discursive positivities more generally.

What does the analysis of rarity look like? Consider again an earlier example: though as an attributive adjective *outrageous* could acceptably modify any (or every) noun, in the Corpus of Contemporary American English (1990–2015) it describes only people's ideas, speech, actions, and their consequences. In the pre-1700 texts of Early English Books Online (EEBO), by contrast, *outrageous* is also used to modify words for supernatural phenomena, such as *rivers, tempests, firespouts, waves, winds, storms*, or, as in *Hamlet, fortune*.[69] Narrowing takes place neither in the meaning of the word *outrageous* nor in the bare form of the attributive adjective but rather in background conceptions of what kind of things possess agency and moral responsibility and therefore warrant outrage. In any event, we cannot make visible the regularities in the use of *outrageous* as an attributive adjective by comparing the noun *fortune* with its synonyms, much less with all nouns in the dictionary. Only by studying the nouns that *outrageous* has actually modified across distinct sets of utterances can we make visible its increasing rarity. Cyberformalist inquiry is all the richer for trafficking in the poverty of actual utterances instead of in the notional plenitude of all possible utterances.

### Fragments of Fragments

Search engines are useful for cultural and historical research only when, as with Stephenson's Librarian, they dance spiderlike across a vast web of texts. And the philological narratives produced by cyberformalist inquiry will only be as good as the digital archives on which they are based. It is not enough to learn search languages and become adept at reading results; scholars also need to understand, concretely and theoretically, the archives in which they carry out their searches.

Concretely, understanding even a single digital archive is a colossal task involving prodigious bibliographic and historical knowledge.[70] As I write this, the archive most central to my research in early modern literature, EEBO, contains more than 130,000 titles printed between 1473 and 1700, with 44,314 of those titles available as full texts for searching through the Text Creation Partnership (TCP). These texts are manually keyed digital transcriptions of digital facsimiles of black-and-white microfilm photographs of early modern printed documents. Each stage of remediation introduces compounding error into the archive, and the automated standardization and annotation requisite for searching using POS tags or parsing introduces more error still. Just as crucially, the full-text searchable documents of EEBO-TCP are not the full linguistic culture or even the full printed record of early modern Britain. We can conceive of its coverage in terms of successively smaller concentric circles: all the language produced in Britain between 1473 and 1700; only written documents; only printed documents; only documents that were, as Ian Gadd writes, "either printed in the British Isles or its colonies or, if printed elsewhere in the world . . . printed in English or any other British language";[71] only those that survived to be photographed by University Microfilms starting in 1938; only copies, in "major" libraries, selected to be microfilmed; only those microfilms selected for digitization; only those digitized facsimiles selected for keying. EEBO full texts represent, in effect, a copy of a copy of a copy of a copy of a fraction of a fraction (and so on) of the *parole* of early modern Britain. Nevertheless, students of the early modern Anglophone world are extraordinarily advantaged in their access to digital texts. For all its flaws and limitations, EEBO is a relatively accurate, transparent, and well-cataloged scholarly archive, a field of light compared with which Google Books, with its tens of millions of digitized volumes made available for full-text searching through error-prone automated optical character recognition, is a dark forest indeed.

Digital archives, like archives more generally, are effects of power as well as contingency. Their inclusions and exclusions are not innocent. They are never comprehensive or representatively random or even effectively random, however large they may grow. We know this.[72] But how power and contingency have shaped the largest digital archives is an open empirical question. Here quantitative digital humanities have a marquee role to play. In collections of tens of thousands or tens of millions of documents, only large-scale computational analysis is positioned to offer answers to the most fundamental ontological question of digital archives: what is there? What kinds of discourses and genres on what topics written by what kinds of writers from what times and places are represented, and in what proportions?[73] The follow-up question will need to be answered by scholars working in physical archives and libraries: what else was there? What documents and voices have been excluded from or underrepresented in digital archives as they are now constituted? Without answers to these questions, we will not have the most basic grasp of the texts we are searching in and through.

Though archives are effects of power, it would be a mistake to suppose that even the most durable structures of exclusion and marginalization translate directly into the makeup or availability of digital texts. Digitization has in some cases jumbled longstanding hierarchies, usually as the direct result of the efforts of scholars and institutions to remediate the work of underrepresented or marginalized groups. There are many outstanding examples, but one will suffice here.[74] Starting in the late 1980s, the Brown Women Writers Project sought, as the project's history recounts, "to reclaim the cultural importance of early women's writing and bring it back into our modern field of vision."[75] It did so at a moment when "the electronic archive seemed like the ideal successor to the physical archive, since it promised to overcome the problems of inaccessibility and scarcity which had rendered women's writing invisible for so long." The project made hundreds of full texts by early modern women writers available for searching nearly a decade before the first phase of the TCP would finish doing the same for twenty-five thousand of the overwhelmingly male-authored texts in EEBO.

Yet in other cases digital remediation troublingly threatens to entrench existing hierarchies and exclusions. I restrict myself to a single, albeit massive example. Medievalists have long sought to challenge what Andrew Cole has called "the wholesale omission of the great middle of intellectual history, the medieval period, which . . . makes the crossing of the ancient and the modern possible in the first place," and what David Aers has described as the "systematic and institutionalized amnesia" that erases more than a thousand years of literature and culture from the stories we tell about who we are.[76] Yet attempts to treat this amnesia face mounting technological challenges. Scholars working on English history, literature, and culture from 1473 (the year of the first printed English-language book) to 1922 (the year after which copyright limits consumptive access to texts) can turn to impressively large and growing centralized archives of full texts, produced through keying or optical character recognition, to aid them in their research.[77] Classicists too have long been able to work with archives containing full-text versions of surviving documents. But medievalists working in English, as in other modern languages, lack any archive comparable to these in size and scope, and the obstacles to creating such an archive are immense. While manuscript pages are perhaps no more difficult to photograph than printed pages, optical character recognition is at present incapable of generating full texts from manuscripts, which require significantly more care, labor, and scholarly expertise (in paleography, codicology, and the history of language) than printed texts to transcribe.[78] The linguistic diversity of medieval English and the high degree of orthographic variation in medieval texts makes spelling standardization, lemmatization, POS tagging, and other kinds of natural language parsing extremely difficult, though not impossible.[79] Medieval manuscripts rarely fit the taxonomic categories of *book*, *work*, or *edition*, by which printed texts are generally classified and included in digital archives. Yet if medieval documents are not made available as digital full texts, they will be left out of work that relies on digital methods, quantitative and qualitative alike. The period Petrarch polemically described as "The Dark Ages" threatens to grow a little darker still.[80] As in the case of women's writing, the efforts of committed scholars and librarians are needed to prevent the reproduction and entrenchment of longstanding exclusions. Any cure for amnesia will need to put medieval manuscripts in reach of the full range of finding tools.

The concrete limitations of digital archives require humility about any and every set of search results. While this humility should not stop scholars from seeking to tell new kinds of philological narratives using digital search, it should prompt them to recognize that different archives, comprising other documents, will produce different results and thus different evidence for the existence, identity, meaning, and history of linguistic entities.

### Archive and Corpus

The consequences of archival finitude are theoretical as well as concrete. Quantitative analysis and cyberformalism inquire into different objects of knowledge that may nevertheless be made up of identical documents. As Saussure put it, "The object is not given in advance of the viewpoint"; rather, "it is the viewpoint adopted which creates the object."[81] Quantitative analysis characterizes a *corpus*, a closed body of texts selected according to specific criteria. The selection criterion for Franco Moretti's corpus in one article is "British Novels, 1740–1850."[82] When Michael Witmore and Jonathan Hope perform statistical analyses of Shakespeare's plays, they work on one corpus; when their analysis grows to include early English drama or early English print, their corpus, and with it their selection criteria, changes.[83] A corpus is always closed—made into a self-contained whole—by an act of stipulation: a choice of which texts to include and which to exclude. This is true even if the corpus may later expand or change based on new criteria or the availability of new texts.[84]

The stipulated closure of a corpus means either that it *stands as* the totality of a set of documents (as with the corpus of Shakespeare's works) or that it *stands in for* a larger totality, as a representative sample. Sampling is a statistical response to incompleteness. Though no sample is definitive, scholars can do better or worse jobs of sampling, make better and worse choices about representativeness, and stipulate better or worse criteria for inclusion. Stipulating a set of documents to stand as or stand in for the whole licenses the use of measures based on relative frequency, frequency of parts relative to the whole. It fixes the number of sides on the dice to make it possible to calculate the probability of any particular throw.

The cyberformalist, by contrast, carries out inquiries in *archives* rather than corpora. Archives are discovered rather than stipulated. Scholars construct corpora, adding documents to satisfy criteria of completeness or representativeness, but scholars are parachuted into archives and must find their way around. Lacking an act of stipulative closure, archives are constitutively open. The die of the archive has no total number of sides, no total denominator relative to which frequencies can be assessed. To posit a denominator, to fix the number of sides on the die, is once again to make the archive into a corpus by stipulating that it stands as or stands in for a whole. In the archive, there is always at least one text missing, outstanding, yet to be added; at any moment the archive is always $n-1$, even as it continues to grow and include more texts.

The epistemological differences between corpora and archives matter even when they contain the very same documents. As a representative corpus grows in size, measures of it become increasingly robust, so that in a sufficiently large corpus a single missing document will have virtually no statistically significant effects. What matter if one document is omitted from a trend line generated out of thirty-six million documents? The robustness of statistical measures in a corpus means that they can be invalidated only by systematic distortions in the data, not by the addition or subtraction of a small number of texts. By comparison, the qualitative philological narratives produced from search results, as from their print predecessors, are inherently fragile. Fragility is the price cyberformalism, like its philological predecessors, pays for its responsiveness to the singular, its unwillingness to rule out the possibility that the one text that is always, constitutively missing from an archive has the potential to transform an entire story, revise or discredit a claim, dispense with some explanations and suggest new ones, or upset accounts of origin, influence, and diffusion. In the corpus, as corpus linguists are fond of saying, *Einmal ist Keinmal* (once is never); in the archive, one additional instance has the potential to alter everything.

Searching in an archive nevertheless shares with statistical methods what we might call *procedural egalitarianism*. By this I mean that a search in a database will retrieve matches from an archive regardless of whether they appear in Hegel's *Phenomenology of Spirit* or in a letter to the editor of the *Iowa City Press Citizen*. Without the interference of ranking algorithms, searches match the pattern specified by a string, attaching no greater value or meaning to products of self-aware artistry than to the most banal repetitions of a cliché. Search is color- and gender-blind unless or until we supply the proper metadata to sort texts by race and gender. Each result is counted as one; every instance is *an* instance. Yet this egalitarianism is limited. First, as already mentioned, archives are in their very constitution inegalitarian and exclusionary products of power. Second, the cyberformalist breaks from egalitarianism almost immediately, as soon as he or she begins to comb through results to identify articulate texts and piece together a story. All search results are created equal, but (to twist George Orwell) some are more equal than others. The cyberformalist is inevitably faced with the task of determining salience and exemplarity, separating wheat from chaff, sorting instances into categories, arranging them into a sequence, an order, which is to say a hierarchy of importance. Not only is it not the case that *Einmal ist Keinmal*; when building a philological narrative, *Einmal* isn't even *Einmal*. And there is, of course, no reason to suppose the hierarchies necessarily constructed by the cyberformalist will be less biased or more just than those of print scholars.

Quantitative digital humanities scholarship has often looked to the social sciences for models and methods of inquiry.[85] Cyberformalism looks back to a rather different set of exemplars. In the early days of print, Lorenzo Valla wrote a Latin grammar textbook based on classical usage; Niccolò Perotti and Ambrogio Calepino compiled Latin dictionaries; Erasmus reconstructed the pronunciation of classical Latin and Greek; Julius Caesar Scaliger formulated the principles of Latin grammar and style; Gerardus Vossius attempted to derive the Greek etymologies of Latin words. Renaissance humanists, in other words, took upon themselves the task of building the infrastructural print tools necessary for the progress of philology. These tools and their descendants continue to support ongoing inquiry into the words that have been key to cultural studies. Working in a later age and a new medium, present day humanists should recognize that a motley assembly of corporations, librarians, and corpus linguists have bequeathed us many of the digital search tools necessary for extending our philological understanding of language, history, and culture, and we should use them. Where these tools fall short—where they are insufficient to retrieve an expanded range of abstract and complex linguistic entities—we should partner with programmers, computational linguists, and machine-learning specialists to develop new ones.

# STUDIES

## 3

## *Was It for This?* and the Study of Influence

And what is Poetic Influence anyway? Can the study of it really be
anything more than the wearisome industry of source-hunting, of
allusion-counting, an industry that will soon touch apocalypse anyway
when it passes from scholars to computers?

Harold Bloom, *The Anxiety of Influence*

### Source Hunting

Harold Bloom's question in *The Anxiety of Influence* (1973) is at once
derisive and prophetic. Derision is directed at the intellectual wage laborers who perform the nearly mechanical task of recording the way words and
phrases, plots and characters, formulas and conventions move between
literary works. For these laborers, Bloom prophesies a radical transformation in the means of scholarly production. Like the manufacturing jobs
replaced by increasing automation, this "industry" will eventually be populated solely by weariless computers that can better perform the chores of
"source-hunting" and "allusion-counting." The move "from scholars to
computers" is apocalyptic because with it the typical study of "Poetic Influence" will finally become the spiritless activity, mechanical in truth, it had
always been.

Bloom's purpose in envisaging the unraveling of the source-hunting industry is primarily to clear room for his own theory of poetic influence,
which replaces sources with Oedipal fathers and allusions with struggles for
priority, yet as far as prophecies go, his has fared well. Computers are indeed
transforming the means of scholarly production, the conditions of literary-
critical labor, and especially the study of influence, as work by numerous

digital humanists, such as David Bamman, Gregory Crane, Franco Moretti, Matthew Jockers, and others, amply shows.[1] But while Bloom's prophecy captures the profundity of the change, it nevertheless misconstrues its character. This chapter offers a corrective vision in which the consequence of digital tools for the study of influence (including study conducted under the aegis of intertextuality) is less apocalypse than revelation. Labor does not merely "pass" from scholars to computers. Nor do computers simply allow us to do what we already do with greater speed and efficiency. Rather, computers have the capacity to deepen, complicate, systematize, and ultimately transform the study of influence. A change in the conditions of academic labor amounts, in this case, to a change in the possibilities of understanding. More specifically, full-text searchable archives allow us to turn our attention from the local task of hunting and counting to the systematic project of discovering and reassembling literary networks of diffusion. Modeled on the "actor networks" of the sociologists Bruno Latour and John Law, such networks reveal the reductionist assumptions that underlie many of influence study's basic concepts, concepts as basic as "commonplace," "source," "author," and "text."[2] By helping us to reassemble networks of diffusion, digital tools allow us to do justice to the plurality, materiality, and irreducible heterogeneity of literary influence.[3]

As a case study in reassembling a network of diffusion, this chapter focuses on a phrase that has already received intense critical attention, *Was it for this*, which initiates the poem that became the seed of William Wordsworth's *The Prelude* (1850). Attending at some length to previous scholarship on the phrase's origins will give us a starting point for further investigation, and it will also allow us to differentiate the digital study of influence from its predecessors. An untitled draft manuscript fragment of 150 lines that Wordsworth composed in Germany in October 1798 begins midline and perhaps midsentence:

> was it for this
> That one, the fairest of all rivers, loved
> To blend his murmurs with my nurse's song,
> And from his alder shades and rocky falls,
> And from his fords and shallows, sent a voice
> To intertwine my dreams? For this . . .
>
> (lines 1–6)[4]

Lines 20–23 ring the note again: "Was it for this that I, a four years' child / . . . / Basked in the sun, or plunged into their streams?" The question serves both as introduction and also, in the truncated variation, "For this," as structuring refrain. The second verse paragraph begins, "For this in springtime" (30), and the fourth, "For this, when on the withered mountain-slope" (76). When Wordsworth incorporated the draft fragment into the two-part *Prelude* of 1799, he jettisoned or wholly altered many of its lines, yet he still began the poem with *Was it for this*. The 1804, 1805, and 1850 versions of the *Prelude* retain the phrase but relocate it some 270 lines into the first book, to a different context, where it no longer serves an inaugural or structuring role.

The scholarly search for the sources of William Wordsworth's question began in earnest on 18 April 1975, when a letter to the editor by Jonathan Wordsworth (the great-great-grandnephew of the poet and a romanticist at Oxford) appeared in the *Times Literary Supplement*. The letter begins, "Sir,— May I ask for your readers' help over one of the odder *Prelude* echoes?" before offering Alexander Pope's *Rape of the Lock* (1712) as one possible source:

Was it for this you took such constant Care
The Bodkin, Comb, and Essence to prepare;
For this your Locks in Paper-Durance bound,
For this with tort'ring Irons wreath'd around?
For this with Fillets strain'd your tender Head,
And bravely bore the double Loads of Lead?

(4.97–102)

While it is "inconceivable," the letter continues, that the elder Wordsworth did not know Pope's lines, Jonathan nevertheless wonders whether there is "in fact a shared classical source."[5]

Other readers were quick to heed the call for help. Less than a month later the Harvard scholar Walter Kaiser wrote in with an echo in W. B. Yeats's "September 1913": "Was it for this the wild geese spread / The grey wing upon every tide?"[6] On 6 June the editorial page featured two further replies. The first, from John Woolford, nominates a passage from John Milton's *Samson Agonistes* (1671), spoken by Samson's father, Manoa: "For this did the angel twice descend? For this / Ordained thy nurture holy, as of a plant; / Select, and sacred?" (361–63). He argues that Milton's omission of the initial "Was it" is "unimportant weighed against Wordsworth's situation and Samson's"—both failed to fulfill their earlier promise—and he asks whether Pope's passage may not also "be derived from *Samson*," especially since "it is concerned with precisely the loss of hair which brought about Samson's downfall."[7] In the second reply, Jonathan Wordsworth updates readers on the progress of his investigation. He acknowledges Yeats's echo and adds Wilfred Owen's "Futility" (1918)—"Was it for this the clay grew tall?"—before addressing a further source, brought to his attention by a private letter from Henry Woudhuysen, then an undergraduate. "Equidistant between Pope and Wordsworth," Jonathan writes, is William Shenstone's "Elegy XVIII": "Was it for this, by constant vigils worn, / I met the terrours of an early grave? / For this . . . / For this. . . ." Despite having amassed a small collection of uses, Jonathan Wordsworth nevertheless continues "to think there probably was a source" behind all of them, most likely "classical." He offers one Latin parallel, *Aeneid* 2.664, "hoc erat, alma parens . . ." (Was it for this, nurturing mother . . . ), but cautions that "the initial question is not developed either by Virgil, or by Dryden" in his translation.[8]

Jonathan Wordsworth shared further updates in July. The classicists C. D. Gilbert and Michael Reeve had alerted him to two possible Latin "parallels" that made comparable use of a repeated formula, Cicero's *Pro Caelio* 14.34 and Seneca's satire *Apocolocyntosis* 10, while his own reading had yielded "an important link in the English chain," the eighteenth-century Scottish poet James Thomson's "Autumn" (1730): "And was it then for this you roam'd the Spring/ . . . for this you toil'd/ . . . / For this in Autumn search'd the blooming waste, / . . . for this sad fate?" Thomson's poem offers a blank-verse counterpart to Pope's heroic couplets, on the basis of which Jonathan Wordsworth hypothesizes a split tradition: "One might guess that Shenstone derives from Thomson, and that [Richard] Jago (*The Goldfinches, An Elegy* [1747]; sent by Roger Lonsdale) and Byron (*Don Juan* [1819] 1.148ff; sent by Ian Donaldson) come from Pope." Though doubtless aware of Pope, Wordsworth was "more likely . . . to be drawing on Thomson."[9]

Not all contributions to the correspondence appear to have been accepted. Paul Haeffner's improbable proposal of *The Revenger's Tragedy* ("Does the silkworm expend her yellow labours / For thee? For thee does she undo herself?") received no further comment.[10] But others added significant new information. In September, Howard Erskine-Hill wrote that Ludovico

Ariosto's *Orlando Furioso* (1516) provides "an earlier and more exact analogue" than those previously mentioned. Melissa, disguised as Ruggiero's sage tutor Atlanta, reproaches the hero for luxuriating in the palace of the sorceress Alcina:

> È questo dunque il frutto ch'io
> lungamente atteso ho del sudor mio?
> di medolle già d'orsi e di leoni
> ti porsi io dunque li primi alimenti
>
> (canto 7, stanzas 56–57)

The similarity to Wordsworth's phrase is not especially evident in the Italian, but it is unmistakable in the first English translation of Ariosto, published by John Harington in 1591:

> What was't for this that I in youth thee fed,
> With marrow of the Beares and Lions fell?
> That I through caues and deserts haue thee led,
> Where serpents of most vgly shape do dwell,
> Where Tygers fierce and cruell Leopards bred,
> And taught thee how their forces all to quell

Erskine-Hill cautions that accepting this source does not "deny the central position, in the descent thus revealed, of Manoa's question to Samson"; rather, Wordsworth, Milton, and Pope may all have alluded to this moment in the *Furioso*. In any event, he suggests, the connection to Ariosto reveals the importance of "heroic story" to *The Prelude*.[11]

In November 1977 Jonathan Wordsworth used a review of Stephen Parrish's edition of *The Prelude* to tie up the loose ends of the correspondence he had begun more than two years earlier, which had petered out after November 1975, probably for lack of new discoveries.[12] After quoting Wordsworth's opening question, he endorses Woolford's contribution, acknowledging that while other sources are available, "Milton's lines" from *Samson Agonistes* are "especially important," since in failing to write *The Recluse* Wordsworth is similar to Samson, who failed to free the Israelites. Jonathan Wordsworth closes the discussion of *Was it for this* in Bloomian fashion, asserting, "If ever there was a case of the anxiety of influence it must be this," regardless of whether the "echo" was "conscious" or not, and asks us to imagine "Milton's presence looking over the effete's [sic] shoulder as he writes."[13]

### The Source and the Commonplace

Though the *TLS* correspondence is somewhat haphazard, it nevertheless operates under a clear set of guiding presuppositions and aims that it shares with source hunting more generally.[14] There is, from the outset, an acknowledgment of multiple possible sources; Pope is offered only as the first of others to come. Yet beneath the acknowledgment of plurality is the drive toward discovering a single, definitive precursor, "a source," or as Woolford puts it, "*the* source," rather than sources. In keeping with this drive, multiple appearances of the phrase are treated as the offspring of a single predecessor. Jonathan Wordsworth begins the investigation as a search for a "shared classical source," where *classical* initially means Greek or Latin but eventually comes, in scare quotes, to mean definitive and aboriginal, needing no further source, such that Milton can be described as the "classical" source of both Pope and Wordsworth. Erskine-Hill's discovery of the phrase in Harington's translation of Ariosto allows him to propose a still earlier, shared source for all three poets.

The "importance" of a source is evaluated through similarity—not only similarity of phrasing, which is prerequisite, but of situation, subject matter, generic form, and so on. The difference between Milton's "For this" and Wordsworth's "Was it for this" is ultimately outweighed by the similarity between Samson's situation and Wordsworth's. Because they wrote rhyming verse, Jago and Byron are thought to look back to Pope, whereas Wordsworth and Shenstone, writing in blank verse, look back to Thomson. Finally, all uses of *Was it for this* prior to Wordsworth are assigned to the category *source*, or, in more tentative formulations that avoid causal assertion, *parallel, analogue*, or *echo*.

The inquiry into poetic influence that unfolds on the *TLS* correspondence page drew on the public and private labor of a broad community of scholars, researchers, and undergraduates from multiple fields, disciplines, institutions, and countries. Ten named and a number of unnamed investigators turned up eleven sources (depending on how one counts), a few of them clearly significant, as well as two subsequent echoes. While a critic like Bloom would question the intellectual worth of such an investigation, in scholarly terms it was unmistakably productive: the following decades saw numerous articles and book chapters, often by notable scholars, returning to the correspondence to add sources, reconsider influences, and draw on its discoveries for interpretive purposes, making Wordsworth's phrase one of the most discussed in twentieth-century studies of influence.[15]

The participants in the *TLS* correspondence were under no illusion that they had found all possible sources, parallels, or analogues. Yet they would probably have been surprised to learn how many uses of the phrase they could have discovered with world enough and time—or a good search engine. A Google Books search for the exact phrase *was it for this* prior to 1798, when Wordsworth composed the lines that burgeoned into *The Prelude*, returns 2,350 matches. Using the Text Creation Partnership engine to search Early English Books Online returns 153 matches in 118 works, all before 1700. Literature Online, a collection of 350,000 full texts, returns 176 matches in 228 works prior to 1798, which it breaks down into 63 poems, 101 dramas, and 12 prose texts.[16] Not all these matches are genuine. Many are duplicates, especially because they are drawn from archives that cover overlapping periods. Some works, depending on their popularity, appear in multiple editions, collections, and anthologies. In some proportion of matches the phrase is not used conventionally, since *Was it for this* was (and remains) a perfectly colloquial phrase that could have been written or spoken by any competent user of the English language without drawing on previous texts or traditions. In others it has a different syntax, or is used with a different aim, as when the natural philosopher Joseph Glanvill asks, "Was it for this man's sin or his Father's [that he was struck blind]?," using "this" as a determiner modifying "man" rather than as a demonstrative pronoun.[17] Excluding duplicates and false matches leaves, in a conservative estimate, more than a thousand unique uses of the phrase in published English works prior to 1798, though the precise number is ultimately beside the point, especially since it could easily grow as the archives mentioned above expand or as further archives are consulted. What is important for present purposes is that a thousand is a big number, bigger than could be made sense of under the investigative presuppositions of the *TLS* correspondence or of traditional source study more generally.

To the examples uncovered by Jonathan Wordsworth and his interlocutors, digital searches add works by luminaries like Fulke Greville, John Webster, Abraham Cowley, Michael Drayton, John Dryden, Tobias Smollett, John Gay, and Jonathan Swift (or perhaps another of the Scriblerians), as well as by lesser lights like Samuel Brandon, the brothers Francis and John Quarles, Robert Gomersall, Shackerly Marmion, John Banks, Elkanah Settle, and Stephen Duck. The male participants in the *TLS* correspondence mention only male authors, but female authors such as Ann Radcliffe, Eliza Haywood, Aphra Behn (twice, in a fictional love letter and a comedy), and Lady Mary Wroth also used the phrase prior to 1798. In addition to appearing in the lyric, dramatic, and heroic poetry mentioned in the correspondence, the phrase also appeared in emblem poems, epistolary novels, translations, polemical pamphlets, sermons, newspaper columns, protestant meditations, Montaigne-inspired essays, antipapist polemical tracts, devotional poems, courtesy books, and gothic romances; in English-language texts published in Paris, Amsterdam, Edinburgh, Dublin, and Philadelphia, as well as London. It was used wistfully, tragically, elegiacally, bitterly, reproachfully, farcically, satirically, and frequently (to my ear at least) woodenly; by suicidal heroes, jealous villains, disappointed parents, deceived friends, spurned lovers, betrayed empresses, zealous nationalists, fiery revolutionaries, fervent pilgrims, and repentant sinners. In the two centuries preceding the composition of *The Prelude* one would be nearly as hard pressed to find an author, and especially a poet or playwright, who did not use the phrase as to find one who did.

A single individual possessing no extraordinary technical skill, sitting alone at a computer with Internet access and a full complement of library subscriptions, can now uncover these uses of the phrase in an afternoon of leisurely searching, though of course doing anything with them—reading, sorting, understanding—takes a more considerable investment. Is this the apocalypse prophesied by Bloom? It does represent a radical change in the conditions of academic labor, as I explore shortly. The pressing matter here is what a thousand-odd sources do to our understanding of influence. They should, to start, challenge the notion that one could, through any further evidence or consideration, arrive at a single, definitive source for Wordsworth's inaugural question. To be sure, some texts do consciously allude or unconsciously borrow from a single source, but the a priori presupposition of such a source is untenable. Wordsworth likely encountered the phrase in a multitude of texts: not only in those mentioned in the *TLS* correspondence but also in a poem by an acquaintance, Francis Wrangham, "The Destruction of Babylon" (1795);[18] in *Things as They Are, or The Adventures of Caleb Williams* (1794), a novel by his early philosophical exemplar,

William Godwin; in Ann Radcliffe's *Mysteries of Udolpho* (1794); in at least six issues of *Gentleman's Magazine* (1731–1922); in four of the poems and plays anthologized in Vicesimus Knox's *Extracts, Elegant, Instructive, and Entertaining* (1791), the standard poetry anthology of the day; and in a host of other texts that he could have read or that scholars have claimed, with varying degrees of confidence, that he actually did read.[19] Although he encountered the phrase in multiple places, as Wordsworth sat down to compose the lines that would grow into *The Prelude* he may have had in mind a single work, or two, or twenty, or indeed none at all—only a mere phrase ringing in his ear, detached from any particular text or author, its plural origins merged, or simplified, or conflated, or forgotten, or half-forgotten. As Ezra Pound puts it, "The domain of culture begins when one HAS 'forgotten-what-book.'"[20]

Nor can we justly elevate one of Wordsworth's predecessors to a decisive role based on similarities of situation, as the *TLS* correspondence presupposes from the outset. To judge that in composing his opening lines Wordsworth is, for example, more like Milton's Samson, or Ariosto's Ruggiero, or Virgil's Aeneas, or even Pope's Belinda is to assess the *extent* of similarity by deciding on the *criteria* of similarity. If we elect Milton as chief precursor, for example, we have implicitly decided that similarity of phrasing is less important than similarity of situation and that who is speaking is less important than what is said, since Wordsworth, like Aeneas, asks the question himself, whereas Manoa asks the question for Samson. We must decide, if only tacitly, on further criteria that allow us to judge that Samson's failure to liberate Israel is a closer match than Ruggiero's failure to resist feminine luxuriousness; or that Wordsworth utters the lines with a heroic voice (as Milton and Harington's Ariosto do) rather than a pastoral elegiac voice (as Shenstone and Thomson do). Such criteria are arbitrary enough when judging three or four texts, but when judging twenty or a hundred, much less a thousand, they are nonsensical. Even if one could decide on the relevant criteria with which to nominate a single, decisive predecessor, doing so overlooks a still more basic fact. Writers are in the business of wresting phrases from their previous contexts of use and repurposing them. The recontextualizability of *Was it for this* is a precondition of its appearance in a vast array of genres, voices, and situations. Judging the importance of sources by their similarity neglects the capacity of poets to pluck beautiful fruit from the tree of the other as well as from the tree of the same.

Harold Bloom's oft-quoted claim that "criticism is the art of knowing the hidden roads that go from poem to poem" is surely right.[21] But while his Freudian account invariably reduces "roads" to a single "road," a *via sacra* that leads from one Oedipal father, priest, or poet to another, every text is more properly understood as a turn lane, filling station, or chop shop at the intersection of a complex and overlapping network of local byways and transnational highways. The digital archive helps us to put these hidden roads on the map.

If Wordsworth's inaugural question does not have a single origin, conscious or otherwise, does it therefore follow that it is commonplace? In present-day scholarly usage (as opposed to the usage of Aristotle or Renaissance humanists), to describe something as *commonplace* is simply to assert that it is pervasive (and perhaps to slight it as banal or trite). This is clearly true of *Was it for this* in the seventeenth and eighteenth centuries.[22] The designation helpfully avoids the error of presupposing that the phrase has a single, identifiable source. It also has the convenience of stopping at the point of acknowledging that the phrase is widespread without probing into why or how it became so. But this is precisely the problem: declaring something commonplace pulls inquiry up short at the boundary of what we already know. The term functions as what Latour calls a *black box*:[23] it is useful precisely because it conceals complex processes of diffusion from view. The black-boxing of diffusion is especially evident when scholars casually refer to an idea or phrase as being "in the air" or, in a more recent idiom that evokes fluoridation conspiracies, "in the water." Such idioms are used metaphorically—no one, I take it, actually means to propose the cultural equivalent of miasma or ether—but they perform the work of concealing all the same.[24] We use them when, as with the now-inert jokes of Elizabethan playwrights about cuckolds having horns, we see something's presence everywhere and the signs of its genesis and diffusion nowhere. The *common* of the commonplace is the end product of a process of diffusion that is forgotten (as in Pound's "forgotten-what-book") or hidden from view.

The kind of scholarly ignorance such ways of speaking represent would be unobjectionable enough, since we cannot know or inquire into everything, and the process by which the common becomes common is often difficult to ascertain. What makes this kind of ignorance objectionable is that it redoubles itself. A black box that began as a useful tool ended up hiding from view the very processes that it is used to illuminate, the very workings of culture. The term *commonplace* has allowed the discipline of literary studies to use its knowledge of a thing's pervasiveness to conceal its ignorance of the mechanisms by which it came to be pervasive. It lets scholars operate under the assumption that because they cannot identify the specific, singular somewhere from which an author receives a phrase or idea, it must therefore be from an unspecified everywhere or, in what amounts to the same thing, an idealized nowhere. In contemporary literary scholarship, the commonplace is the workmanlike companion of Virgil's Fama (Rumor), the god of many mouths, voices, tongues, eyes, and ears, who (*mirabile dictu*) spreads truth and falsehood far and wide. But Virgil at least recognized Fama as a fictional stand-in for a complex process of diffusion that is only infrequently open to inspection.

Only by material processes of transmission, only by the work of coordinated humans and nonhuman things, does something widespread come to be spread so widely. There is no reservoir of cultural material (ideas, words, images, background assumptions, discursive rules, etc.) independent of concrete mechanisms of diffusion. No utterance reproduces itself without matter in motion, without the work of tongues, pens, or presses. Phrases or ideas are "in the air" only in the wholly literal sense that vibrations carry them from mouth to ear, light carries them from surface to eye, or, more recently, radio waves or pulses of light carry them from transmitter to receiver. The drive to identify a single source mistakenly seeks to pierce through a phrase's plurality; by positing it as inexplicably everywhere at once, the category of the commonplace mystifies the materiality of the processes by which a phrase becomes common.

### Standards and Formulas

The thousand-odd uses of *Was it for this* do not merely disabuse us of some widely accepted methodological assumptions; they also call for explanation. Traditional source study has focused on the individual author and the work—its sources, significance, and meaning. Accounting for the phrase's plurality, by contrast, requires a new set of questions: Why did this particular phrase spread so widely? What media, what agencies, what things, transmitted it? Why did it flourish in a particular environment? What were its variations, how did they arise, and which were influential? How did it move between groups (English and Irish writers, for example, or poets and playwrights)? What made some groups (poets, heroic poets, rhyming poets, etc.) particularly susceptible? Asking these kinds of questions does not make Wordsworth disappear, but it does displace him from the center of investigation. He becomes one (admittedly consequential) node, his debts a subset of edges, in a larger network of diffusion.

Though these questions inquire about the dynamics of a network, they do not obviate close attention to the phrase's verbal intricacies. *Was it for this* is so readily transmissible because of its linguistic form.[25] The phrase's twin pronouns—the impersonal "it" and the demonstrative "this"—hook seamlessly into a wide variety of contexts. *It* and *this* are what Roman Jakobson called *shifters*, linguistic signs that gain their indexical meaning (meaning as pointers) from the context in which they are uttered.[26] Unlike aphorisms, maxims, or adages such as "Friends share all things in common," which convey situation-independent meaning, the phrase taken on its own is semantically poor, with *was* and *for* serving grammatical rather than lexical functions and *it* and *this* pointing only to empty or unspecified particulars.

Yet the phrase's semantic poverty is the condition of its combinatory opulence. While its referential and semantic openness makes it portable, the specificity of its form makes it worth porting. It initiates utterances that fill in, with various degrees of definition, answers to the questions posed by its pronouns, utterances of the form *Was it for this [that] X [in order to] Y*, where *X* describes a propitious past and *Y* the deficient present. (The *X* and *Y* variables are reversible and may both be left unexpressed, or implied, or gestured to with a deictic sweep of the hand.) For the author sitting down to compose, the phrase offers an instrument of invention or way to begin writing, a *seed phrase* that bears within it a set of complex syntactic, temporal, and narrative relations, as well as the moods, attitudes, and conventional speech acts that go with them—the generative origins, in other words, not simply of a sentence but of an entire dramatic situation. Consider a stanza by Mary Leapor, the daughter of a Northamptonshire gardener who for much of her short life (1722–46) worked as a domestic servant; the stanza likens the rejection of her play script to the humiliation of an errant child:

> Was it for this, O graceless child!
>    Was it for this you learn'd to spell?
> Thy face and credit both are spoiled:
>    Go drown thyself in yonder well.

The whole matter of the stanza is anticipated in, and can be folded back into, its initiating phrase: "Was it [learning to spell] for this [the spoiling of thy face and credit both]?"[27] In much the same way that a seed contains the structure of a tree, or in Wordsworth's terms, that "the child is father of the man," so does the phrase comprehend and dictate the form of both the sentence and the situation that follows from it.

In Leapor's poem as elsewhere, the *it* refers to the promise of the past, the *this* to the failure of that promise in the present. Because the phrase retrospectively takes measure of the disparity between past and present, registering the frailty of human hopes and expectations, it is usually uttered with disappointment, regret, resentment, rage, or despair; speakers use it to initiate the conventional speech acts of mourning, lamenting, complaining, reproaching, and chastising. A range of intricate dramatic situations are tightly coiled into four colloquial, monosyllabic, Anglo-Saxon words. (In digital terms, the phrase is composed entirely of *stop words*, which are usually filtered out before text processing.)[28] While it can initiate the most formal of set pieces and acquires an especially ceremonial character when used as a refrain, it does not sound out of place in the prose of the forum or the marketplace. Meter matters too: the phrase is made up of two iambs (Was *it* for *this*) or, as need dictates, a trochee and an iamb (*Was* it for *this*), allowing it to be easily integrated into the most common verse forms of the day.

The humanist culture of early modern England, obsessed with recovering and imitating classical antiquity, proved highly susceptible to the phrase. Through the work of early translators, it arrived stamped with the most prestigious of associations—with the premier form of literary art, the heroic poem, and with that form's most exemplary practitioner, Publius Vergilius Maro. In book 2 of Virgil's *Aeneid*, after witnessing Troy in flames, Aeneas is rescued by his mother, Venus, from marauding Greeks. Resolved to die fighting, he returns to his home and bewails his and his family's fate:

> hoc erat, alma parens, quod me per tela, per ignis
> eripis, ut mediis hostem in penetralibus utque
> Ascanium patremque meum iuxtaque Creusam
> altered in alterius mactatos sanguine cernam?
>
> (2.664–67)

(Was it for this, gracious mother, that thou savest me amid fire and sword, to see the foe in the heart of my home, and Ascanius, and my father, and Creüsa at their side, slaughtered in each other's blood?)[29]

This lament represents the nadir of Aeneas's fortunes; his hopes are soon restored by a prophecy that his son Ascanius will found the Roman race. But light in Troy gives way to darkness in Carthage. A version of Aeneas's "hoc erat . . . quod" appears again in book 4, which relates his love affair with Dido, his eventual departure, and her subsequent suicide. Dido impales herself and casts her dying body on the pyre supposedly meant to immolate the possessions Aeneas has left behind. When Anna, her sister, returns to find her corpse, she despairs:

hoc illud, germana, fuit? me fraude petebas?
hoc rogus iste mihi, hoc ignes araeque parabens?

(4.675–76)

(Was it for this, sister? Didst thou aim thy fraud at me? Was this for me the meaning of thy pyre, this of thy altar and fires?)[30]

Where Aeneas exclaims "this" (*hoc*) only once, Anna beats out the demonstrative pronoun three times: "this . . . this . . . this." Where his despair gives rise to hope, hers leads to ghastly suicide.

Wordsworth studied Virgil's lines during his education at the Free Grammar School at Hawkshead, which was endowed and founded by the archbishop of York in the late sixteenth century.[31] The standard grammar curriculum focused heavily on classical languages and literatures and especially on Latin texts; with some exceptions, this curriculum stayed remarkably stable for nearly four centuries.[32] Along with Milton, Pope, Dryden, Shenstone, Thomson, Cowley, and Harington—indeed all the male authors of the previous two centuries who received a classical education—Wordsworth would have come to know the *Aeneid* in school through repeated reading, translation, double translation (from Latin to the vernacular and back again), memorization, and imitation. As an exemplary object, Virgil's poem received especially close study, more than even most other Latin literature.[33] Though English grammar-school boys usually read the entire epic, they often gave special attention to books 2 and 4, which contain Aeneas's and Anna's laments.[34] By putting students on intimate terms with these books of Virgil's Latin poem, the grammar schools of the sixteenth, seventeenth, and eighteenth centuries established the conditions for the spread of *Was it for this* throughout the educated English populace.

Evidence of Wordsworth's classical education survives in the first volume of Christopher Pitt's translation of the *Aeneid*, a volume he owned and shared with his three brothers.[35] Published in 1736, Pitt's *Aeneid* was acquired by the Wordsworths as early as 1784, when William was fourteen years old and, with his father dead a year, newly orphaned. Duncan Wu helpfully describes the copy's markings: "The verso of the first flyleaf bears the inscription, 'J Wordsworth 1784'; the recto of the second flyleaf bears the inscriptions, 'Rd & Wm Wordsworth 1784' and, beneath it, 'John Wordsworth's Book 1787.'"[36] In addition, the recto of the final flyleaf bears the inscriptions "Richard," "C Wordsworth," and "John Wordsworth," pen trials as much as marks of ownership.[37] Based on the evidence of the book's inscriptions, it is likely that William and his brothers used Pitt's *Aeneid* as what later came to be called a "crib," "pony," or "trot,"[38] an aid to translation that allowed them to complete their lessons without consulting a dictionary or Latin grammar. They appear to have passed the book down from older brother to younger, Richard to William to John to Christopher, so that each could use it to tackle Virgil's Latin at the appointed time in the curriculum. Pitt's translation has Anna, discovering the body of Dido, wail, "Was it for this my hands prepar'd the pyre / The fatal altar, and the funeral fire?" (4.971–72). Even after he finished his schooling, Wordsworth continued his intimacy with the *Aeneid*. He later acquired and annotated a copy of John Ogilby's *Works of Publius Virgilius Maro I* (1649), and in 1823–24, dissatisfied with existing translations, he set out to make his own, though discouragement from patrons, and especially from his friend Coleridge, led him to halt the project after completing only the first three books.[39]

The romanticist John Hodgson first noted the Virgilian resonance of Wordsworth's question in 1991, reversing Jonathan Wordsworth's earlier dismissal of the *Aeneid*. Hodgson concludes that Virgil's poem is "the source" for Wordsworth and other English poets who used the phrase, or more exactly, that it contains "two sources," in books 2 and 4.[40] Hodgson is surely right that the *Aeneid* played an indispensable role in the spread of *Was it for this*, but it does not follow that it is the phrase's "source." Most obviously,

*Was it for this* is an English, not a Latin, phrase. It does not have a natural, necessary, or unequivocal Latin counterpart. What Hodgson calls its "two sources" are far from identical. Though Anna echoes Aeneas's "hoc," she does not utter the same words: he begins with "Hoc erat . . . quod," while she begins with "Hoc illud . . . fuit." Nor do they utter a classical formula, since the words, order, syntax, grammar (functional roles), and meter of their questions differ.[41] Hodgson asserts that "the Englishing of Aeneas's and Anna's questions as 'Was it for this?' would have been straightforward."[42] Yet the history of the *Aeneid* in English shows that this translation was hardly straightforward, much less necessary or inevitable. James Harrington did not use the phrase in his 1659 translation, nor did Edmund Waller and Sidney Godolphin in theirs. In his influential *Aeneid* of 1697, Dryden renders Aeneas's lament: "Did you, for this, unhappy me convey / Through foes and fires, to see my house a prey!" (2.903–4). His Anna asks, "Was all that pomp of woe for this prepared?" (4.970). In translating Virgil, Wordsworth himself avoids the full phrase he had used as the seed of *The Prelude* a quarter century earlier; his Aeneas begins instead with the truncated form: "For this, benignant Mother! Didst thou lead / My steps along a way from danger freed."[43] Even when translators did use the full phrase, they rarely did so for both Aeneas and Anna. Though Pitt's Anna utters "Was it for this," his Aeneas avoids any version of it: "Why, heavenly mother! did thy guardian care / Snatch me from fires, and shield me in the war?"[44]

*Was it for this* was not from the outset the standard ("straightforward," idiomatic, natural, etc.) English rendering of Virgil's "hoc erat . . . quod" or "hoc illud . . . fuit"—the rendering, that is, from which all others are departures. It only *became* standard (though never necessary or invariable) through the agency of multiple English translators and other writers. By the middle of the nineteenth century, critical, scholarly, and pedagogical editions of the Latin text would consistently annotate line 2.664 as "Was it for this."[45] But translations of the *Aeneid* before 1798 show the early, still incomplete stages of this standardization process. The phrase first appears, albeit in a nonstandard form, in Henry Howard, Earl of Surrey's 1557 translation of Aeneas's lament. In the first published blank verse in the English language, Surrey renders Virgil's "hoc erat, alma parens, quod me per tela, per ignis / eripis, ut mediis hostem" (2.664–65) as "O sacred Mother! Was it then for this / That you led me through flame, and weapons sharp?" (2.874–75).[46]

In 1583, translating the same passage into English hexameters rather than the conventional pentameters, Richard Stanyhurst shortened the phrase through syncope: "Was't for this (moother) that mee through danger unharmed / You led?"[47] The truncated reprise, "for this," first appears in the lament of Surrey's Anna: "Sister! for this with craft did you me bourd [deceive]?" (4.900). Though eighteenth-century translators like Pitt did not need to establish *Was it for this* as standard, since earlier translators had effectively completed this process, they maintained it as standard by repeating it. Without such establishment and maintenance, there would be no standard translation and no recognizably Virgilian English phrase that we could speak of as persisting from one text to the next over time.[48]

Acknowledging the standard as the product of translation rather than its precondition does not imply that we should regard Surrey (or Stanyhurst, or the others that follow them) rather than Virgil as the phrase's source, but rather that for the study of influence the very concept *source* is insufficient to capture all the necessary distinctions. Its etymology suggests the wellspring from which a river or stream takes its origin.[49] The same substance, the same liquid, emerges and flows from one text to another. (The liquid metaphor is built as well into the word *influence*, from the Latin *fluo, fluere*, meaning "to flow.") In the *TLS* correspondence, as in the source study more generally, the "source" names a single, undifferentiated category to which all prior appearances of a phrase can, at least potentially, be consigned. But this category conceals the way a phrase changes, as it travels through the literary network, in its composition, meaning, and use. *Was it for this* only became the phrase that appears in Wordsworth's *Prelude* (instead of Virgil's "Hoc erat . . . quod" or Surrey's "Was it then for this") by undergoing a multitude of transformations as it moved from one author, text, language, nation, age, genre, and verse form to another. Even when the actual sequence of words that composed the phrase remained identical, their use and meaning changed. As the product of multiple agencies, it has an ultimate source or origin in none of them.[50]

Instead of joining the *TLS* correspondence in regarding all thousand-odd pre-1798 uses of the phrase as candidate sources, reassembling a network of diffusion requires that we differentiate them according to their various functional roles. This means enlarging our descriptive vocabulary and, where ready terms are not available, drawing on analogies to nonliterary domains. I suppose that it is sufficient, for example, to say that Surrey is a translator—the first, so far as I can discover, to render a line of the *Aeneid* in a particular and contingent way. But we lack a ready term to describe a poet who, like Virgil, is the cause of a widespread phrase in a different language. The *Aeneid* is less like the wellspring of a stream than, to borrow from epidemiology, the disease reservoir (such as a flock of birds or herd of swine) from which a virus repeatedly crosses over to humans. Asymptomatic in the reservoir, the virus becomes contagious and virulent only in its new (English-speaking) hosts. Or to vary the analogy, in his translation Stanyhurst is like the early adopter who purchases a new technology before it has become standard, thereby lowering the cost and risk for subsequent buyers. The provenance of such analogies matters less than that they adequately capture the differentiated roles entities play in the network of diffusion. As Bruno Latour explains, "agencies" must "always be presented in an account as *doing* something . . . transforming As into Bs"; there is "no meaningful argument to be made about a given agency, no detectable frame of reference" unless it makes some difference in a state of affairs, even if that difference is a matter of maintenance and standardization rather than of revision or transformation.[51] Of course, in any network agency will be unequally distributed, with some actors exercising an outsize influence. Though he never uses the phrase, Virgil's role in the diffusion of *Was it for this* is far more consequential than that of most poets who do.

Other texts differentiate themselves not only by the extent of their agency but also by the variety and centrality of the functional roles they play in the network of diffusion. As we saw earlier, Erskine-Hill proposes Harington's 1591 translation of Ariosto's *Orlando Furioso* as a possible source for *The Prelude*: "What was't for this that I in youth thee fed, / With marrow of the Beares and Lions fell?"[52] He might also have remarked Harington's use of the phrase in the "Apologie of Poetrie," which prefaces the translation. After quoting the rebuke of Melissa, who is disguised as Ruggiero's tutor, Atlanta, Harington imagines what his own tutor, Samuel Fleming, might say to him upon learning he had Englished Ariosto: "Was it for this, that I read *Aristotle* and *Plato* to you, and instructed you so carefully both in Greek and Latin? to have you now become a translator of

Italian toyes?"[53] In a remarkable act of appropriation, Harington transfers *Was it for this* not simply from one heroic poem to another, from *Aeneid* to *Orlando Furioso*, but from a heroic context to an autobiographical one. The ghost of his tutor laments the betrayed promise of his classical education, the very education that exposed him to books 2 and 4 of the *Aeneid* and, we might suspect, the phrase *Was it for this*, quite likely in the translations of Surrey or Stanyhurst. Harington summons this tutelary spirit in order to justify himself and his translation of Ariosto before it. For its part, the *Furioso* serves (to use a horticultural analogy) as the lattice or truss on which Harington's Virgilian innovations grow and climb.

In using *Was it for this* to reflect on his own education, Harington develops in the phrase a potentiality that romantic poets would exploit and develop nearly two centuries later. In a short poem entitled "History," for example, Robert Southey imagines the muse of history, Clio, rebuking him for retreating from the cruel deeds of men to the bower of poetic fantasy:

> Was it for this I waken'd thy young mind?
> Was it for this I made thy swelling heart
> Throb at the deeds of Greece, and thy boy's eye
> So kindle when that glorious Spartan died.[54]

She speaks to him in the role of a forgotten tutor (like Atlanta or Samuel Fleming), reminding him of his boyish encounter with classical history and its enlivening effect on his youthful emotions and intellect.

When Wordsworth sets out to describe "The Growth of a Poet's Mind," he further expands the educative potentiality of the phrase, transforming it into a *Bildungs*-block, a conventional way of evoking, reflecting on, and accounting for his spiritual growth (*Bildung*). Instead of imagining a scolding teacher, he poses the question to himself; instead of formal, institutional education, he depicts the more comprehensive process of self-cultivation in all its forms; instead of in the schoolhouse, his study takes place in the grander schoolhouse of Nature. Where Harington appropriates the phrase for a brief discussion of his own life, Wordsworth uses it to inaugurate an autobiographical poem, an epic of the self. As he wrote in a letter to Sir George Beaumont in April 1805, it was "a thing unprecedented in literary history that a man should talk so much about himself."[55] The phrase spread rapidly in the sixteenth and seventeenth centuries partly because of its association with Virgilian epic; it continued to attract poets in the eighteenth and nineteenth centuries partly because of its association with education and spiritual self-formation.

Harington's functional role in the diffusion of *Was it for this* goes deeper than content. Whereas Surrey and Stanyhurst had fashioned the early versions of the English phrase in the project of translation, he first mobilizes it as a formula separable from its initial context of use and transferrable to new contexts. (Derrida taught us to see that every phrase or syntagm is by its very nature iterable,[56] but it takes a specific act to demonstrate why anyone might wish to iterate one phrase rather than any other.) When, in *Orlando Furioso*, Melissa rebukes Ruggiero for his "wanton womanish behavior" (7.42), she does so with the words "È questo dunque il frutto," literally, "Is this then the fruit?" Whether Ariosto is here imitating Virgil is uncertain; that Harington is doing so in his translation, "Was't for this," is clear. Indeed, his "Apologie" compares *Orlando Furioso* to the *Aeneid* throughout, seeking to legitimize the Italian romance by likening it to the Latin epic. Using a Virgilian English phrase to translate a line of Ariosto is a subtle part of the same justificatory project. When, after quoting Melissa's reproof, he ventriloquizes his tutor Samuel Fleming, he places the phrase's mobile, formulaic character directly before his readers, even those unaware of its Virgilian origins. By repurposing the phrase, he also illustrates the process of standardization in small: the "Was't for this" of the verse translation becomes, in his tutor's prose rebuke, the *Was it for this* that spreads most widely throughout the literature of the next two centuries. That the phrase could be used as a standard formula was not lost on other poets, like Thomas Collins, who in his 1615 pastoral poem *The Teares of Cupid* has the likely distinction of being both the first to adapt the phrase to a woman's toilet, preceding Pope by nearly a century, and the first poet, though hardly the only one, to repeat the phrase ad nauseam:

> Was it for this Dame Nature did her best,
> To frame my face more fayrer then the rest?
> Was it for this I did reiect so many,
> And (but that one) could loue or like of any?
> Was it for this, that I would go so trim,
> To gaine his loue, then be beguild of him?
> Was it for this, that I did tricke my hayre,
> And sought all meanes to make me supreme fayre?

Was it for this, that I so carelesly
Forsooke my flockes, to keepe him company?
Was it for this, that I tooke no delight
In any thing, but onely in his sight?[57]

Through sheer, insipid repetition Collins continues the process, inaugurated by Harington, of transforming the phrase into a mobile formula.

Harington and other early poets and translators make *Was it for this* into the standard rendering of two half lines of the *Aeneid*, a seed phrase, and a mobile formula; they also turn it, retrospectively, into a "classical" formula. In early modern texts characters from antiquity frequently utter the phrase, as when, in a 1598 tragicomedy by Samuel Brandon, Octavia rebukes Marc Antony:

Was it for this thou shedst those teares,
O Crocodile un kinde,
When lastly thou didst part from me,
With shew of constant minde?[58]

But the classical character of the formula is only fully evident in translations of non-Virgilian Latin texts. Thomas Heywood's massively synthetic epic *Troia Britannica, or Great Britain's Troy* (1609) incorporates two of Ovid's *Epistulae Herodium* (*Heroides*), the first a letter from Paris to Helen, the second Helen's reply. Coyly deflecting Paris's marriage suit, Helen asks, "Was it for this, our free Tenarian Port, / Receiu'd thee and thy traine, in friendly sort?"[59] Heywood's "Was it for this" translates Ovid's "scilicet idcirco," literally, "certainly for this reason" or "of course on this account." Subsequent translators of Ovid followed Heywood's lead; in 1717 John Gay also uses the phrase to render a simple "ergo" (therefore) in the *Metamorphoses* (9.1082), when Hercules, dying from the poisoned shirt of Nessus, recalls his past labors, "Was it for this [ergo] Busiris was subdu'd, / Whose barb'rous Temples reek'd with Stranger's Blood?"[60] Over the course of the seventeenth century the same English phrase, in other words, came to be a standard translation of four, fully distinct Latin phrases: Ovid's "silicet idcirco" and "ergo," Virgil's "hoc erat . . . quod" and "hoc illud . . . fuit." It became a "classical" formula in English even though it corresponds to no such formula in the Latin it translates. By the early eighteenth century the phrase's "classical" back-formation may even have partially displaced its association with Virgil, as

English writers came to see the opening of Aeneas's lament not as the phrase's point of origin but as one instantiation of a widespread formula.[61] In any event, writers used *Was it for this* as a mark of distinction, an understated but obvious enough sign of their classical training and easy familiarity with Latin authors.

The functional role a text plays in the network of diffusion need not be as grand and far reaching as the *Orlando Furioso* or even the *Troia Britannica*, as long as it does something with, makes some difference to, what it reproduces and transmits.[62] To return to an "echo" mentioned in the *TLS* correspondence, W. B. Yeats's poem "September 1913," though a late adopter to be sure, nevertheless repurposes the phrase as a reflection on Irish politics and particularly on the apparent demise of Irish nationalist hopes at the hands of middle-class greed and fear:

> Was it for this the wild geese spread
> The grey wing upon every tide;
> For this that all that blood was shed,
> For this Edward Fitzgerald died,
> And Robert Emmet and Wolfe Tone,
> All that delirium of the brave;
> Romantic Ireland's dead and gone,
> It's with O'Leary in the grave.

The title of the book published by John Waters, a columnist for the *Irish Times*, in May 2012—*Was it For this? Why Ireland Lost the Plot*, about the collapse of Ireland's economic hopes in the wake of financial crisis—clearly alludes to Yeats, and not Wordsworth or Virgil, much less Surrey or Harington or Collins. In Yeats's hands the phrase became a question about the fate of Irish sovereignty; this potentiality then became available for others to take up, exploit, and transform in turn.

### Sets and Associations

The aims and methods of the current investigation are dramatically different from the aims and methods of the scholarly "notes" that appear in journals like *Notes and Queries*. Instead of suggesting a new source or sources, I have sought to sketch a network of diffusion. Instead of explaining the appearance of a phrase in a single poem like *The Prelude*, I have sought to explain its appearance in English texts prior to 1798. Instead of discovering an earlier use of the phrase through hours, days, weeks, or years of reading with an eye out for echoes and similarities, I have "discovered" a thousand uses of the phrase in the time it took to run a few searches in various digital archives. Discovery, for the methodology of the note, is expensive in terms of both labor and exchange value. Yet thanks to the outlays of corporations like Google and ProQuest and the labor of numerous programmers, librarians, photographers, and typists to create archives of digital texts, discovery is now cheap. Constructing a network of diffusion requires that scholars spend labor not on discovery but on arrangement, placing the discovered uses, so far as possible, into relation with one another.

Far from calling down the apocalypse, digital tools make possible a redistribution of labor. Search engines discern similitude in dissimilitude, culling from thousands or millions of different texts those that contain the same sequence of words, so that scholars may spend their efforts discerning dissimilitude in similitude, differentiating the culled texts according to their functional roles and relationships. They generate nodes, but it is up to us to connect those nodes with edges and determine their agency in the network. The repeated acts of informed judgment, comparison, inference, and discretion that are characteristic of the best source study are no less requisite in reassembling a network. Investigative and speculative work likewise remain necessary, especially regarding the early stages of a phrase's development, before it has achieved its "standard" form or forms. Without a carefully formulated search string, a search engine will not find variants like Surrey's "Was it then for this," Harington's "Was't for this," the truncated "for this," or, for that matter, Virgil's "hoc erat . . . quod." Search engines offer digital texts as nodes, but it is often to physical texts, like the Pitt translation of the *Aeneid* owned by the Wordsworth family, that we must look for evidence of the material channels by which those nodes were connected. And just as one can contest a source, so too can one contest the configuration of the network, proposing different functional relations, different means of diffusion, different processes of origination, standardization, and variation. I have given an account of the spread of *Was it for this* that centers on late-sixteenth-century translations of Virgil, but I do not doubt that other accounts, complementary or contradictory, are possible.

Earlier studies of influence engaged in the business of reconstructing networks even when they did not theorize it as such. When Jonathan

Wordsworth speculates that though all uses derive finally from a "classical" source, Byron's and Jago's uses of *Was it for this* come from Pope, whereas Wordsworth and Shenstone's look back to Thomson, he implicitly constructs an arboreal network, where the root of a single tradition branches off into various subdivisions. Duncan Wu's insuperable two-volume work of reference, *Wordsworth's Reading*, which aims "to provide the fullest account possible of the scholarship concerning Wordsworth's reading," reconstructs a massive network in the figure of a hub and spokes. Wordsworth rests securely at the center of inquiry, while an estimable circle of authors and volumes are arrayed around him. The network developed in this chapter synthesizes the genealogical tree with the hub and spokes into a third figure, a constellation. In the constellation, each node is a potential hub with an array of spokes stretching out to other hubs. Like the tree, the constellation charts multiple degrees of separation—not just which texts Wordsworth read but what the authors of those texts read in turn—what we might, with an obligatory wink, call Wordsworth's "extended network." Also like the tree, the constellation takes into account sequence: some stars appear on the horizon before others. By combining the forking relationships of the tree with the radial relationships of the hub and spokes, the constellation is also able to represent triangular relationships. Triangles, and the sequence of ordered polygons built from triangles, allow the constellation to capture close-knit groups in which an agent's associates are also associated with one another. They can account for both indirect associations and what the sociologist Mark S. Granovetter has called the "strength of weak ties," the role of weak associations in creating bridges between otherwise distant groups.[63] In the constellation partially mapped here, it matters not just that (*a*) Wordsworth encountered *Was it for this* in Pope's *Rape of the Lock* and (*b*) Wordsworth read the *Aeneid*, but also that (*c*) Pope also read the *Aeneid* and even (*d*) Wordsworth knew that Pope read the *Aeneid* and used *Was it for this* as a Virgilian formula. The figure of the constellation acknowledges these relationships at multiple degrees of difference. In the division of labor described here, the search engine discovers the stars, including those not usually visible to the naked eye, but it remains to us to trace the edges that connect them.

One might object that the network approach merely replaces the classical vocabulary of authors and sources or the postmodern vocabulary of texts and intertexts with yet another, technologically motivated vocabulary of nodes and edges.[64] But these words do not name basic elements or constituent parts. There are no "nodes" in early modern England, though it feels funny to say so. Instead these words name the cosmographer's tools, the means of representing the heterogeneous multitude of entities and relations between entities that play a role in diffusion. They are useful precisely because they cannot easily be taken—as texts, sources, or authors can—for real things in themselves; they are obviously, ostentatiously empty and unreal categories (saying that two texts "share an edge" or "are associated" tells us virtually nothing) in need of further elaboration and functional differentiation. In other words, it is their sheer, obtrusive abstraction that makes a network vocabulary suitable for representing the heterogeneity and materiality of diffusion. Though nodes and edges are empty categories, they do not accommodate any and all content; because they traverse space without filling it, edges force us to specify the actors that are veiled or forgotten by concepts (like fields, spaces, spheres, or the "commonplace") that purport to fill space without traversing it, thereby placing the process of diffusion in a black box.

There are significant limits to what any attempt to reassemble a network can hope to achieve. In some cases, it may be possible to establish the concrete associations by which diffusion occurs. Consider the Southey poem "History," mentioned earlier, in which Clio, the muse of history, reminds the poet of his youthful enthusiasm: "Was it for this I waken'd thy young mind?" Like Wordsworth, Southey probably read the phrase in a multitude of texts. Yet there is clear textual evidence of at least two of those encounters. In a footnote to *Letters Written During a Short Residence in Spain and Portugal* (1797), he reproduces in full a "beautiful poem on monastic life" from Francis Quarles's emblem book *Hieroglyphikes of the Life of Man*, which begins, "Was it for this, the breath of Heav'n was blown / Into the nostrils of this heavenly creature?"[65] He also knew the poem "The Abuse of the Gospel," from William Cowper's *Olney Hymns*, which rhetorically asks, "Was it for this, ye lawless tribe, / The dear Redeemer bled?" Southey edited Cowper's *Works* for their 1854 publication, though he may have read the poem much earlier.[66] Because traces of these connections have been preserved, we know that Southey passed *Was it for this* on to subsequent readers not just as an author and poet but also as an editor and epistolarian.

Yet not all associations leave these sorts of documentary traces. Bringing to a close a digital study of seven thousand novel titles from the period

1740–1850, Franco Moretti quotes Goethe's wistful observation in *Wilhelm Meister's Journeyman Years, or the Renunciants*. "Literature is the fragment of fragments," writes Goethe, "the least part of all that ever happened and was spoken was written down, and of what was written only the least part has survived."[67] Despite Moretti's use of the quotation, "all that . . . was spoken" does not pose a problem for his project, which focuses on the genre of the novel, nor would it be a problem for the study of, say, the sonnet or the tragedy. Simply put, people don't speak in novels, sonnets, or tragedies, but they do speak in phrases and linguistic forms. A short phrase like *Was it for this* and the sentences it initiates may well have been common parts of daily conversation, at least in certain educated circles. It is possible that a significant portion of the phrase's diffusion may have occurred through speech. Yet this potentially crucial part of the network, like the prophecies of Virgil's Cumaean Sibyl, has been scattered to the winds. Especially for words, phrases, and linguistic forms, the network of diffusion will, in spite of increasingly powerful search engines and ever-growing digital archives, always remain incomplete.

There are, however, better responses to speech and to the lack of documentary traces more generally than merely throwing up our hands. Though the network cannot recover spoken conversations, it can outline the institutional spaces (in the most literal sense: a particular classroom, library, or lecture hall) in which scenes of instruction would have been likely to take place. In the English grammar school, for example, masters would have prompted and corrected the translations of their pupils, who would also have shared translations with one another, as the orphaned Wordsworth brothers clearly did.[68] Further, unrecorded conversations tend to take place through already existing associations that may leave other kinds of traces. Letters and diaries offer a fairly detailed portrait, for example, not simply of Wordsworth's reading but also of his intellectual companions and interlocutors at various points in his life.[69] Our ability to reassemble a network of diffusion, and particularly to detect its lacunae, will always depend on our existing knowledge of other, overlapping networks.

A more far-reaching response to the ephemerality of speech is to complement the tracing of *associations* with the construction of *sets*. Associations, as I use the term here, are actual, material connections between agents, like that between mother and son, author and reader, translator and text, or sender and receiver. Literary scholars study associations when they inquire into Milton's meetings with Hugo Grotius and Galileo during his grand tour, the dynamics of his relationship with Cromwell during the Protectorate, or the allusions to the *Aeneid* in *Paradise Lost*. Sets, by contrast, are abstract or notional categories to which agents can belong by virtue of any shared attribute. Scholars debate about sets when they ask whether Milton was or was not a Puritan, an Arian, an iconoclast, a Republican, or a liberal (a category that was not available to Milton in the sense in which it is currently used).

The distinction between sets and associations introduces two crucial questions, the first about construction: To what degree are sets made out of associations? Murasaki and Jane Austen both belong to the set "female novelists," though one lived in eleventh-century Japan and the other in eighteenth-century England. A purely notional set of this sort is susceptible to conceptual analysis but not to network analysis. Other sets, like the coterie, manuscript circle, or writer's workshop, are fully associative (made up of material associations) and can therefore in principle be reconstructed as a network.[70] Still other sets are, as it were, amphibious. When F. R. Leavis begins *The Great Tradition* with "The great English novelists are . . ." he appears to stipulate a purely notional set.[71] Yet membership in this set depends on associations with previous members (hence the *tradition* of the title): George Eliot is tapped by Leavis as a "great" novelist in part because she read and responded to the work of Jane Austen.

One of my claims throughout this chapter has been that the search-engine-generated set "texts that use the formula 'Was it for this' prior to 1798" is like a temporally and spatially elongated coterie or circle rather than like the notional set "female novelists." But the question of construction becomes more difficult when we consider smaller subsets. Is the set "texts that use *Was it for this* as a *Bildungs*-block" an associative or a notional set? The question is difficult because it is empirical rather than definitional: we cannot answer it without inquiring into the actual texts that participate in the set and the relations between them. The question of construction could be productively asked of different kinds of sets, not just those based on shared phrases, formulas, forms, or metaphors. It applies, in principle, to all pregiven ubiquities, all concepts that, like the term *commonplace*, designate something that is everywhere, while forgetting or concealing the process by which it became so. To the category of pregiven ubiquities we can add terms as basic to the current practice of literary criticism as *culture*, *society*,

Bourdieu's *fields*, Fredric Jameson's *political unconscious*, Foucault's *discursive regimes*, and even Heidegger's *world*. Networks provide us with the means to reassemble the processes by which these ubiquities have been (and continue to be) constructed.

The second question, following on that of construction, is about knowledge: given that a set is at least partially made up of associations, to what extent can we trace those associations? Media like email, blogs, or tweets, which document their own transmission with time, date, and routing stamps, often make it possible to trace all associations fully. Other associative sets leave virtually no traces, whether incidentally (a casual conversation) or by design (a backroom negotiation, burned manuscript, or silenced voice). The crucial, albeit difficult task is to keep construction and knowledge—what is the case and what we can know to be the case—distinct. Even were we to accept Foucault's discourses as entirely associative, for example, the associations that compose them—those by which the rules that condition the possibility of utterance are transmitted—might nevertheless remain largely or wholly untraceable. Conversely, we cannot conclude that Foucault's discourses are purely notional simply because we are unable, or have been so far unable, to trace the associations out of which they are made. Conflating what is with our knowledge of what is has given rise to many of the reductionist errors cataloged earlier in this chapter. Attending to the difference between sets and associations, conversely, is not a path to certainty, but it does allow us to mark the limits of our knowledge, to see as clearly as possible what it is that we do not know, and in some cases may never know, about diffusion. Although Virgil's Fama cannot be eradicated, she can be diminished and, like her Spenserian successor, the Blatant Beast, at least provisionally bound.

### Heterogeneous Networks

A writer reads a phrase in one or two or more texts and then reproduces it in another text that is read, if he or she is lucky, by one or two other writers or perhaps more. The collective result of these individual encounters, without which nothing could become common, is an enormous and enormously complex web of associations, what John Law calls a "heterogeneous network."[72] The network is heterogeneous because its participants are not made up of or reducible to any single kind of entity. Most obviously, a literary network comprises authors and their texts—texts not just as ideal types but as the material books that carry them, like the Wordsworth brothers' hand-me-down translation of the *Aeneid*. Yet authors and texts, which have received most of our attention here, do not begin to exhaust the heterogeneity of the network, which necessarily overlaps with other, complex networks. While we have noted the crucial role that English grammar schools played in the spread of *Was it for this*, we have left largely uncharted this enormous constellation of pupils and teachers, administrators and parents, as well as its vibrant economy of official pedagogical texts (textbooks, translations, commentaries, curricula) and unofficial student texts (trots, ponies, cribs, cheat sheets, etc.). The pervasiveness and persistence of this institution, with its relatively uniform classical curriculum, contributed to the diffusion, standardization, and maintenance of *Was it for this*, but it is itself the product of processes of standardization, diffusion, and maintenance. As book historians have taught us to see, the material texts by which the phrase was transmitted are also products of complex relations of tradesmen, papermakers, printers, and publishers, as well as of physical objects like presses and paper mills, which were in turn constructed by other craftsmen with other tools. Lending libraries, private libraries, book societies, and booksellers are products of similarly complex relations.[73] All these heterogeneous entities, linked together through multiple associations, contributed in different ways, at different degrees of separation, to the spread of *Was it for this*. The vast network they produce is, in answer to Marx's rhetorical question, "what becomes of Fama alongside Printing House Square."[74]

The heterogeneity and magnitude of such networks eventually and perhaps inevitably lead us, at some point, to stop tracing associations and instead gesture, as I did a few paragraphs earlier, to a "context" like "the humanist culture of early modern England." When Latour writes that "context stinks," since it is "simply a way of stopping the description when you are too tired or lazy to go on," his charge is wrong only insofar as it is uncharitable.[75] The inevitability with which we cease to trace associations between heterogeneous entities is not necessarily a consequence of fatigue or laziness (though it is sometimes that) but of real limitations—limitations on our time, work, scope, interest, and tools. Description always stops somewhere, even if associations do not, at which point the task of reassembly falls to the community of intellectual laborers at large rather than any single individual. We all depend on the networks traced by our predecessors, as I do on the reconstruction of Wordsworth's reading by Duncan Wu or of his schooling by Richard W. Clancey, T. W. Thompson, and Ben Ross Schneiderman, and we leave still other networks for our successors to re-assemble. Gesturing toward a context like "the humanist culture of early modern England" need not "stink" so long as we recognize it as a book-mark for where we've left off tracing rather than as a reservoir of explana-tory power in itself.

The heterogeneity of networks requires us, despite our limitations, to reject two kinds of reductionism that have dominated the study of literary influence. The first kind, which I will call *personalism*, includes any account that disregards relations of influence that are not conceivable as relation-ships between people. Personalism describes influence solely in terms of friends and lovers, borrowers and stealers, teachers and pupils. The great-est of the personalists is Harold Bloom, who systematically personifies re-lations of influence. Though the anxiety of influence is primarily textual rather than psychic, "achieved in and by the story, novel, play, poem, or essay" rather than the mind of its author,[76] Bloom practices a "historicism" that, by his own account, "deliberately reduces to the interplay of person-alities."[77] "A poem is always a person," he writes, and "a poem is a response to a poem, as a poet is a response to a poet, or a person to his parent."[78] This is why Bloom writes with open derision of "source hunting," "allusion count-ing," and indeed all studies of influence based on "verbal resemblances."[79] His Freudian family takes no account of the way writers absorb and reuse material from texts that have no personal or familial resonance, that are neither fathers nor substitutes for fathers, neither sublimations of Oedipal desires nor displacements of the primary object of affection.[80]

It is true that one rarely reads a novel or a poem without connecting it to a particular author or at least an author function. Yet personalist models disregard the way writers encounter a multitude of short syntagms—phrases, formulas, linguistic forms—without ever associating them with a person at all. The impersonality of influence is no doubt heightened by the paradoxical solitude and connectivity of the Internet, which delivers a barrage of anonymous words, phrases, and sentences with every mouse click. But this impersonality is inherent in writing as such, specifically the necessity that a text be legible in the absence of its originator. Though phrases may reach us stripped of an author, they still necessarily arrive by way of a medium. Materiality is requisite even when personality is not. Finally, even when a phrase does come attached to a name, an author, or a personality, it can nevertheless become depersonalized through plurality, by appearing in a multiplicity of other works by different authors—as when a translation of Virgil came to be understood as a widespread "classical" formula.[81] The process of forgetting by which a phrase comes to be described as "commonplace" effectively divests it from any particular person, making it the property of everyone and, in what amounts to the same, no one.

We can justly call the second kind of reduction *impersonalism* (or *apersonalism*), though it is most often associated with terms like postmodernism and poststructuralism. Impersonality in this sense is not, as in T. S. Eliot's "Tradition and the Individual Talent," an aesthetic and ethical ideal for which the poet must strive; rather, it is the basic condition of textuality as such.[82] The prototypical impersonalists are Julia Kristeva and Roland Barthes, for whom the key term *intertextuality* designates not a field of positive inquiry (as it would for many later scholars) but a radical philosophical concept.[83] Rather than originating in the mind of an individual author, every text is, in the well-known formulation of Barthes, a "tissue of quotations," the compilation or intersection of other texts.[84] To the extent that an impersonalist speaks of persons, subjects, authors, or agents, it is as effects of texts rather than as their causes. Where personalists reduce textuality to persons (poets and their precursors), and relations of influence to relations between persons, impersonalists reduce persons (authors, subjects) to texts and relations of influence to relationships between texts.

The reassembling of a network, by contrast, does not seek to reduce texts to persons, persons to texts, or indeed any kind of entity to any other. Taking its cue from Latour's notion of *irreduction*, it aims to see more kinds of agencies—not just the author and, as Milton puts it, the "purest efficacie and extraction of that living intellect," the text, but all the various nonhuman agents (books, presses, grammar schools, schoolhouses, curricula, etc.) that play a role in diffusion.[85] The concepts *author* and *text* do pose a problem, as they have for the last half century of literary theory, but the problem is not that either is a mere cypher for or effect of the other; rather, like the concept *source*, both are too low-resolution to capture the differentiated functional roles that compose networks of diffusion. For texts we need an elaborate parade of disease reservoirs, lattices and trusses, intersections, pit stops, and chop shops, seed phrases and *Bildungs*-blocks. For authors we need a mobile army of translators, early and late adopters, formulators, standardizers, and repurposers of all sorts. In the network, the author inevitably has many functions. As long as fathers and sons, precursors and ephebes do not drive out all other impersonal roles, there is no reason why they should not assume their distinctive place in the network as well. As with the term *source*, we need not discard terms like *author* or *text* so long as we recognize them as the names of genera containing functionally differentiated species. Even as we expand our vocabulary, we cannot decide in advance what kind of terms will be needed to describe any particular network adequately. The spread of *Was it for this* depended on specific roles that were neither necessary nor exhaustive; other networks of diffusion will depend on different roles and therefore require different terms and analogies.

Because the network approach seeks to diversify rather than reduce the kinds of visible entities, it must forgo the grand reveal in which Wordsworth is shown to be either, as in M. H. Abrams's personalist reading, the heroic poet who has achieved "a stage of self-coherence, self-awareness, and assured power that is its own reward" or, as in impersonalist accounts, the "Aeolian harp" across which the winds of history and textuality play.[86] The network neither exalts nor deflates authorial agency, but instead multiplies and dislocates it, showing how it is at once constituted, constrained, and enabled by the widest possible range of other agencies. In accord with the impersonalists, Wordsworth is only a node, a nonextended point in the network formed by the intersection of edges leading to other nodes. He writes *Was it for this* only by rewriting it, copying the phrase from other texts. In accord with the personalists, authorial nodes are themselves ineliminable and active constituents of the network. They play real functional roles, creating and structuring the network by exercising agency, often at multiple degrees of separation, in concert with various other human and nonhuman agencies. Without nodes, no edges, since authors like Wordsworth work in concert with other agencies to standardize, formularize, develop, change, and spread "Was it for this." Without edges, no nodes, since Wordsworth only shows up in the network at all because of his relation to other agencies. In the network of diffusion the author is neither dead nor deified, only distributed.[87]

Though reassembling a network primarily explains how a phrase came to be where it is rather than what it means once it gets there, it can nevertheless contribute to our interpretation of individual works. It allows us to see which earlier potentialities a poem takes up, develops, or alters, sharpening some claims of exceptionality while dispelling others.[88] Multiplying associations tends to make us warier of particular claims of influence, along with the interpretive claims that rest on them. The account of Wordsworth as a second Aeneas and the image of "Milton's presence looking over the effete's [sic] shoulder as he writes" become less persuasive once we bring into view the multitude of other texts in which he did read or could have read the phrase.

Reassembling a network can also generate new interpretations. Discouraged by his failure to begin "The Recluse," Wordsworth, like other writers before him, may have found in *Was it for this* a new seed of poetic invention, a reminder of his schoolboy training, and a reassuring connection to classical tradition and Virgilian epic. Alternatively, the phrase that was for so many of his peers and predecessors a mark of cultural capital may for him have been a sign of imaginative impoverishment and vitiation, one of "the mean and vulgar works of man" (1805 *Prelude* 1.435) separating him from the purer influences of his childhood. *Was it for this*, in this second reading, stands for the very creative enervation the poem laments. Both readings are finally inextricable: the instrument of invention is also a mark of imaginative insufficiency; the prosthetic extension is also a crutch; to mark one's cultural accomplishments with a widespread formula (what later came to be called a cliché) is to betray them. It is the peculiar power of Wordsworth's poem, with its sophisticated deployment of generic conventions and its longing for the uncorrupted responsiveness of youth, to place both alternatives in the balance.

Networks can help us to think about the provenance of poems, but a more radical possibility is that poems can, in some cases, help us to think about networks. Here again, at somewhat greater length, are the opening lines of Wordsworth's draft fragment of 1798, which were incorporated, with minor alterations, into subsequent revisions of the *Prelude*:

> was it for this
> That one, the fairest of all rivers, loved
> To blend his murmurs with my nurse's song,
> And from his alder shades and rocky falls,
> And from his fords and shallows, sent a voice

> To intertwine my dreams? For this didst thou,
> O Derwent, travelling over the green plains
> Near my "sweet birthplace," didst thou, beauteous stream
> Make ceaseless music through the night and day
> Which with its steady cadence, tempering
> Our human waywardness, composed by thoughts
> To more than infant softness, giving me
> Among the fretful dwellings of mankind,
> A knowledge, a dim earnest, of the calm
> Which nature breathes among the hills and groves.
>
> (1–15)

The lines bear witness to the influence of multiple voices, not just the "nurse's song" but the "murmurs" and "ceaseless music" of the river Derwent that "blend" and "intertwine" with the poet's dreams. Wordsworth acknowledges that such agencies, human and nonhuman alike, shaped him right from his "infant softness." And they do not merely speak for themselves, delivering their own messages; in the course of its travels, the Derwent delivers both "knowledge" and a vague pledge ("dim earnest") of "the calm / Which nature breathes," mediating nature's "calm" by means of a "steady cadence." The two-part *Prelude* of 1799 alters the second half of line 11 from "composed by thoughts" to "composed my thoughts," making unmistakable the force of such agencies on the poet's self and, through the connotations of "composed," his writing. In the 1799 poem we are also told, in case we missed it, how "The mind of man is fashioned and built up, / Even as a strain of music" (1.67–68).

Wordsworth's lines, in short, articulate a network far more heterogeneous than the limited one sketched in this chapter, illustrating the relative narrowness of the kinds of entities we are able to see and put in meaningful relation. The lines likewise elaborate a set of richly metaphorical, often musical descriptions of the functional associations between agencies as they blend, intertwine, temper, and compose the poet's mind. *Was it for this* does not simply introduce the poem's recognition and disposition of agencies into a network; it also represents an agency in its own right, one that speaks (in contrast to the "nurse's song," which is marked as a naïve, feminine, folk melody) with the voice of a Latin-educated, masculine, humanist literary elite. The phrase is the key point of contact between the small but heterogeneous network portrayed within the poem and the larger though necessarily more homogeneous network—of poets and poems, translators and translations, texts and books, publishers, printers, and grammar schools—in which the *Prelude* is but a single node. Wordsworth's lines challenge us to explain how we can understand these two disparate networks as finally one and the same. It is difficult enough to conceive of a network of diffusion that includes entities as heterogeneous as John Harington, the volume of Pitt's *Aeneid* owned by the Wordsworths, and Hawkshead Grammar School.[89] But how, without lapsing into incoherence, could such a network also include the river Derwent? Though the digital archive puts us in a position to ask this kind of question in a detailed and meaningful way, it is no more capable of providing an answer than the print media used by earlier scholars. The study of influence has yet to "touch apocalypse" as Bloom prophesied, but it remains in need of further revelation.

4

## *Act as If* and Useful Fictions

### A Technology of the Self

In a letter to the editor of the black newspaper the *Weekly Louisianian*, on 8 November 1879, a correspondent identified as "a Republican Scout" with the pen name Irrepressible proposes a strategy for achieving electoral victory in the precinct of Orleans.[1] After advising the party to put aside favoritism and nominate the most qualified leaders, organize canvassing committees that include as many white men as possible, register all Republican voters, and get them to the ballot box on voting day, the scout turns to address voters directly. "Unless each man will regard this fight as his own," the letter warns, "a campaign is useless." Voters must "act as if" the Republican ticket "would have no votes but your own. Act, as if your candidates will have a majority of but one vote, and as if each man thought that *one* would be *his* vote." In a democracy of any size, the vote of a single citizen is highly unlikely to determine the final outcome. No doubt this was especially true for citizens who had only been emancipated from slavery a decade and a half earlier; who had, for purposes of representation, been counted as three-fifths of a person before emancipation; and who were, in 1879, witnessing the early stages of disenfranchisement strategies that continue to the present day. Yet the letter counsels the paper's readers to set aside this discouraging reality and instead act according to a self-conscious fiction in which one vote—the reader's own—would make the crucial difference.

This chapter contends that the counsel offered by the "Republican Scout" is part of a long tradition that threads its way through the works of Seneca,

Saint Paul, Blaise Pascal, Immanuel Kant, William James, and Hans Vaihinger, among other notable figures, but ends, in a period of flourishing, with the self-help and pop-psychology industries of the twentieth and twenty-first centuries. Dr. Reverend Gary Brodsky sells *Act as if* books and CDs on his website with the promise that to "free yourself from the root cause of diseases, loneliness, poverty and powerlessness . . . all you need is to learn to ACT AS IF."[2] Holly Boyd, a self-described "Christian Professional Organizer," calls the title of her book, *Act as If*, the "key to happiness" and "one of the oldest formulas in the world." (As we will see, this last claim is not wholly inaccurate.)[3] In *Reallionaire: Nine Steps to Becoming Rich from the Inside Out*, Farrah Gray advises readers to "act as if someone is watching you—because someone always is."[4] Alcoholics Anonymous frequently pairs *act as if* with another popular slogan, "fake it till you make it."[5] The following lines may strike dismay into the hearts of poets and poetry lovers, but in the last two decades few verses have been circulated so widely, appearing (in sundry variations) on greeting cards and housewarming gifts, in graduation speeches, country-music lyrics, and positive-psychology handbooks.

> You've gotta dance like there's nobody watching,
> Love like you'll never be hurt,
> Sing like there's nobody listening,
> And live like it's heaven on earth,
> And speak from the heart to be heard.[6]

*Act as if* has become a nearly ubiquitous slogan in motivational speeches, sales and management seminars, twelve-step programs, prosperity Bible sermons, and half-time pep talks. For all those who promise to make us fitter, happier, more productive, comfortable, at ease, calm, confident, prosperous, organized, and successful—all those professional purveyors of what Michel Foucault called "technologies of the self"—*act as if* is both a central piece of intellectual machinery and a well-worn calling card.[7]

How and why did *act as if* become a pervasive linguistic resource for self-fashioning? This chapter attempts to recover the history, not of a fixed phrase, but rather of practical counsel of the form *X as if Y*, in which *X* is a verb (often, though not always, imperative) and *Y* is a sentence expressing a false or hypothetical proposition.[8] *Behave as though* and *do it like* function in much the same way, as do the Greek *hōs, hōs ei (hōsei)*, and *hōs ei te*; the Latin *quasi, sicut, ac si*, and *tamquam*; the French *comme si*; the Italian *come se*; the Spanish *como si*; and the German *als ob* and *wie wenn*. For the sake of convenience, *act as if* will serve as a shorthand for this family of forms across various languages. The pages that follow trace the development of *act as if* through works of moral and theoretical philosophy, advice manuals, poems, autobiographies, self-help books, psychological treatises, sermons, and films. Because *act as if* has served as a technology of the self at least since classical antiquity, the story told here is not an attempt to establish a clear origin. Rather, this chapter traces the consequential developments that the form underwent over the last four centuries, accruing significant new intellectual functions as it spread across multiple genres, disciplines, and discourses. In its use as a practical imperative, the form did not merely appear sporadically in unrelated texts but was increasingly handed down from writer to writer, thinker to thinker, in a coherent and identifiable tradition.

Yet a history of individual writers, however influential, or of individual disciplines, however comprehensive, cannot on its own explain why this particular imperative has been so widely adopted. In addition to examining the texts that shaped and popularized *act as if*, this chapter offers an explanation for the development and spread of the form in recent centuries. From its earliest recorded uses to its present-day role in self-fashioning, the form has had a complicated and troubled relationship to religious faith. Beginning in the latter half of the seventeenth century, writers mobilized it as a practical response to, and a reaction against, the threat of an increasingly secular age. When belief in God and the mind-independent laws underwritten by God could no longer be taken for granted, so that religious belief became, as Charles Taylor has put it, "one option . . . one human possibility among others," writers used the form as a strategic supplement to faith, a means of combatting doubt and unbelief.[9] Instead of asking readers to govern themselves in accordance with firmly held convictions and independently available norms, writers began to advise them to act as if those convictions were true and those norms were in effect. Enlisting *act as if* in reaction to the incursions of secular doubt led, however, to a kind of historical irony. As an unwieldy supplement to belief, the form ended up exacerbating the problem it was brought in to remedy, hastening the very crises of faith it had been employed to halt or forestall.

### Speculator Omnium

The use of *act as if* as a positive imperative goes back at least to ancient Greece and Rome. Defending himself against the charges of M. Licin-
ius Crassus in 54 BCE, the republican orator Cicero writes, "We ought at all
times to act as if we were standing [*stare enim omnes debemus tamquam*] in
some revolving orb of the republic, and as that turns round we ought to
choose that part to which the advantage and safety of the republic direct
us."[10] Cicero advises his listeners to govern themselves according to the demands of the republic, and his metaphor of a revolving orb suggests how
fluid and complex these demands may be. In his commentary on the
*Enchiridion* of Epictetus (ca. 450 CE), the Neoplatonist Simplicius instructs
his readers, "If you are not like [Socrates], you would do well to endeavor it;
and, whatever you want of his Perfections at present, live with that exact-
ness, as if you meant and hoped one day to equal them."[11] Here the form is
used to recommend Socrates as an exemplar whom we cannot hope to equal
but whom we should work to imitate nonetheless. It posits an imagined
future, "one day," in which we might gain his perfections.

In classical antiquity a particularly influential version of the practical
imperative involved imagining a witness or spectator. Epicurus is reported
by Seneca (64 CE) to have told his followers, "Act as if Epicurus were always
watching you" (Sic fac omnia tamquam spectet Epicurus).[12] This may at first
seem like the ancient equivalent of *don't do anything I wouldn't do*, but it is,
as Seneca explains, an important aid to morality. The problem, he writes, is
that solitude moves us to all kinds of evil ("omnia nobis mala solitudo per-
suadet"), and the solution is to choose an imagined guardian to witness our
thoughts and actions even when we are alone. Ideally we would choose from
respectable men ("boni viri") like Cato, Scipio, or Laelius, but it is enough to
act as if anyone is watching ("tamquam spectet aliquis"). Seneca's eighty-third
epistle extends this kind of moral reasoning one step further: "It is thus
that we should live, as if we lived in plain sight of all men [*tamquam in con-
spectu vivamus*]; and it is thus that we should think, as if there were someone
who could look into our inmost souls [*tamquam aliquis in pectus intimum
introspicere possit*] . . . and there is one who can so look. For what avails it
that something is hidden from man? Nothing is shut off from the sight of
God" (83.1). Seneca ends by asserting the reality of the God he had initially
only imagined. Whether a real but invisible God or a merely imagined Cato,
the spectator does not directly dictate what we ought to do but rather aids

us in our deliberations in a way that is at once intuitive and comprehensive: intuitive because it extends to solitary life the well-developed, public morality that we already possess; comprehensive because it can be applied to nearly all situations without requiring the articulation of subprinciples. The spectator is motivational as well as deliberative; a public gaze helps us to discern the right thing to do and urges us to do it. If the superego is, as Freud proposed, an internalization of the law initially imposed by the father, then Seneca's *act as if* re-externalizes the superego as an observing other.

Early modern humanists found in Seneca's advice an important source of guidance. In *Religio Medici* (1642), Thomas Browne admits that he has "practiced that honest artifice of *Seneca*, and in my retired and solitary imaginations, to detaine me from the foulenesse of vice, have fancied to myself the presence of my deare and worthiest friends."[13] Browne emulates Seneca's "honest artifice," though not his syntax, but other writers, like John Tillotson (1630–1677), archbishop of Canterbury, do both. In a sermon on the knowledge of God, Tillotson offers complicated counsel. First he asserts that we are being watched at all times, since "God is every where" and omniscient. But since God's ever-vigilant gaze is not sufficient to inspire the same "Shame and Fear" as the gaze of other men, he joins Seneca and Epicurus in proposing that we "live as if" a morally authoritative person were observing us:

> Live as those that believe this; be continually under the power of this Apprehension, That God takes a particular and exact notice of all thy Actions. The firm Belief of this would have a double influence upon us, it would encourage us in well-doing, and be a restraint upon us as to sin; *sic vivamus tanquam in conspectu vivamus, Sen.* It were well if Men would live as if any body saw them; but to live as if some Worthy and Excellent Person were always present with us, and did observe us, this will be a far greater curb upon us.[14]

For Tillotson, the shame and fear inspired by the imagined gaze of another person, a "Worthy and Excellent" one or, in a pinch, "any body," provides a greater moral check than the real and unblinking gaze of God ever can.

The New Testament provides a second ancient source text for the imperative use of *act as if*. The appropriate attitude of a Christian toward this world is described in 1 Corinthians 7:29–31: "This therefore I say, brethren; the time is short; it remaineth, that they also who have wives, be as if they had none [*oi echontes gunaikas ōs mē echontes ōsin*]; And they that weep, as though they wept not; and they that rejoice, as if they rejoiced not; and they that buy, as though they possessed not; And they that use this world, as if they used it not [*kai oi chrōmenoi ton kosmon ōs mē katachrōmenoi*]: for the fashion of this world passeth away."[15] Paul counsels a split consciousness. He does not direct followers of Christ to leave their families, cease mourning and rejoicing, or stop doing business, but rather to regard these activities as temporary and inessential. Our actions take place in this world, but our care is to be directed toward the world to come, in which our families, attachments, and possessions will, in the twinkling of an eye, have ceased to exist. The literal meaning of the Greek word *katachrōmenoi* is not to pervert or "to abuse" (as the King James Version translates it) but rather "to make full use of" or "to be fully engrossed in," and it is this engrossment that we are warned to avoid. Paul's list—wives, weeping, rejoicing, buying, using—is intended to be partial, synecdochic, and therefore generalizable to all the things and activities of this world.

The influence of the Pauline *act as if* is somewhat harder to assess than that of Seneca. In his *Spiritual Exercises* Ignatius of Loyola likely recalls Paul when he writes, with regard to alms giving, "I will consider, as if I were at the point of death [*considerar como si estuviesse en el artículo de la muerte*], what form and measure I will at that time wish I had used in the discharge of my administration. Then, guiding myself by this, I will apply it to my act of distribution."[16] Like Paul, Ignatius uses *act as if* to interpose the distance, detachment, and awareness of human finitude afforded by the "point of death." We are presumably more likely to give alms freely, without regard for our own worldly needs, *en el artículo de la muerte*, since money will no longer be of use. Jonathan Edwards likewise uses a Pauline *act as if* when he exhorts his parishioners to "have no dependence on any future time . . . hear every sermon, as if it were the last that you shall ever hear . . . in all your dealings with your neighbors, act as if you were never to make another bargain. Behave in your families every day, as though you depended on no other, than to take the final leave of them before another day."[17] In his counsel we can see the functional identity of "act as if" and "behave . . . as though"; both imaginatively remove us to the moment of our death. Where the Senecan imperative calls heaven closer to witness our solitary actions, the Pauline imperative pushes us to the brink of heaven so that we may consider our daily business as a final transaction with a fleeting world.

Not all modern uses of *act as if* have obvious predecessors.[18] Machiavelli's *The Prince* and Erasmus's *Education of a Christian Prince*, two humanist treatises on governance written within three years of each other (1513 and 1516, respectively) furnish instances of imperatives that are either *sui generis* or only loosely related to the Senecan or Pauline uses. Machiavelli warns that when noblemen will not bind themselves to their ruler, choosing instead to pursue their own ends, "a prince ought to guard against such, and to fear them as if they were open enemies [*come se fussino scoperti inimici*], because in adversity they always help to ruin him." A prince ought, in other words, to fear disobedient nobles now because they will be outright enemies in the future. Erasmus similarly seeks to account for the future by way of a double precept: "Conduct your own rule as if you were striving to ensure that no successor could be your equal [*sic imperato, quasi certes in hoc, ne quis tui similis queat*], but all the time prepare your children for their future reign as if to ensure that a better man would indeed succeed you [*tamquam id agas, ut tibi succedat te melior*]."[19] The two futures these precepts propose are incompatible, which accounts for their aphoristic charge: a ruler either will or will not be succeeded by a "better man." Yet the actions these imagined futures inspire are wholly compatible: to raise and educate one's children well is simply one duty of a good ruler. What matters, for the purposes of Erasmus's advice, is practical, not theoretical, concord.

### As If They Believe

All of the imperatives examined so far are heuristic. They imagine a state of affairs—a real or imagined observer, future consequences, or a counterfactual present—that can direct our conduct in a wide range of contexts. The purpose of such imperatives is not to obligate us directly but rather to make our obligations intuitively evident and motivate us to fulfill them. In the *Pensées* (1669), Blaise Pascal both participates in and decisively transforms the heuristic tradition of *act as if*. The influence of the Pauline imperative, with its emphasis on human finitude, is especially evident in note 203, "That passion may not harm us, let us act as if we had only [*comme s'il n'y avait que*] eight hours to live," and note 211, ". . . we shall die alone. We should therefore act as if we were alone [*faire comme si on était seul*]."[20] While these imperatives use an imagined account of the world to guide action, the passage headed "infini-rien" (n. 233), best known as "Pascal's Wager," reverses this causality, using action to shape our account of the world. Pascal adopts this reversed *act as if* to bridge a final gap in his argumentation.

Famously, his wager does not seek to demonstrate God's existence. Instead of logical or empirical evidence, it offers a purely prudential justification of belief, extending to otherworldly concerns the practical reasoning that ordinary, rational, self-interested individuals use to evaluate worldly risks like gambling or insurance.[21] But Pascal's prudential argument runs into a difficulty. Even if we accept that a belief in God is in our interest, such a belief is not so easy to come by. We can no more choose to believe that God exists than we can choose to believe that left is right or up is down. After finishing the probabilistic arguments for faith, Pascal offers a plan to overcome this final obstacle:

> You would like to attain faith, and do not know the way; you would like to cure yourself of unbelief, and ask the remedy for it. Learn of those who have been bound like you, and who now stake all their possessions. These are people who know the way which you would follow, and who are cured of an ill of which you would be cured. Follow the way by which they began; by acting as if they believed [*c'est en faisant tout comme s'ils croyaient*], taking the holy water, having masses said, etc. Even this will naturally make you believe, and deaden your acuteness [*vous abêtira*].

By advising us to act as if we believe things we do not (yet) believe, Pascal opens himself to the charge that he is proposing hypocrisy. Yet the path he proposes is only proximate, not identical, to hypocrisy. He does not endorse dissimulation. The goal is not to persuade others of your piety but to persuade yourself. The discrepancy between belief and action is intended to bring belief into eventual congruity with action. Pascal recommends that we follow those who "faisant tout comme s'ils croyaient" as a technology for placing our beliefs under our own control.

The main argument of the wager shifts the burden of justifying belief in God from theoretical reason to practical reason; "comme s'ils croyaient" shifts the cause of belief from existence to praxis. Instead of accepting that God exists because God exists, we accept that God exists as a consequence of our own repeated actions. In Louis Althusser's resonant paraphrase, "Kneel down, move your lips in prayer, and you will believe."[22] The manner and context in which these actions are carried out matters too: we ought to perform them regularly, using the appurtenances of faith, with masses ringing in our ears, surround by "people who know the way."[23] In stressing the importance of habitual actions, Pascal draws on a long tradition of ethical thought leading back to Aristotle, who claims that one becomes virtuous by the repeated performance of virtuous actions. Hamlet exemplifies this tradition when he counsels his mother, Gertrude, to "assume a virtue if you have it not."[24] Yet Hamlet and Aristotle speak only of the role habit plays in the constitution of virtues and vices; unlike Pascal, they do not propose that we should use habitual actions to reprogram our beliefs.[25] Where Aristotle holds that thoughts (including beliefs) arise from and are likenesses of things, Pascal locates the origin of belief in our habits.[26] Despite his divergence from the philosophical tradition, Pascal does not suggest that this method of producing belief is his own invention; to the contrary, he says the faithful have always arrived at their piety through habitual action. They too have "been bound like you" and have also sought to "deaden" themselves to doubt, to "lessen the passions" and remove the "stumbling blocks" to faith. In pursuit of belief we should do likewise.

The verb *abêtir*, here translated as "deaden" and sometimes rendered as "stupefy," means more literally to imbrute oneself, to become a beast (*bête*) or animal reliant not on rational capacity but on habituation. In note 252 Pascal explains that in most cases it is our animal nature, not reason, that produces faith: "We are as much automatic as intellectual; and hence it comes that the instrument by which conviction is attained is not demonstration alone. How few things are demonstrated! Proofs only convince the mind. Custom is the source of our strongest and most believed proofs." Because it appeals to our feeling and does not need to rely on the "violence" or "art" of argumentation, custom is a more powerful and pervasive cause of belief than reason. Custom instills belief directly into our body, which Pascal variously calls "the automaton" or "the machine." "It is custom that makes so many men Christians," he writes, "custom that makes them Turks, heathens, artisans, soldiers, etc." Only after custom has produced conviction do the higher faculties step in to ratify our beliefs. The heart has its reasons, which reason knows only after the fact.

Pascal's recommendations for engendering belief find an unlikely companion in the Anglican preacher, mystic, and meditative poet Thomas Traherne. Traherne rehearses arguments similar to Pascal's in 1675, six years after the first publication of the *Pensées* in France. His *Christian Ethicks*, usually considered to be the fullest statement of his philosophical beliefs, contains the following verses:

For Man to Act as if his Soul did see
The very Brightness of Eternity;
For Man to Act as if his Love did burn
Above the Spheres, even while it's in its Urne;
For Man to Act even in the Wilderness,
As if he did those Sovereign Joys possess,
Which do at once confirm, stir up, enflame,
And perfect Angels; having not the same!
It doth increase the Value of his Deeds,
In this a Man a Seraphim exceeds.[27]

These verses may appear to propose a heuristic imperative along the lines of Seneca, Erasmus, or Tillotson. Yet Traherne goes on to explain that our "natural complexion" can be dramatically altered by "care and study." The "humors of the soul," he writes, are "tractable things" that can be made "subject to the will." Because custom and habit together form a "second nature," each of us is a "made up man . . . artificial, and not natural."[28] As with Pascal, Traherne's *act as if* is the linguistic form of the artifice by which we create ourselves. Yet because he is more sanguine about the consequences of self-creation, Traherne eschews Pascal's *abêtir*. The virtuous man can, he argues, "put off and on, as he sees occasion" the second natures that he has created through custom and habit—becoming, like Paul, "all things to all men"—without having to imbrute or stupefy himself. That we are artificial, in Traherne's view, need not consign us to the status of automaton. Where Pascal's *comme s'ils croyaient* is a way of binding oneself to a particular set of beliefs, Traherne's *act as if* is a way of moving freely between different beliefs, different value commitments, and even different selves.

A further theological concern underwrites Traherne's use of *act as if*. The repetition of the phrase accentuates our epistemological finitude, the limits of our knowledge. Unlike that of angels, who look directly on eternity, our access to the divine is always blocked or interrupted. Lost in the wilderness, man can only "Act as if" he possesses the "Sovereign Joys" of the angels. Yet our separation from God redounds to our benefit, allowing us to exceed even the perfections of the seraphim, since it creates the possibility both for faith and the "Deeds" to which faith gives issue. "To Love GOD in the clear and perfect Light is a cheap and Easie Thing," he writes, while love shown "to an absent Object" is "far deeper."[29] Traherne's poem celebrates our epistemological finitude because it makes room for a faith more pro-found and virtuous than the unmediated vision of the angels.

### Regulative Principles and Categorical Imperatives

Seventeenth-century divines used *act as if* as a rule of thumb to guide private conduct. Pascal's altered *act as if*, which appears only once in the *Penseés*, proposes instead that we use our habitual actions to refashion our beliefs. The critical philosophy of Immanuel Kant takes a step back from both, using the form to express what he takes to be the necessary presup-positions of both our moral deliberations and our scientific investigations. The section of the *Critique of Pure Reason* (1781) on the *ideas of reason* argues for the necessary role of metaphysical illusion in our empirical study of the natural world.[30] Kant argues that the "interest of reason" (A666/B694), which always looks beyond the order of natural causes for a first cause, an uncaused cause, cannot do without the ideas of God, the soul, and a purpo-sive universe. Although they are mere "thought-entities" (*Gedankenwesen*) (A673/B701), the ideas of reason are necessary conditions of inquiry because they underwrite the "systematic unity" that our investigations must presup-pose in order to proceed in accord with the "harmonious use of reason" (A693/B721). Put more simply, only these illusions allow us to investigate the universe with the assurance that everything fits together in a rational way.[31] Voltaire's famous dictum is, for Kant, literally true: "If God did not exist, it would be necessary to invent him."[32] Since the ideas of reason cannot be simply jettisoned—since, Kant argues, they are presupposed whenever one engages in systematic inquiry—they must be construed regulatively, as "subjective principles of reason" (A616/B644) that have no correspond-ing object.

By describing ideas as "regulative," Kant means that they direct the un-derstanding toward a goal in a rule-guided way. He compares regulative ideas to the vanishing point (*focus imaginarius*) in a perspectival draw-ing (A664/B672). Although this point is never actually represented, it still organizes the space of the drawing. Throughout the first critique, Kant expresses regulative ideas in a standard linguistic form, usually with empha-sis: "Things in the world must be considered **as if [als ob]** they had gotten their existence from a highest intelligence" (A671/B699).[33] This form re-mains constant even as the domain of inquiry shifts. In psychology we must "connect all appearances, actions, and receptivity of our mind to the guiding thread of inner experience **as if** the mind were a simple substance" (A672/B700). In cosmology, we must "pursue the conditions of . . . nature through an investigation that will nowhere be completed, **as if** nature were infinite in itself and without a first or supreme member" (A672/B700). In theology, we necessarily "consider . . . experience **as if** this experience constituted an absolute unity . . . yet at the same time **as if** the sum total of all appearances had a single supreme and all-sufficient ground outside its range, namely an independent, original, and creative reason" (A672/B700). More generally, we must "[see] all combinations **as if** they were ordained by a highest reason of which our reason is only a weak copy" (A678/B706). Kant sums up: "The regulative law of systematic unity would have us study nature as if systematic and purposive unity together with the greatest possible manifoldness were to be encountered everywhere to infinity" (A700/B728).

Consider, connect, pursue, see, and study "als ob": in all but the final case, Kant's repetition and emphasis suggest that he was conscious of these statements' linguistic form as well as their conceptual content. In each restatement, *as if* draws a bright line between ideas in their constitutive and merely regulative use, serving as a prophylactic against the two related errors that Kant identifies as the basis of metaphysical illusion: *hypostatization*, in which an idea is turned into a thing, and *subreption*, in which a concept or principle appropriate only for empirical use is applied to things in themselves. While *God exists* expresses a dogmatic proposition, *study as if God exists* expresses a necessary presupposition of scientific inquiry. The Kantian *as if* keeps illusion in its proper place by designating it *as* an illusion.

While *act as if* first appears in Kant's epistemological thought, the form plays a similarly prominent role in his ethics. In the *Groundwork of the Metaphysics of Morals*, which aims to establish "*the supreme principle of morality*," Kant reformulates the categorical imperative in a variety of ways. The second variation, the *Naturgesetzformel*, or Formula of the Law of Nature (FLN), reads, "Act as if the maxim of your action were to become by your will a universal [natural] law" (*Handle so, als ob die Maxime deiner Handlung durch deinen Willen zum **allgemeinen Naturgesetze** werden sollte*).[34] The FLN makes the categorical imperative practically applicable by asking us to think of our maxim, as Allen Wood writes, "not as a normative law (a law *simpliciter*) but as a law *of nature*, that is, a law which is necessary in a different sense—a universal rule against which it is *causally impossible* for anyone to act."[35] Because of its applicability, Kant goes on to use the FLN to show how the categorical imperative can provide practical guidance in four concrete examples, in each case asking whether a maxim "could become a universal law of nature" (4:422).

We are of course not meant to suppose that our maxims *will* become universal laws of nature. Unlike other formulations of the categorical imperative, the FLN is expressly counterfactual. Instead we are meant only to test whether a maxim is capable of being a causal law. A maxim that can be willed categorically must be able to takes its place in the kingdom of ends, which is considered by "analogy" to the kingdom of nature, an order of "externally necessitated efficient causes" (4:438). The FLN in effect uses the laws of nature as a template for the laws of freedom. Similarly, when Kant writes, in a variation on the Formula of the Kingdom of Ends (FKE), that "every rational being must act as if he were by his maxims at all times a lawgiving member of the universal kingdom of ends" (4:438), the clear implication is that we are *not* lawgiving members of a universal kingdom of ends. The *as if* indicates that the kingdom of ends remains "merely possible," since, Kant writes, "even though a rational being scrupulously follows this maxim himself, he cannot for that reason count upon any other to be faithful to the same maxim nor can he count upon the kingdom of nature and its purposive order to harmonize with him" (4:439). Because our maxims remain merely subjective, in other words, the legislating we do through our actions will remain largely unacknowledged by other rational beings as well as by the natural world.

Both uses of *act as if*, in the *Critique of Pure Reason* and the *Groundwork*, are products of a critical philosophy that seeks to limit ideas to their proper domain of application. Even as they evoke the transcendent domain of metaphysical ideas like God and the soul, regulative ideas are applicable only within the immanent domain of natural causes. Even as they evoke the immanent causal order of nature, the FLN and the FKE are applicable only within the transcendent domain of freedom. In both cases, the *as if* functions as a cut, a clear incision between immanent and transcendent, theoretical and practical, regulative and constitutive use.

The most obvious ancestors of the FLN and the FKE are Kant's own formulations of the regulative ideas in the first critique. They are the categorical imperative expressed in the linguistic form of a regulative idea.

Much as Kant judges regulative ideas necessary to establish the systematic character of scientific inquiry, the FLN tests our maxims by seeing how they fit into a larger system of laws. But if the regulative idea is the most obvious and proximate ancestor of the FLN, it does not follow that it is the only one. Kant's correspondence with Markus Hertz in 1771 indicates that he was familiar with Adam Smith's *Theory of Moral Sentiments*.[36] Smith's account of the "general Rules of Morality"[37] includes an intriguing potential predecessor for the Kantian *act as if*. He describes a man who, having "received great benefits from another person," nevertheless feels "but a very small degree of the sentiment of gratitude." Through a virtuous education, however, this kind of man will "often have been made to observe how odious those actions appear which denote a want of this sentiment, and how amiable the contrary." In this peculiar case, moral conditioning circumvents genuine moral sentiment to induce the actions that are sentiment's usual consequence: "Tho' his heart therefore is not warmed with any grateful affection, he will strive to act as if it was, and will endeavour to pay all those regards and attentions to his patron which the liveliest gratitude could suggest."[38] This cold-hearted man performs all the actions of one moved by moral sentiment, but he is actually moved only by "a reverence for the established rule of duty, a serious and earnest desire of acting, in every respect, according to the law of gratitude." As if to drive the point (and perhaps also the linguistic form) of this moral type home, Smith describes a second agent, a wife who feels no "tender regard" for her husband: "If she has been virtuously educated, however, she will endeavour to act as if she felt it, to be careful, officious, faithful and sincere, and to be deficient in none of those attentions which the sentiment of conjugal affection could have prompted her to perform."[39] Coldness and lack of feeling lead Smith to judge that "such a friend, and such a wife, are neither of them, undoubtedly, the very best of their kinds"; despite their "serious and earnest desire to fulfil every part of their duty," they fall short of "those of the happiest mould," who are "capable of suiting, with exact justness, their sentiments and behaviour to the smallest difference of situation."[40]

Kant inverts Smith's moral hierarchy. For him, agents motivated solely by "reverence for . . . duty" and a "desire of acting, in every respect . . . according to the law" (Kant calls this *Achtung*) are more deserving of approbation than those who are moved by "tender regard" or "grateful affection." Although he rejects Smith's ethics, along with all ethics based on empirical inclination, Kant nevertheless preserves Smith's syntax. He re-formulates the categorical imperative as a universal law of nature so that it may serve as a practically applicable moral principle for those who act out of respect for law rather than sentiment.

The Kantian *act as if*, like the rest of his philosophy, had an extensive afterlife in epistemology, ethics, and practical morality, but it attracted no follower more dedicated than Hans Vaihinger.[41] In 1911 Vaihinger published the *Philosophie des Als Ob* (translated by C. K. Ogden in 1924 as *The Philosophy of "As if"*), which expands Kant's regulative ideas beyond the domain of scientific inquiry to include all aspects of human life. For Kant, only ideas that we cannot know to be false, and that therefore have the possibility of being true, can be regulative, but Vaihinger proposes that an "idea whose theoretical untruth or incorrectness, and therewith its falsity, is admitted, is not for that reason practically valueless and useless."[42] He argues that not only metaphysics and theology but also the natural sciences, mathematics, ethics, economics, and law are populated with "useful fictions," ideas that, while false, "provide us with an *instrument for finding our way about more easily in this world*" (15). Where Kant's regulative ideas are necessary suppositions—systematic inquiry cannot take place without them—Vaihinger's useful fictions are tools that can be taken up and employed at will. Latent in all of these fictions, according to Vaihinger, is an unexpressed *as if* (95). So, for example, he restates the premise of Leibnitz's calculus as "every curved line is to be thought of (may be thought of, must be thought of) *as if* it consisted of an infinite number of infinitely small straight lines" (91). He likewise restates the enabling assumption of Adam Smith's theory of political economy as follows: "all human actions . . . could be looked upon *as if* their driving force lay in but one single factor—egoism" (20).

Vaihinger's central contention is that the utility and the truth of ideas must be judged independently. This claim steers a middle path between two contrary positions. Most philosophers since Socrates have held that, at least in the final analysis, only true ideas are useful; by the same token, false ideas (such as Francis Bacon's "idols of the mind") are harmful or at best useless. On the other side, pragmatists like Charles Peirce and William James aim to collapse the distinction between truth and utility. Pragmatists understand the claim that only true ideas are useful as a tautology. *True*, for the pragmatist, is simply the word we use to describe ideas that work, while the term *useful fiction* amounts to an oxymoron.[43] Like Friedrich Nietzsche, who was one of his main influences, Vaihinger rejected both the pragmatist's identification of the true and the useful and the natural scientist's conviction that although truth and utility are different, only true ideas are (finally) useful. For him, the false, the fictional, and the demonstrably untrue have countless indispensable applications for human thought and action.

While Vaihinger's claims are primarily philosophical, they hinge on his analysis of a linguistic form. He analyzes the meaning of *as if* into the meaning of its particles: *as*, which signals a comparison, and *if*, which signals an unreal or impossible condition (92). Between these particles lies "something else hidden":

> What, then, is contained in the as if? There must apparently be something else hidden in it apart from the unreality and impossibility of the assumption in the conditional sentence. These particles clearly also imply a decision to maintain the assumption *formally, in spite of these difficulties.* Between the *as* and *if, wie* and *wenn, als* and *ob, comme* and *si, qua-si,* a whole sentence lies implied. What, then, does it mean if we say that matter must be treated *as if* it consisted of atoms? It can only mean that empirically given matter must be treated *as* it would be treated *if* it consisted of atoms. (93, Vaihinger's italics)

This analysis makes evident that *act as if* is a counterpart to the linguistic form that I examine in the following chapter, *WWJD?* Both forms express half of a conditional sentence. *Act as if* expresses the condition but (usually) leaves the consequence hidden; the question *what would Jesus do?* expresses the consequence but leaves the condition implicit. Especially when expanded to its fullest form, *as if,* for Vaihinger, is a marker of fictionality. He observes that fictions share the same linguistic form as hypotheses, similes, and errors, and he writes that a fiction is merely a *"more conscious, more practical and more fruitful error"* (94; Vaihinger's italics). By calling *as if* sentences *"more conscious,"* he means that the admission of fictionality is built into the form of their expression. Useful fictions are false, but deliberately, self-consciously, knowingly false.

### The *Act as If* Method

The history of *act as if* proceeds by accumulation rather than succession. Newer uses of the form do not simply supplant older uses. Instead, older and newer uses live alongside each other, the Senecan and Pauline alongside the Pascalian and the Kantian. Subsequent thinkers and writers sometimes take up earlier uses and breathe new vitality into them, as the pragmatist William James did with Pascal's *act as if*. James ends the chapter in *Principles of Psychology* (1890) entitled "The Perception of Reality" with a short "practical observation." Given that beliefs are the attitude we take toward things that are outside our control, how, asks James, can we "believe at will"? His answer is that while we cannot will ourselves to believe instantaneously, "*gradually* our will can lead us to the same results by a very simple method":

> We need only in cold blood ACT *as if the thing in question were real, and keep acting as if it were real, and it will infallibly end by growing into such a connection with our life that it will become real.* It will become so knit with habit and emotion that our interests in it will be those which characterize belief. Those to whom "God" and "Duty" are now mere names can make them much more than that, if they make a little sacrifice to them every day.[44]

In saying that the thing in question will "become real," James is of course describing a psychological process rather than a magical transformation. He argues that we invest belief in those things (physical objects, abstract ideas, religious doctrines, whatever) that have "intimate and continuous connection" with our experience (298). The word *reality* does not point to an attribute that things have in themselves but instead signifies their "relation to our emotional and active life" (295). To make ourselves believe and feel that a thing is real, which is equivalent, for James, to making it real, we need only bring it into connection with our day-to-day existence through habitual action. James famously adopted Charles Peirce's definition of belief as a "rule for action" (he calls this "the principle of Peirce, the principle of pragmatism").[45] The *act as if* "method" reads the principle of pragmatism in reverse, generating beliefs by acting according to their rule.

Two of James's later works suggest that Kant and Pascal directly influenced his syntax as well as his philosophy, although in different ways. *The Will to Believe*, published in 1896, begins with a loose translation of Pascal's wager, note 233. The similarity between Pascal's philosophy and James's is clear enough: both propose a technique for transforming will into belief through habitual action. But it is striking that James omits a key line from Pascal's argument. He closes the translation as follows:

If there were an infinity of chances, and only one for God in this wager, still you ought to stake your all on God; for though you surely risk a finite loss by this procedure, and finite loss is reasonable, even a certain one is reasonable, if there is but the possibility of infinite gain. Go, then, and take holy water, and have masses said; belief will come and stupefy your scruples,—*Cela vous fera croire et vous abêtira.* Why should you not? At bottom, what have you to lose?[46]

James goes on to voice a number of criticisms of Pascal's reasoning, declaring that in the terms presented in the wager the will to believe appears either "silly" or "vile": silly because no one has ever been persuaded to convert from one faith to another by probabilistic reasoning ("certainly no Turk ever took to masses or holy water on its account"); vile because the faith produced is ersatz, "mechanical," lacking "the inner soul of faith's reality."[47] Yet the hyperbole of these criticisms alert us that James is practicing polemical ventriloquism, giving voice to the possible objections of his readers so that he can refute them. And indeed, he writes a few pages later that "Pascal's argument, instead of being powerless, then seems a regular clincher, and is the last stroke needed to make our faith in masses and holy water complete."[48] Yet absent from James's rehearsal of Pascal's argument is the key line: "faisant tout comme s'ils croyaient," the *act as if they believe* that, as we have seen, had been a central part of James's practical psychology at least since 1890. In the subsequent essay, "Is Life Worth Living?," James delivers his own version of the formula: "To trust our religious demands means first of all to live in light of them, and to act as if the invisible world which they suggest were real."[49] While James is usually scrupulous about acknowledging his precursors, often to the point of ascribing his own ideas to them, he omits Pascal's counsel only to present it later as his own. Pascal proposed *act as if* as a way of manipulating our beliefs. James renovates the form so that it can also be used to manipulate the basic constituents of reality, including God, morality, and the self.

While James's *act as if* is uncomfortably close to Pascal's, it is pointedly opposed to Kant's. In his lectures on "natural theology" delivered at the University of Edinburgh between 1901 and 1902 and then published as *The Varieties of Religious Experience*, he writes,

Immanuel Kant held a curious doctrine about such objects of belief as God, the design of creation, the soul, its freedom, and the life hereafter. These things, he said, are properly not objects of knowledge at all. Our conceptions always require a sense-content to work with, and as the words "soul," "God," "immortality," cover no distinctive sense-content whatever, it follows that theoretically speaking they are words devoid of any significance. Yet strangely enough they have a definite meaning *for our practice*. We can act *as if* there were a God; feel *as if* we were free; consider Nature *as if* she were full of special designs; lay plans *as if* we were to be immortal; and we find then that these words do make a genuine difference in our moral life. Our faith *that* these unintelligible objects actually exist proves thus to be a full equivalent in *praktischer Einsicht* [practical judgment], as Kant calls it, or from the point of view of our action, for a knowledge of *what* they might be, in case we were permitted positively to conceive them.[50]

James is especially critical of "this particularly uncouth part" of Kant's philosophy. For him, to say that something exists or is real means only that it has "a definite meaning *for our practice*" and makes "a genuine difference in our moral life." He rejects the positivist restriction of knowledge to the objects of "sense-content," as well as the distinction between practical and theoretical perspectives that Kant's regulative ideas entail.

James sought to bring his psychological theory and its practical applications to a broader public. "The Gospel of Relaxation," which he first delivered as a graduation speech at Wellesley and then published in *Scribner's Magazine* in 1899, sets out to demonstrate the "practical applications" of his psychological doctrines to the "hygiene of our American life."[51] Amid a hodgepodge of anecdotes about prominent psychologists (including "a Viennese neurologist of considerable reputation") and observations on national character (he describes American women as "bottled lightning"), James writes:

> Action seems to follow feeling, but really action and feeling go together; and by regulating the action, which is under the more direct control of the will, we can indirectly regulate the feeling, which is not. Thus the sovereign voluntary path to cheerfulness, if our spontaneous cheerfulness be lost, is to sit up cheerfully, to look round cheerfully, and to act and speak as if cheerfulness were already there. If such conduct doesn't make you soon feel cheerful, nothing else on that occasion can. So to feel brave, act as if we *were* brave. (500)

The *act as if* method apparently made a strong impression on James's protégés at Harvard. Teddy Roosevelt, one of James's early students, used the method to work up his courage: "There were all kinds of things of which I was afraid at first, ranging from grizzly bears to 'mean' horses and gunfighters; but by acting as if I was not afraid I gradually ceased to be afraid. Most men can have the same experience if they choose."[52] But not all James's students adopted his usage and rejected Kant's. The reporter and political thinker Walter Lippmann, who studied with James three decades after Roosevelt, uses the form to indicate the necessity of relying on imperfect knowledge when making political decisions. "We have to act on what we believe, on half-knowledge, illusion, and error," he writes. "Experience itself will reveal our mistakes; research and criticism may convert them into wisdom. But we must act, and act as if we know the nature of man and proposed to satisfy his needs."[53] Like Kant, Lippmann proposes an imperative that underwrites our political actions in the face of limited knowledge, not one that reprograms our beliefs or alters the constituents of reality itself.

The students of James, despite their prominence, were not the ones to bring his *act as if* method to the attention of the wider public. That task fell to Dale Carnegie, whose *How to Win Friends and Influence People* (1937), the best-known and best-selling example of the self-help genre, reproduces the paragraph from the "The Gospel of Relaxation" that I quote above.[54] While Carnegie reasonably enough detached James's quotation from its philosophical underpinnings, he also managed to misinterpret James's advice, following it with this commentary: "Everybody in the world is seeking happiness—and there is one sure way to find it. That is by controlling your thoughts. Happiness doesn't depend on outward conditions. It depends on inner conditions." Carnegie supplies a Stoic moral to a pragmatic technique. James's *act as if* method does not depend on a stable, persistent self that can insulate itself from "outward conditions." It seeks, rather, to break down the very distinction between "inner" and "outward" conditions by showing their causal inextricability. It is precisely because outward action and inner feeling "go together," in James's phrase, that the former can be used to alter the latter. More recent books of self-help, positive thinking, and popular psychology regularly refer to James as the founder of the *act as if* technique. Because they are usually little more than collections of inspirational commonplaces, they tend to quote or rather paraphrase only one or two short aphorisms, most frequently, "If you want a quality, act as if you already had it" and "Act as if what you do makes a difference. It does."[55]

### Regulative and Pragmatic Imperatives

Like most of its descendants in the self-help industry, James's *act as if* is a technical or instrumental imperative. It is employed as a means to a given end and is therefore conditional on the end for which it is employed. We act as if we believe in God so that we will believe in him, making use of a conditional supposition in order to achieve a real aim. The heuristic imperatives of Seneca and Saint Paul are similarly conditional; as moral expedients they aid our deliberations but are not necessary to them. It may be helpful to imagine that we are being watched or are on the point of death, but we can act virtuously without ever needing to do so. The Kantian *act as if*, by contrast, is categorical; it does not depend on particular situations, like being alone and unwatched, or our particular aims or desires. Always in effect for rational beings, it obligates us without further conditions.[56]

Yet an even more decisive distinction divides the *act as if* tradition into two strands. What we might term a *pragmatic* imperative aims to defictionalize its presupposition, to make the counterfactual *were* into an indicative *is*. James's advice, to "ACT *as if the thing in question were real*," is pragmatic because it aims to make the thing real. We act as if we were brave so that we may be brave. Hans Vaihinger warns that our counterfactuals tend to slide from fiction into belief (he calls this "ideational shift"),[57] and James, like Pascal and Traherne before him, aims to induce precisely this slide.

In what might, by contrast, be called *regulative* imperatives, the presupposition and the aim remain distinct. When an inspirational poem or the lyrics of a song instruct us, in an updated version of Seneca's heuristic, to "dance like there's nobody watching," the goal is not to scare away all observers (though that may sometimes be the actual effect) but rather to change the way we dance. The presupposition of a regulative imperative remains counterfactual or merely possible even as it exercises real causality. In some cases, as when we act as if we were lawgiving members of a kingdom of ends, we may make infinite progress toward an ideal aim. But this progress is asymptotic, such that the real always remains distinct from the ideal, possible but never wholly actual. Vaihinger's entire philosophy is a defense of regulative imperatives. Because they are, as he puts it, "conscious" of their own fictionality, these imperatives keep subjective judgments distinct from objective judgments, thought entities distinct from real entities, practical reasoning distinct from theoretical reasoning. Where the regulative *act as if* is a metaphysical border patrol, policing the line between fact and fiction, practice and speculation, immanence and transcendence, the pragmatic *act as if* is a *bureau de change*, converting fiction into action, will into belief, practice into faith, the useful into the true.

The two strands of imperatives that make up the modern tradition of *act as if* present inverse *mnemonic* problems, problems of memory. For Kant and Vaihinger the problem is amnesia, the forgetting of the transcendental distinction (and thus the fictionality denoted by *as if*) that leads to subreption and hypostasis. What is legitimate for practical reason can be illegitimately attributed to theoretical reason. Useful fictions, as Vaihinger notes, tend to slide into dogmatic error. Kantian critique administers a kind of anamnesis, reminding reason of its own limits, retracing the line between objects of knowledge and practical presuppositions, putting concepts back into their proper sphere of application.

For the pragmatic imperative, by contrast, the problem is remembering and the solution is amnesia. As Vaihinger observes, *act as if* carries an admission of fictionality in its very form. It denies its own truth, marking out a transcendental distinction in spite of itself. Yet the slide into belief requires that we forget or erase markers of fictionality. Pascal's *abêtir*— working beneath the threshold of reason in order to instill belief through one's animal nature—is a crucial, perhaps even necessary step in using the form to program belief. The sheer imbrutement of habit allows us, in Frank Kermode's words, to "forget that fictions are fictive."[58] It is not enough to practice the *act as if* method; for it to be effective one must cease to recognize it *as* a method even as one puts it into practice. Stated in a different way, the pragmatic and regulative uses of *act as if* interfere with each other. Each is tripped up by sharing its linguistic form with the other.

Because of their shared form, it is sometimes unclear whether a particular utterance of *act as if* is a pragmatic or regulative imperative. When Steve Chandler, an author of business motivational books, instructs customer service representatives to "act as if [the customer] is the most important person in the world to you," it would appear at first to be a regulative imperative, a consciously held fiction used only to guide behavior. But Chandler goes on to assert that "by acting as if [customers] are important, you have made them important."[59] If we take him at his word, "importance" can be created or redistributed based on the actions of a customer service representative. Crucially, whether an utterance of *act as if* is pragmatic or regulative is not apparent in the utterance itself but depends on the context of use. More specifically, it depends on a contextual understanding of which features of the world are constant or beyond control and which can be deliberately altered. We can roughly categorize those who counsel us to *act as if* based on their sense of the manipulability of the real: for Seneca, the presence or absence of an observer is a fact that does not depend on one's actions; for Kant, metaphysical ideas exist or not independently of our assertions about them; for Pascal, our beliefs can be reprogrammed by our habits; for James, our habits shape and determine our beliefs and even reality itself, including the reality of God.

Although pragmatic and regulative imperatives function in opposed ways, it would be a mistake to regard these modern strands of *act as if* as necessarily incompatible. In the self-help industries of the twentieth century, these imperatives cohabit without obvious tension or distinction. Consider the speech that Ben Affleck, playing a cocky, hard-driving senior stock broker, delivers to a board room of nervous, young, white male associates in the 2000 film *Boiler Room* (with apologies for obscenity): "There's an important phrase that we use here, and I think it's time that you all learned it. Act as if. You understand what that means? Act as if you are the fucking president of this firm. Act as if you got a nine-inch cock. Okay? Act as if."[60] Affleck's professional imperative is pragmatic, while the sexual imperative, I presume, is not, yet both fit together without tension or distinction. His advice also nicely illustrates the most recent development in the *act as if* tradition, a development so recent that we are still in its midst. The form's *Y* variable has accommodated a broad range of fictional contents, but it has increasingly operated apart from any content, as in Affleck's first and final repetitions. When delivered as *act as if,* full stop, the form directs us not to any specific fiction as the regulative principle of our actions but rather to fiction in the abstract, fiction *as such.* The early roots of the form's abstraction are to be found in Kant's categorical imperative, which Kant presents merely as the *form of law*—a form that obligates us regardless of the particular maxim we seek to test. In its contentlessness, the abstracted imperative is like Rilke's famous dictum "Du musst dein Leben ändern" (You must change your life), which enjoins change itself rather than any specific change that can be specified in advance.[61] Shorn of particular fictions, *act as if* expresses only the obligation to live one's life according to fiction itself. In the brokerage firm dramatized by Affleck, which draws on and caricatures the world of positive psychology and managerial philosophy, the only imperative is to fictionalize.

### Genuine Options

At the outset I proposed that around the latter half of the seventeenth century practical imperatives of the form *X as if Y* began to develop new functions as a response to and a reaction against what Charles Taylor calls our secular age. Unlike the "subtraction narratives" of Weber and Durkheim, which suppose that the rise of a rationalized modernity leads inevitably to the decline of faith or at least to its evacuation from the public sphere, Taylor's account of secularism is concerned with changes in the conditions of belief, the context of understanding or social "background" against which belief or unbelief occurs. The flaw of subtraction narratives, in Taylor's view, is that they seek to compare different phenomena that share the name *belief*, whereas belief means something very different at the start of the seventeenth century, when it was "virtually impossible not to believe in God," and in the present day, when "faith, even for the staunchest believer, is one human possibility among others."[62] The experience and significance of belief radically changes when there are other viable alternatives, chief among them the purely immanent understanding of the world and of human flourishing that Taylor calls *exclusive humanism*.

While Taylor's notion of *background* is borrowed from phenomenologists like Maurice Merleau-Ponty, Hubert Dreyfus, and especially Martin Heidegger, his understanding of secularism is derived primarily from William James. In *The Varieties of Religion Today*, a series of lectures he used to prepare for writing *A Secular Age*, Taylor observes, "James is our great philosopher of the cusp. He tells us more than anyone else about what it's like to stand in that open space and feel the winds pulling you now here, now there. He describes a crucial site of modernity and articulates the decisive drama enacted there."[63] By the "cusp" or the "open space" Taylor means precisely the condition of our secular age, in which one is pulled between the "great options" of theism and exclusive humanism. James is the great philosopher of the secular condition, Taylor argues, because he was pulled strongly in both directions and "could feel and articulate the continuing ambivalence." Taylor finds in James's personal account of his own situation the "decisive drama" of secular modernity.

James's *act as if* method, in its original application, was a way of coping with the "open space" between the great options, a technology of the self designed to help one escape, to the extent possible, the ambivalence of our secular age, with all its attendant anxieties and ironies. The method seeks to allow its users to step down off the cusp to embrace one of the options fully. In a secular age, when unconditional commitments are hard to come by, James's method helps us to forge such commitments out of deliberately chosen habits of action. Pascal, James's obliquely acknowledged predecessor, uses *comme s'ils croyaient* in response to a similar but not identical "open space." The wager, which asks its readers to decide between two possibilities, *infini-rien*, infinity or nothing, contemplates a space that is at once narrower and starker than it would be for James more than two centuries later. James stands uneasily in the "open space," whereas Pascal is closely bound in the probabilistic quadrangle of the bettor and the game theorist.

While Taylor is particularly focused on the question of belief, his account of secularism is also concerned with changes in the way we make choices, live together, and govern ourselves. He claims that our social world is, as Peter Gordon puts it, "now sufficiently pluralistic about faith-commitments that as a society we no longer regard religion as providing us with the default normative foundations for all collective action."[64] Kant's place in this narrative is, as Taylor acknowledges, especially complicated. Because Kant's ethics invests normativity in the law we give to ourselves (autonomy) rather than the law given to us by another (heteronomy), his philosophy is often regarded as a key step in the development of exclusive humanism.[65] The categorical imperative, including its formulation as a law of nature (FLN), does not derive its value or legitimacy from the existence or nonexistence of God. As the first critique argues, we can only have knowledge of entities that we encounter in experience, within the limits of what Taylor calls the *immanent frame*. God, immortality, and the soul fall outside this frame and so cannot be objects of knowledge.

Yet what Kant discards with one hand he preserves with the other. He does not think we can abandon the metaphysical ideas, since they play an indispensable role in morality and scientific inquiry. Although we can say nothing about God or the soul, even to affirm their existence, we must postulate them nonetheless. James gets Kant right on this point: for purposes of practical judgment, he summarizes, we must "act *as if* there were a God; feel *as if* we were free . . . lay plans *as if* we were to be immortal." Instead of banishing metaphysical ideas entirely, Kant displaces them from theoretical to practical philosophy. He seeks to remove them from the domain of verification and falsification so as to preserve them for the sake of ethics and scientific inquiry. They survive as mere postulates that allow us to hope that the world is not finally indifferent to our moral or rationally inquisitive ends.

*Act as if* has been the object not only of invention and development but also of contestation. As we have seen, James rejects Kant's understanding of the *as if* in order to offer his own. Sigmund Freud goes a step further by rejecting the philosophy of *as if* altogether.[66] Although he singles out Vaihinger for criticism in *The Future of an Illusion*, he uses him as a representative of Kant and Kantianism more generally.[67] "A man whose thinking is not influenced by the artifices of philosophy," he writes, will invariably rebuff the *as if* since "it cannot be expected of him that precisely in treating his most important interests he shall forgo the guarantees he requires for all his ordinary activities." Freud remains optimistic that "people will soon behave" with disdain "towards fairy tales of religion, in spite of the advocacy of 'as if.'"[68] For him, *as if* stands alongside Tertullian's "Credo quia absurdum" (I believe because it is absurd) as a final, desperate attempt to evade the edicts of reason and evidence, the last remainder of an illusion that has passed its expiration date.[69]

Pascal and James use *act as if* to create willed belief in the context of a pluralistic world. Kant mobilizes it to preserve a practical role for the metaphysical ideas that his epistemology places beyond the bounds of knowledge. Yet the formula is not intrinsically suited to the task of contesting secularism. *X as if Y* is capable of accommodating a hypothetically infinite range of actions for the *X* variable and conditions for the *Y* variable. As a technology, like a hammer or a knife, it can be repurposed according to the aims of its users, but like other tools, it does not always serve the purposes of its wielder. Developed as a response to and a reaction against an increasingly secular age, *act as if* paradoxically ends up hastening on the process of secularization. James, Pascal, and Kant all employ the form with regard to the traditional set of metaphysical ideas, but twentieth-century writers reoriented it primarily to worldly concerns. After developing his method to produce deliberate belief in God, freedom, and the soul, James himself applied it to "moral hygiene" as well as to otherworldly commitments. He instructed readers to act as if they had an immortal soul but also to act as if they were cheerful, confident, and brave. Carnegie and his self-help acolytes deployed the form in a wide range of uses related solely to human flourishing in the immanent frame.

Pragmatic imperatives like those used by Pascal and James were designed to produce belief, but they also undermined belief by unveiling its worldly origins. When Pascal offers the form as a means to attain faith, he also suggests, with no evident reservations, that those who already possess faith arrived at it by the same means. Religious belief, in note 233 of the *Pensées*, is the product of self-manipulation undertaken for one's own advantage. Its ground lies in the psyche of the believer, not in evidence for or a demonstration of existence, and it is therefore not transferrable from one person to another. That you have willed yourself to believe gives me no grounds for willing myself to do the same. Those who possess faith, Pascal implies, begin with artifice and then manage to forget or deaden themselves to its artificiality. Revealing the origins of confidence or courage does not undermine their authority or legitimacy. Those who act confidently and regard themselves as confident simply *are* confident. But locating the origins of religious belief in the psyche of the believer only affirms the skepticism of Freud and other exclusive humanists who seek religion's origins solely in the immanent frame. For these humanists, *act as if* reveals the emperor in the process of putting on his imaginary clothes.

The form hastens on secularism in a still more basic way. In both its pragmatic and regulative forms, it is the vehicle of a kind of practical antifoundationalism. It offers us a way of getting on with things without needing to make claims about the way the world actually is, and thus without needing to have propositional beliefs about it. When we follow advice to "act as if you are confident," we make no claim about whether or not we are confident; the self is regarded as an object of manipulation rather than of belief. Likewise, those who reject moral realism—the view that moral propositions are true features of the world—can still act as if moral norms are in effect, whether by imagining a virtuous observer, divine legislator, or universalized maxim. The fully abstracted *act as if*, which expresses the bare obligation to live by and through fictions, is merely the totalization of this antifoundationalism. In its variability, the form serves as the vehicle for the unbounded instantiation of practices that are acknowledged to be without grounds. The Kantian *act as if* opens up a new modality—mere possibility—in which God and the soul can be preserved as the guides for empirical inquiry and practice without requiring, or allowing for, assertion or denial. Belief in God is not, in this modality, what James terms a "forced" option. Consigning metaphysical ideas to a purely regulative role makes the "open space" of secular modernity at once more open and even habitable in its own right.

### A History of Various Statements

The present-day self-help industry inherited *act as if*, primarily by way of Dale Carnegie, from William James, but it also looks back to the imagined spectators of Epicurus and Seneca. James acknowledges Pascal as a veiled precedent for, and Kant as an explicit obstacle to, his *act as if* method. Freud rejects the *as if* of Vaihinger and Kantians more generally. Kant's reformulation of the categorical imperative as a law of nature is indebted to his own account of the regulative ideas in the first critique and possibly to Adam Smith as well. Pascal employs Pauline regulative imperatives even as he reworks *act as if* into a pragmatic supplement to his wager. Though these relationships (among the others I have described) do not exhaust the history of the form, cataloging every distinction of its meaning and use, they do map its main thoroughfares, those that have had continued consequence even up to the present day. This history constitutes a relatively coherent tradition, a simplified network of diffusion with two main branches, stretching across at least seven Western languages (Greek, Latin, French, Italian, Spanish, German, and English), in which writers adopt a linguistic form from their predecessors, adapt it to their own purposes, and make it available to their successors. Further explorations may uncover continuous or analogous traditions, with other points of articulation and other causes, in other languages and discourses. But in this tradition, at least as I have construed it, the form is developed primarily by a series of intellectuals and systematic thinkers before gaining wide purchase in popular discourse and practice, where it has come to serve as a pervasive technology of the self.

Though this tradition traverses multiple discourses and disciplines of knowledge—moral instruction, Christian apologetics, theoretical and ethical philosophy, pragmatism and pop psychology—it cannot be fully assimilated to any of them. Likewise, over the course of its history the linguistic form has been associated with and analyzed in terms of a broad and sometimes incompatible array of general and specialized concepts: fiction, error, artifice, hypothesis, habit, and belief, as well as the useful, practical, categorical, merely regulative, merely possible, ideal, real, and imaginary. What the form's history shows, however, is that its relation to *any* of these various concepts is contingent and conventional rather than necessary and permanent. From our current vantage, it is no doubt especially tempting to understand the history of *act as if*, retrospectively, as an outgrowth or province of the history of what Vaihinger called "useful fictions." And indeed the linguistic form has in the last century come to serve as a key thoroughfare between fiction, on the one hand, and conduct, practice, belief, and reality, on the other, so that it would be difficult to study the relationship between these concepts without also grasping the role of *act as if* in regulating the traffic between them. Yet the identification of the linguistic form with the concept of the "useful fiction" is a late development, one that is projected back to its earlier use in writers like Traherne, Pascal, or Kant only with violence.

To my knowledge, intellectual historians have yet to study traditions like the one sketched here. Over the past century, they have produced countless histories of words, concepts, ideas, and phrases, whether studied under the rubric of philology, intellectual history, lexicography, *Begriffsgeschichte* (history of concepts), historical semantics, cultural history, or the history of ideas. A student of ethics looking to understand the origins of the keywords employed in his or her discipline will not be at a loss for fine histories of justice, human rights, autonomy, or natural law.[70] Where intellectual historians in the wake of Arthur Lovejoy traced the history of unit-ideas across long swaths of history, more recent work has sought to include the broader discourses, language games, social and linguistic contexts, *mentalités*, epistemes, forms of life, and cultures in which words and concepts are situated. Yet somewhere in the transition from studying unit-ideas to studying broader contexts, histories of linguistic forms have been neglected. Why should this be?

I suggested in chapter 1 that general technological limitations, coupled with longstanding lexicocentric assumptions, have prevented inquiry into linguistic forms like *X as if Y*. But there are also, I believe, obstacles peculiar to the recent discipline of intellectual history. Beginning in the late sixties, Quentin Skinner, J. G. A. Pocock, and other members of the Cambridge School of intellectual history launched a philosophically nuanced and highly cogent critique of what Lovejoy had named *the history of ideas*. Skinner in particular targeted the anachronism, presentism, and essentialism that led historians to understand earlier thinkers as precursors or anticipations of later intellectual movements.[71] Because of their essentialist assumptions, he argued, the historian of ideas attributed to earlier thinkers intentions they could not possibly have had given the time and context in which they wrote. The proper task of the intellectual historian, as Skinner conceived it, is to understand the utterances of thinkers in relationship to the context of use in which they originated. In practice this meant reading a wide range of lesser-known authors alongside the better-known ones to develop a holistic understand of the discursive conditions in which individual texts and utterances emerged. Skinner's critique took aim not only at those within the discipline of intellectual history proper; it extended as well to the apparently modest project of Raymond Williams's *Keywords* (and by extension to the philological enterprise more broadly).[72] Tracing the meaning of words across multiple periods, he warned, isolates them from the various discursive contexts in which they were employed. This isolation risks elevating keywords to timeless essences, and it also occludes the diverse social processes that cause the meanings of words to change.

Although Skinner's arguments have been vigorously and frequently contested, they have had a significant influence on the discipline of intellectual history, as well as a less definitive but still considerable influence on literary studies.[73] Of course, historians did not, in the wake of Skinner's critique, stop publishing books and articles that spanned periods, but the discipline as a whole became wary of engaging in the kind of transhistorical inquiry that he had sought either to proscribe or to narrowly circumscribe. For subsequent intellectual historians, the cardinal sin has been anachronism, and the cardinal virtue a thorough grasp of an author's or work's local, discursive context.

Yet Skinner's arguments against anachronism need not discourage us from the investigation of the *longue durée* necessary for understanding the full life span of a linguistic form. To the contrary, he raises the possibility of just such an inquiry in an often-overlooked passage near the close of his seminal article, "Meaning and Understanding in the History of Ideas." After forcefully concluding that "the project of studying histories of 'ideas,' *tout court*, must rest on a fundamental philosophical mistake,"[74] he writes that "the only history to be written is thus a history of the various statements made with [a] given expression."[75] A history of a linguistic form of the kind attempted here is precisely a history of the various statements made with various expressions, albeit expressions defined by their form rather than by the words they comprise and the concepts they name. Such a history does not presume to study, as Skinner puts it, "all the various situations, which may change in complex ways, in which the given form of words can logically be used,"[76] since the logically possible situations in which a given form of words can be used are necessarily unbounded. Instead it confines itself to the actual situations in which the forms have been used. Linguistic forms, as opposed to individual words, are less easily mistaken for bearers of "essential" meaning. One cannot simply point to a formula's denotation, in the way that one generally can with a single word. Investigating the histories of forms asks us, in the dictum Skinner borrows from post-Wittgensteinian analytical philosophy, to "study not the meaning of the words, but their use."[77] To write the history of a form is to write a history of its changing discursive function over time. Understanding the specificity of a form's use in one period or context requires comparing it with the use of the form in other periods and contexts. While such a history of various statements would be, in Skinner's terms, "conceptually proper," he warns that it "would of course be an almost absurdly ambitious enterprise."[78] Growing digital archives and increasingly sophisticated search engines temper, though they do not wholly eliminate, the ambition of the enterprise; whether that ambition remains "absurd" I leave others to judge.

Even if we accept that the history of various statements that instantiate a particular linguistic form is, by Skinner's lights, "conceptually proper," it is no doubt more susceptible to charges of anachronism than other forms of historical inquiry, if only because it must examine brief passages, often individual sentences, from many different writers spread over centuries or even millennia. Yet this kind of inquiry risks anachronism precisely for the sake of deepening our understanding of anachronism itself. More than five centuries ago, in one of the greatest triumphs of the new humanist philology, Lorenzo Valla deployed the concept of anachronism (though not the word) to demonstrate that the *Donation of Constantine*, a document that supported the pope's claim to temporal, political authority, was a forgery. Examining the titles given to public officials in the document, he wrote, "Why do you want to bring in *satraps*? . . . Who ever heard of satraps being named in the deliberations of the Romans? I cannot recall reading that anyone, either in Rome or even in the provinces of the Romans, was ever named a satrap."[79] Valla's Latinity, his extraordinarily wide and careful reading of classical Latin, was sufficient for him to judge that the word *satrap*, and by extension the document of which it was a part, was the spurious invention of a later age. While I do not suppose that the history of linguistic forms will be used to discredit religious or legal documents anytime soon, it does allow us to extend the kind of judgments made by Valla to a new domain. For example, I have not discovered any instance of *X as if Y* used to produce belief prior to Pascal's *Pensées*. This claim, no less than Valla's, is falsifiable. The results of my repeated searches are, no less than his extensive reading, constitutively incomplete. Philology in all of its forms is, as Erich Auerbach puts it, an "infinite task."[80] One may well discover an earlier use of the Latin *satrapes* or an earlier pragmatic use of *act as if*. But this is only to point out that judgments of anachronism, like all historical judgments, are not logical and necessary but empirical and contingent, dependent on the documents and research tools available to us.

The philological study of anachronism entails a specific awareness of the difference of the linguistic past, but it also serves as a general reminder of the unforeseeable difference of the linguistic future. Some of the trends discussed in this chapter—the increasing prevalence of *act as if* as a means of self-fashioning, the coexistence and mingling of pragmatic and regulative imperatives, the abstraction of the linguistic form from any particular content—seem likely to continue. Yet past usage is not a sure guide to the future. The linguistic form will doubtless shift and change in the hands and on the tongues of unexpected poets, philosophers, preachers, and life counselors; in social and discursive contexts that have not yet come into being; to address cultural and intellectual tensions of which we are not yet cognizant. Like words, linguistic forms change their meaning and use over time; like metaphors, they are waiting to be reconfigured and made new.

# *WWJD?* and the History of *Imitatio Christi*

## Who Would Jesus Bomb?

Over the past twenty years, *WWJD?* and the question it abbreviates, *What would Jesus do?*, have become prominent features of American culture, appearing on book covers, buttons, bracelets, blue jeans, board games, bumper stickers, teddy bears, T-shirts, ties, key chains, coffee mugs, pencils, and even women's underwear. (This last item is truly a complex cultural artifact: is it worn by the devout or the derisive, to deter seducer or seducee, and by aesthetic or ethical deterrence?) In more recent years, the question has given rise to scores of spin-offs, devout and derisive alike. The book *How Would Jesus Vote?* aims to help readers determine whether their "political views really align with the Bible."[1] Those seeking a "Christian nutrition handbook" need look no further than *What Would Jesus Eat?*, which bills itself as a "healthier, Bible-based eating program."[2] (Think water, bread, and *lots* of fish.) The Evangelical Environmental Network, a progressive evangelical group, launched the "What Would Jesus Drive?" ad campaign in 2002; now the question appears on bumpers across the nation.[3]

Parodic spin-offs of *WWJD?* sometimes retain the moral ambitions of the original. Antiwar protesters hold up signs that read "Who Would Jesus Bomb?" Other popular variations, in which *Jesus* is replaced with another name (usually that of a popular athlete), are markedly less rich in satire and ethical intent: few have received genuine moral guidance from asking themselves "What would Johnny Damon do?" or "What would Michael Jordan do?"[4] The question and its derivatives have even edged their way into academia. John D. Caputo, a notable scholar of deconstruction and proponent of theopoetics, published *What Would Jesus Deconstruct?*[5] The 2008 Modern

Language Association convention featured a panel entitled "WWWD? What Would Wharton Do? Edith Wharton and Politics." A diverse array of names of secular as well as sacred exemplars now substitute for *Jesus*: a Google search for the string *"what would * * do"* retrieves instances in which the wildcards are matched by *Buddha, Muhammad, Gandhi, Aristotle, Shakespeare, Nietzsche, Reagan, Bernie Sanders, Trump, Atticus Finch, Jane Austen, Steve Jobs, Rosa Parks,* and many, many others.

For many Christians inside and outside the evangelical community, *WWJD?* has become the ethical question par excellence. Like the Golden Rule, the categorical imperative, the principle of utility, or the veil of ignorance, it serves as a distinctive kind of moral deliberation. We might hypothesize that at present *WWJD?* is a more popular ethical guide than the systems offered by Immanuel Kant, J. S. Mill, and John Rawls, although perhaps not the Golden Rule. And while some Christians turn to the question in times of moral difficulty, others use it to direct every aspect of their daily lives. The question of what Jesus would do is, in one sense, an old one. It is part of the tradition of *imitatio Christi*, in which believers model their actions on the pattern set forth in the life of Jesus as described in the Gospels. But it is also, in another sense, far more recent, a novel form of a practice some two millennia old.

The phrase *What would Jesus do?* has usually been traced back to the late nineteenth century, to a short novel by Charles Sheldon called *In His Steps*.[6] While Sheldon's novel is an influential document, and one that I will discuss at some length, it is only a waypoint in a longer history that runs back at least to late-sixteenth- and early-seventeenth-century England, when preachers and theologians increasingly began to use a new kind of ethical formulation that challenged Christians to do not as Christ *did* but rather as he *would do*. The advent of the conditional in the discourse of *imitatio Christi* is among the most consequential events of the practice's two-thousand-year history, marking a dramatic change in the dynamics of imitation. The cause of this modal shift, I argue, was a deepening sense of the disparity between the modern world and the authoritative past of the Gospels. The conditional (specifically the unreal or counterfactual conditional) entered the discourse of *imitatio Christi* as a means of overcoming this disparity, imaginatively bridging the historical gap between the life of Jesus and the lives of his followers and allowing his example to serve as a guide even in a radically changed world. The effects of this modal shift reach well beyond the religious and ethical spheres into modern philosophy, literature, politics, and popular culture. Especially among North American Protestants, the conditional question (especially the fixed phrase *What would Jesus do?*) has become the dominant form of *imitatio Christi* in modernity. In what follows I attempt to establish the provenance of conditional imitation and then sketch out its history to the present day.

### "Do as I Have Done"

Numerous passages from the New Testament have motivated and guided the imitation of Christ for the nearly two millennia of the practice's history. Some enjoin Christians to "follow" Christ, since "he that taketh not his cross, and followeth after me, is not worthy of me" (Matt. 10:38). Others are written in the language of likeness and exemplarity: "For I have given you an example, that ye should do as I have done to you" (John 13:15). Presenting himself as a model that leads us back to Christ's own, Paul enjoins his readers to "be followers of me, as I am of Christ" (1 Cor. 11:1). As the first epistle of John 2:6 instructs, "He that saith he abideth in him ought himself so to walk, even as he walked." In Romans we are told to "put ye on the Lord Jesus Christ" (13:14) and directed "to be conformed to the image" of the Son (8:29). Charles Sheldon's novel *In His Steps* takes its title from 1 Peter 2:21: "Christ also suffered for us, leaving us an example, that ye should follow his steps." For our present purposes we need only notice one thing about these passages: they all exhort us to imitate what Christ *did do*, not what he *would do*, although the grammatical resources for indicating the conditional were present in the Koine Greek of the New Testament no less than in the English of the King James translation quoted here.

These passages of scripture provide the vocabulary and set the mood, as it were, for over a millennium and a half of writing about *imitatio Christi*. In one sermon Origen addresses his counsel to "you who follow Christ and are His imitator." Cyprian gives a near synopsis of scriptural proof texts when he writes, "He follows Christ who follows His precepts, walks by the path of His teaching, pursues His steps and ways, [and] who imitates that which Christ both taught and did." Ambrose insists that "he who follows Christ should according to his abilities imitate Him, in order to meditate within himself His precepts and examples of divine deeds." Jerome cautions that as adults we cannot copy Christ in every detail: "Since we are men, and cannot imitate the nativity of the Saviour, we at least imitate His way of life."[7] Augustine asserts in *The City of God* that "the highest duty of religion is to imitate him whom you worship."[8] Pierre Abélard claims that God became incarnate "in order to instruct us truly in the doctrine of justice both by preaching and also by the example of His bodily way of life."[9] Thomas Aquinas writes that Christ allowed himself to undergo temptations at the hands of Satan "to give us an example: to teach us, namely, how to overcome the temptations of the devil," although he argues that no less than Christ's entire life as a man on earth should be regarded as a model of Christian behavior.[10]

Every aspect of Christ's humanity was seen as an ideal for imitation. A sermon by Bernard of Clairvaux has Christ, speaking *in propria persona*, say that he went through each stage of human life "in order that My conception may cleanse yours, My life instruct yours, My death destroy yours, My resurrection proceed yours, My ascension prepare for yours."[11] Special note should be given to the fifteenth-century *Imitation of Christ*, widely ascribed to Thomas à Kempis. Although written as a manual for monastics and ascetics, it became one of the most popular devotional works among lay Catholics and Protestants alike. Its opening passage begins with quotation ("Oure lord saiþ, 'he þat folowiþ me goþ not in darkenes'"), moves on to explication ("we are amonysshed to folowe his lyf and his maners"), and then ends with exhortation ("Wherefore lete oure souereyn studia be in þe lif of Ihesu crist").[12] This progression, from indicative to imperative, from exposition to admonition, is repeated throughout the work.

The relative consistency of these utterances, written over a span of nearly sixteen hundred years, accompanied enormous variations in practice. For some, imitating Christ demanded simple charity to one's neighbors; for others, like Margery Kemp, it required traveling to the Holy Land to visit the Stations of the Cross; while for still others, like Saint Francis of Assisi, it involved receiving the stigmata, the bodily marks of Christ's suffering.[13] Nicholas Love's proem to *The Mirror of the Blessed Life of Jesus Christ*, an early-fifteenth-century translation of the pseudo-Bonaventuran *Meditationes vita Christi*, illustrates the adaptive fluidity of medieval accounts of imitation. One of the chief tasks of the proem is to explain why the "meditacions" it precedes are able to narrate "cristes lyfe more pleyne in certeyne partyes þan is expressed in the gospell of þe four euaungelistes." The pseudo-Bonaventuran text adds new details and events to the authoritative accounts of scripture and even includes descriptions of "speches or dedis of god in heuen & angels or oþere gostly substances." Love excuses this "drawynge oute" of the "boke of cristes lyfe" on the grounds that it is "moste spedefull & edifyng to hem þat bene [of] symple vndirstondyng." The stirring of devotion in "symple soules" justifies, for Love, the attempt to "ymagine and þenk diuerse wordes & dedes . . . and oþer" events that are "not writen" in the Gospels. Even as he acknowledges that his book represents "diuerse ymaginacions," Love defends its truthfulness by quoting the Gospel of John's admission that "alle þo þinges that Jesus dide, bene not written in Þe Gospelle" (see John 21:25). In other words, *The Mirror of the Blessed Life of Jesus Christ* imagines a great deal, but what it imagines might nevertheless have been real. For Love, the only limitation on such imagining is that it should not be "aȝeyns þe byleue or gude maneres" of its readers. This principle offers wide interpretive and imaginative latitude. One may imagine deeds and actions not recorded in the Bible when it is appropriate and "edifyng"—useful for moral instruction. And yet even in their reliance on "ymaginacion," the meditations firmly bind themselves to the indicative description of what Christ did do. The conditional question of what Jesus would do in "oþer" circumstances is never raised.[14]

In addition to seeing many medieval imitative practices as idolatrous rituals, the Reformation challenged the larger importance and centrality of *imitatio Christi*. Because Martin Luther held faith rather than works to be the cause of salvation, he promoted Christ's role as "sacrament" above his role as "exemplar." And yet he too enjoins imitation in much the same manner as his predecessors: "In Christ we see the height of patience, gentleness, and love, and an admirable moderation in all things. We ought to put on this adornment of Christ, that is, imitate these virtues of His."[15] Like those who precede him, Luther speaks of *imitatio Christi* as a form of mimetic reproduction, instructing believers to reproduce Christ's example within their own lives.

### "Were He in Our Case and Condition"

Extensive searching suggests that the earliest instance of conditional imitation appeared in 1590, in a sermon on Romans 13:14, "Put yee on the Lord Jesus Christ," by the Anglican preacher Henry "Silver-Tongued" Smith.[16] It is because Christ's "example will teach" the Christian "what hee shall follow, and what he shall flee better then all preceptes in the world," writes Smith, that it is "the best thought in every action for a man to think, what Christ would do." Before speaking, we should ask "whether he would speak so, and consider before we doe whether he would doe so, and doe all by his example."[17] He promises, "If thou resolvest to speak & doe no otherwise then Christ wold speake and doe himselfe, thou shalt bee sure to doe all thinges well, because thou followest a straight patterne."[18] Seventeenth-century English preachers and theologians across sectarian divides increasingly spoke of imitating Christ in this new modality. In 1631 Edward Reynolds, a prominent Presbyterian preacher who would later become bishop of Norwich, enjoins his readers: "What ever action therefore you goe about, doe it by *Rule*, enquire out of the scriptures whether Christ would have done it or no, at least whether he allow it or no."[19] Reynolds expands the imitation of Christ to include not only those actions he in fact performed but also those he enjoined by means of a general rule, or allowed, or would have performed himself. The conditional does not, of course, immediately displace more customary, indicative ways of speaking about imitation; the two often appear together, as complements. The great divine, Jeremy Taylor, writes in his 1656 *Holy Living* that "when you are to do an action, consider how Christ did, or would do, the like, and do you imitate his example, and transcribe his copy."[20] Here the conditional *would do* is introduced only as a qualification, working alongside the past indicative *did* to cover all instances of moral action.

The seventeenth-century preachers and divines who employ the conditional often express concerns about the disparity between Christ's life and their own. In 1649 Taylor concedes that Jesus's life is not able to provide an appropriate model for all his seventeenth-century peers and parishioners. "Some states of life also there are," he writes, "which Jesus never lead [*sic*]." In the lives of his readers, however, "many cases do occurre, which need a president, and the vivacity of an excellent example." Examples are necessary because rules do not make "provision for all contingencies," and they are, in any case, easily perverted by the "subtlity" of men. Taylor counsels those who lead lives that Christ never led, and who confront "cases" and "contingencies" he never encountered, to consider "what he would have done in the like case . . . in such cases we must alwayes judge on the strictest side of piety and charity . . . for so would the righteous and mercifull Jesus have done."[21]

There is much virtue in *would*; it allows even those who lead radically different lives from Christ, and who live in radically different worlds, to look to him as a pattern of moral behavior. In 1672 the preacher Thomas White laid out the logic for considering Christ's example in the conditional, pledging that he "shall endeavour in every action that I do, and word that I speak, to remember if I can, whether there be any parallel instance in the life of Christ, if there be, I shall make that my pattern, and do likewise, but if there be none, that I can think of, then I would do that which in my conscience I think Christ would have done in like case."[22] In White's account, believers should practice indicative imitation, doing as Christ did, when they are able to discern congruity or parallelism between his life and their own, and should practice conditional imitation ("would have done") only when faced with incongruity. The conditional thus functions as a practical response—a linguistic adaptation—to a perceived difference.

Conditional sentences are composed of two parts: a protasis, which states a hypothesis, the *if . . .* ; and an apodosis, which states the consequence, the *then. . . .* The use of the modal auxiliary *would* plus an infinitive main verb in the apodosis implies a counterfactual or unreal protasis, one the speaker regards as false or at least unlikely, even when the protasis remains unexpressed. The question *who would Jesus bomb?* is implicitly accompanied by something like the hypothesis *if Jesus had possessed bombs*, though a range of other acceptable hypotheses could also be supplied: *if Jesus were alive now, if he had been confronted with similar threats, as commander in chief, in our situation,* and so on. The hypothesis controls for the relevant differences between Jesus's world and our own by pointing to a possible world in which the question can be meaningfully asked. This world is constructed either by drawing Christ's world incrementally closer to the speaker's own (*if he had possessed bombs*) or by drawing the speaker's world incrementally closer to Christ's (*if he were alive now*).

While twenty-first-century Christians tend to leave the condition unstated, seventeenth-century writers often state or, in the case of the mystic John Everard, overstate the condition. Follow Christ "as our pattern," Everard exhorts his readers in 1657, "that *in what condition soever we are in,* whatever *in such a condition* Christ himself would do, *were he in our case and condition,* the same do we." Later he directs his readers to do "the same things as our Saviour would do *in thy case, were he upon earth.*" Later still he rolls out the condition no less than three times, recommending "that what ever Christ would do *were he on earth, in my case, in my calling and condition* the same do we."[23] Everard's contemporaries usually express the hypothesis in less emphatic terms. The nonconformist minister Richard Steele instructs his readers to treat others "as you think *David, Paul, or Christ* would do *if they were here.*"[24] The hypothesis sometimes controls for differences less general than case, condition, contingency, time, place, or presence. In a 1653 pamphlet, the pastor John Carter urges Christians to ask, "how would Christ carry himself in my Calling, in my Relation?" Magistrates "going to the Bench" should inquire "how would Christ proceed in executing Judgment *if he were in my room?*," and the "Minister . . . Trades-man . . . Husband-man . . . Servant . . . and Child" should likewise ask the question with a profession-specific hypothesis.[25]

In the indicative modality characteristic of medieval imitation, Christ's example posits a definite set of events, experiences, and actions that should be ritualistically repeated in the life of all believers. As I stressed earlier, this repetition leads to a vast diversity of practices and should not be conceived of as thoughtless or mechanical repetition. Even so, the believer begins with Christ's pattern and then shapes his or her own life accordingly. The conditional reverses this priority. The believer begins with his or her own present situation (what should I do in case $X$? how ought I to chose between $Y$ and $Z$?) and then turns to Christ's life as a way of imagining the right answer. No longer are actions obligatory merely because Jesus performed them. The conditional allows Christians to perform Christlike actions that Christ himself never performed even as it frees them from the obligation to perform all or even any of Christ's actions in order to be Christlike. What Taylor called the great exemplar ceases to be an obligatory pattern. Indicative *imitatio Christi* had involved a range of outward, ritualized actions and visible, bodily marks as well as affective identification with Christ's suffering. Conditional imitation, by contrast, retreats from public view, to serve as a procedure of inward deliberation. Asking what Jesus would do prompts the believer to imagine Christ's response to his or her own ethical situation. Joseph Hall, bishop of Norwich, offered his readers this meditation in 1652: "What ever I am about to do, or speak, or affect; let me think: If my Saviour were now upon earth, would he do this that I am now putting my hand unto? would he speak these words that I am now uttering? would he be thus disposed as I now feel my self? Let me not yeeld my self to any thought, word or action which my Saviour would be ashamed to own."[26] These questions are not concerned with direct mimesis; there are no definite actions enjoined or prohibited. Instead they are concerned with the process of deliberation itself, filtered through the imagined perspective of Christ. From this per-spective the deliberator considers what Christ would do and also what he would feel, his affective disposition, and whether he would be ashamed in a similar situation.[27] This meditation, which creates a sense of intimate contact across vast differences of history and culture, is licensed by the counterfactual hypothesis "If my Saviour were now upon earth."

### "A Different Age"

Although the conditional continues to appear throughout the eigh-teenth century, only about the middle of the nineteenth does it become a pervasive way of talking about *imitatio Christi*.[28] Naturally, discussions of Christ's example occur most frequently in the works of preachers and reli-gious writers, in collected sermons, periodicals, and the rapidly expanding varieties of popular devotional materials that followed upon the reawaken-ing religious sensibilities of the period. In a fragment from his collected works, published in 1836, the Reverend Richard Cecil cautions that hetero-geneity and difference must be attended to even when employing the con-ditional: "We must take care when we draw parallel cases, not to take such as are not or cannot be made parallel. For instance—we may ask, before we act, 'What would Jesus Christ do in this case? or what would St. Paul?' but we cannot be guided by this rule in every thing, because Christ's mission was peculiar: it was an unparalleled event." Cecil is not simply insisting on the inimitability of Christ's divine or supernatural role; he warns that "in the conduct peculiar to our station, our application of these examples must be governed by circumstances."[29]

By the late nineteenth century conditional imitation had become espe-cially prevalent among American evangelicals; the prominent evangelist D. L. Moody instructs his audience, "Whenever we are tempted, if we would just ask the question, 'I wonder if Jesus would do it if He were here?' and be willing to take Him as our guide, what a help it would be!"[30] But such ques-tions were not asked only by evangelicals; an article in an 1848 issue of the *Church of England Magazine*, a periodical produced by the Clergymen of the United Church of England and Ireland, advises, "Often put yourself in these inquiries: what am I doing? Where am I? What would Jesus Christ have been doing in my circumstances?"[31] It was in the second half of the nineteenth century that the question *What would Jesus do?* became a con-ventionalized fixed phrase that speakers learned, remembered, and used as a prefabricated unit rather than generated anew each time, and it was this phrase, not simply the conditional as such, that spread from sermons and tracts into popular religious poems, hymns, short stories, and novels. *Friendly Words for Our Girls*, published in 1875 for the Members of the Girl's Friendly Society, an organization founded by the Church of England to help urban women working in textile mills, includes a hymn that opens with these lines:

> If to sinful deeds and actions
> Men are tempting you,
> Stop and ask yourself the question, "What would Jesus do?"[32]

In an 1880 digest, a vicar from Hampstead reported having seen the "words 'What Would Jesus Do?' hanging as an illuminated motto on the wall of an orphanage."[33] And an 1889 issue of the *Home Missionary*, the periodical of an interdenominational organization that aimed to assist in the development of Christian congregations, included a poem entitled "What Would Jesus Do?" The closing lines begin by echoing 1 Peter 2:21:

> Now if it be our purpose
> To walk where Christ has led,
> To follow in his footsteps
> With ever careful tread;
> O let this be our watchword,
> Twill help both me and you,
> To ask in each temptation,
> "What would Jesus Do?"

The poem is followed by this entreaty: "Dear Young Friends—Will you take this as your watchword for 1889—'WHAT WOULD JESUS DO?'"[34]

While these instances placed special emphasis on established Christian virtues like temperance and chastity, conditional imitation also cleared space for disruptive questioning. Exemplary in this regard was *The True History of Joshua Davidson*, an 1872 novel by Elizabeth Linton, an agnostic, a fierce critic of the Church of England, and the first woman in England to draw a salary as a journalist.[35] Linton's tale of "practical Christianity" narrates the life of Joshua, a nineteenth-century carpenter who decides to live according to the example of Christ. But he soon comes to find that example limited by the historical conditions in which Christ lived. Jesus was "the product of His time," Joshua argues, and while he "did His best to remedy" suffering and injustice "by proclaiming the spiritual equality of all men," he nevertheless "left the social question where He found it." Christ's failure to advocate "radical revolution" leads Joshua to a shocking assertion: "The modern Christ would be a politician." Instead of "mak[ing] the poor contented" with their miserable conditions, the modern Christ "would raise the whole platform of society" and "would work at the destruction of caste, which is the vice at the root of all our creeds and institutions."[36] He would, in short, be a communist. Like many present-day spin-off questions, these assertions display a spirit of overt opposition. Joshua uses the conditional to expose the historical limits of Christ's example and, more pointedly, the failure of the church in Linton's day to go beyond those limits. What Jesus would do functions not merely as a complement to but as a criticism of indicative imitation of his life. (Linton's novel ends, it is worth noting, with the leaders of the Church of England kicking Joshua to death.)

In the later years of the century the example of Christ was more commonly employed to advocate Christian reform than it was to promote communist revolution. Gregory S. Jackson observes that "homiletic novels," which "aimed to facilitate private devotion, strengthen moral autonomy, and foster social engagement," were "largely discussed in the subjunctive mood."[37] The homiletic novel of greatest historical significance is Sheldon's *In His Steps*, the subtitle and slogan of which is *What Would Jesus Do?* As we noted, this question has a long history and was already current in the culture when Sheldon, a preacher from Topeka, Kansas, and an adherent of the Social Gospel movement, began in 1891 to write the narrative sermons that eventually constituted his most popular novel. But there is little doubt that *In His Steps* is responsible for establishing the conditional question's immense popularity even up to the present day. First published serially in 1896 and then as a novel in 1897, it is by many estimates the best-selling novel of the nineteenth century.[38]

Sheldon tells the story of a small-town congregation that pledges "for an entire year, not to do anything without first asking the question, 'What would Jesus do?' "[39] Those who take the pledge dramatically upend their lives in order to help the poor, strengthen the faith, and fight the evils of liquor (Sheldon was an ardent prohibitionist). The novel is a testament to how dominant conditional imitation had become by the end of the nineteenth century. To the novel's characters, the passages of scripture that enjoin the imitation of Christ's life seem unfamiliar and lifeless, like relics from a distant past in need of decoding and explanation. After listening to a competent but uninspired sermon on 1 Peter 2.21—"Christ also suffered for you, leaving you an example, that ye should follow his steps" (1)—one character asks, "What would Jesus do? Is that what you mean by following His steps?"[40] Only when accompanied by or translated into the conditional do scriptural instructions begin to have transformative power, providing characters with an intuitive way of conquering their selfish instincts for the sake of true Christian morality.

Sheldon's characters are explicitly and acutely aware of the disparity between Christ's world and their own. They acknowledge that they can only ever imitate "Jesus' probable action" and must therefore rely on their own uncertain judgments.[41] When first taking the pledge to follow Christ, one young woman asks, "Who is to decide for me just what He would do in my case? It is a different age. There are many perplexing questions in our civilization that are not mentioned in the teachings of Jesus. How am I going to tell what He would do?"[42] Sheldon himself develops the problem of historical difference in the preface to *Jesus Is Here!*, the sequel to *In His Steps*, writing that "the world to-day is far different from the world into which the historical Jesus was born. It is so different, that entirely new problems relating to human conduct face the modern Christian." Despite these differences, he argues, we must "ask what would be the attitude of Jesus as he faced the complex conditions of modern society."[43] For Sheldon and his characters, *What would Jesus do?* is a practical way to connect "the world to-day" ever more closely to the "different age" of the Gospels.

Throughout *In His Steps*, characters ask themselves variations on the novel's titular question, such as "What would Jesus do as Edward Norman, editor of a daily newspaper in Raymond?,"[44] that cannot be meaningfully asked in the indicative. Jesus Christ did not *do* anything as Edward Norman, editor of the daily newspaper in Raymond. By the same token, we can ask, *What would Jesus drive?*, but Jesus did not, of course, *drive* anything (apart, that is, from a donkey and, if we trust Milton, a flying chariot). The conditional opens up the imitation of Christ to the potentially infinite set of moral issues that confront us now, in our own world, and in worlds more different still. In the writings of Sheldon and his successors, these possibilities are reflected in the proliferation of questions based upon the conditional. Published twenty-five years after the original novel, Sheldon's

*In His Steps Today* addressed the pressing issues of the early twentieth century through a series of ten chapters titled with questions. Each question begins, "What Would Jesus Do" and then continues, "In the Coal Fields," "In Politics," "With the Press," "In the Railroad World," "With International Affairs," and so on.[45] This proliferation of questions has, as we began this essay by observing, continued on a still larger scale in our own day.

Sheldon's novel and its central moral question attracted serious criticism even as they gained widespread popularity. In a sermon published three years after the debut of *In His Steps*, the Unitarian preacher John White Chadwick argued that the question *What would Jesus do?* is an unsatisfactory and potentially misleading guide to ethical deliberation. In his reading, the "question really asked" in Sheldon's book "is not 'What steps did Jesus take?' or 'What would Jesus do?' but 'What ought we to do in this last decade of the nineteenth century, conditioned and environed as we are?'" since there are abundant "situations in our modern life which could not possibly exist in the old time Galilee or Judea." The problem with asking such questions is that they merely provoke "a vicious circle" in which Christians, "to find out what they should do, ask what Jesus would do; and, to find out what Jesus would do, they ask what they should do." The viciousness of the circle is why Sheldon, instead of conforming his life to the life of Jesus, "makes Jesus a mouthpiece of his personal conviction," finding justification for his own teetotalism even in the story of someone who turned water into wine at the wedding of Cana.[46] Rather than a bridge that allows for moral instruction to traverse the gulf of radical cultural difference, Chadwick argues, the conditional question is a dark mirror in which Christians misrecognize their own alienated beliefs and prejudices as the exemplarity of Christ.

### Historical Solitude

It is in Sheldon's acknowledgment that "the world to-day is far different from the world into which the historical Jesus was born," no less than in Chadwick's acknowledgment that "our modern life . . . could not possibly exist in the old time Galilee or Judea," that we find the most plausible explanation for the modal shift that had taken place in the discourse of *imitatio Christi* more than three centuries earlier. Such acknowledgments exhibit what Thomas Greene has notably described as "historical solitude." According to Greene's thesis, no one before Dante was "fully sensitive to the fact of radical cultural change." Only in the Renaissance did writers and thinkers develop a sense of "estrangement," "remoteness," and "cultural distance" from a past that was, they realized, "never fully recoverable." And yet early moderns saw cultural discontinuity not simply as a fact to be accepted but rather as a predicament to be dealt with, struggled against. It is because of this struggle that Renaissance art and thought display what Greene calls "the rage for contact with the past."[47]

The modal shift that began to spread in the late sixteenth and early seventeenth centuries is one relatively quiet indicator of this rage, a linguistic means of making contact with an increasingly remote past. But a weak version of historical solitude, one less monumental and more flexible than Greene supposed, provides a better explanation for this shift. We need not contend that the awareness of radical cultural change arose like a tropical dawn in the minds of Dante and Petrarch. A weak version of the thesis would allow for an awareness that deepened and spread over time, sometimes gradually, sometimes in fits and starts. Greene associates historical solitude with the study of classical texts by fourteenth- and fifteenth-century humanists, but a weak version must allow for asynchronous development across discourses if it is to explain why an awareness of rupture only begins to appear in discussions of *imitatio Christi* nearly two centuries later. The larger implication of this asynchronous development is that historical solitude occurs in particular discourses rather than in the minds of individuals. An early-sixteenth-century humanist may be fully conscious of the remoteness of ancient Greece or Rome, for example, and yet still maintain an intuitive sense of closeness and contemporaneity with first-century Christians. We will later see that Erasmus exhibits precisely this disjunction.

The circumstances, contingencies, conditions, and cases mentioned by early modern preachers enjoining the imitation of Christ suggest a relatively diffuse sense of cultural change, while in other imitative discourses, regarding other exemplars, the change is quite concrete and well defined. Galileo's *Dialogue Concerning the Two Chief World Systems*, published in Florence in 1632, stages a debate on the role of Aristotle in our knowledge of the cosmos. Although Salviati, Galileo's empirically minded and mathematically skilled champion of the Copernican world system, supposes that belief is warranted by evidence and argument rather than by the *ipse dixit* of any ancient *autorità*, he does not seek simply to discredit or dismiss Aristotle but to recuperate his authority for his own position. Of his Peripatetic opponent, Simplicio, he asks:

> Are you so credulous as not to understand that if Aristotle had been present [*quando Aristotile fusse stato presente*] and heard this doctor who wanted to make him inventor of the telescope [*autor del telescopio*], he would have been [*si sarebbe*] much angrier with him than with those who laughed at this doctor and his interpretations? Is it possible for you to doubt that if Aristotle should see the new discoveries in the sky [*quando Aristotile vedesse le novità scoperte in cielo*] he would change his opinions and correct his books and embrace the most sensible doctrines [*e' non fusse per mutar opinione e per emendar i suoi libri e per accostarsi alle più sensate dottrine*], casting away from himself those people so weak-minded as to be induced to go on abjectly maintaining everything he had ever said?[48]

This passage imagines a technologically up-to-date Aristotle who stands in opposition to dogmatic Aristotelianism. Aristotle's (counterfactual) embrace of Copernicanism follows explicitly from his (counterfactual) witnessing of the new discoveries made possible by his (counterfactual) invention of the telescope. A difference in instrumentation precipitates a difference in doctrine, but in all other respects the world is left unchanged.[49] Historical solitude is in this case specified as technological progress.

In addition to locating historical solitude in asynchronous discourses rather than individual minds, a weak version of Greene's thesis must also account for the fact that changes in usage bear a complex causal relation to awareness. The conditional may precede or follow, as either a leading or lagging indicator, a conscious or express sense of remoteness. It may function as an adaptive response to a burgeoning awareness of cultural distance that is not fully manifest and, conversely, precipitate further such awareness. While the seventeenth-century writers quoted above employ the conditional primarily to control for differences in what Jeremy Taylor calls "cases" and "contingencies," they do not, as Linton, Sheldon, or Chadwick do more than two hundred and fifty years later, explicitly identify or thematize it as the result of historical or cultural change, the disparities between "modern life" and "the old time Galilee or Judea."

In a strong version of historical solitude, conditional *imitatio Christi* might be taken as the smoke rising from a newly kindled consciousness of radical cultural change. It is more likely that this shift in modality displaced or compensated for earlier strategies of bridging historical difference that had grown less viable or effective.[50] In the Roman Catholic reading practices that Thomas Aquinas codified in the four senses of scripture, the literal or historical meaning of the text was accompanied by three spiritual meanings,[51] of which the tropological or moral sense allowed Catholic readers to discern, in the historical events recounted in the Old and New Testaments, lessons (or, in the case of the *vita Christi*, patterns) for how to live in the present. Dante gives the example of the exodus of the Israelites from Egypt, which in its tropological sense is the story of "the conversion of the soul from the sorrow and misery of sin to a state of grace."[52] Scholars have recognized that in spite of the Reformation insistence on the one, true, literal sense of scripture, early modern Protestants did not cease reading scripture figuratively.[53] Yet by using the conditional as a means of spanning the gap between Christ's life and their own, they could avoid relying on reading practices they associated with a discredited Catholic hermeneutics.[54] Rather than creating the space into which it emerged, conditional imitation stepped into a functional role at least partially vacated by tropological reading.

Finally, a weak account of historical solitude cautions us against seeing the growth of historical consciousness as an unequivocal story of epistemological progress. While the shift to conditional imitation signals a deepening sense of difference, it does not therefore represent an unqualified advance from historical blindness to historical insight. Rather, asking what Jesus would do introduces its own kind of blindness. In seeking to join together the immediate ethical demands of the present and the example of the distant past, the condition ("If my Saviour were now upon earth") effectively elides everything that stands between. Early modern Protestants often spoke of the period that stood between them and Christ as a dark age or era of pathless error and corruption.[55] In the present day what stands between believers and the historical life of Christ lacks a name, but conditional imitation elides it nonetheless. Though asking what Jesus would do is a response to the discontinuity of past and present, the question is unable to take account of history as the process of continuity, incremental change, accretion, and tradition that provides the only connection between past and present. When present-day Christians ask themselves what Jesus would eat, for example, they consider both Christ's diet and their own, but they invariably (and quite practically) ignore the vast and complex history of dietary practices that link the two together. Blindness to historical process is the price the modern *imitatio Christi* pays for its ability to overcome historical difference.

### Search and the Conditional

I have attempted thus far to narrate the history of the counterfactual conditional in the discourse of *imitatio Christi*, arguing that the shift to imitating what Jesus would do rather than what he did do was a response to changes in historical understanding. As with earlier chapters, my ability to tell this story has depended on a number of digital archives: primarily Early English Books Online, Google Book Search, Eighteenth-Century Collections Online, and the Patrologia Latina Database.[56] Even tentative answers to the questions I have asked would not have been forthcoming in the absence of these digital resources, many of which are still growing. Consider the empirical claim I made earlier, that the conditional appears in the tradition of *imitatio Christi* for the first time in 1590. This claim is subject to falsification and requires some qualification. Because of the kinds of documents that have been digitized as full text, I can make the claim with greater confidence for texts in English and Latin than for texts in other modern languages. An earlier instance is always possible, of course, since the absence of conditional imitation even in an archive of texts larger than anyone could read in a lifetime does not entail its absence in all. Conversely, my claim is buttressed by the absence of the conditional in earlier canonical writings on *imitatio Christi* by Augustine, à Kempis, Luther, and Calvin, as well as in the texts of the Corpus of Middle English Prose and Verse.[57] Even after the first attestation of conditional *imitatio Christi* in 1590, its spread is slow and halting. A second attestation appears more than forty years later, in 1631. In 1602 the Anglican clergyman Christopher Sutton could still publish a devotional manual that manages to show, in more than six hundred pages, "that the life of Christ is the most perfect patterne of direction to the life of a Christian," without asking, at any point, what Christ would do.[58] Though an earlier attestation of conditional *imitatio* might modify the timeline, it would not necessarily overturn the larger narrative I offer here. I rehearse these qualifications, however, to suggest that they will become, if never entirely superfluous, then at least less necessary. In growing digital archives, a well-wrought search string will constitute increasingly compelling evidence for a claim of the kind I make above.[59] Scholars who wish to refute such claims will proceed by formulating a better search string (one with higher recall), trawling more capacious archives, or both.

My ability to trace modal shifts in *imitatio Christi* depends on the capabilities of current search tools and their suitability to the particular ways that modality is indicated in different languages. There is no direct means of searching for the conditional, no box you can check that will retrieve all and only the apodoses of conditional sentences in an archive of digital texts. But it is possible to search for the ways different languages signify conditional modality. Because inflected languages like Latin and Greek indicate the conditional with a variety of morphological markers, locating conditional *imitatio Christi* in an archive such as the Patrologia Latina Online involves searching for conjugations of verbs in the third-person present (*\*et, \*eat, \*at, \*iat*) and the pluperfect subjunctive (*\*isset*) in proximity to *Iesus, Christus, filius, salvator, dominus,* and so on. English, as we have noted, indicates the conditional with the modal auxiliary *would* plus an infinitive main verb (*do* or *say*, but not *did* or *says*; or, for the past tense, *have* plus a past participle like *did* or *said*). In questions this order is inverted, with the auxiliary placed before the subject, as in *Would Jesus have done this?* Finding instances of conditional imitation in English is thus a matter of locating utterances in which *would* (in its various spellings) appears either before or after *Jesus, Christ, Lord, Savior,* and so on.[60] Searches in a POS-tagged corpus can be further constrained to utterances in which *would* is accompanied, before or after the subject, by a finite verb.

While instances of conditional imitation are reliably indicated by the presence of *would*, not all appearances of *would* denote the conditional, since the word serves multiple lexical and grammatical functions. The past tense of *will*, *would* also indicates future actions from a past perspective ("I . . . told my bretheren . . . afore hand what wold falle in the ende"),[61] habitual or repeated actions (*He would pray every morning*), and volition or desire ("that peace, whyche Christe wold haue betwene god and man"),[62] among other senses. These senses are not fully distinct: anterior future and conditional uses of *would*, for instance, are often shaded with volition or desire.[63] Rather than being a fully automated process, locating instances of conditional *imitatio Christi* in an archive requires the researcher to perform considerable interpretive work, which means that others might interpret the same search results quite differently.

### Rarity, Conventionalization, Productivity

The kind of history made possible by these search methods aims to deepen our understanding of both the linguistic resources available to writers in different periods and the particular use to which they put those resources. In other domains such understanding is relatively well established. We know that Milton could not have written a haiku. This judgment is not concerned with the empty issue of logical possibility. Milton was unable to write a haiku because that verse form was not available at the time he wrote. (I leave aside the vexed question of what it would have meant for Milton to have *invented* the haiku.) With regard to generic forms, such judgments are relatively clear, well developed, and testable against the history of literature as we presently have it. Our knowledge of the lexicon is similarly well developed. Philologists have long produced accounts of coinages, first attestations, and changes in definition and usage. We know that Milton could not have described *Paradise Lost* as a theodicy, even though we now recognize it as one, because Leibniz invented the word *theodicy* some thirty-five years after Milton's death. Finally, historical linguists have for more than five decades produced detailed knowledge of changes in the grammar of English and other languages. We know that multiple negation (as in Chaucer's translation of Boethius: "it **ne** mai **not** well in **no** manere be desired **ne** requerid") had fallen out of use, especially in formal registers, by the time Milton wrote *Paradise Lost*.[64]

Compared with the history of genres, words, and grammars, the history of conditional *imitatio Christi* is of an unfamiliar and undeveloped kind. This history falls into three phases, though marking precise boundaries between phases is difficult even with the extensive evidence provided by digital archives. The first phase involved a change not in linguistic competence but in the kind of discursive regularity that Foucault calls "rarity": of all the utterances it is possible to say with the given combinatory resources of a language, only the smallest sliver are ever said.[65] Like writers in other modern and ancient European languages, English writers before 1590 possessed the lexicogrammatical knowledge—all the words and linguistic forms—they needed to formulate counterfactual conditional sentences regarding the imitation of Christ: "Yf hyt were dylygently laburyd," wrote Thomas Lupset in 1538, "hyt wold bryng forth frute."[66] The change that takes place in the late sixteenth and early seventeenth centuries is thus not a change in writers' linguistic knowledge but in how they employed that knowledge across discourses, with regard to different topics; more specifically, it was a change in how they filled abstract forms with particular lexical constituents. There is, moreover, nothing to suggest that conditional *imitatio Christi* was traditional, something that one writer or speaker learned from another (though this possibility cannot be ruled out). I have found no evidence, for example, that Edward Reynolds learned to write about imitating what Jesus *would do* from Henry Smith, or that Jeremy Taylor learned to do so from Edward Reynolds or anyone else. Absent such evidence, we should not suppose that in this first phase conditional *imitatio Christi* spread through a network of diffusion of the kind described in chapter 3. Rather, following 1590 a range of English Protestants were increasingly motivated by historical solitude to use their existing linguistic resources to enjoin the imitation of what Christ would do rather than what he did do.[67]

No figure better exemplifies the complexities of discursive rarity than the humanist and theologian Erasmus of Rotterdam. Because of his engagement with both classical and Christian cultures, Erasmus wrote extensively about imitating two different models: Christ and Cicero. In his *Enchiridion Militis Christiani* (Handbook for the Christian soldier), first translated into English in 1534, Erasmus promotes Christ as the only perfect model for imitation. He writes that Christians must "neuer swarue nor go from the trewe patron [pattern] and example of Christe." Whoever "wryeth one ynche or nayle brede" from this example "gothe besydes the ryght pathe and ronneth out of ye way." Displaying far more rigidity than Nicholas Love, he insists that we must "counterfayte" the life of Christ "without excepcion."[68] Like his predecessors, and like other writers until the late sixteenth century, Erasmus enjoins the imitation of Christ solely in the indicative.

In part because he held Christ to be the only model worth following, Erasmus was skeptical of those who sought out other models. Many humanists saw Cicero as the ideal orator and therefore aimed to copy his style as closely as possible in their own writing. Erasmus regarded such dogged imitation as unnecessary and ridiculous but also as a kind of idolatry. His *Ciceronianus*, a dialogue between Nosoponus (a caricature of Ciceronianism) and Bulephorus (Erasmus's avatar), lampoons those who believe they can obtain eloquence by slavishly copying a single past model. Nosoponus at one point outrageously admits that he would rather be accounted a true imitator of Cicero than a faithful Christian. Bulephorus counters that rather than simply imitating his writings, we should consider what Cicero would say were he alive in changed (i.e., Christian) circumstances. He concludes that "if Cicero were alive now [*si viveret*] . . . he would speak today as a Christian among Christians [*dicturus esset hodie Christianus apud Christianos*]."[69]

It is striking that Erasmus wrote of what Cicero would do (using the Latin subjunctive to indicate the conditional) even though he did not write in this way about Christ. Conditional imitation does appear, albeit infrequently, at other points in the classical tradition, with regard to other exemplars. In his own *Enchiridion*, for example, Epictetus advises that when meeting famous people we should ask ourselves, "What would Socrates or Zeno have done [*epoiēsen*] under these circumstances [*en toutōi*]?"[70] Yet Erasmus uses the conditional for the opposite end to which it would eventually be widely used in the *imitatio Christi* tradition. By noting that Cicero would behave very differently in the present, he accentuates the disparity between pagan and Christian ages and shows the absurdity that results from transferring a fixed model from one to another. "Thus it can happen," he writes, calling attention to this absurdity with a paradox, "that he is most a Ciceronian who is most unlike Cicero [*Ciceronianus sit maxime, qui Ciceroni sit dissimillimus*]."[71]

In a second phase, *What would Jesus do?* became a conventionalized fixed phrase of the sort that by the second half of the nineteenth century could be hung on an orphanage wall or serve as a watchword, a ballad refrain, a book subtitle, or the central heuristic in a method of ethical deliberation. Though nineteenth-century English speakers, like their seventeenth-century predecessors, were of course capable both of formulating this question anew and of figuring out its meaning on the basis of more general linguistic knowledge, the evidence of the archive suggests that they also read or heard, learned, remembered, recognized and repeated it as an idiomatic unit, passing it down from one person and text to the next.[72]

In a third phase, the fixed phrase *What would Jesus do?* served as the prototype of a productive linguistic form, a phrasal template, or *snowclone*, with open blanks that speakers and writers could fill in various ways: *[Wh-Word] would X Y?*[73] The X and Y blanks became open or variable at different times: writers like Charles Sheldon had already begun to fill the Y blank with verbs such as *say* and *think* by the end of the nineteenth century, but only in the final decade of the twentieth century did writers regularly begin filling the X blank with the names of different exemplars.

The *Y* blank is a classical category, defined by a set of shared properties: all its members will be infinitive verbs. The most frequent filler of the *Y* category, *do*, is also the most generic or abstract; other fillers—*say, eat, think, drive, deconstruct, bomb*—are specifications of *do*.[74] By contrast, the *X* blank is structured as what George Lakoff calls a "radial category," with *Jesus* as the prototype or "best example" on which others members are analogically based.[75] When someone asks, "What would Michael Jordan do?," the implication (whatever the relation between tongue and cheek) is that Michael Jordan is the Jesus of basketball. Some members of the *X* category are evidently closer or more similar to Jesus than others. In the book title *What Would Google Do?* we are to understand *Google* as the corporate equivalent of the "great exemplar" and therefore as worthy of imitation by other corporations. Likewise, a T-shirt printed with the question "What Would Cthulhu do?" asks observers with the requisite knowledge to take measure of the analogical distance separating H. P. Lovecraft's Elder God from Christ.[76] Where Jesus saves, Cthulhu horrifies and devours. This and other *clone* questions, like the initialisms (WWMJD? WWCD?) that sometimes accompany or displace them, are parasitic: their meaning depends on the meaning of a prototypical sign that is unexpressed, absent but nevertheless implied by the linguistic form. Someone who does not know the conventional expression *What would Jesus do?* or who fails to grasp the analogical relation of other instantiations to it will fail to understand their full meaning.[77] Because the radial structure of the *X* blank (though not the classical structure of the *Y* blank) is specific to the form *[Wh-Word] would X Y?*, this radial structure vanishes with the form. If I ask, *would you take the job?*, the meaning of *you* is in no way based on a relation to *Jesus*, though *take the job* still participates in the verb-phrase category of which *do* is the most generic member. In sum, *What would Jesus do?* began as the product of more general linguistic knowledge, but through a process of conventionalization and abstraction it became a productive signifying unit—a bit of linguistic knowledge—learned in its own right: productive because it generates a range of distinct utterances; signifying because it contributes to those utterances a meaning that cannot be fully predicted from the other signs that compose them.

Whither *WWJD?* Speculating on future or ongoing linguistic developments is risky, but it appears that the form *[Wh-Word] would X Y?* is now in the midst of a further change. Those learning the language now will likely encounter *What would Jesus do?* as one instantiation of the form alongside many others, including *What would Muhammed do?* and *What would Buddha do?*[78] For these speakers, the form is increasingly an independent sign unit, no longer parasitic on the fixed phrase *What would Jesus do?* The radial structure of the *X* category is flattening out, deradializing, to become a classical category with membership defined by shared characteristics. Unless new speakers continue to infer prototypicality through frequency or other cues, *Jesus* will become one constituent among many; conversely, *Muhammed*, *Buddha*, and others will appear not as secondary or derivative, motivated by analogy to *Jesus*, but as equal constituents, fillers of the *X* blank, in their own right.[79] Though *[Wh-Word] would X Y?* arose in the discourse of *imitatio Christi*, the form is becoming equally available for use in any and every imitative discourse.

The history recounted here and projected (however tentatively) into the future raises an array of empirical, interpretive, and explanatory questions. Why did one seventeenth-century divine, Jeremy Taylor, adopt the conditional, while another, Richard Baxter, did not? Why did conditional *imitatio Christi* become prominent in one cultus or denomination but not others? (I have not, for example, found instances in pre-nineteenth-century Catholic writings.) The historical and cultural significance (as distinct from the semantics) of conditional *imitatio Christ* cannot be grasped by meditating on an isolated WWJD? key chain or teddy bear or even the central slogan of Charles Sheldon's influential novels; rather, it becomes visible only through "the systematic study of how forms vary in space and time" that Franco Moretti, borrowing a term from biology, calls *comparative morphology*.[80] Though my current argument has focused on the Western, Christian discourse of *imitatio Christi*, with sidelong glances at the imitation of Aristotle and Cicero, the frame of morphological comparison can in principle be extended beyond all national and linguistic borders. Every culture has its exemplars. Every culture—the weakest of universals—looks to the past for models of how to live. Did other imitative discourses, in other cultures, with different exemplars, undergo conditionalization in response to radical cultural change? Have other discourses undergone similarly unnoticed tectonic shifts without the least alteration to their vocabulary?

That it is now possible to ask such questions (and in some case propose answers) in the indicative rather than conditional mood suggests the extent to which, in an era of digital archives and advanced search tools, the philological enterprise must take measure of its separation from its own past exemplars—a task for which it is uniquely prepared by its very character as a discipline. Though this separation from the past is hardly "radical," in Greene's sense, since it has not by any means become illegitimate to follow in the steps of, say, a Valla or Vico, a Bopp or Benveniste—to study what they studied, with a similar scope and scale, using the tools they used— philology will be better served by imitating what these exemplars would do in changed and still changing circumstances, whether to preserve a connection with the past or, as in Erasmus, Galileo, and Linton, to heighten and make visible our growing estrangement, making it stranger still.

# Milton's Depictives and the History of Style

## Depictive Secondary Predicates

When English speakers say *She drove **drunk*** or *He cooked **naked*** or *I walked home **alone***, they use the adjectives that linguists call *subject-oriented depictive secondary predicates*, or *depictives* for short.[1] Though these adjectives modify the subject of the sentence, they are part of the predicate and syntactically dependent on the verb. Because they describe the state of the subject during the event expressed by the verb, the sentences above can generally be paraphrased as *When she drove, she was drunk*; *When he cooked, he was naked*; and so on. Depictives are more abstract than the linguistic forms studied in the previous chapters; unlike *Was it for this?* or *X as if Y* or *What would X Y?*, they have no fixed lexical content and no specified word order whatsoever. Though depictives are an unexceptional part of English, as they are of many other languages, I hope to show that John Milton puts them to special use in his epic poem *Paradise Lost*. When the demons in hell raise themselves up off a lake of fire in response to Satan's call, we read that "to their general's voice they soon obeyed / **Innumerable**" (1.337–38).[2] When the Son of God reenters heaven following the six days of creation, the angels sing that "the great Creator from his work returned / **Magnificent**" (7.567–68). Depictives like these, about which this chapter has much to say, are telltale markers of Milton's epic style; they generate some of the most distinctive aesthetic and semantic effects of *Paradise Lost*. They are an essential part of how Milton made the poem, how the poem means, and how it guides the responses of readers. Nevertheless, this chapter is not primarily concerned to offer a reading of Milton's epic. Instead it attends to the poem's depictives in order to challenge the kinds of stories that scholars have told about the history of style and to propose in their place the rudiments of a different kind of story.

Twentieth-century histories of style largely followed the work of Erich Auerbach in telling stories about the succession and development of Ciceronian *genera dicendi*, the doctrinal types, levels, kinds, or registers of style.[3] In these histories, types play the role of protagonists: Attic and Asiatic, high and low, painted and plain, grand and humble styles do battle in the literary field, develop through conflict, ally with ascendant cultural forces, achieve their apotheosis in the works of exemplary authors, and fall into subsequent desuetude. Breaking with the ostensible impressionism and imprecision of Ciceronian types, quantitative stylistics began to accumulate epistemological prestige and forensic success as early as 1964, when Frederick Mosteller and David Wallace hand-counted function words to determine which of the disputed *Federalist Papers* had been written by Hamilton, Madison, or Jay.[4] The growth of computing power has since made style an increasingly tractable object of quantitative study, with authorship attribution providing the most prominent success stories. Instead of dusting kits and glass slides, digital Pudd'nhead Wilsons now use off-the-shelf plagiarism software and statistical suites like R to discover the fingerprints of an author's style. By counting and computing the frequency and distribution of individual words, clusters of words (collocations), n-grams (phrases of word length n), or, more recently, skip-grams (sequences of nonadjacent words), they have reshaped the *oeuvres* of writers like Samuel Taylor Coleridge, Thomas Kyd, and William Shakespeare.[5] Computational approaches to style have not limited themselves to answering forensic questions. In seeking to uncover trends that contribute to meaning and reception, they have occupied territory that has, with a few exceptions (like the recent interest in "late style"), largely been ceded by qualitative literary inquiry.[6] When the relative frequencies of quantitative stylistics are plotted across time, the history of style appears as the rise and fall of trend lines.[7]

This chapter argues that the history of style is the history of the reproduction of stylistic markers, which neither the stylistician's trend lines nor Cicero's *genera dicendi* can adequately account for. It looks instead to Seneca's parable of the bees for an early treatment of the mechanisms of gathering, extraction, and imitation by which markers are reproduced. Markers accumulate significance as they pass through successive texts, come into conjunction with and travel in the company of other markers, become objects of experience and interpretation for successive readers, and are used (or avoided) by different writers for different ends. They carry the sedimented memory of their past use with them as the potential for further invention. By helping us to unearth the diverse careers of markers, digital search tools allow us to understand a style neither as the expression of a personality or period, nor as a set of quantitative measures, nor as an instantiation of one *genus* or another, but as a composite of markers, each with a past of its own, and thus as a repository and workshop of cultural memory.

The chapter opens with a theoretical consideration of style, especially of what it means to speak of style as having a history; then it rolls out, under the sponsorship of Seneca, an approach to narrating the history of style as a history of markers. As a case study for this approach, it attends closely to the structure, aesthetics, meaning, and social function of Milton's depictives, locating them in a larger historical trajectory. It closes by considering how a history attentive to the individuation and reproduction of stylistic markers might be reconciled with the computational approaches that currently dominate the study of style.

### The History of Style

Writing the history of style is complicated by the fact that long-dominant conceptions of style deny that it has a history. When Georges-Louis Leclerc, Comte de Buffon, declared in 1753 that "le style est l'homme même" (style is the man himself), he was restating the association between style and personality that had been conventional since at least the seventeenth century.[8] But he was also asserting that style is unlike "the knowledge, the facts, the discoveries," and other "things outside the man" (*choses . . . hors de l'homme*) that can be passed down from one person to another and that can "gain by being placed in more able hands [*mains plus habiles*]." Because of its identity with—its interiority to—the individual person, a style "cannot be taken, transported, or altered [*ne peut donc ni s'enlever, ni se transporter, ni s'altérer*]." It is intransmissible and immune to change, beyond the circulation or manipulation of subsequent hands; yet when sufficiently "elevated, noble, and sublime" it can become "eternal," "admired in all times," partaking in the "durability" of Truth. History requires both continuity and change: without continuity there is no history of a thing; without change a thing has no history. Yet a style, in Buffon's view, is at once too singular and too transcendent for history: it manifests only once in the sequence of time, but once manifest it has the potential to endure unchanged for all time. Because it is incapable of being taken, transported, or altered, it lacks the narrative and causal continuity requisite for history as such.[9] Its past, to draw a distinction from Hayden White, can only be written as a chronicle, a disconnected series of individual men themselves, one following another, so that every artist, as Charles Baudelaire later put it, "stems only from himself" and "dies childless."[10]

It is tempting to dismiss the individualism and idealism of Buffon's conception of style, but present-day intuitions also threaten to place style beyond the reach of history. I refer especially to the intuition of holism, which holds that a style is more than the sum of its parts. For Leo Spitzer, the philologist grasps style "not only by the gradual progression from one detail to another detail, but the anticipation or divination of the whole."[11] Jeff Dolven writes that while "the path that has been taken by stylistics as a subdiscipline is to speak of style as an aggregation of discrete characteristics," there is necessarily "something holistic, integrated and integrating" about the draw of style, "something that is anathema to the idea of style as a matter of discrete elements," such that "integration is part of style's promise."[12] It is the "integrated and integrating" promise of style that makes reading the opening pages of a novel less like noticing a set of features (syntactic, semantic, prosodic, phonological, etc.) than like practicing a new skill, finding one's way around a built environment, or even, as Dolven suggests, adopting a kind of life.[13] Though style's holism is most often invoked in relation to personality (*l'homme même*), we conventionally associate it with other, overlapping principles of integration, speaking also of the styles characteristic of periods (*stile antico*), genres (epistolary style), phases of an artist's career (*Spätstil*), discourses (*style indirect libre*), institutions (house style), the decorum of occasions and topics (*genera dicendi*), movements (*dulce stil nuovo*), professions (curial style), places (Gangnam Style), genders (*écriture féminine*), and so on. The diversity of these integrating principles is a reflection of the fact that, as Paul Valéry famously wrote, "every work is the work of many things besides an author."[14]

For all its appeal, holism poses no less of an obstacle to history than Buffon's idealism, for it is impossible to take and transport a style as an integrated whole, impossible to wrest and reconstitute it apart from the specific person, place, and time that is the principle of its integration.

Borges brilliantly imagines the limit of such impossibility in his short piece "Pierre Menard, Author of the Quixote." Menard, a "*Symboliste* from Nîmes," did not set out "to compose *another* Quixote, which surely is easy enough—he wanted to compose *the* Quixote," copying it word for word. Nonetheless, Borges's narrator remarks that the "contrast in style" between this secondary text and Cervantes's original is "vivid": "The archaic style of Menard—who is, in addition, not a native speaker of the language in which he writes—is somewhat affected. Not so the style of his precursor, who employs the Spanish of his time with complete naturalness."[15] Menard's style differs from that of Cervantes not because his words differ but because he and his world do. In the most fully holistic conception, style is defined not simply by the features of the text but by the text's situation in a total lifeworld, such that one cannot appropriate a text's style even by reproducing it exactly. Transporting alters, and altering demolishes. Like ice sculptures or spider webs, integrated styles do not travel. They appear, as in Buffon's conception, as the proper subjects of discontinuous chronicles, lacking the continuity and portability necessary for historical narrative.

However strong the intuition of holism may be, our use of the concept "style" entails a contrary requirement. Every style must be susceptible to imitation and therefore to alteration, whether as mimicry, parody, or pastiche. The "Oxen of the Sun" chapter of James Joyce's *Ulysses*, which marches through the styles characteristic of successive periods of English literary history, is only the most virtuosic demonstration of this requirement. In Jacques Derrida's terms, style is necessarily iterable, capable of being repeated in new texts and situations. The iterability of style has typically been understood in terms of the distinction between form and content. Arthur Schopenhauer writes that style "shows the *formal* nature [*die **formelle** Beschaffenheit*] of all a man's thoughts, a formal nature that must stay always the same whatever he may think about." In the same sentence he goes on, somewhat disconcertingly, to compare style to "the dough [*den Teig*] out of which all of his thoughts are kneaded, however different they may be."[16] Style is allied either with the form that imposes itself on the variable content of thought or with the doughlike substance that persists through the imposition of thought's variable forms. Tellingly, whether style *is* form or substance makes no difference: Schopenhauer's purpose in distinguishing the two is only to allow for one to persist or remain the same through changes in the other. Style is necessarily iterable even when, as Nelson Goodman has urged, we dispense with the opposition between content and form.[17] What is needed for a style to travel is not the abstraction of a contentless form from a formless content but rather a minimum of selfsameness and identity that persists across difference.[18]

### The Example of the Bees

Because a style is necessarily iterable, its holistic promise can be fulfilled only at its own expense. Full identification with the whole—whether the "man himself," the text situated in its world, or any other principle of integration—denatures the very concept of style. As long as we are unwilling to dispense with the term *style* as hopelessly confused (as some have suggested)[19] or to disambiguate it into at least two distinct concepts, any attempt to write its history will be structured by an antinomy that demands that it be integrated—ever more identical to a total way of being in the world—and at the same time iterable—capable of being taken and transported to a different place and time. The antinomy is nicely encapsulated in the linguistic form with which we speak of someone writing, playing, painting, or dressing *in the style of* another, which testifies at once to the propriety of style and its appropriability. A style belongs to a particular person, period, or place that it is *of*, even as other writers, players, painters, or dressers can always place themselves *in* it, inhabiting and thereby dislocating and altering it.[20]

Erich Auerbach's *Mimesis* is the most elegant and influential attempt to write a history of style that positions itself within this antinomy.[21] Despite the apparently inductive method of his chapters, which begin with an extended close reading of a long quotation, Auerbach also regards each work of literature as a stage or instantiation of a single underlying narrative, generated by the development of opposed levels of style, at various times identified with Homer and the Bible, the Hellenic and the Hebraic, the *sublime* and the *humile*, pure and mixed, high and low. He writes that these "styles, in their opposition, represent basic types" that "exercised their determining influence upon the representation of reality in European literature" (23). The "basic types" persist unchanged even as they "determine" the course of literary history, so that the style peculiar to each subsequent work in the tradition is the product of their "antithetical fusion" (153).[22] Auerbach's account is normative as well as descriptive, celebrating literature to the extent that it fuses opposed styles and subjects. He declares Dante's *Divine Comedy* "a well-nigh incomprehensible miracle" (182) in terms both of "subject matter" and "stylistic form" for its ability to "represent a mixture of sublimity and triviality" (184). The end product of Auerbach's Hegelian history is "emancipation" from the classical doctrine of the levels of style (554). Even as they endure unaltered, the "basic types," in their opposition, are both the drivers of style's history and the chains from which style eventually liberates itself. The elegance of this dialectical resolution is that it presents, in the discontinuous, chroniclelike structure of its chapters, successive passages as representatives of individuated styles unique to their authors and periods. But it also figures those styles as mixtures, syntheses of opposites, that provide not just the continuity necessary for history but the teleology, arc, and motivation characteristic of the most satisfying metanarratives.

In his eighty-fourth letter to Lucilius, the Roman Stoic and dramatist Seneca offers a profoundly different vision of the history of style, proposing that writers

> should follow . . . the example of the bees, who flit about and cull the flowers that are suitable for producing honey, and then arrange and assort in their cells all that they have brought in. . . . We also, I say, ought to copy these bees, and sift whatever we have gathered from a varied course of reading, for such things are better preserved if they are kept separate; then, by applying the supervising care which our nature has endowed us,—in other words, our natural gifts,— we should so blend those several flavors into one delicious compound that even though it betrays its origin, yet it nevertheless is clearly a different thing from that whence it came.[23]

He describes a material process of gathering, extracting, sifting, and blending, with the resulting compound bearing witness to its various origins (*unde sumptum sit*) even as it differentiates itself from them (*aliud quam unde sumptum est*). The simile of the bees and the similes of digestion, procreation, and choral harmony that follow are models of what writers *should* do, but they also articulate a powerful account of what writers *necessarily* do. Some writers, to be sure, cull the markers that make up their style from a wider range of texts than do others, but not even the most zealous disciples of a single exemplar can keep their style pure, free from the contamination of multiple influences. Writers set out to imitate the styles (*orationem* [84.8]) of others, but they cannot avoid doing so. Seneca's metaphors describe the processes by which markers are gathered and blended with others to produce new wholes. By expanding our ability to trace the honey's floral inheritance and differentiate it from other blends, search engines make feasible a reinvigorated Senecanism.

Roland Barthes developed a fundamentally Senecan account of style in a conference paper he delivered in 1969 and then published in 1971 as the essay "Style and its Image."[24] He argued that "literary writing must be placed, not only in reference to its closest neighbors, but also to . . . syntagmatic patterns, fragments typical of sentences, formulae if one likes . . . which form a part of the collective memory of literature" (8). The study of style would consequently be driven by "the conviction that style is essentially a citational process, a body of formulae, a memory (almost in the cybernetic sense of the word)" (9), with *cybernetic*, derived from Norbert Wiener's coinage in 1948, denoting something like a self-regulating system of internal feedback mechanisms operating without human supervision.[25] Though Barthes argues that stylistic analysis is necessarily a "search" for various linguistic "models, or patterns: sentence structures, syntagmatic clichés, divisions and clausulae of sentences," he rightly cautions against hunting for "*sources* in the philological sense of the term" (8) since "origins" are finally "unrecoverable" (9) and writing is "a kind of hereditary process, heredity without end" (14).

Where rhetorical approaches had treated style as a deviation from a norm, whether in the form of everyday spoken language, normal usage, or an unspoken code, Barthes argues instead for studying style as a chain or system of differences (6). The method of "search" Barthes proposes has "some affinity" with transformational grammar, since it understands every marker of a style as a "transformation" of another model, but it diverges "in a fundamental point" from the "ideological" approach of Chomskyan stylisticians like Richard Ohmann, Donald Freeman, and E. D. Hirsch Jr. in rejecting the notion of "'deep structures,' universal forms issuing from a psychological logic" (10).[26] Individual utterances are instead "repetitions, not essential elements; citations, not expressions; stereotypes, not archetypes" and must be understood in reference to "models" that are only ever "the depositaries of culture (even if they seem very old)."[27] In Barthes's account, there is no transcendent category above and no foundational category below the flat, immanent plane of utterance—of the various things spoken or inscribed. Advanced search tools prosthetically extend our ability to carry out the program of research envisioned by Barthes, allowing us to (1) investigate a stylistic marker not as a deviation from a "deep," ideal, essential, archetypal, or universal norm posited in advance of history but in its difference from other, analogous markers dispersed throughout history; (2) treat "normal" or "ordinary" utterances themselves as transformations, as deviations from previous deviations; (3) study style as a way of marking social differentiation and affiliation—of being with others and standing apart from them—not simply along the vertical axis of high and low but along many axes for which Ciceronian levels or types of style are insufficient descriptors; (4) understand the style of each work as a composite of markers and therefore of multiple histories; and (5) elaborate difference within the bounds of a single work (like Barthes's *Sarrasine*) and within a collective, almost "cybernetic" cultural memory, at least insofar as it is deposited in digital archives and accessible by search tools.

Why should we prefer a Senecan history of markers to a history of doctrinal types? Why tell stories about the often fussy procedures of gathering and extracting, repetition and transformation, similarity and difference, rather than grand dialectical stories of "antithetical fusion" and "emancipation"? Why displace Auerbach's tragicomedy with myriad picaresques of markers that are inassimilable to a unified narrative of opposition and synthesis?[28]

First, Auerbach understands history as posing a single question—how to reconcile high and low in order to represent reality—to which successive styles are responses that succeed (as with Dante) or fail (as with neoclassical literature) to varying degrees. It may well be the case that the *Commedia* aspired to wed the opposed styles of Homer and the Bible, but it is a mistake to regard other stylistic aspirations as so many diversionary liaisons. Writers, periods, and movements seek what Milton called an "answerable style" in response to a bewilderingly large and amorphous range of questions—questions of desire, identity, ideology, distinction, politics, the market, and so on. Their responses draw from a diverse repertoire of markers, made available by literary history and preserved in material texts, that have no necessary, fixed, or even consistent relationship with any doctrinal type. Stylistic markers locate texts and speakers more precisely than any of our social or stylistic categories, marking not only the brute fact of inclusion and exclusion, as Carlo Ginzburg has argued, but also position within and relative to groups.[29] Because markers can be extracted, altered, and blended together, they enable writers to compose (or fall into) supple and distinct styles in response to the fullest range of historical and social questions.

Second, a Senecan account allows an integrated style to play a local, partial, but nonetheless indispensable historical role without elevating (or reducing) it to the status of a determining principle, basic type, or instantiation of preexisting *genera dicendi*. For it is only as part of styles as integrated wholes that markers appear, respond to the diverse questions posed by history, combine with other markers, take on new resonances, vary their significance, and become available for further repetition in still other wholes. A Senecan history, no less than Auerbach's Ciceronian one, positions itself within the antinomy of holism and iterability, propriety and appropriability, but it proposes a different compromise. Only markers of style can be taken and transported; they, rather than basic *genera*, provide continuity across difference. The emulator, mimic, parodist, *pasticheur*, or forger always ends up imitating markers rather than the whole, even when it is the apprehension of the whole that arouses imitative desire. The necessary partiality of imitation is the corollary of its necessary impurity. When markers travel, integrated styles are free to stay put, to remain fully embedded in their world, identical only to themselves and discontinuous with what comes before and after. In the network vocabulary developed in chapter 3, integrated styles can be stable nodes because markers trace the edges between them.

Doctrinal types of style such as Cicero's *genera dicendi* do not drop out of a Senecan account, but rather than constituting the substance of style's history, they take up residence in a parallel discourse *about* style that is only loosely and irregularly related to it. They serve as rough principles of evaluation and selection, normative rather than strictly analytical terms, that say, in effect, "imitate these markers but not those . . . desire these words, these linguistic forms, these tropes figures and cadences, but not those." The principles are rough, in the sense of historically diverse and variable, because they are repeatedly contested and revised. A writer never imitates the plain style or any other *genera dicendi* as such. Yet the concept of a plain style can, with varying degrees of explicitness, shape the subset of the larger repertoire of markers that are suitable for imitation.[30] Conversely, a work or author may, when consecrated as the highest or purest instantiation of a doctrinal type, become the chief storehouse of markers for subsequent, doctrinally motivated writers. Though Milton did not imitate and could not have imitated the epic style or the *genus grande* as such, these idealized types undoubtedly guided him, in his search for an answerable style, to take up and imitate the markers he found in the Bible, Homer, Virgil, and a sizable array of Continental epics. No doctrinal type is sufficient to explain the use of depictives in *Paradise Lost* or, for that matter, their absence in other epic poems of the period, such as Abraham Cowley's *Davideis*, that presumably were guided by a similar set of doctrinal types. Yet subsequent writers, largely as a consequence of *Paradise Lost*, came to understand depictive adjectives as markers distinctive to the grand style.

### Who Will Mark the Flowing Unchanging Line?

Before turning to Milton and the history of depictives, we need to answer a basic question: what is a marker of style? More pointedly, what counts as *a* marker of style, a thing distinct from others? In the second of two essays attacking the early enterprise of stylistics, Stanley Fish argued that formal patterns "do not announce themselves naturally; they are picked out by an interested perception, and a perception otherwise interested will pick out another pattern."[31] Because the "descriptive categories" (syntactic, prosodic, phonetic, semantic, etc.) we use in describing markers "are themselves interpretive . . . they are constitutive of their object rather than being faithful (or unfaithful) to it," so that there is "no fact or pattern that is *independently* specifiable" (263). What counts as a marker of style will therefore be "interpretive from first to last" (266). Styles do not have natural or self-evident joints at which they can simply be cut and parceled out. Markers are the products, not the raw data, of interpretive acts.

Fish's claim for the interpretive constitution of markers chastened an earlier wave of stylisticians, but a Senecan approach begins by admitting his claim as its founding and enabling assumption. The assumption is enabling because it allows us to understand the history of style as nothing other than a history of interpretive acts: the acts of individuating, extracting, and blending that Seneca captures with the metaphor of the bees. Consciously or unconsciously—it scarcely matters—writers establish the identity of markers when they pick them out, detach them from one context, and reproduce them in a new one. As Goethe writes in the prelude to the first part of *Faust*, it is the poet "who marks out the flowing unchanging line," and poets do so not once and for all but every time they go about the business of writing.[32] What counts as a marker of style is neither necessary nor arbitrary but contingent and, more importantly, conventional. A marker's existence (what marks it out as a *thing*) and individuation (what marks it out as *a* thing) is the product of repeated, convention-making acts, whether of imitation, description, naming, or analysis. A marker's significance, to the extent that it acquires one, is no less conventional than its identity. Fish rightly rejects the notion of an "inventory in which formal items will be linked in a fixed relationship to semantic and psychological values" (75), or, more basically, the "assumption that formal features *possess* meaning" (78). Rather, meaning is conferred on markers, turning them into meaning-bearing signs, through acts of interpretation in a way that is neither arbitrary (since conventions guide the acts) nor fixed (since the conventions are themselves instituted and altered by these acts).

The conventionality of markers means that not every fact—every true proposition—about a text is a marker of style. It is possible to divide any text into an infinite number of facts, including compound, relative, and negative facts. (The inclusion of negative facts is not a philosophical subtlety: for style, what is absent may matter no less than what is present. In Georges Perec's *Les revenentes* the surfeit of the vowel *e* is no more significant than— is indeed a correlate of—the absence of all other vowels, while the converse is true for his earlier *La disparition*.) Over the course of history relatively few of these infinite facts, a finite subset, have been picked out as markers of style. Which of these facts get picked out differs in different times and places, meaning that what counts as a marker of style changes. The admittedly difficult task of determining which facts entered the sunlit domain of markers in a particular time and place is a question of historical phenomenology that can be revisited in light of new evidence or new interpretations of existing evidence. I will return shortly to those un-illumined facts that are not, or until recently have not been, markers.

The conventionality of markers means also that they do not make up a repertoire of basic, indivisible units of language out of which every text is composed and into which it can be analyzed. They are instead structured and unstable mixtures—already composites rather than atoms—given unity by the activities of reading and writing, comprehending and speaking. The composite nature of markers means that they are thoroughly historical: the conventional acts that establish them can also alter them, and their persistence through time and across texts is relative. Some parts and relations may prove durable, while others are more readily shed or replaced.

It is because markers are conventional that advanced search tools are especially vital to a Senecan account of style. Once a marker is understood not as any fact or pattern whatsoever but as the product of interpretive activities guided by the conventions and categories of a period or culture, it can no longer be discerned in itself, in the self-evidence of its singular existence. As an object defined by its iteration, it must be studied comparatively, with attention to how it has been reproduced and altered within and across texts, *oeuvres*, periods, and so on. As Leo Spitzer complains of the pedagogy of his mentor, the philologist Wilhelm Meyer-Lübke: "We were never allowed to contemplate a phenomenon in its quiet being, to look into its face: we always looked at its neighbors and predecessors."[33] Quite right.

Advanced search engines extend our capacity to gather the evidence needed to trouble the "quiet being" of the stylistic phenomenon. Yet the conventionality of markers puts definite, nontechnical limits on what search can do. Even though it can retrieve a wide array of results, a search engine cannot distinguish which results, if any, were markers under a given set of interpretive conventions. The cyberformalist must discern what was and was not perceptible and imitable in a particular period by reconstructing and thereby partaking in the interpretive economy that established a marker's identity and iterability in the first place. All that can be achieved is a rough agreement between the specification of the search and the minimum identity conditions by which a marker was established. Search is also limited by the obvious fact that it retrieves results according to a fixed specification, while markers can, by their very nature, shift and change. Etymologists have long acknowledged this challenge: just as the history of a word lies in other words (to the extent that it is not constructed at random, one lexeme is always derived from another), so too does the history of a marker lie in other markers.

Perhaps most crucially, search retrieves only one kind of evidence for the interpretive activity of writers. Further evidence resides in practices of imitation and the material traces they leave behind. Early modern humanists extracted adages, aphorisms, maxims, and *sententiae*—witty, widely applicable sayings—from classical authorities and disposed of them under various topic headings. The resulting commonplace books and florilegia, from the Latin *flos* (flowers) and *legere* (to gather or select), offer the most tangible evidence of how writers divided the texts of their predecessors into discrete units for further use in composition.[34] The linguistic forms of the *auctores* were objects of humanist desire no less than their *sententiae*. In his educational treatise *The scholemaster*, Roger Ascham recommended that students seeking to imitate the eloquence of ancients like Homer and Virgil begin by comparing them with one another, attending to differences in "handlyng of their matter," "proprietie of words," and "forme of sentences."[35]

Humanists displayed a remarkable appetite for identifying these forms using labels borrowed from the traditions of classical rhetoric and Latin grammar. Henry Peacham, for example, devotes a sizable portion of *The Garden of Eloquence*—some forty-six figures in all—to "Schemats Syntactical, or Figures of constructions."[36] Yet taxonomies like Peacham's did not name all the markers that were available for imitation, nor did they limit imitation to markers that could be named. (Milton could surely pick out and employ adjectival constructions that he took no account of in the grammar he published in 1669.)[37] Instead they trained readers in the strategies of identifying and culling markers from existing texts for reuse in their own. Rather than establishing a final and exhaustive repertoire of markers, early modern rhetorical handbooks, commonplace books, grammar texts, and pedagogical practices evidence the larger categories of textual facts that were present to writers in the period as markers of style.[38] The explicitness and visibility of humanist imitative practices are exceptional, but other periods, earlier and later, had their own, diverse practices and instruments for identifying, extracting, and imitating markers.[39]

### Markers of Milton's Style

Interpretive, material, and imitative practices offer some evidence of which elements of texts were visible and available for repetition, but they cannot tell us whether writers actually repeated them. For that we must look to the texts themselves, subjecting them to close and comparative analysis. Through such analysis we can begin to establish the identity and coherence of a marker, defining the conditions of its iteration and individuation from other markers. Scholars have studied Milton's style in detail for as long as there has been commentary on the poem, and they have attended as well to his distinctive use of adjectives, which *Paradise Lost* conspicuously postposes (as in "darkness **visible**" [1.63]) and deploys in what Ronald

Emma calls "divided pairs," with attributive and postpositive adjectives modifying a single noun.[40] The phrase "**human** face **divine**" (3.44), for example, studiously avoids subordinating the face's humanity to its divinity, or vice versa, as it would if both adjectives were attributive (*divine human face* or *human divine face*).[41] In rarer cases critics have moved past describing and evaluating the markers of Milton's style to suggest their provenance. Hilda M. Hulme supposes that on reading Belial's account of the fallen angels' plight—"**Unrespited, unpitied, unreprieved,** / Ages of hopeless end" (2.185–86)—"English readers will recall at once the similarly constructed line of *Hamlet*," in which the Ghost laments his murder in blossoms of his sin, "**Unhousel'd, disappointed, unanel'd**" (1.5.77).[42] The construction of the line—three negated, multisyllabic, passive past participles in succession—is one to which *Paradise Lost* returns with degrees of variation. Grace, the Son says, "Comes **unprevented, unimplor'd, unsought**" (3.23); the choir of angels regales God as "**Immutable, Immortal, Infinite**" (3.373); the "bought smile" of the harlot is "**loveless, joyless, unendeared**" (4.765–66); Abdiel stands among the false angels "**unmoved,** / **Unshaken, unseduced, unterrified**" (5.898–900). The form, in other words, has a history within the poem as well as one preceding it.

Depictive adjectives are subtler, easier to pass over without notice, than divided pairs or repeated constructions. Consider the "mantling vine," which "Lays forth her purple grape, and gently creeps / **Luxuriant**" (4.257–60). By the middle of the seventeenth century writers used *luxuriant* to describe plants as "growing profusely."[43] The notion of a luxuriant vine is unexceptional. What is exceptional is that "luxuriant" is divorced from the noun it modifies and placed after the verb "creeps." It is neither attributive nor postpositive, nor does it function as a complement, which occurs only with a limited range of verbs like *to be* ("God saw that it was good"), *seem*, *feel*, *appear*, *become*, *remain*, *stay*, and other copulas and quasi-copulas. What it means to *be* or *seem luxuriant* is clear enough, but what does it mean to *creep luxuriant*?[44]

In some cases it is difficult or impossible to distinguish depictives from *flat adverbs* (adverbs that do not end in *ly*), which modify the verb rather than the subject.[45] Janette Richardson has argued that in his regular substitution of adjectives for adverbs Milton is adopting a marker "typical of Virgil's style," which in English "creates an unexpected caesura and achieves almost the effect of a parenthetical afterthought." She compares a line like "thee I revisit **safe**" (3.21), in which we can understand "safe" as "safely," to a line from the *Aeneid*: "Ipsa Paphum sublimis abit, sedisque revisit/**laeta** suas" (She to Paphos went away on high and her temples **happy** revisited) (1.415–16).[46] Contesting Richardson's Virgilian provenance, Emma notes that such substitution was common Elizabethan practice even among men of "little Latin" like Shakespeare, who wrote of the Prince of Wales that he "raged more **fierce**."[47]

The adverbial force of Milton's adjectives is more evident in some cases than in others. When Satan, in flight, "ascending rides/**Audacious**" (2.930–31), it is easy to see how the riding may itself be performed audaciously. When "Death/Grinned **horrible** a ghastly smile" (2.845–46), Death was horrible and he grinned horribly. Speaking to a disguised Satan, Uriel recounts how at the creation of the universe the fifth element, or "ethereal quintessence . . . /Flew upward, spirited with various forms,/That rolled **orbicular**, and turned to stars/ Numberless, as thou seest, and how they move" (3.718–19). *Orbicular* means both circular and in circles, and it can be taken to describe either the shape of the "various forms" assumed by the element or "how they move," the manner in which they roll: in effect, the orbicular elements roll orbicularly.[48] There are orbits within orbits here, both in the multiple syntactic roles of "orbicular" and in the cosmos it is used to describe.

The ambiguity of depictive adjectives is no less evident when Eve declares her submission to Adam in book 4: "what thou bidst/**Unargued** I obey" (4.635–36). There is little doubt about what this means: she says that she follows Adam's commands implicitly. But we formulate this meaning without a single construal of the role played by "Unargued" in the sentence. As a passive participle, it can modify the object, "what," but not the subject of the sentence, "I." As an adverb meaning roughly "without argument," it can modify "bidst" and perhaps, at a stretch, "obey." "Unargued" can also be taken in two slightly different senses: Adam, in bidding, offers no reasons, and Eve, in obeying, requires none. Milton's depictives are predominantly *subject-oriented*, meaning that they modify the subject of the verb, but in some cases, as with "Unargued," they can be construed as *object-oriented* as well. Only context lets us know that in *He ate the vegetables **raw*** the depictive modifies the object, but in *He ate the vegetables **naked*** it modifies the subject, a fact Milton exploits. The Latin case system would make the attachment of the adjective unmistakable, but in present-day English divorcing the adjective from a single noun head produces luxuriant attachments, multiple possible construals that cannot easily be disregarded or ruled out.

Like adverbs, depictives are a kind of adjunct, which means that they add information to the sentence but are structurally dispensable. Unlike verb complements (*She is **angry***), they can be omitted without disrupting the predicative structure of the sentence or changing the relationship between other constituents. Like adverbs, depictives are highly mobile within the sentence.[49] You can say *I taught **unprepared***, or ***Unprepared**, I taught*, or *I, **unprepared**, taught*. In the same way, "Unargued" could comfortably occupy the position of the second, third, fourth, or sixth word in Eve's declaration of submission, or it could disappear altogether without changing the sentence's predicative structure. Compared with attributives, depictives are a conservative category, accommodating some but not all adjectives. We can say *She played injured*, but in most idiolects *She played talented* and *She played old* are unacceptable. Noam Chomsky's famous example "Colorless green ideas sleep furiously" is grammatically acceptable nonsense; by contrast, *Green ideas furiously sleep colorless* will register to most present-day English speakers as incorrect or at least awkward nonsense, syntactically as well as semantically ill-formed, because *sleep colorless* is an unacceptable pairing of verb and depictive.[50] One can *drive drunk* or *die alone*, but it is a question whether one can *drive chubby* or *die imprecise*.

The answers to such questions are governed by rules that linguists have sought to reconstruct with much difficulty and only mixed success.[51] In pairing verbs with depictives, Milton works on the blurry edge of those rules. *Creep luxuriant, roll orbicular, ride audacious, obey innumerable*: each exceptional verb + depictive pair widens the thoroughfare of language as it marches through, putting pressure not simply on the semantic boundary between sense and nonsense but on the grammatical boundary between acceptable and unacceptable. I have no evidence to show that T. S. Eliot was thinking specifically of Milton's use of depictives when he described *Paradise Lost* as "a perpetual sequence of original acts of lawlessness," but the comment is appropriate all the same.[52] The poem bridles not only under what Milton called the "modern bondage" of rhyming but under all forms of linguistic constraint.[53]

In Stanley Fish's famous account of *Paradise Lost*, the poem's style functions as a "programme of reader harassment" that works to pull its readers up short, to "complicate or contradict" our previous expectations, and

thereby convict us of our own fallenness.[54] Fish is particularly adept at identifying sentences in which a belated verb, negation, or qualification contra-
dicts or dissolves the meaning built up earlier, forcing the reader to parse its
syntax anew. As in the cases Fish describes, Milton's depictives are belated—
they come after the reader has already made preliminary decisions about
how to parse and construe a sentence. Since they are adjuncts, adding to a
predictive structure that is complete in their absence, no earlier constituents of the sentence lead the reader to expect them. Yet their effect is not to
surprise us by contradicting what has come before but rather to enhance
it with complementary or convergent meanings, meanings that sometimes
verge on redundancy or tautology, as when Milton begs Urania to

Return me to my native element:
Lest from this flying steed unreined, . . .
. . . . . . . . . . . . . . . . . . . . . . . . . . . . . . . . .
Dismounted, on the Aleian field I fall,
**Erroneous** there to wander, and forlorn.

(7.16–20)

Does "Erroneous," as an adjective, modify "I"? Or does it, as an adverb, modify "fall" or "wander"? Because of its role in the sentence, its attachments
are multiple, excessive, but its meaning, like that of "Unargued," is scarcely
in doubt. From the Latin *errare* (to wander), "Erroneous" anticipates the
meaning of the verb "to wander." As Earl Miner notes, the name Aleian is
also from the Greek for wandering, so that the lines propose a manifold re-
duplication: on the field of wandering I, wandering, fall, there to wander
wanderingly.

The luxuriant attachments of the depictive leave Milton open to the
charge of overemphasis—of needless repetition and wastefulness—that
Christopher Ricks occasionally levels at *Paradise Lost* and regards as a dis-
abling flaw of *Paradise Regained*.[55] When the angels sing, "The great Creator
from his work returned / **Magnificent**, his six days work, a World" (7.567–
68), "Magnificent," from the Latin *magnus + ficere* (great making), does
scarcely more than repeat the appellation "great Creator" of the previous
line, a repetition of which Milton, who coined the words *omnific* and *petrific*
from the same Latin root, was undoubtedly aware. Once again, "Magnificent" can be taken as an adjective describing the "Creator" or an adverb

describing the manner in which he "returned," but from an interpretive standpoint it scarcely matters how we choose to parse it, if choose we must. In the sentence's curiously orbicular syntax, the luxuriant possible construals converge on a single or barely differentiated meaning.

In most cases, depictives allow the poem to achieve delicate enhancements in meaning without repetition or waste. When Satan resolves to "leave / Unworshipt, unobeyed, the throne supreme, / **Contemptuous**," he is contemptuous and displays his contempt through omission. When the remnants of the satanic host with "fear surprised, and sense of pain, / Fled **ignominious**" (6.394–95), they retreat in a shameful manner, and they are quite literally without name (from the Latin in- + *nomen*, "no name"), having been, as Raphael reports, "by doom / Cancelled from Heav'n and sacred memory" and left "Nameless in dark oblivion" (6.379–80). Instead of reversal, contradiction, correction, *aporia*, or vertiginous irony, these adjectives multiply small, compatible, overlapping variations in meaning. They generate semantic density with syntactic economy.

This economy is beautifully evident when Milton describes how "the parting sun / Beyond the Earth's green Cape and verdant Isles / **Hesperian** sets" (8.630–32). Editors have noted that Milton's "Hesperian" has two senses. In its general, directional sense, as Patrick Hume first noted, it means simply "placed in the west," where the sun sets.[56] In its second, mythologically specific sense, it refers to the Isles of the Blessed (sometimes identified with the Canaries), where the daughters of Hesperus guard the golden apples that grow in their father's garden. What editors have not noted is that the multiple attachments of "Hesperian" bring forth the word's various senses. The sentence may be parsed in two different ways. The first, "the sun [beyond the isles Hesperian] sets," foregrounds the adjective's mythological meaning by attaching it to the isles as a postpositive; the second, "the sun [beyond the isles] Hesperian sets," foregrounds its directional meaning by attaching it to the sun as a depictive. Between the two parses, and the two meanings, there is difference but not discrepancy. The semantic density of the lines is a result not only of what William Empson called the "structure" of a complex word like *Hesperian* but of a complex linguistic form as well.

Other adjectives similarly function as at once postpositive and depictive. Shortly after declaring the great Creator magnificent, the angels repeat their call for the doors of heaven to "Open, and henceforth oft; for God will deign / To visit oft the dwellings of just men / **Delighted**" (7.569–71). "Delighted" is the postpositive member of a divided pair, "**just** men / **Delighted**," but it also prompts the reader to look back across two line breaks and ten words to modify the subject of the sentence, "God." It describes both God and men because God's frequent visitations will be delightful to both. The word does double duty, so to speak, because the feeling is mutual. The multiple attachments produced by the delay of the depictive, over two line breaks and eleven words after the subject, "God," toward which it is oriented, result not simply in a convergence but in an outright reciprocity of meaning.

We can understand the syntactic compression enacted by depictive adjectives in one final way. In early modern as in modern English, some verbs, like *stand*, *sit*, and *fall*, regularly function as copulas or quasi-copulas; like *is* or *become*, they link the subject to an adjectival predicate.[57] When Zephon compares Satan's diminished brightness with "when thou stoodest in Heaven **upright** and **pure**," we understand that Satan stood in heaven and was both upright and pure. When the angels address their song to God, "where thou sit'st / **Throned inaccessible**" (3.376–77), God sits, is throned, is inaccessible, and is also inaccessibly throned. Yet *Paradise Lost* rarely employs quasi-copulas in a solely copulative (grammatical) role; it also reactivates their intransitive (lexical) meaning. *Fall*, an obviously charged word in a poem about the Fall, has since the fourteenth-century served as an equivalent to *become*, without implying literal downward motion, as when we speak of someone falling sick, or silent, or asleep.[58] Yet when Adam recounts how he met the "Presence divine" and how "In adoration at his feet I fell / **Submiss**," "fell" means both that he became submissive and also, as an intransitive verb, that he literally dropped to the ground, a meaning to which "submiss"—from the Latin *submissus* (put low)—orbicularly returns. Eve likewise at Adam's feet "Fell **humble**," from the Latin *humile* (low), itself from *humus* (dirt, ground). In the troubled dream Eve relates to Adam, she cannot *fall asleep* without at the same time moving downward: "I, methought, sunk down, / And fell **asleep**." After the Fall, Adam and Eve together go to the place where they were judged by God to "prostrate fall / Before him **reverent**," at once falling prostrate (lying flat) and falling into a reverent state. Nor does Milton keep to the usual range of copulas and quasi-copulas. Depictives effectively enlist a broad array of transitive and intransitive verbs to perform the work of copulation. Raphael's promise to Adam and

Eve that "Your bodies may . . . / . . . ascend / **Ethereal**, as we" (5.497–99),
folds the promise of becoming and being ethereal into the upward motion
of "ascend."

Though the depictives Milton uses throughout *Paradise Lost* are distinguished primarily by their syntactic roles, they tend to share other, extra-
syntactic characteristics. They are almost always multisyllabic Latinate
words (*Luxuriant, Innumerable, Magnificent, Delighted, Unargued, Erroneous,
orbicular, ignominious, Hesperian, Contemptuous, Audacious, Ethereal, horrible*).
As adjuncts divorced from direct proximity to a single noun head, Milton's
depictives are highly mobile, able to wander erroneous within the structure
of the sentence. He takes advantage of this mobility by frequently positioning them at the beginning of lines, giving them special prominence and
separating them visually and prosodically from the sentence constituents
they modify. His blank verse allows them to assume this place in the line in
a way rhymed verse, especially when end-stopped, does only with difficulty.

### Detective Work

This close formal analysis of *Paradise Lost* has allowed us to pick out
and individuate a particular marker of Milton's style; illustrate its diversity and establish its coherence; evaluate its aesthetic affordances, treating it
as a kind of script or recipe for the experience of a reader; and assess its
role in the production of meaning. The procedures for such analyses are at
once indispensable and decidedly familiar; scholars of literature will likely
have witnessed, taken part in, and performed many similar analyses over
the course of their careers. One could pursue—though I will not—further
formalist procedures: Leo Spitzer's method of using the surface "details" of
a work to "divine" or "anticipate" the "inward form" or "etymon" of the work
as a whole, or Christopher Ricks's marshaling of readings into a strenuous
defense of Milton's style as possessing "epic grandeur" as well as "delicate
and subtle life" and "infinite suggestiveness."[59]

Yet historical and contextual analysis of such a marker is as unfamiliar
as these procedures of formal analysis are familiar. Confronted with relatively simple questions—Where did Milton's depictive adjectives come
from? How did *Paradise Lost* come to use an unexceptional linguistic form
in such a distinctive way? How were depictives situated in the literature of
the period? In what kinds of texts do they appear? How were they related
to doctrinal types? What sorts of social work did they do? How, if at all, were

they taken up, imitated, and transformed by later texts?—a scholar will find few established methodologies and few suitable tools or works of reference. Historicism has yet to develop adequate resources and practices for historicizing style. Fredericus Theodorus Visser's monumental *Historical Syntax of the English Language* informs us that depictives have been part of the language from its earliest origins and offers a useful chart of conventional copulas and quasi-copulas, but its concern is with the general history of the grammar rather than with style, literature, or culture. Since depictives share no fixed word or phrase, no string for which to search, conventional search capacities are scarcely more helpful. The very aspects of the depictive that make it an aesthetically and semantically distinctive marker of Milton's style also make it exceptionally difficult to locate in a full-text archive of any size. Retrieving subject-oriented depictive adjectives with reasonable recall and precision would require distinguishing them from other parts of speech as well as from attributive, postpositive, and complement adjectives, flat adverbs, resultatives, and object-oriented depictives. Current natural language processing is not up to the task.[60]

The absence of the search tools needed for a fully methodical inquiry does not render us completely helpless, but it does throw us back either on the vagaries of our past reading, our memories (as when Belial's "Unrespited, unpitied, unreprieved" leads readers to recall Hamlet's "Unhousel'd, disappointed, unanel'd"); on generalized assertions of Milton's Latinity; or on our knowledge of established lines of influence (tracing, for example, the substitution of adjectives for adverbs back to Virgil or Shakespeare). More generally, it throws us back on a kind of makeshift detective work. The actual depictive adjectives *Paradise Lost* uses provide valuable clues to that marker's history. As it happens, Milton uses one depictive adjective repeatedly:

> the empyreal host
> Of Angels by imperial summons called,
> **Innumerable** before the Almighty's throne
>
> (5.585)

> How first began this Heaven which we behold
> Distant so high, with moving fires adorned
> **Innumerable**
>
> (7.86–88)

Locating a linguistic form, whether using search engines or print finding tools, is considerably simplified when it travels with a particular lexical content. So far as I can tell, Virgil does not make analogous use of *innumerable* in Latin, but Homer does so in Greek.[61] Here are lines from book 2 of the *Iliad*, shortly before the catalog of ships:

> estan d' en leimōni Skamandriōi anthemoenti
> murioi, hossa te phulla kai anthea gignetai horēi
>
> (2.467–68)
>
> (And they stood in the flowery meadow of Scamander, countless, as are the leaves and flowers in their season.)

*Murios*, in Homeric Greek, denotes a specific quantity, ten thousand, but it also means countless, beyond number, innumerable. Here it modifies a plural noun (presumably the subject of the previous sentence, "ethnea polla," the many tribes of Achaeans) that is expressed in the sentence only in the verb "estan" (they stood), the third-person aorist indicative of *histēmi*.[62] *Murios* occupies the same syntactic and prosodic position in other lines of the *Iliad* and the *Odyssey*, but none so remarkably similar to the line from *Paradise Lost* with which we began: "Yet to their General's voice they soon obeyed/**Innumerable**" (1.337–38). Homer's "murioi" closely precedes the catalog of ships, Milton's "Innumerable" the catalog of demons; Homer's numbers (or rather fails to number) the Achaean troops, Milton's the troops of "bad Angels." Both come in the midst of a series of epic similes suggesting the immensity of their respective forces. Homer likens them to forest fires, winged birds, swarming flies, flocks of goats, and flowers and leaves; Milton to swarming locusts, barbarian hordes, and scattered leaves. Milton's early biographers claimed that he could repeat Homer almost without book and that his daughter, Deborah, could recite "considerable verses" from the *Iliad* and the *Odyssey* as well.[63] Milton adopted a syntactic, prosodic, and lexical marker of Homer's style as part of the larger machinery of the epic catalog, though there's no reason to suppose that Homer was his sole predecessor. If he is in fact imitating Homer's syntax here, then Gregory Machacek's exceptionally inclusive term, *phraseological adaptation*, is not inclusive enough, since what is taken up, transformed from a nominative attributive adjective to a depictive, and reinstantiated throughout *Paradise Lost* is not a phrase at all but an abstract linguistic form.[64]

Following the well-traveled roads of literary influence also partly reveals the afterlife of Milton's depictive adjectives. The most canonical of his successors, William Wordsworth, signals his stylistic debts throughout the published *Prelude* of 1850. Like Milton, he sometimes divides his adjectives: "Days of sweet leisure, taxed with **patient** thought / **Abstruse**, nor wanting **punctual** service **high**" (1.45–46).[65] In moments of sublime description, his adjectives become still more distinctly Miltonic, as in the ascent of Mount Snowdon:

> Not distant from the shore whereon we stood,
> A fixed, abysmal, gloomy, breathing-place—
> Mounted the roar of waters, torrents, streams
> **Innumerable**, roaring with one voice!
>
> (14.58–61)

Or when he pulls back from observing a small town gathering to observe how

>                Immense
> Is the recess, the circumambient world
> **Magnificent**, by which they are embraced
>
> (8.56–58)

"Innumerable" and "Magnificent," though imitations of the lexis and prosody of *Paradise Lost*, are postpositives, not depictives. Their functional roles are single and unambiguous, their attachments limited. Seeking the sublime, Wordsworth puts Milton's big Latin words up front.

Wallace Stevens may also evoke Milton by the placement of adjectives in the line, as in stanza 3 of "Sunday Morning":

> Jove in the clouds had his inhuman birth.
> No mother suckled him, no sweet land gave
> Large-mannered motions to his mythy mind.
> He moved among us, as a muttering king,
> **Magnificent**, would move among his hinds,
> Until our blood, commingling, virginal,
> With heaven, brought such requital to desire
> The very hinds discerned it, in a star.[66]

This is what an enchanted world-view sounds like to a secular atheist sitting comfortably at home on a Sunday morning. In its secular syncretism, pagan and Christian mythoi are scarcely distinguished or distinguishable. As in *The Prelude*, Stevens's "Magnificent" is lexically and prosodically, though not syntactically, analogous to Milton's. Even though the poem is pervaded, as *Paradise Lost* is, with fruit and the flutter of wings, the word is not, I think, an allusion to Milton. Rather, it is one note of the music that a "mythy mind" makes—what the poem earlier calls the "holy hush of ancient sacrifice." Like the use of "hinds" to refer to household servants, the word and its position in the line are an archaism, a way of intimating at once the solemnity and the obsolescence of the sacred. When Stevens imagines the way faith is recollected by the faithless, it is Milton's verse that he recalls. True depictive adjectives appear only later, in a final stanza that presents the world in the present tense, stripped of metaphysical struts:

> We live in an old chaos of the sun,
> Or an old dependency of day and night,
> Or island solitude, **unsponsored**, **free**,
> Of that wide water, inescapable.
>
> (stanza 8)

Like Milton's *obey innumerable*, *ride audacious*, or *roll orbicular*, Stevens's "live . . . unsponsored, free" is luxuriant. His lines ask us to perform an exceptional kind of syntactic work to see that "unsponsored" and "free" do not describe the noun, "solitude," they immediately follow, but are instead predicates of the verb "live," two lines earlier, and modify the subject, "We." In discerning their attachments to us and the manner of our existence in the absence of divinity, we perform the interpretive labor necessary to bestow meaning on an "old chaos of the sun."

Detective work of this sort is hardly an unproductive or unpleasant pursuit, yet it is by definition unsystematic and impressionistic. No doubt a Vendler or a Ricks, not to mention a Spitzer or an Auerbach, could through sheer erudition summon numerous other examples and perhaps establish a more satisfying narrative. But that narrative would still be constrained by an individual's reading and memory. More worryingly, it would be enthralled to existing accounts of the shape of literary traditions, canons, cultures, and lines of influence. Digital tools do not, of course, allow us to proceed free of investigative assumptions, nor do they make interpretive judgment and skill any less necessary, but they can help us to push investigation beyond the partiality of current canons and the limited reading of individual critics.

### Finding Tools

Moving beyond the limits of individual reading requires finding the right finding tools, tools that do what print-based detective work cannot, in some cases making it possible to identify potential predecessors and successors to Milton's depictives. In the BYU EEBO corpus, for example, the search string *[v\*] [innumerable]* retrieves all instances of verbs followed immediately by the adjective *innumerable*. As one would expect, the search returns mostly forms of *to be* and *to have*, but the sixth most frequent combination is striking: "creeping innumerable," which the BYU interface retrieves in twenty-eight of the TCP texts from the period 1570–1680, all of them direct quotations or close paraphrases of Psalms 104:25. In the Coverdale Bible of 1535 the verse is given as, "So is this greate and wyde see also, wherin are thinges crepinge innumerable, both small and great beastes," with the relevant phrase *things creeping innumerable* preserved in both the Geneva and Authorized translations.[67] Innumerable things creeping? Innumerable creeping things? Things creeping innumerably? No: things creeping innumerable. In *Paradise Regained* the Son describes the psalms as the origins of pagan as well as sacred song, "with artful terms inscribed"; Mary Ann Radzinowicz has argued that as a stylist Milton "saw in the psalms the truest poetry," looking to them as exemplars of poetic sublimity, divinely inspired attempts to capture the immensity and teeming multiplicity of the Creation in language.[68] He may also have found in them a precedent both for pairing an unaccustomed depictive with the verb *creep* ("creeps luxuriant") and for pairing the depictive *innumerable* with an unaccustomed verb ("obey innumerable").

A search for pairings of verbs with a particular depictive can likewise yield possible successors to Milton's depictive adjectives. So, for example, in CQPweb the search string *_V\* luxuriant* reveals only one writer in the period besides Milton who used the adjective *luxuriant* as a depictive with a verb other than *grow*. John Dryden, who approved of Milton's imitation of Virgil's "Latin Elegancies" as well as his imitation of Homer's "Grecisms," and who in 1674 rewrote *Paradise Lost* as a stage play, translates a passage in book 11 of the *Aeneid* comparing Turnus to a "wanton Courser" that "prances o're the Plains": "To quench his Thirst, and cool his fiery Blood: / He swims **luxuriant**, in the liquid Plain."[69] We need not conclude that Dryden took the use of *luxuriant* as a depictive from *Paradise Lost*, but he certainly did encounter it there, and it is likely that he would have encountered it nowhere else. Milton's depictives widen the thoroughfare of language not just for their own passage, but so that other writers can march through as well.

Queries need not be limited to searches for possible predecessors or successors; they also make it possible to discern the dispersion of particular depictives within the literature of the period. CQPweb makes it possible to read through the hundreds of thousands of verb + adjective bigrams in the EEBO-TCP corpus, though lexically focused searches are obviously more practical. For example, only *Paradise Lost*, of the forty-four thousand–odd full texts in the corpus, uses *magnificent* as a depictive following *return*, or *luxuriant* as a depictive following *creep*. *Orbicular* was routinely (in 649 instances) used to describe both shape and manner of motion; other texts use it as a depictive, but *Paradise Lost* is the only one to pair it with *roll*.[70] Unsurprisingly, Milton alone uses the adjective *Hesperian* (or as the 1667 and 1674 publications spell it, *Hesperean*) as a depictive. In some cases, attending to specific depictives can allow us to locate *Paradise Lost* in a broader social milieu. For example, the angel Zephon is not the only one to use the idiom *standing pure* in the years before the first edition of *Paradise Lost* appeared in 1667. A CQPweb query for "{stand} {pure}," which searches for all forms of each lexeme, returns ten uses between 1646 and 1667: five in tracts by Quaker preachers like Richard Farnsworth, Samuel Fisher, and James Whitehead; two in translations of treatises by the mystic Jakob Boehme; one in a 1649 pamphlet by the Digger Gerard Winstanley; one in a translation of a biblical commentary by the Socinian Johan Crell; and one in Milton's own *Likeliest Means to Remove Hirelings*. Five of these uses appear in tracts or pamphlets sold by the Puritan bookseller Giles Calvert. In a 1664 letter, to quote only one instance, James Whitehead prays that "ye may be strengthened against every appearance of evil, and stand pure in a righteous holy, blameless life."[71] Zephon's reminder to Satan that "thou stoodest in Heaven **upright** and **pure**" need not be taken as evidence that either Zephon or Satan or Milton was allied with any of these writers, but in the years leading up to the publication of *Paradise Lost* this pairing of verb and adjective was the distinct property of antinomians, mystics, and perfectionists—those who rejected the Calvinist doctrine of total depravity and regarded human purity as a possibility in this world. This affiliation resides not simply in the use of the verb *to stand* or the adjective *pure*, since many writers of the period employed these words to various ideological and religious ends, but in their combination as a verb + depictive pair.

### Making Markers

Is the Senecan approach to the history of style, which I have both theorized and then tested out with available search tools, compatible with the quantitative methods that are dominant in digital humanities scholarship? To what extent is the study of stylistic markers compatible with quantification, calculation, and statistical description? Like statistics, the Senecan study of markers seeks a finer-grained alternative to Ciceronian histories of doctrinal types. And it clearly matters not just that Milton used depictive adjectives but that he used them quite frequently—far more frequently in some works (*Paradise Lost*) than in others (*Paradise Regained*). Frequency is consequential not just for Milton's style but for its place in the literature of his day and in the longer history of style. We can suppose that writers like Dryden, Wordsworth, and Stevens were more likely to notice and imitate the depictives of *Paradise Lost* because those adjectives are repeated more rather than less frequently. Markers are defined by iterability, and iterations are by definition enumerable. To be a *mark* of style is to be *a* mark, one mark that can be added to others. "Style," as Franco Moretti puts it, "is *always* a matter of relative frequency"—frequency relative not only to a single document or *oeuvre* but potentially to all the various, overlapping principles of stylistic integration.[72] Relative frequency is already implicit, if vaguely, in the kinds of assertions critics (including me) unavoidably make when talking about style, as when we say that Milton *tends* to use a construction this way, or that he does so *often* or *habitually* or *rarely*, or that his usage is *uncommon* or *conventional* or *idiomatic*.

Yet there are substantial challenges to unifying the computational and Senecan approaches. The first is technical: computation, and with it a significant degree of uncertainty, is already built into searches that use POS tagging or other kinds of probabilistic natural language processing. The precision of quantitative analysis is better suited to features of a text, like words or strings, that a computer can identify and count with perfect or near-perfect recall and precision. Of course, human readers can reliably identify complex syntactic constructions in a relatively small sample of texts before turning them over to computers for statistical analysis, as

Thomas Corns did in his 1990 study, *Milton's Language*.[73] But if the goal is to discover how a marker of style has been used in a huge and growing archive of texts, then classifying thousands or millions of sentences by hand is self-defeating. Nevertheless, this challenge is merely technical and will likely recede at least somewhat as natural language processing methods become more reliable.[74]

The second challenge runs deeper. Here is a truism: a complex array of exemplars, ideals, doctrinal types, categories, grammatical rules, rhetorical taxonomies, habits, and conventions guided the writing of every sentence Milton ever wrote. The average length of the sentences in *Paradise Lost* (24.6 words in the sample of Tom Corns) is the product of these conventions and of Milton's desire to write a poem in which the sense is "variously drawn out from one verse into the next."[75] Yet average sentence length, measured in words, is epiphenomenal, an effect of these complex practices and conventions that does not play a further causal role in them. Milton did not set out to attain this average length or any other; nor did he imitate the average sentence length of his predecessors; nor did successors like Wordsworth, Dryden, or Stevens imitate his. Milton and these successors wrote within a set of conventions that never employed the categories that would be required to pick out and imitate (consciously or not) average sentence length, to say nothing of more nuanced measures like frequency distribution or relational measures like tf-idf, chi-square, or log likelihood.[76] They could of course have added up the words in a poem and divided the number by the total number of sentences. But there were no strategies for making the product of this simple calculation into a marker of style to be desired or avoided; still more obviously, there were no conventions for situating it in semiotic space and conferring meaning or value on it. For the vast majority of literary history, aggregate quantitative measures have not been markers of style, even when the things they measure and aggregate have been. That is, even conventions finely attuned to the length of individual sentences and to the succession of long and short sentences were nevertheless mute regarding average sentence length. (If this claim sounds tendentious, simply substitute a more sophisticated statistical measure, such as log likelihood.) Until relatively recently—and how recently is a question for historical inquiry—aggregate quantitative measures have existed outside the conventions that make it possible to perceive, imitate, and confer meaning on some facts and patterns rather than others.

The claims of the previous paragraph, because they are about conventions and practices rather than, say, transcendent categories of the understanding, are themselves contingent and subject to change. It is easy to imagine different circumstances in which writers vigilantly monitor the average sentence length of a document as a whole—easy because those circumstances already exist, albeit in a limited sphere. Popular print media, educational-textbook publishers, the Department of Defense, and other bureaucratic agencies routinely measure (and revise accordingly) the documents they produce using average word and sentence length as well as the readability statistics, such as the Flesch-Kincaid Grade Level, derived from them.[77] Widely used word-processing programs like Microsoft Word now generate these statistics automatically. By providing the material, instrumental means to identify statistics like sentence length or readability scores, word processors *make* them into markers of style. Hugh Craig writes that forensic studies of style "avoid perceptible features if possible, working at the base strata of language where imitation or deliberate variation can be ruled out," but such studies, and the text-analysis tools they build and use, simultaneously enlarge the domain of the perceptible and imitable they seek to avoid.[78] There is no stable, ahistorical base stratum of language that will forever elude notice and manipulation. In the most recent stage of an arms race that is as old as philology itself, the computationally intensive metrics generated by the analysis of digital texts become part of the toolkit of the forger no less than that of the stylistic sleuth. Authors seeking to dissimulate the telltale fingerprints of their identities can now acquire the instruments to manipulate the sentence-length distributions, the relative frequency of definite and indefinite articles, and even function-word skipgrams of a document. By measuring the inimitable fingerprints of style, computational stylistics makes those fingerprints imitable, expanding the domain of perceptible and imitable markers rather than merely discerning a domain already in existence.

Drawing on the philosophy of speculative realists like Quentin Meillassoux and Ray Brassier, Michael Witmore has proposed that quantitative measures specify a set of formal, mathematical relations that transcend the correlates of human consciousness to characterize the real nature of texts directly, as they are in themselves.[79] He argues that "PCA [principal component analysis], cluster analysis and the other techniques we use are clearly *inhuman* in the number of comparisons they are able to make." For Witmore, "the detour through mathematics is a detour *away* from consciousness" even if mathematical characterizations in some cases converge with human interpretive categories. Yet what is transcended is not the domain of human consciousness and interpretation *tout court* but rather the domain marked out by earlier interpretive conventions. (Principal component analysis was invented in 1901, cluster analysis in 1932, and they have been applied to textual analysis only much more recently.) Computers and the algorithms that run on them are just the latest in a long line of prostheses used to characterize, manipulate, and cull texts. These tools are constitutive of the humans we are—or, if one prefers, the humans we have never been, since any original state of preprosthetic humanity is surely imaginary.[80] Computational analyses of digital texts enlarge the repertoire of markers, the set of facts and patterns we can identify and imitate. They turn new patterns and facts into correlates of perception.

In expanding the domain of stylistic markers, however, statistical analysis risks forsaking the project of literary history by transcending the past rather than seeking to describe it. Under computational analysis, *Paradise Lost* has more, or at least different, markers of style than it did for Milton and his readers. Stephen Ramsay has defended the legitimacy of algorithmic criticism by arguing that all interpretations necessarily deform the text and that the deformation of counting and computing, however unfamiliar, does not differ in kind from other interpretive practices.[81] If we accept (as Fish and Nietzsche would not) that there is a text prior to interpretive deformance, then Ramsay's argument is correct, but for the purposes of literary history it is beside the point, since the goal is not to practice any mode of deforming texts that promises "liberating visions of potentiality"[82] but rather to reconstruct how Milton (and other readers and writers) *actually* deformed the texts of their predecessors and had their texts deformed in turn. Without some minimal epistemological fidelity to the actual past instead of the transcendence of the merely potential, one cannot be said to be doing history at all.

### Translation Problems

An aggregate quantitative measure becomes an object of imitation, enters the semiotic domain, and serves as a mark bearing cultural meaning and memory only if and insofar as it shows up within a period's interpretive conventions, categories, and practices. It makes no difference unless it manifests as a difference. I refer to the process of manifestation as *translation* because, like the translation between languages, it always leaves a remainder or excess on both sides.[83] The proposition that a poem has an average sentence length of 24.6 words states both more and less than the proposition that it was written in long sentences. In some cases it is possible to reenact the translation process by treating statistics as precisifications of vague concepts. We might decide, for example, that all sentences containing more than, say, fifteen words count as long. Yet the very process of precisification entails all the philosophical problems of vagueness, including higher-order vagueness, in which the ostensible boundaries of vague concepts are themselves vague, and so on.[84] We might also ask what is to be gained by seeking quantitative precision in the first place, especially since vagueness was and remains a constitutive feature, not a failing, of concepts like *long* and *short*. For the project of literary history, a precise judgment may prove less accurate than the vague one it seeks to supplant.[85]

Translation is especially tricky with regard to causal inferences. On the one hand, scholars studying earlier periods can justly regard trends in aggregate measures as effects and therefore as indicative of changes in the conventions that caused them; translation takes place in the very process of explanation. Ted Underwood and Jordan Sellers perform translation when they explain the divergence of literary diction from that of nonfiction prose—literature's increasing use, beginning in the eighteenth century, of words that entered the language before the twelfth century—as the consequence of a "longer debate about language," in which poets and fiction writers sought to specialize "in the direction of old words that would appear plain, common, and universal."[86] Causality runs from conventions to measures, and explanation traces the reverse course. Yet aggregate measures are not merely epiphenomenal, effects that emerge from a system without playing a further causal role in it. The yearly ratio of pre- to post-twelfth-century vocabulary caused nothing directly in itself; it exerted further influence only insofar as it was translated into the conventions that guided the interpretive acts of individual readers and writers.[87] Aggregate measures of texts or groups of texts were facts even when no one could see, identify, or imitate them. Before computational analysis, they existed in themselves, but not (yet) for readers and writers, and thus had no independent causal efficacy, no way of producing changes either in themselves or in the phenomenal world except insofar as they were phenomenalized. The way out of the semiotic domain is easy, but the way back is long and hard.

The problem of translating relative frequencies into perceptible signs is redoubled by the necessity of breaking a text up into discrete units, a process known as *tokenization*. The elements, or *tokens*, can in principle be any kind of consistent units (letters, morphemes, words, clauses, sentences, etc.). Tokenization is necessary because it is only as a fraction of the total number of tokens in a document or corpus that any sort of relative measure of distinct kinds of units, or *types*, can be calculated. Yet it is far from obvious that the conventions of earlier periods identified all markers of style as types of a token. As long as they are not working with *scriptio continua*, studies of diction can reasonably tokenize texts into words, since the very concept *diction* refers to the provenance of words. But what is the tokenization scheme proper to depictive adjectives? Should their frequency be measured relative to the total number of words, or adjectives, or predicate adjectives, or verb phrases, or sentences? Though one answer may prove more computationally tractable or yield more interesting or appealing results, from a historical standpoint there is no correct answer, since Milton and his contemporaries neither judged, nor had the interpretive practices to judge, this marker in relation to *any* single, consistent tokenization scheme. Such schemes are the product of computational needs rather than of language use or the concept of style.[88]

Despite these difficulties, the move from precise (24.8 words per sentence) to vague (really long) measures is the *least* complicated kind of translation, since it renders one judgment of magnitude in terms of another. Translations between quantities and qualitative concepts are far more difficult. Corns, for example, offers a quantitative analysis of the "Latinity" of Milton's style. On the grounds that "Milton is not likelier than the generality of other poets to conclude complex sentences with the main clause," he asserts that "syntactically, Milton dances to a thoroughly English tune."[89] Yet in drawing this conclusion he forgets or disregards his caution, only a page earlier, that "the concept of Latinity embraces larger and vaguer aspects of style than the sorts of postponement which may seem reminiscent of Latin periodic constructions."[90] In its early use, the term *Latinity* arose from early modern humanists' rich, if constitutively vague, understanding of the Latin language—its grammar, lexis, idioms, cadences, and so on.[91] Judging the issue of Latinity on the basis of a single syntactic measure (such as postponement, or the ratio of right-branching to left-branching sentences) is a consequence, so to speak, of poor translation, translation that empties the original concept of nearly all its content.

The computational response might be to translate a complex concept like Latinity into a set of weighted measures or to model it with a set of variable thresholds. Yet even this more sophisticated approach encounters a significant conceptual obstacle, an obstacle that can be understood through the distinction between an aggregate and a composite. Consider the following sentence, which appears shortly after the invocation to book 1 of *Paradise Lost*:

> Him the Almighty Power
> Hurled headlong flaming from th' ethereal sky,
> With hideous ruin and combustion down
> To bottomless perdition, there to dwell
> In adamantine chains and penal fire,
> Who durst defy th' Omnipotent to arms.

(1.44–49)

One might point to a number of possible markers as evidence of this sentence's Latinity: the syntactic inversion that Ezra Pound regarded as a "wrong" against Milton's "mother tongue," which places the object, "Him," before the subject and verb;[92] the long-delayed relative clause, "Who durst defy . . . ," which modifies the object fully five lines earlier; the use of words of Latin origin ("ethereal," "hideous," "ruin," "combustion," "perdition," "adamantine," "Omnipotent"); the delay of "flaming" (an object-oriented depictive) after the pronoun it modifies, "Him"; and so on. One might equally point to the absence of other markers, like the postponement of the relative clause ("Who durst defy . . .") to the end of the sentence, as well as the position of this sentence in the temporal and spatial unfolding of the poem and its relationship to the sentences that precede and follow it. The syntactic inversion that fronts "Him" is less jarring, less indicative of what Samuel Johnson called a "foreign idiom," because this sentence, like the preceding one, which begins, "Th' infernal serpent; he it was," is responding to a question asked eleven lines earlier: "Who first seduced them to that foul revolt?" "Him" is uttered not simply as an accusative but as an accusation. No one of these markers, divorced from the others, is sufficient evidence for or against the Latinity of the sentence (much less *Paradise Lost* as a whole).[93] They have evidentiary force only when considered together, in relation to one other, in the very structure and disposition of their appearance, as parts of a larger composite.

Computational analysis decomposes composites in order to measure them as aggregates; this is not incidental to but the basis of its analytical power. A particularly sophisticated analysis might be able to tally each of the markers of style mentioned above as tokens of various types and use them to generate an overall measure of Latinity. But the very act of counting and aggregating abstracts markers from their relationship to one another. Counting the fronted "Him" as a single instance of syntactic inversion removes it from the earlier sentences that distinguish it as an answer to a question. Likewise, it is only notable, as evidence of Latinity, that the sentence ends with a relative clause because it is relative *to* the first word of the sentence, five lines earlier. Computation decomposes composites regardless of the granularity of the measurement procedures: in measuring the frequency of these markers in the sentence itself (as opposed to in the corpus, document, book, or text chunk of set length), one would simply consider the markers relative to themselves, in the total density of their appearance, but get no closer to their compositionality. Moretti is right to insist that style is always a matter of relative frequency, but it is never just a matter of relative frequency. A Senecan approach studies the way markers are extracted from some composites and recomposed into others. But these compositions are precisely the aspect of style that computational analysis must decompose in order to count and compute.

Finally, even when one can, in retrospect, plausibly translate a quantity back into the categories and conventions of an earlier period, this is not by itself a reason to believe that translation actually took place. Infinite textual facts (patterns, properties, attributes, components, what have you) remained wholly untranslated, and thus invisible, in earlier periods, just as infinite facts still remain invisible to us now. In the terms that Graham Harman's object-oriented ontology adopts from Martin Heidegger, all texts partly "withdraw" (*zurückziehen*) from their relation to us.[94] Because our conceptual resources, tools, practices, and motives are limited, the historical domain of markers will only ever be a limited subset of a text's infinite reserve. No matter what tools or methods we bring to bear, the perceptible domain of markers will always be finite, while the shadowy domain of textual facts will persist innumerable, unmeasured, unimitated, withdrawn from presence.

The historical limits on the domain of markers, along with the resulting translation problems, currently prevent the Senecan and computational approaches from forming a single, unified or synthetic method of inquiry into the history of style. Instead these approaches constitute, in their nonunity, a negative dialectic, with each serving as a continuous reminder or critique of the other's limitations. I have devoted attention to what the Senecan approach reveals about the limits of computation, but computation reveals the limits of Senecanism in turn. Because the study of individual markers grasps composites *as* composites, it must perpetually defer the characterization of the whole that statistical measures achieve through aggregation. Without quantification, moreover, it can only grasp markers of style, like Milton's depictive adjectives, that appear infrequently enough to examine individually, case by case, as they are integrated into larger composites. It would be inadequate, for example, as a method of characterizing all biclausal sentences in a sizable corpus of novels, as the Stanford Literary Lab has done.[95] Without quantification, the approach to style proposed here can suggest, in Seneca's terms, the flowers that compose the honey but never specify the proportions of the blend, much less how those proportions change over time, between genres, across larger collections of texts, and so on. Befitting the antinomies of the concept of style, the negative relationship between Senecan and computational approaches is liable to endure—and with it the nonidentity of style and thought.

# CONCLUSIONS

# 7

## Shakespeare's Constructicon

### More Than Words, Words, Words

Shakespeare's works have long been the sandbox of philologists, historical linguists, and especially lexicographers, who for more than two centuries have produced an impressive array of general and specialized dictionaries, glossaries, lexicons, and *Wörterbucher*. David and Ben Crystal's *Shakespeare's Words* (2002) is a recent and popular representative of a long line of lexicons stretching back at least to Thomas Dolby's *The Shakespearian Dictionary: Forming a General Index to All the Popular Expressions, and Most Striking Passages in the Works of Shakespeare*, which was published in 1832.[1] As Dolby's title suggests, early Shakespeare dictionaries were not fully distinct from other reference genres like indexes, concordances, or phrase books.[2] In an age when computers produce concordances with the click of a mouse, it is easy to forget that works like *A Concordance to Shakespeare*, compiled by Andrew Becket in 1787, and *An Index to the Remarkable Passages and Words Made Use of by Shakespeare*, which Samuel Ayscough, affectionately known as "the prince of index makers," published in 1790, were monuments of lexicographical labor, scholarship, and erudition in their own right.[3] The last century and a half has witnessed more general Shakespeare dictionaries, lexicons, indexes, concordances, phrase books, and collections of quotations than I have purpose to mention here, and the last seventy-five years have increasingly given rise to works of specialized lexicography, of which Eric Partridge's *Shakespeare's Bawdy*, a 1947 essay followed by a glossary of naughty words, is the most influential example.[4]

The specialized business of Shakespeare dictionaries is by all appearances flourishing. In 2011 Bloomsbury purchased Continuum, and with it

Continuum's series of dictionaries on particular topics within Shakespeare, now published (and often reprinted) in the Arden Shakespeare Dictionary series. A curious student can consult *Shakespeare's Religious Language: A Dictionary*, *Shakespeare's Demonology: A Dictionary*, *Shakespeare's Plants and Gardens: A Dictionary*, and so on for women, music, books, medical language, political and economic language, and class and society, with more titles to come.[5] Suffice it to say that Shakespeare has sponsored a significant portion of the English lexicographical enterprise.

I come to praise, not to bury, the massive, collective, philological achievement of more than two hundred years of Shakespeare scholarship, and yet I want to argue that lexicographical reference works, even in the aggregate, are far from cataloging the symbolic resources that Shakespeare employed in writing the plays and poems. Existing lexicons inventory words and sometimes fixed expressions (lines, phrases, "popular expressions," "remarkable passages"). But with a notable exception that this chapter returns to later, they have no purchase on the abstract, variable, and productive Saussurean signs that I have been calling linguistic forms. From the culture of his day Shakespeare inherited not only words but also an immense repertoire of forms that he put to both conventional and innovative use in his poems and plays.

This chapter proposes a new work of philological reference that will incorporate Shakespeare's linguistic forms as well as his fixed words and phrases. Cognitive and constructional linguists have taken to calling this kind of reference work a *constructicon*, a word coined by analogy to *lexicon*, no doubt with a tip of the hat to the team of evil construction vehicles in the cartoon series *Transformers*.[6] A linguistic constructicon is a structured repertoire of constructions—conventional signifier-signified pairings of varying complexity and abstractness. In order of increasing abstraction, the full continuum of constructions includes the following:

— Individual morphemes: the *er* in *wrestler* and *minister*
— Words found in lexicons: cozener, coxcomb
— Fixed idioms and conventional multiword expressions: "let be" (*Hamlet* 5.2.233, *Antony and Cleopatra* 4.4.9, *Winter's Tale* 5.3.75), "in faith" (*Merchant of Venice* 1.3.164, 2.4.13, 5.1.155, 5.1.179, etc.)[7]
— Variable idioms: "giving him the lie," "gave thee the lie" (*Macbeth* 2.3.37, 39)

— Partially unfilled or lexically open constructions like the *way*-construction: "presently you take your way for home" (*All's Well that Ends Well* 2.5.68), "thou dost make thy way / To noble fortunes," "Go thrust him out at gates, and let him smell / His way to Dover" (*King Lear* 5.3.34–35, 3.7.113–14)[8]

— Wholly unfilled constructions or phrasal patterns with no fixed lexical components, like the ditransitive *Subj V Obj₁ Obj₂*: "the fated sky / Gives us free scope" (*All's Well that Ends Well* 1.2.223–24), "Deliver me the key" (*Merchant of Venice* 2.8.65)[9]

— Constructions as abstract, pervasive, and semantically general as *[Subject] [Predicate]*: "He dies" (*Julius Caesar* 5.5.57 stage direction), "It wearies me" (*Merchant of Venice* 1.1.2), "You come most carefully upon your hour" (*Hamlet* 1.1.6).

The term *linguistic form*, as I have been using it, refers only to those constructions that are at least partially lexically unfilled, abstract, variable, and therefore capable of producing and being instantiated in multiple distinct utterances. In what follows I share three examples of the kinds of linguistic forms that could eventually become entries in a Shakespeare constructicon. Building this new kind of reference genre is a distinctly twenty-first-century project, and not least, as I have already suggested, because discovering the linguistic forms that Shakespeare inherited and employed requires advanced query tools, like CQPweb (cqpweb.lancs.ac.uk), that can search the roughly forty-four thousand–odd Early English Books Online Text Creation Partnership (EEBO-TCP) Phase I and Phase II full texts using POS tags and regular expressions.[10] In addition, the complex task of organizing the constructicon in a way that both represents its conceptual structure and allows users to consult it conveniently will require hypertext media and relational databases.

Building a constructicon is not simply a positivist exercise—an excuse to collect and catalog more facts about Shakespeare's language—but a challenge to some of the most durable and entrenched notions of how language works. A Shakespeare constructicon will require expanding our account of the conventional linguistic knowledge Shakespeare learned through experience as well as our account of how he employed that knowledge in writing the plays and poems as we have them. The very notion of a constructicon, as a single repertoire of combinatory symbolic units of varying complexity and abstraction, puts pressure on the longstanding separation of grammar from lexicon. I propose building a *Shakespeare Constructicon*, then, as a way to prompt reconsideration both of Shakespeare's linguistic creativity and of his dependence on the linguistic culture that Stephen Greenblatt has rightly called "the supreme instance of a collective creation."[11]

### Filling Forms

There is no reason to suppose, and no evidence to suggest, that anyone had ever previously spoken or penned the particular sequence of nine words with which Hamlet begins his second soliloquy: "O, what a rogue and peasant slave am I!" (2.2.577). Obviously, Shakespeare learned each of this line's component words and their meanings from his experience of talking to people and reading texts. It is possible to look up each of its lexical items—*rogue*, *peasant*, *slave*—in a general dictionary like the *Oxford English Dictionary*, a general Shakespeare dictionary, or, as of 2007, Paul Innes's *Class and Society in Shakespeare: A Dictionary*.[12] We might also research the history of the ostensibly pleonastic bigram *peasant slave*, which Shakespeare could have encountered in a 1581 English translation of Seneca.[13] Turning to formal considerations, we might note that Hamlet's line is an exclamation, one marked by the initial "O," the funny use of "what," and, in most modern editions, an exclamation point, though in the First Folio it was punctuated by a question mark. It contains a trope related but not identical to *hendiadys*, the expression of a single idea through two coordinated elements (from the Greek *hen dia duoin*, "one through two"), as when Macbeth uses *sound and fury* (*Macbeth* 5.5.30) in place of *furious sound*. Here, by contrast, three semantically proximate words—*rogue*, *slave*, and *peasant*—are arranged into two coordinated noun heads, with the third word (*peasant*) subordinated to the second as an adjective.[14]

Working within the framework of transformational grammar, an earlier generation of critics like Richard Ohmann, Donald Freeman, and Seymour Chatman might also have offered a rule-based account of the grammar of Hamlet's exclamation, first reconstructing a semantically determinative *deep structure*, *I am a rogue and peasant slave*, formulated according to a system of *base* or *phrase structure* rules, and then deriving from it the *surface structure* that we hear on stage or read on the page through the transformation known as *wh-movement*, which accounts both for the fronting of

**Table 1**

| Date | Result | Date | Result |
|------|--------|------|--------|
| 1547 | what a wretch & Caitiff am I | 1593 | what a notable Ass indeed was I |
| 1549 | what a fool am I | 1593 | What a Calimunco am I |
| 1562 | what a man am I | 1593 | what a fool am I |
| 1566 | what a mad man am I | 1594 | what a miserable wretch am I |
| 1568 | what a nody was I | 1596 | what a fool am I |
| 1572 | what a fool were I | 1596 | what a fool am I |
| 1573 | what a gross hedded fool am I | 1596 | what a doting fool was I |
| 1574 | what a foreign Being am I | 1597 | what a fool was I |
| 1574 | what a lively picture am I | 1597 | What a wretch was I |
| 1579 | what a wretch am I | 1598 | what a fool am I |
| 1579 | what a coward am I | 1598 | what a fool am I |
| 1582 | what a wretch and caitiff am I | 1599 | what a fool am I |
| 1582 | what a state am I | 1599 | what a wretch am I |
| 1583 | What a yeoman is I | 1599 | what a pussell am I |
| 1585 | What a drunken wooer am I | 1599 | what a stock am I |
| 1589 | What a wretched fool am I | 1599 | what a trouble am I |
| 1589 | what a doleful case am I | 1599 | What a villain was I |
| 1590 | what a lamentable case were I | 1599 | what a villain am I |
| 1590 | what a fool am I | 1600 | what an horrible monster am I |
| 1590 | what a traitor am I | 1601 | what a Caitiff am I |
| 1592 | What a Calimunco am I | 1602 | what a beast am I |
| 1592 | What a fool was I | 1603 | what a dunghill idiot slave am I |

"what" and the subject-auxiliary inversion "am I."[15] Digitally assisted inquiry suggests a different mode of analysis, one that proceeds by comparing the utterance not to a posited deep structure but to other actual, historically proximate utterances that share the same form. Shakespeare could have encountered more than sixty instantiations of the linguistic form *what [Indefinite Noun Phrase] [Copula] I* in published texts prior to the entry of *Hamlet* into the Stationers' Register in July 1602, a number that obviously takes no account of the form's prevalence in spoken language (table 1).

The utterances in table 1 were retrieved using the search string *what _ AT\* | \* \* \* \*_VB\*I*, where _AT\* matches all articles (*a, an, the*), + \* \* \* \* matches between one and five words, and _VB\* matches any form of the verb *to be*.[16] Taken together, they offer considerable evidence that Hamlet's opening line was produced by filling an inherited linguistic form for which the noun-phrase blank specifies an insult and the resulting utterance serves as a self-reproach, lament, or self-accusation. Hamlet himself returns to the same linguistic form again, filling it still more conventionally, only slightly later in the second soliloquy: "Why, what an ass am I!" (2.2.611). The first quarto (Q1) publication of *Hamlet*, in 1603, long thought to be a memorial reconstruction by the actor who played Marcellus, gives the soliloquy's opening self-reproach as "Why what a dunghill idiote slave am I?"[17] Whoever misremembered, rewrote, or wrote the Q1 line employed the same linguistic form, with the same semantics, pragmatics, and indeed prosody, as the Folio and other quarto versions but filled it with a different phrasal constituent.[18]

We can imagine Hamlet acceptably filling the linguistic form with an approbative noun phrase (*What a fair creature am I!*), but it would have been a deviation from the semantic and pragmatic conventions established by repeated use, conventions to which Shakespeare adhered over the entirety of his career. In his final exit from the stage, a disillusioned Caliban uses the form in the past tense to reproach himself for serving Stephano:

> I'll be wise hereafter
> And seek for grace. What a thrice-double ass
> Was I to take this drunkard for a god,
> And worship this dull fool!
>
> (*The Tempest* 5.1.351–54)

Throughout its instantiations in the First Folio, the noun phrase, the tense of the copula, and the indefinite article *a/an* vary, but the form and its function as self-accusation persist unchanged:

— what a thrice double Ass Was I
— what a beast am I
— what a fool am I
— what a beast was I
— What a wicked Beast was I
— What an Ass am I
— what a Rogue and Peasant slave am I[19]

With more time, one might make the argument that *what [Indefinite Noun Phrase] [Copula] I* acquired its self-accusatory function within an English Protestant culture increasingly focused on what the *Thirty-Nine Articles of Religion* termed the "fault and corruption of the nature of every man," a doctrine that held that no one, as Hamlet says, "should 'scape whipping"

(2.2.555–57).[20] Developing this argument would require one not simply to identify semantic and pragmatic consistency but actually to read through the various instances of the form in context, asking the kinds of concrete philological questions that have long guided the study of words and phrases: who was using it? for what ends? in what kinds of documents? A Shakespeare constructicon would thus necessarily look beyond Shakespeare's works to study the linguistic resources available in Elizabethan and Jacobean England. Only through comparison with other texts (as opposed to a deep structure) is it possible to make a credible case that "O, what a rogue and peasant slave am I!" instantiates a form that Shakespeare learned and used to produce new utterances. One cannot understand the linguistic form of this utterance in isolation any more than one can understand sonnet form by reading a single sonnet. The analysis of linguistic forms does more than describe the abstract, grammatical structure of Shakespeare's utterances; it also ascertains, through comparison, those forms' conventional discursive function within the linguistic culture of Shakespeare's day.

A second example of a linguistic form that might earn an entry in a Shakespeare constructicon makes evident the explicitly social stakes of this philological project. The ghost of the dead king Hamlet returns to tell his son that he was "Cut off, even in the blossoms of my sin, / Unhouseled, disappointed, unaneled" (*Hamlet* 1.5.83–84). The words in the second of these lines each warrant an entry in a general Shakespeare lexicon, as well as in most editorial notes. The third-series Arden *Hamlet*, for example, glosses *unhouseled* as "without having taken the sacrament"; *disappointed* as "unprepared"; *unaneled* as "not anointed, i.e. without having taken extreme unction."[21] Using digital archives, it would be easy enough to explore the history of these words, the various contexts of their use, their illocutionary force, and so on. But this would tell us nothing of the linguistic form of the line: three coordinated, negated, multisyllabic, past (passive) participles in succession. Like the words it accommodates, this lexically unfilled form is also a sign that has a history, a discursive function, a meaning. The search query _VVN * _VVN * _VVN in CQPweb matches three past participles in succession, with the optional token symbol (*), or wildcard, allowing for commas or concatenators.[22] The search string produces 2,139 matches in 1,007 texts between 1470 and 1610.

That's a lot to read through instance by instance, even in an efficient snippet format, but grouping by frequency makes some patterns evident.

**Table 2**

| Search Result | Occurrences | Percentage |
| --- | --- | --- |
| hanged, drawn and quartered | 146 | 1.31 |
| revealed and made known | 102 | 0.92 |
| drawn, hanged and quartered | 95 | 0.85 |
| published and made known | 62 | 0.56 |
| hanged drawn and quartered | 53 | 0.48 |
| manifested and made known | 47 | 0.42 |
| granted, bargained and sold | 43 | 0.39 |
| drawn hanged and quartered | 27 | 0.24 |
| discovered and made known | 27 | 0.24 |
| concluded, accorded and agreed | 27 | 0.24 |
| Levied, Collected and paid | 26 | 0.23 |
| admitted, Instituted and Inducted | 25 | 0.22 |
| declared and made known | 24 | 0.22 |
| elected, called, justified | 22 | 0.20 |
| adjudged, deemed and taken | 22 | 0.20 |
| supposed and taken for granted | 20 | 0.18 |
| Printed and Published. Given | 19 | 0.17 |
| read, published and Registered | 18 | 0.16 |
| given, granted and confirmed | 18 | 0.16 |
| made known and discovered | 17 | 0.15 |
| devised, advised or required | 16 | 0.14 |
| covenanted, granted and agreed | 16 | 0.14 |
| limited, expressed and declared | 14 | 0.13 |
| laid, assessed, raised | 14 | 0.13 |
| assessed, raised and levied | 14 | 0.13 |
| preached and made known | 14 | 0.13 |
| predestined, called, justified | 14 | 0.13 |
| promulgated and made known | 14 | 0.13 |
| presented, instituted and inducted | 14 | 0.13 |
| given, taken and eaten | 13 | 0.12 |
| known, observed and practised | 13 | 0.12 |
| Raised, Levied and Paid | 13 | 0.12 |
| Seen and allowed. Imprinted | 12 | 0.11 |
| made known and revealed | 12 | 0.11 |
| opened and made known | 11 | 0.10 |
| covenanted, concluded and agreed | 11 | 0.10 |

Table 2 lists the most frequent instantiations of this form in the sixteenth and seventeenth centuries. Such a list has the potential to produce surprises in its own right: one hopes the variation in the order of the formula "hanged, drawn and quartered" was not reflected in the sequence of the punishments.[23] But reading down the list, a well-defined pattern emerges. With remarkable consistency, three passive past participles were in Shakespeare's day used in legal or liturgical formulas: "read, published and Registered," "made, promised, and subscribed," "covenanted, granted and agreed," "granted, bargained and sold" "predestined, called, justified." This form persists, with the same discursive function, in present-day English, perhaps most memorably in the Stevie Wonder song "Signed, Sealed, Delivered I'm Yours." In legal and liturgical contexts, the sequence of participles names and even performs official or ceremonial actions. The form is filled by *passive* participles so that those who perform the actions—the agents who will hang, draw, and quarter; or read, publish, and register; or agree, appoint, and accord; or housel, appoint, and anneal—may do so as the indifferent and substitutable representatives of a corporate agency like the state or the church. It is filled by *past* participles because its function is to announce completed (or *perfect*) actions—proclamations irrevocably proclaimed; ceremonies concluded; contracts signed, sealed, and delivered. Hamlet's father negates each of participles in the conventional form to describe rites that have gone uncompleted, unfinished, unperformed—with hellish consequences. The entry for this form in Shakespeare's Constructicon would not be just about its use in *Hamlet*. It would record the social provenance of the form, showing how it derives from and retains the imprint of a particular sphere of life—how, as Mikhail Bakhtin writes, it is "populated—overpopulated—with the intentions of others."[24] It would also observe the way Shakespeare alters the inherited form, adapting it to the dramatic situation of the play through negation (*un-*, *dis-*, *un-*). Without the ability to identify and study the derivation of even lexically unfilled forms like this one, we will be unable to hear a significant section of the social chorus in which Shakespeare sang, much less the peculiar and inventive ways that he joined his own voice to that chorus.[25]

Neither of the linguistic forms I have explored so far were necessary elements of the grammar of early modern English, elements without which Shakespeare would not have been a competent user of the language. He could have written the opening line of Hamlet's second soliloquy without participating in the form *what [Indefinite Noun Phrase] [Copula] I*, since the line could be an instantiation of a more general, abstract, and semantically neutral form (or indeed a repetition of an utterance he heard elsewhere). Likewise, he did not need a tripartite linguistic form inherited from legal or liturgical utterances to write the line "Unhouseled, disappointed, unaneled"; he could have concatenated and negated three past participles without having heard or seen others doing so. For this reason linguistic forms of this kind make no appearance in traditional grammars, prescriptive or descriptive, and traditional grammars, conversely, tell us nothing about linguistic forms of this kind beyond whether they are grammatically acceptable or not. A Shakespeare constructicon, by contrast, would inventory the forms he necessarily possessed in common with his linguistic community at large, as well as the contingent forms that he in fact possessed, though many other members of his community may not have. While the rules of Shakespeare's grammar, traditionally conceived, differ little or at all from those of early modern English more generally, a constructicon would catalog his idiolectal repertoire of linguistic forms, a repertoire that differs (as his lexicon does) from that of every other English speaker before or since.

Though Shakespeare need not have possessed a linguistic form consisting in a sequence of three, concatenated past participles, this form, as I have described it, has a legal and ceremonial significance, a meaning and discursive function, that was not associated with past participles taken individually, with their concatenation, or with the word *unhouseled*, *disappointed*, or *unaneled*. Lexical analysis is unable to take account of this form's semantic and pragmatic role in the line. Whether the line is in fact an instantiation of this form as Shakespeare had learned it from his linguistic community and whether it consequently merits inclusion in a Shakespeare constructicon is a question not of logical or formal necessity but of philological judgment based on evaluating comparative and historical evidence (drawn from corpora like EEBO) as well as the evidence of Shakespeare's works themselves. For the sake of inclusion in a constructicon, one need only use this evidence to make the probable, contingent, historical case that a form was actually part of Shakespeare's linguistic repertoire and, as an abstract linguistic sign, was associated with a particular meaning and discursive function.

If scholars were to undertake the project of reassembling Shakespeare's repertoire of linguistic forms, they would have at least one distinguished predecessor: Alexander Schmidt, whose *Shakespeare-Lexicon*, a massive work of nineteenth-century German philology that was first published in 1874 and was still in print, in updated editions, as late as 1987 with the added English subtitle *A Complete Dictionary of All the English Words, Phrases, and Constructions in the Works of the Poet*.[26] Schmidt's reference work lists the kinds of abstract and variable constructions that I have been calling linguistic forms under alphabetical word entries, with the consequence that the entries for grammatical function words like articles, prepositions, and the verb *to be* are exceptionally long. Consider extracts from the multicolumn entry for the article *the*:

> **The** (often apostrophized before vowels . . . )
>
> the definite article, employed in general as at present: "the sun," Ven. 1. . . .
>
> Sometimes instead of the possessive pronoun: . . . "he bites the lip," R3 IV, 2, 27. . . .
>
> Before two comparatives, denoting corresponding gradation (cf. Much): "the mightier man, the mightier is the thing that makes him honoured," Lucr. 1004. . . .
>
> The first comparative replaced by another form of expression, or supplied in thought: "her words are done, her woes the more increasing," Ven. 254. "and that his beauty may the better thrive, with Death she humbly doth insinuate."

Under the heading of the word *the*, Schmidt describes what present-day linguists sometimes call the *comparative correlative* or *The Xer the Yer* construction.[27] In addition to giving a definition of *the*, he uses the entry to classify a linguistic form in which it plays a prominent role. (I see no indication that Schmidt was aware, as linguists later established, that the *the* in the comparative correlative is not the definite article at all but a descendant of the Old English demonstrative *Þe*.) David and Ben Crystal's *Shakespeare's Words* does not have an entry for *the*.

The example of Schmidt's *Shakespeare-Lexicon* is doubly instructive. First, it suggests that the project of inventorying the repertoire of Shakespeare's linguistic forms is not just the product of a faddish linguistic theory or technological optimism but has fairly deep philological roots. Second, it illustrates some of the constraints that print tools and lexical organizational schemes have historically placed on the project of discovering, studying, collecting, and organizing Shakespeare's linguistic forms and words. The alphabetical order of Schmidt's volume is inadequate to the array of linguistic entities it aims to inventory and make available for consultation. Under what heading does a lexicon place linguistic forms that have more than one fixed lexical component, such as *what [Indefinite Noun Phrase] [Copula] I*? Where does it record abstract linguistic forms that have variable word order and therefore no first letter by which they can be alphabetized? There is no way to know, and the preface to Schmidt's work does not address the matter. It is unlikely, at any rate, that a speaker's grasp of the definite article *the* is sufficient to explain his or her ability to understand or use the comparative correlative. Still more seriously, alphabetical order is obviously inadequate for storing and retrieving linguistic forms (like the sequence of three past participles) that have *no* fixed or necessary lexical content and therefore no alphabetical content whatsoever. Finally, even if it were capable of supporting consultation, Schmidt's volume has no mechanism for expressing the network of hierarchical and lateral relations between linguistic forms—no way, to adopt a different idiom, of locating forms in relation to their parents, children, or siblings.

Where print reference works fall short, the affordances of digital tools like hypertext media and relational databases offer promising though by no means simple or readymade solutions to the challenge of organizing a constructicon. Though determining the hierarchical and lateral relations between linguistic forms will be especially tricky, Shakespeare constructi-cographers can begin by looking both to the work of linguists like Charles J. Fillmore and Adele E. Goldberg and to the model provided by the Berkeley FrameNet project, so far the only serious attempt to plan and execute a digital constructicon of late modern English.[28] Linguistic forms also pose a taxonomy problem that is lessened, though not solved, by databases and hypertext. As I mentioned in chapter 1, words wear their own nametags, while linguistic forms, in their abstraction and variability, are naturally anonymous. This means that if we wish to organize them, they must come forward, as do the animals in Genesis, to be given a name—or at the very least an address where they can be called on. FrameNet relies on an unavoidably technical and idiosyncratic assortment of descriptive names that linguists have accreted over decades: names like "long.NPI," "Reciprocal_predicate_pumping," and even "Count-to-Mass.meat." The form *X [Copula] X*, for which the prototypical instance is *when men were men*, is labeled the "tautology.nostagia" construction, which is sensible enough, if hardly transparent. But how many humanists will gather from its name what the "Degree_qualifier_realization" is or means unless they undertake substantial training?

The taxonomy problem grows as the number of linguistic forms does. While a Shakespeare constructicon will not be able to sidestep entirely the need for a descriptive taxonomy of linguistic forms, it could, I believe, be accessed and consulted in a more convenient and intuitive way than a general constructicon of the language could, since it would aim to inventory only the linguistic forms that are instantiated in a finite and relatively small corpus: Shakespeare's works. (Because it inventories only the sign units found in Shakespeare's works, rather than all the units that were part of his linguistic competence, we might prefer to call this a *constructicordance*, on the model of concordance, rather than a constructicon.) The utterances in his works would provide exemplars—representative instantiations—of all the linguistic forms inventoried in the constructicon; they would also serve, consequently, as addresses where those forms could be found. A user who wished to look up the form or forms instantiated by "O what a rogue and peasant slave am I!" would not be required to memorize or recall the names of these forms but would instead search for or browse through to this line in *Hamlet*. Clicking on the line would bring up links to entries on the forms it instantiates, each with an account of its fixed and variable parts, discursive function, provenance, and relations to other forms. Clicking on a form like *what [Indefinite Noun Phrase] [Copula] I* would, in turn, bring up a list of the utterances in Shakespeare that instantiate it: Hamlet's subsequent "Why, what an ass am I," Caliban's "What a thrice-double ass / Was I," and so on. Especially for those who already know the plays and poems by heart, this organizational scheme would make it relatively easy to consult and navigate the full repertoire of symbolic units, of varying abstractness and complexity, that Shakespeare employed in his writings.

No less crucially, a digital constructicon could support, as a printed reference volume could not, ongoing debate over the linguistic form of Shakespeare's utterances. Consider the opening words of Hamlet's most famous soliloquy, "To be or not to be" (3.1.64), which Peter Stallybrass takes as an illustration of how Shakespeare "appropriated for his own use what he read or heard."[29] Treating the soliloquy as a "tissue of quotations," a phrase he quotes from Roland Barthes, Stallybrass offers examples of texts leading up to the publication of the second quarto of *Hamlet* that employ the same fixed sequence of six words, albeit with slight variation in orthography and punctuation:

1573 Ralph Lever: "to be or not to bée"
1584 Dudley Fenner: "to bee or not to be"

> 1588 Abraham Fraunce: "to bée, or not to bée"
> 1596 William Perkins: "to be or not to be"
> 1601 John Deacon: "to be, or not to be"
> 1603 Robert Rollock: "to be or not to be"
> 1604 Henoch Clapham: "to be, or not to be"
> 1604 William Shakespeare: "to be, or not to be"[30]

Stallybrass is right to use database search results like these to "help free us from the tyranny of proprietary authors" and to challenge the *sui generis* originality of Hamlet's utterance by placing it alongside other utterances available in Shakespeare's linguistic community.[31] Yet the examples he gives, no less than Barthes's concept of "quotation," suppose an insupportably narrow account both of Shakespeare's creativity and of his capacity to appropriate. Like any competent speaker, Shakespeare had the capacity to learn linguistic forms by generalizing across utterances, abstracting from words and phrasal constituents to variable categories. Like any competent speaker, he could also fill those categories in new yet situationally appropriate ways. An approach to intertextuality that limits appropriation to the quotation of fixed sequences of words does more than deflate notions of authorial propriety; it also restricts our understanding of how even new utterances, unattested sequences of words, are dependent on a larger linguistic community for their form.

A constructicon entry for Hamlet's "To be or not to be" would include multiple, potentially conflicting accounts of the linguistic knowledge Shakespeare employed in writing the phrase. Presumably this knowledge included the words *to*, *be*, *or*, and *not* and their meanings, as well how to employ *to* and *be* together as an infinitive verb, *or* as a disjunctive, and *not* as a negation.[32] Though this knowledge alone may be sufficient to account for the composition of the line, we should not rule out the possibility that he appropriated and repeated the fixed sequence of words *to be or not to be*, whether from one or more of the texts listed by Stallybrass or from some other source. Yet such appropriation is not as simple as the extracts offered by Stallybrass make it appear. Though Fraunce and Rollock, like the other authors on the list, wrote precisely the same sequence of words as Shakespeare, they nevertheless wrote that sequence as part of a different phrase structure in which *to be or not to be* takes a predicative complement: in Rollock's religious treatise, "after his death"; in Fraunce's

**Table 3**

| Search Result | Occurrences | Percentage |
| --- | --- | --- |
| to do, or not to do | 10 | 5.26 |
| to be or not to be | 10 | 5.26 |
| to believe or not to believe | 9 | 4.74 |
| to do or not to do | 7 | 3.68 |
| to eat or not to eat | 7 | 3.68 |
| To marry or not to marry | 6 | 3.16 |
| to be done or not to be done | 6 | 3.16 |
| to believe, or not to believe | 5 | 2.63 |
| to use or not to use | 5 | 2.63 |
| to use, or not to use | 3 | 1.58 |

logic handbook, "the cause, or effect."[33] Appropriating Hamlet's phrase from either of these sources would have required altering its phrasal structure, truncating the complement and reinterpreting the copular use of *to be* as an existential, an assertion of existence or life. Appropriation is only sometimes a matter of quotation or repetition; it often entails complex grammatical knowledge and linguistic creativity in its own right.

A POS-tagged corpus like CQPweb makes it feasible to consider comparative evidence for one further account of the phrase's linguistic form, *to X or not to X*, where *X* is an infinitive verb. Ordered by frequency, the 190 results returned by the search string *to _V+I * or not to _V+I* (in which *_V+I* matches all infinitive verbs including *be* and *have*) suggest the prevalence of this form in texts published before 1600 (table 3). In its most general use, *to X or not to X* denotes the disjunction between contradictory alternatives.[34] But the form also acquired a more specific function in the Reformation discourse of Christian liberty, as a 1591 pamphlet by the clergyman George Gifford makes evident:

> There are certayne middle actions, and things, which we call indifferent, because if we simply respect them in themselves, or in their owne nature, they bee neither good nor euil. In these consisteth one part of Christian libertie **to use or not to use** with knowledge and discretion. Now if we respect y^e very nature of these things, no Prince or church can change it, as to make them to become necessarily good, or necessarily euil in themselves to the conscience.[35]

In this discourse, *to X or not to X* indicates actions that are at once contradictory and indifferent—actions that, because they are neither commanded nor prohibited by scripture, good nor evil in themselves, Christians are free to perform or omit.[36] Glossing the First Epistle to the Corinthians 7:23, "Ye are bought with a price, be not the servants of men," the Protestant polemicist (and former Catholic priest) Thomas Bell writes in 1596 that it is "as if [Paul] had said, **to marrie or not to marrie** is in your owne election, let therefore neither Jew nor Gentile ouerrule your libertie, let none entangle your consciences, let none bring you into faithlesse bondage, let none impose that heauy yoke vpon your necks, which yee are no way able to beare."[37] Though discussions of this sort occurred most frequently in theological writings, Elizabethan parishioners attending Sunday services each week would have likely heard preachers fill *to X or not to X* with a variety of verbs (*do, use, marry, eat, drink, give, lend, write, abstain, confess, sing*), especially when they took their proof texts from Paul's epistles.

Did Shakespeare read or hear one or more of these utterances? He was certainly capable of abstracting from them to the linguistic form *to X or not to X*, but did he in fact do so? Is "to be or not to be" an instantiation of this form with the specific function it acquired in Reformation discourse? Would the audience of *Hamlet* (including Shakespeare himself, if only as a reader and reviser of his own writing) have understood it as such? Though it is impossible to say for certain, we cannot rule out an affirmative answer to these questions any more than we can rule out the possibility that Hamlet's words are merely a quotation. The plausibility of an affirmative answer depends on more than the evidence of the archive. We should be compelled by an analysis of an utterance's linguistic form when it aids in successful, fruitful, plausible interpretation. If Hamlet utters "to be or not to be" as an instantiation of the discursively specific form *to X or not to X*, he does so not simply as the expression of an abstract choice between contradictory alternatives, being and not being. Rather, in his despondency he considers nothing less than his own life under the category of things indifferent. He regards his own continued existence as neither good nor bad in itself. As he says to Rosencrantz and Guildenstern in the previous act, "There is nothing either good or bad but thinking makes it so" (2.2.268–70). In Hamlet's thinking, the domain of *adiaphora* extends well beyond its conventional scope in Protestant theology to encompass even suicide, so that making one's own quietus, if not prescribed, is not proscribed either. Rather than simply weighing the benefits of life and death, the lines that follow are Hamlet's attempt to make or discover, in the space of indifference opened by the evacuation of law, the minimal difference that he calls "the rub" (3.1.73) as the ground for further deliberation and choice.

A scholar adds to the inventory of Shakespeare's linguistic repertoire by giving a new account of the form of one of the utterances in the poems and plays. Such accounts will inevitably lead to debate, which a Shakespeare constructicon will need to support. A debate about the form of an utterance is also, as we have seen, a debate about what symbolic units compose it and consequently how to interpret its meaning and use. These debates promise to grow and mature as scholars use new digital corpora and corpus query tools to assemble the evidence necessary for developing multiple, interpretively consequential, and potentially incompatible accounts of the form of even ostensibly simple utterances like "to be or not to be."

### The Kingdoms of Language

Literary scholarship has long studied the way that texts are made of other texts, making use of Barthes's "tissue of quotations" as well as Julia Kristeva's concept of "intertextuality," Derrida's "citationality" and "grafting," and Bakhtin's "dialogism" and "heteroglossia," to show the dependence of every utterance on other utterances from literary and nonliterary spheres. A constructicon would be a systematic attempt to study the way Shakespeare inherited his syntactic no less than his lexical resources from specific spheres of early modern social life. Though it adopts Bakhtin's thesis that "verbal discourse is a social phenomenon—social throughout its entire range and in each and every of its factors," it would move beyond what he calls the "internal dialogism of the word" to hear the "variety of alien voices" in more abstract and complex sign units as well.[38] We live not only "in a world of others' words" but in a world of others' linguistic forms, forms that are abstracted from the "already uttered."[39] We systematically underestimate the already-made-ness of language when we conceive of it only in terms of words or phrases cut out from previous texts and pasted together, as in a ransom note. Replacing every instance of *word* in Bakhtin's writings with *linguistic form* would neither falsify nor diminish the force of his claims. Using searchable digital archives, the cyberformalist seeks to excavate the heteroglossic diversity of an utterance's form as the product not just of typified "social dialects . . . professional jargons, generic languages, languages of generations and age groups" but of other, actual utterances inscribed in other, socially located texts.[40] For every linguistic form, we seek to show, with Bakhtin, that it does not pass "freely and easily into the private property of the speaker's intentions" but is instead "populated—overpopulated—with the intentions of others."[41]

Building a Shakespeare constructicon would also represent a practical attempt to reunite the domains of lexicon and grammar into a single kingdom of sign units of varying complexity and abstraction and thereby to reject the de facto confinement of cultural and historicist literary studies to the lexicon.[42] That the current separation of grammar and lexicon still structures and limits our understanding of Shakespeare's language is most plainly manifest in the existence of two different genres of reference works. Centuries of dictionaries, glossaries, indexes, concordances, and vocabularies, as I have noted, represent the lexical domain. The ongoing publication of these lexical reference works suggests that they are in perennial need of revision, elaboration, and specification, much as plays warrant being restaged over and over again. In the past century and a half, by contrast, only four works of Shakespeare reference have systematically represented the domain of grammar: Edwin Abbott Abbott's *A Shakespearian Grammar* (1869), Wilhelm Franz's *Shakespeare-Grammatik* (1897, written in German), N. F. Blake's *A Grammar of Shakespeare's Language* (2001), and Jonathan Hope's *Shakespeare's Grammar* (2003).[43] While the lexicons have proliferated in ever more specialized forms to accommodate the rich, messy, and idiosyncratic vocabulary of Elizabethan and Jacobean culture, the intermittent grammars are works of exacting parsimony. In its Platonic ideal, a constructicon would obviate the need for separate Shakespeare dictionaries and grammars, capturing and making available for consultation the full range of Shakespeare's linguistic knowledge in a single organon.

Much of what would be included in a Shakespeare constructicon is already known. The field of Shakespeare's words has been harvested for many seasons. New accounts of the most pervasive, abstract, and semantically general forms, like the noun phrase or the passive voice, are unlikely to differ much, if at all, from the accounts already developed in the grammars of Blake and Hope. Yet there are more things in Shakespeare's language than are cataloged in our lexicons or grammars. Reunifying the kingdom of language would bring into view the vast and largely undiscovered country of partially and wholly unfilled forms that lies between the well-charted domain of concrete words and phrases to the south and the well-charted domain of the most abstract grammatical categories and structures to the north. Exploring this country—what we might think of as the overlooked midlands of Shakespeare's language—will require scholars to get comfortable using the kinds of digital tools made by corpus linguists, but it will otherwise employ, in the study of abstract linguistic entities, the philological skills and the literary and cultural expertise they already possess. If the project of building a systematic constructicon from scratch is too daunting, we might begin more modestly by gathering a collection of Shakespeare's most culturally consequential keyforms on the model of Raymond Williams's *Keywords*.[44] I began this chapter by noting that Shakespeare has long sponsored a sizable portion of English lexicography; I close with a wager that as a name, a figure, and a body of texts he remains capable of sponsoring new kinds of philological inquiry as well.

## 8

## God Is Dead, Long Live Philology

It is by touching, however lightly, on man's relation to the signifier . . .
changing the procedures of exegesis—that one changes the course of his
history by modifying the moorings of his being.

Jacques Lacan, "The Instance of the Letter in the Unconscious"

The previous chapters of this book employ a vocabulary, an idiom,
and indeed a repertoire of forms associated with empirical philological inquiry. They set out to define the abstract sign units I have called linguistic
forms as objects of knowledge and to show that they warrant historical and
cultural study; to describe the emerging techno-methodological conditions
of such study; to establish facts about the meaning, provenance, diffusion,
and variation of forms; to propose cultural and material explanations for
these facts; and even, in the preceding chapter, to envision the encyclope-
dization of forms in a systematic and consultable work of reference, a constructicon. Where there is language, there are linguistic forms. These forms
and their histories matter to the key concepts, narratives, and debates of
humanists. We should seek to understand them and tell their histories. The
preceding chapters show, at a minimum, that we must move the histories
of linguistic forms from the category of things we don't know that we don't
know to that of things we know that we don't know—but should.

Yet I wish to suggest that as a knowledge project cyberformalism stands
in service to the eminently humanistic activity that has long been taken to
oppose empirical inquiry: interpretation.[1] Linguistic forms are part of what
Martin Heidegger calls the as-structure of interpretation.[2] In Heidegger's
account, all experience is the interpretation of something as something. To

interpret an utterance is necessarily to understand it not only as a linear chain of concrete signs—words linked one after another—but also as a stratification of abstract signs—forms layered on and nested inside one another at various levels of abstraction.[3] By recuperating contingent linguistic forms as they have been instantiated in and across linguistic communities, acquainting us with signs that are not (or are no longer) part of our working linguistic knowledge, cyberformalist inquiry has the potential to recover interpretive possibilities for even the most scrutinized and studied of utterances. As we have seen, this is what differentiates cyberformalism most sharply from other, currently dominant modes of digital text analysis: rather than counting well-recognized, pre-individuated signs to produce new aggregate measures, it investigates signs that have otherwise passed without notice, even when they have been silently decoded and understood.[4] By expanding the system of signs beyond words to include linguistic forms, cyberformalism also expands the scope of interpretation, and with it the scope of concepts—ambiguity, polysemy, idiomaticity, indeterminacy—that resist the progressive establishment of positive fact. In this concluding chapter I aim, in a speculative mode, to probe cyberformalism's empirical limits, semiological prospects, and theoretical consequences by attending to its role in interpretation.

### The Stratification of Forms

As a final example of a well-known utterance that the historical study of linguistic forms can help us interpret anew, consider that well-worn slogan of secular modernity, Nietzsche's "Gott ist todt" (God is dead), which appeared first in *The Gay Science* (1882; expanded 2nd ed. 1887) and then in *Thus Spake Zarathustra* (1883).[5] Subsequent thinkers have powerfully reinterpreted this utterance. In Heidegger's reading, "The pronouncement 'God is dead' means: The suprasensory world is without effective power."[6] For him, "God" (*Gott*) refers, as a proper name, to "the Christian God" and also to metaphysics as such; the sense of "dead" (*todt*) is not of an organic body deprived of life but of a philosophy or belief system grown obsolete or impotent. More recently Alain Badiou has asked, "What is God the name of in the formula 'God is dead?'"[7] Dissenting from Heidegger, he argues for understanding the formula "literally" so that the name God refers only to "Isaac, Abraham, and Jacob's God, or the Christ who speaks directly to Pascal in his inner Garden of Gesthemane." The adjective "dead," in this reading, implies that the Christian God was once alive "like all living beings," possessing "the power of living in the pure present."[8] (Neither Heidegger nor Badiou directly explicates the "ist" of "Gott ist todt," though few thinkers have meditated so intensely on the meaning of the copula and its relation to being.)[9]

My aim is not to adjudicate between these competing interpretations but rather to point out the common interpretive assumption from which they proceed. Both Heidegger and Badiou are able to propose, explicate, and defend divergent readings of Nietzsche's pronouncement because the words *God* and *dead* are polysemous signs, signs bearing multiple potential senses and naming multiple potential referents. But while both thinkers variously construe the words of Nietzsche's pronouncement, neither sets out to question or explicate its syntax, with ample reason.

Oversimplifying somewhat, longstanding accounts of syntax distinguish between attachment ambiguities (discussed at some length in chapter 6) and categorization ambiguities. The sentence *The woman saw the man with the telescope* can indicate that either the woman or the man possessed the telescope, because the prepositional phrase *with the telescope* can attach either to the verb phrase *saw the man* or to the subordinate noun phrase *the man*. The newspaper headline "British Left Waffles on Falkland Islands" can mean either that left-wing British politicians reversed their position regarding the Falklands or that the British abandoned their waffles on the islands, since *British* can be categorized as either an adjective or a noun, *left* as a noun or a verb, and *waffles* as a verb or a noun. Both of these sentences have an inherently ambiguous syntax that permits multiple parses; only further context would allow us to select a single correct parse. Even so, all possible parses can be quantified. That is, we can count up the possible categorizations and attachments and from them compute a finite total number of possible acceptable syntaxes.[10]

According to the standard account, Nietzsche's "Gott ist todt" exhibits neither categorization nor attachment ambiguity. It has a single, unequivocal syntax. The predicative adjective, "todt," is linked to the subject, the proper noun "Gott," by the copula "ist." There is no other acceptable way to parse the sentence—to categorize its words or attach them to one another. Nietzsche's pronouncement is an instance of what has long been understood as the most fundamental, unequivocal, and universal linguistic form, the form least open to the contingencies of history, culture, or specific linguistic and discursive communities: simple predication, the joining of subject to predicate, *[Subject][Predicate]*, or *SP* for short. What's more, the predicative form with the copula, *S is P*, has been regarded, from the speculative grammars of the twelfth-century *modistae*, through the *Port-Royal Grammar* (1660) and its successors, to present-day generative grammar, as the primitive or irreducible form that underlies (whether as a logical form, kernel sentence, or deep structure) the multiplicity of possible surface expressions.[11] It is ostensibly to this primitive predicative form, unambiguous in itself, that all ambiguity can be reduced. As the *Port-Royal Grammar* has it, every verb encloses or contains (*enferme*) within it the copula *to be*, so that the sentence "Pierre lives" (*Pierre vit*) contains the claim that "Pierre is living" (*Pierre est vivant*); the "great diversity of verbs in each language" springs forth from the copula, which is alone necessary as the sign of judgment and affirmation.[12] Summarizing the grammarians of the classical period following *Port-Royal*, Michel Foucault writes that the "entire species of the verb may be reduced to the single verb that signifies *to be*. All the others secretly make use of this unique function, but they have hidden it beneath a layer of determinations" such that *to be* "forms the basis of the proposition" and, "by enabling language to affirm what it says, renders it susceptible of truth or error."[13] The form of "Gott ist todt" is all the more canonical because it instantiates, as Heidegger writes, "the third person singular of the present indicative" of the copula (in German, *sein*), which "has dominated our historical being-there since antiquity."[14] When Jacques Derrida writes that "Western metaphysics, as the limitation of the sense of being within the field of presence, is produced as the domination of a linguistic form," he is writing of *S is P*.[15] The preeminence of this form suggests that it is no accident that Nietzsche and his interpreters treat "Gott ist todt," rather than other roughly synonymous utterances such as "Gott starb" (God died), as the preeminent proclamation of divinity's demise.[16]

Yet in describing Nietzsche's pronouncement as an instance of simple predication, I have given only maximally abstract characterizations of its linguistic form. We cannot therefore conclude that *S is P* and predication as such, *SP*, are the only forms in which it participates. For it is both possible and, I will suggest, plausible that even this simplest and most syntactically unequivocal of utterances also, simultaneously and without contradiction, instantiates some number of more idiomatic, culturally specific, and partially unfilled forms.[17] Consider two possibilities:

The first, *God is P*, is what we might call the form of divine predication, a form used in the long tradition of Christian theology to define God and enumerate his perfections. The predicate is conventionally filled in two ways. It can be filled by a nominal, as in the Greek of John 4:8, "ho theos agape estin" (Vulgate's Latin: "Deus caritas est"; Martin Luther's German: "Gott ist Liebe"; the King James Bible's English: "God is love"). Or it can be filled by an adjective, as in Peter Abelard's assertion "Deus est omnipotens, omnisapiens, omnibenignus" (God is all-powerful, all-knowing, all-good); in Martin Luther's translation of 1 Corinthians 10:13, "Gott ist getreu" (King James Version: "God is faithful"); in Luther's translation of the prophet Baruch, "Gott is gerecht" (God is just); or in Nietzsche's own "Gott ist gnädig und barmherzig" (God is gracious and merciful).[18] Though divine predication's customary home is Greek and Latin theology, the form also assumed a prominent role in the philosophical discourse of Nietzsche's Germany. In his 1763 book on the possibility of demonstrating the existence of God, the young Kant offered "Gott ist allmächtig" (God is omnipotent) as a proposition that establishes a logical relation between subject and predicate without thereby asserting the existence of the subject.[19] And when G. W. F. Hegel, in the preface to *The Phenomenology of Spirit* (1806), sought to illustrate both "the nature of judgment or the proposition in general" and its dialectical negation, it was the theological proposition "Gott ist das Seyn" (God is being) that he offered as an example.[20]

The second form, *S is dead*, is abstracted from the cries heard, Ernst Kantorowicz recounts, at "the burials of French kings in the Abby of St.-Denis" as early as the "interment of Louis XII, in 1515": "Le roi est mort! . . . Vive le roi" (The king is dead! . . . Long live the king).[21] As an instantiation of this form, Nietzsche's pronouncement replaces the prototypical subject, *Le roi*, with *Gott*. As with instances of divine predication, the French proclamation of the king's death and continued life was current in Nietzsche's Germany; one German lexicon, published in the same year as the first part of *The Gay Science*, translates it into German as "Der König ist tot es lebe der König."[22]

Both of these intermediate, partially concrete, and idiomatic forms signify discursive functions beyond simple predication. To interpret "Gott ist todt" as an instantiation of either or both of these forms is to change our answer to the question, "What is this utterance doing?" Interpreted as an instantiation of *God is P*, it is the successor to a long tradition of divine predication. Far from being a bare predicate, *todt* is the final, subversive addition to a category prototypically populated by adjectives such as *everliving, omnipotent, omniscient, good, just, perfect, immutable, unchanging,* and *eternal* and, more distantly, by nouns such as *love, being, spirit, truth,* and so on, across multiple languages. By positing *dead* as the last predicate that replaces these prototypical others, the pronouncement's function is not simply to assert a proposition but to end the tradition of divine predication in which it participates, finishing off God's perfections by rendering them finite, mortal.

Interpreted as an instantiation of *S is dead*, "Gott ist todt" extends to God the persistence through death that "Le roi est mort" accords to the king, elevating political theology to theology proper. Nietzsche's pronouncement qualifies the proposition that God is dead through an implicit analogy. Much as the king's body politic, in medieval and early modern theories of regnal succession, survives the death of the king's body natural, so too does God survive his own death, though in a markedly different way. In its first appearance in *The Gay Science*, the announcement of death is followed immediately by an account of survival: "God is dead; given the way people are, there may still for millennia be caves in which they show his shadow.—And we—we must still defeat his shadow as well!"[23] What survives is not an eternal, spiritual body but rather an ideology, the idea of God as it dwells in the minds of humans and in their places of worship. "God is dead," proclaims Nietzsche, but history whispers back, *Long live the shadow of God*.

Here, then, is a provisional list of linguistic forms potentially instantiated in Nietzsche's pronouncement:

— *SP*
— *S is P*
— *God is P*
— *S is dead.*

Words are by their nature exclusive; by saying *no*, I exclude the possibility of saying *yes* at the same time. By contrast, linguistic forms can, as it were, cohabit with one other, accommodating the same utterance at different levels of abstraction without exclusion or contradiction. To the forms listed above we can add the possibility, raised by a number of source studies, that Nietzsche may be directly quoting an earlier text verbatim.[24] I have omitted from consideration a further form, *God [Verb] dead*, not for any a priori reason—no obstacle stands in the way of abstracting to this form and then filling it in a variety of acceptable ways—but because I have found no archival evidence to support its existence as a conventional sign unit.

Humanists are used to debating words, but except in occasional cases of homonymy or textual instability their debates concern how, rather than whether, words like *Gott* and *todt* are used.[25] Yet because linguistic forms are abstract, debates about which form or forms an utterance instantiates cannot be put to rest by pointing to a set of fixed marks on a page or even a parse tree that correctly identifies the categorization of words and their syntactic attachments. How, then, do we decide which forms, of various degrees of idiomaticity and abstractness, Nietzsche's pronouncement instantiates? The decision is not arbitrary, since the knowledge of ingroup speakers or the evidence of an archive may make some alternatives more plausible than others. Yet neither is it fully determinate, since there is always the possibility that an utterance participates in still other historically available forms at different levels of abstractness and idiomaticity, which means that we cannot, in advance of inquiry, compute a total, finite number of potential forms.[26]

Adjudicating between possible forms concerns signifier and signified at once. We ask which forms were current in the linguistic communities, discourses, and intellectual traditions to which Nietzsche belonged: Was *God is P* part of the conventional linguistic knowledge of nineteenth-century Prussian philologists? We ask how potential forms and their associated uses fit into our understanding of the larger textual wholes of which his pronouncement was a part: Did *The Gay Science*, or *Thus Spoke Zarathustra*, or Nietzsche's philosophical project at large aim to subvert theological traditions, and does this pronouncement play a role in achieving that aim?[27] We judge the idiomaticity of the pronouncement against our sense of the idiomaticity of his writings more generally: Was Nietzsche the kind of writer who used fixed phrasal templates, or did he stick to maximally abstract forms such as *SP*? Adjudicating between variously idiomatic forms in this way is not the peculiar activity of scholars. It is something language users do every day, every time they construe a written or spoken utterance. Yet especially when a text is from a different or distant linguistic culture, determining the form of an utterance draws on all the interpretive savvy and linguistic knowledge—all the historical and cultural expertise—that humanities scholars labor to acquire.

A skeptic might, at this point, dismiss both *God is P* and *S is dead* as irrelevant to Nietzsche's pronouncement, to its meaning and force, to his linguistic competence, or to his intentions in writing. It is entirely possible that the function of "Gott ist todt" is simply to assert a proposition such that only the most abstract predicative forms are needed to understand its truth value: "Gott ist todt" is true if and only if God is dead, or (in Heidegger's reading) if the supersensible has become impotent, or (in Badiou's reading) if the Christian religion is obsolete.[28] Yet to dismiss more idiomatic forms is already to make an interpretive judgment—a judgment about the as-structure of Nietzsche's utterance that is also a judgment about what it is doing, how it fits into the larger context of *The Gay Science* or *Zarathustra*, what linguistic conventions it employs, and so on. No a priori principle of economy or parsimony permits us to rule out relatively idiomatic forms such as *God is P*. If we do rule out such forms, we do so not in advance of interpretation but as an outcome of interpretation, not as an escape from the as-structure but as one possible way of inhabiting it.

### Limits and Prospects

I have suggested that cyberformalist inquiry, by increasing the potential semantic density even of utterances as ostensibly simple as Nietzsche's pronouncement, militates against attempts to give an a priori, ahistorical account, as well as a finite accounting, of syntactic ambiguity. Yet the most abstract form of Nietzsche's utterance—simple predication, *SP*—can help to make evident the limits of this method of inquiry itself. Most importantly, this linguistic form represents a transcendental limit. Forms like *God is P*, *[Verb] as if [Sentence]*, and *What would X Y?* are conventional sign units within the empirical field of discourse. They are present in some languages, epochs, cultures, communities, and discourses and not others. But simple predication is not one unfilled or open sign unit, one linguistic object, among others. It is a condition of the possibility of language, discourse, and culture and therefore exists at least partially in excess of any empirical determination. There is no way to say anything about anything without asserting something (a predicate) about something (a subject). Without *SP* it would be impossible, in Aristotle's terms, to accuse (in Greek, *kategorein*, the root of *category*) anything of anything, and therefore equally impossible to plead guilty or innocent.[29] Were, say, *X [be] the new Y* to vanish from living and written memory, English would be but one abstract sign, one contingent form, the poorer. But without *SP* there would be no English, no language at all. It is this form, rather than the copula *to be* or indeed any fixed mark or distribution of lexical marks, that is properly transcendental and transcategorial, transcending the categories it makes possible. Even if lists of words and their associated meanings were still to exist, in the absence of predicative form there would be no means of joining them into unified propositions, whether to categorize (*War is hell*) or to affirm self-identity (*War is war*). Without the glue of predication to bind them together, individual words would remain separate, merely proximate.[30] This transcendental limit imposes itself whether we accept a Husserlian account of predicative form in which *SP* (or, in Husserl's formulation, *Es ist so!*) is a "free ideality," an eternal idea that persists unaltered and unexhausted by any of its historical instantiations or instead regard it as the limit case of abstraction from the assertions of every and any language, and therefore as merely the most general of predicative idioms, the idiom abstracted furthest from idiomaticity.[31] Unlike the contingent panoply of more concrete and idiomatic forms, simple predication necessarily structures every discourse, including discourses that set out to study it (such as the one you are reading right now).

Practical constraints flow from this transcendental limit. As a consequence of its extreme abstraction, predication is instantiated in the full range of propositions: Joseph Conrad's "Mistah Kurtz—he dead," no less than Plato's "Socrates is mortal," no less than a mock newspaper headline such as "Area Man Only One With Problems." So mercurial are the instantiations of predication that no search engine currently in existence could begin to retrieve them all. We will always be at a loss in studying what we lack the instruments to find. Yet overcoming this technical limitation would be of questionable use, since there is little need to search for what we find everywhere. Like the air we breathe, *SP* is all around us, which means that locating it for study is not a technical problem. Where a relatively concrete form like *God is P* will accommodate only a sliver of utterances in any discourse or archive—a sliver, moreover, that is retrievable with simple search strings—the set of utterances that instantiate *SP* is virtually coextensive with discourse itself. Studying the history of predication as such would be like attempting to swallow the world of discourse whole. In the terms of Foucault's archaeology, the predicative form *SP* opens the infinite horizon in which the law of rarity manifests, the notional plenitude in comparison with which any discourse will necessarily be impoverished. But the poverty of any historical discourse, the distribution of its absences, only becomes available to inspection and study in the various ways comparatively concrete forms like *S is dead* are or are not instantiated across languages, periods, cultures, communities, discourses, genres, and so on.

Within the transcendental, practical, and technical boundaries traced out by the form *SP* lies a rich and largely uncharted domain of social and cultural as well as linguistic history. There await myriad histories to tell, facts to establish and explain, discursive functions to explicate, encoded cultural logics to analyze, forms to critique and contest. But the semiological prospects do not stop there. Just as Saussure's conception of the sign as a term within a differential system has had enormous consequences for inquiry well beyond natural language, so too will changes in the conception of the sign ripple out to other semiotic domains as well. How might the inclusion of linguistic forms in the domain of sign units have consequences beyond the philological study of language?

As with language, there is no full understanding of other sign systems— of fashion, or cars, or food, or more complex systems like mass media, cinema, television, and so on—without an understanding of the meaning and combinatory properties of variously complex and partially or wholly unfilled signs.[32] When Roland Barthes analyzed the "fashion system" to demonstrate the power, generality, and scope of semiotics, he had to reject the Saussurean assumption that signs were concrete units, the equivalent of words. "Except in cases of flagrant eccentricity," he writes, "the item signifies nothing." Rather, what signify in dress are "abstract, highly mobile, arbitrary forms," the analogues of what I have been calling linguistic forms.[33] We cannot understand the signifying possibilities of garments as the selection and assembly into outfits of discrete, substantive items, individually produced articles of clothing such as shoes, shirts, and socks (the analogues to the words of a natural language) from paradigms of possible alternatives (black or blue or brown checked socks). Instead we must understand it as a stratification of abstract and complex forms, in which individual items are replaceable. The analogue of a wholly abstract or unfilled linguistic form, for fashion, may be something like *work clothes, cocktail attire, exercise outfit,* or *Sunday best*. Each of these forms imposes a range of constraints on the substantive items of clothing in each paradigm without specifying any particular item (any single skirt or belt or shirt). Merely by choosing to put on a work outfit for my job as an English professor, for example, I know that I will need to wear (among other things) a collared shirt, though not which one, and dress socks, though not which pair. Colleagues likewise, I hope, understand my dress as a work outfit, a sign of at least a minimal threshold of professionalism, across and with a degree of indifference to otherwise signifying differences in, say, the width of my collar or the hue and pattern of my socks. Though the abstract forms of clothing, like linguistic forms, can be filled in variously conventional, innovative, and subversive ways, they will ordinarily be fixed-order templates, with the spatial relation of categories set by the structure of the body.

While the notion of linguistic form can profitably be exported to the study of some signifying systems, others already possess sophisticated conceptions of abstract symbolic units. Music theory, for example, has long analyzed and traced the histories of the motifs, themes, phrases, sentences, progressions, and melodies that maintain their identity and meaning even as they are varied and elaborated in constrained ways and transposed from one key, pitch class, tempo, and opus to another.[34] When such disciplines have well-developed accounts of abstract sign units, scholars of language should seek to learn rather than to teach.

By expanding the field of signs, the study of linguistic forms has the potential to change our understanding of the way various systems of meaning work and even to reconfigure many of the central questions of twentieth-century critical theory, not least the question of what it means to be a subject, a self. Foucault and other twentieth-century antihumanists sought to overgo Nietzsche by proclaiming the death of man as well as the death of God. Foucault weaponized Saussure's account of language as the chief engine in what he termed the "siege" on "the figure of man."[35] He argued that language effaces the illusory sovereignty of the speaking subject, "dissolv[ing]" it into an inhuman system of signs that it does not make and that long precedes it.[36] Yet Foucault's account of language as solvent leaves a human residue, an insoluble remainder. At least until 1966, he followed structuralists in distinguishing the horizontal actuality of the "signifying chain" from the "perpendicular" virtuality of the paradigm that "always produces a possible choice between several words."[37] Man may speak the words of another, but he selects and concatenates them into utterances by means of a grammatical power that nevertheless remains distinctly his own. As Foucault puts it an essay on Blanchot, the speaking subject is "no more than a grammatical fold" in the "continuous streaming of language."[38] In this description the subject is contracted ("no more than") to the minimal difference (a mere "fold") that grammar introduces into language, but grammar is, by same token, subtracted from the historicity of language.[39] The project of assimilating grammar to the system of inherited signs is the project of ironing out this fold. As long as the system of language is constituted solely of words—of what Foucault, citing Mallarmé citing the Gospel of John, calls "the Word itself"—then grammar, as the spontaneous combinatory capacity to generate all and only the infinite well-formed sequences of words in a language, remains the sovereign, species-specific endowment of humanity.[40] To the extent, however, that our grammatical knowledge is a learned repertoire of abstract and complex signs such as *SP* and *S is dead*, it is not an innate power that conditions linguistic acculturation. Instead it is, no less than the lexicon, an element of acculturation "founded on the order of positivities exterior to man," another way that we are passible to an estranged and inhuman system that predates and constitutes us.[41]

Yet it is not so easy to banish the anthropological question, What is man that language speaks through him? Geoffrey Galt Harpham has argued that every antihumanist attempt to dissolve the figure of man into an autonomous and self-contained language, "language itself," leads instead to a "return of man."[42] By redescribing the speaking subject as the possessor of a repertoire of forms as well as words, do we not renew man as an object of study and knowledge? Learning to use linguistic forms does presuppose a rather thick set of cognitive capacities: language users associate signifiers with signifieds; individuate lexical units from the blooming buzzing confusion of sounds and marks; abstract from and generalize over those units to densely structured categories; organize the forms produced by abstraction and generalization into a hierarchical network; and instantiate these forms appropriately, layering them on and nesting them inside one another and filling their blanks to produce unwitnessed utterances.[43] It would seem that Harpham is right to posit a "law of return," in which the speaking subject can only temporarily be repressed or hidden—concealed, as it were, in the "fold" of grammar—rather than fully effaced by the impersonality and inhuman technicity of language.[44] Yet the unification of grammar and lexicon in a single symbolic repertoire may belong to a creature that no longer deserves to be called *man*, a figure of the speaking subject that Foucault regarded as a "recent invention" some 150 years old.[45] What emerges from the extension of the empire of the sign is neither the triumph of a wholly autonomous language, language itself freed from the speaking subject, nor the inescapable return of an irrepressible humanism, but rather a reconfigured figure: the speaking subject as a combinatorial node where the abstract forms of another are filled with the words of another to create (with remarkable frequency) utterances spoken by no other.[46]

The mainstays of nearly any introductory undergraduate critical-theory syllabus—from Lacan, Althusser, and Foucault to Butler, Spivak, and hooks—have sought not only, in a destructive mode, to efface the figure of the human but also to interrogate the processes of subject formation, the ways that language makes us into the concrete, historically specific subjects we are.[47] It is through language that ideology whispers us into being, assigning us social and political roles established in advance by words like *man* and *woman*, *black* and *white*, *queer* and *straight*. Unlike words, linguistic forms do not serve as names for the categories into which people are sorted. The police do not call us a sequence of passive past participles; *to X or not to X* is not written above the doors of public restrooms; no one is required to tick a box next to *God is P* on the census; *X [be] the new Y* is hurled at no one as a slur. Yet these forms, in their contingent historical existence, nonetheless play an indispensable role in the construction of identities and the ideological system they occupy. The form *X as if Y*, as we saw in chapter 4, has long served as an instrument of self-fashioning, but other forms work on us in less deliberate and more oblique ways. When the police hail us, "interpellating" us as subjects of ideology, they do so not only in words ("Hey you!") but in the linguistic forms these words fill.[48] Though *SP* is not a name by which someone could be hailed, it is in and through this form that anyone can be given a name or assigned differentiating predicates. Linguistic forms articulate our identities, defining them by putting them into relation to one another. Every subject is the product of signs more abstract than names. What kinds of subjects do linguistic forms form? How do they work to activate and inform raced, gendered, and classed subjects even without naming them? What kind of self is the correlate of a form's complex mixture of fixed words and unfilled categories, which at once constrain us and provide the framework for innovation? How do these forms encode and carry out the work of ideology? How might the subversion of a form's conventions—as in Nietzsche's replacement of God's traditional perfections with death, as in the innovations characteristic of everyday speech—provide a model for the subject's subversion of social norms? To tell the history of a linguistic form is to tell how we fill preexisting forms and by filling them remake them and are remade.

Digital tools and methods have sometimes been taken, if not to oppose traditional humanistic inquiry, then at least to remove us from (or mercifully set aside) the theoretical and interpretive questions that have occupied the humanities in recent decades of structuralist, poststructuralist, and postmodern thought.[49] Cyberformalism seeks not only to identify new objects of philological knowledge; not only to employ new and emergent digital tools and archives for the pursuit of this knowledge; not only to extend the domain of the Saussurean sign beyond its lexicodogmatic limits to include the combinatory means of language; but also to return us to the questions raised by the nature of the linguistic sign, and to the thinkers who asked those questions, as beginners once again.

# Notes

**Preface**

1. Friedrich Nietzsche, *Daybreak: Thoughts on the Prejudices of Morality*, trans. R. J. Hollingdale (New York: Cambridge UP, 1997), 5; William Shakespeare, *The Tragedy of Hamlet, Prince of Denmark*, ed. Barbara Mowat, Paul Werstine, Michael Poston, and Rebecca Niles (Washington, DC: Folger Shakespeare Library, n.d.), 2.2.210, www .folgerdigitaltexts.org. On the role of "the words on the page" in the New Criticism, see Mark Jacovich, *The Cultural Politics of the New Criticism* (New York: Cambridge UP, 1993), 6; on the distinction between *res* and *verba*, see Terence Cave, *The Cornucopian Text: Problems of Writing in the French Renaissance* (New York: Oxford UP, 1979), xi.

2. Walter Jackson Bate, "The Crisis in English Studies," *Harvard Magazine*, September–October 1982, 46–53, described philology as "the study of words historically" (49). Yet Jan Ziolkowski, "'What Is Philology': Introduction," in *On Philology*, ed. Ziolkowski (University Park: Pennsylvania State UP, 1990), 1–12, rightly points out that "*Wortphilologie* is one of philology's divisions" and that "philology is not just a grand etymological or lexicographic enterprise" (6–7).

3. Paul de Man, "The Return to Philology," in *The Resistance to Theory* (Minneapolis: U of Minnesota P, 1986), 3–26, 23; Gerald Graff, *Professing Literature: An Institutional History* (Chicago: U of Chicago P, 1987), 28–41, 67–69; Edward Said, *Humanism and Democratic Criticism* (New York: Columbia UP, 2004), 61; Jerome McGann, *A New Republic of Letters: Memory and Scholarship in the Age of Digital Reproduction* (Cambridge, MA: Harvard UP, 2014), proposing that *Wortphilologie* (2) should be accompanied by *Sachphilologie*, "a philology of material culture" (3).

4. William Empson, *The Structure of Complex Words* (Ann Arbor: U of Michigan P, 1967), 39.

5. Ralph Waldo Emerson, "The Poet," in *The Complete Works of Ralph Waldo Emerson*, vol. 3 (New York: Houghton Mifflin, 1904), 22; Honoré de Balzac, *Louis Lambert*, in *The Works of Honoré de Balzac*, ed. George Saintsbury, vol. 2 (Boston: Dana Estes, 1901), 147.

6. James Turner, *Philology: The Forgotten Origins of the Modern Humanities* (Princeton, NJ: Princeton UP, 2014), 3–4. On *philology* as the expansive name for, in the words of August Boeckh, "die Erkenntnis des Erkannten" (the knowledge of things known), see Martin Mueller, "The EEBO-TCP Phase I Public Release," *Spenser Review* 44.2.36 (Fall 2014), http://www.english.cam.ac.uk/spenseronline/review/volume-44/442/digital -projects/the-eebo-tcp-phase-i-public-release/. Hans Ulrich Gumbrecht, *The Powers of Philology* (Urbana: U of Illinois P, 2003), offers a contrarian account of philology in which the word refers solely to the discipline of historical text curatorship.

7. Leo Spitzer, *Essays in Historical Semantics* (New York: S. F. Vanni, 1948); Martin Jay, *Cultural Semantics: Keywords of Our Time* (Amherst: U of Massachusetts P, 1998); Roland Greene, *Five Words: Critical Semantics in the Age of Shakespeare and Cervantes* (Chicago: U of Chicago P, 2013).

8. See Marjorie Garber, *Loaded Words* (New York: Fordham UP, 2012); Brian Boyd, ed., *Words That Count: Essays in Honor of MacDonald P. Jackson* (Newark: U of Delaware P, 2004); and Judith H. Anderson, *Words That Matter: Linguistic Perception in Renaissance English* (Stanford, CA: Stanford UP, 1996).

9. Empson, *Structure*; Raymond Williams, *Keywords: A Vocabulary of Culture and Society*, rev. ed. (New York: Oxford UP, 1983). The production of keywords volumes has become a major industry across domains of cultural studies. See, e.g., recent volumes in the Wiley-Blackwell series Keywords in Literature and Culture: Allen J. Frantzen, *Anglo-Saxon Keywords* (Chichester, UK: Wiley-Blackwell, 2012); Melba Cuddy-Kean, Adam Hammond, and Alexandra Peat, eds., *Modernism: Keywords* (Chichester, UK: Wiley-Blackwell, 2014); and Frederick Burwick, *Romanticism: Keywords* (Chichester, UK: Wiley-Blackwell, 2015), with further volumes slated on Middle English and British literature from 1660 to 1789.

10. Judith Butler, *Bodies That Matter: On the Discursive Limits of Sex* (New York: Routledge, 1993), 145.

11. See Jean Laplanche and Jean-Bertand Pontalis, *Vocabulaire de la psychanalyse* (Paris: Presses Universitaires de France, 2007); David Crystal and Ben Crystal, *Shakespeare's Words: A Glossary and Language Companion* (New York: Penguin, 2002); and Annabel M. Patterson, *Milton's Words* (New York: Oxford UP, 2009).

12. See Greene, *Five Words*.

13. Instances abound, but see, for prominent examples, Raymond Williams, *Culture and Society, 1780–1950*, 2nd ed. (New York: Columbia UP, 1983); and Martin Jay, *Songs of Experience* (Berkeley: U of California P, 2006).

14. Samuel Johnson, *A Dictionary of the English Language* (London, 1766), s.v. "lexicographer."

15. For exemplars of recent scholarship that rescues from neglect words and concepts of aesthetic, social, and political consequence, see Sianne Ngai, *Our Aesthetic Categories: Zany, Cute, Interesting* (Cambridge, MA: Harvard UP, 2012); Benedict Robinson, "Disgust c. 1600," *English Literary History* 81.2 (2014): 553–83; John Guillory, "Genesis of the Media Concept," *Critical Inquiry* 36 (2010): 321–62; and Matthew Kaiser, "A History of 'Ludicrous,'" *English Literary History* 71.3 (2004): 631–60.

16. See, e.g., Brian Cummings, *Mortal Thoughts: Religion, Secularity, and Identity in Shakespeare and Early Modern Culture* (London: Oxford UP, 2013), which "deals with the complex history of words such as 'conscience', 'sincere', 'solitude', 'luck', 'suicide', or 'passion'" (17).

17. T. S. Eliot, *Selected Essays, 1917–1932* (London: Faber, 1999), 347–48.

18. The etymology of *tragedy* as "goat song" (Greek *tragos + oda*) is rehearsed in Dante Allegheri's letter to Cangrande della Scala, in *Dante: The Critical Heritage*, ed. Michael Caesar (New York: Routledge, 1999), 94; that of *academia* in John Milton's

*Paradise Regained*, in *The Complete Poetry and Essential Prose of John Milton*, ed. William Kerrigan, John Rumrich, and Stephen Fallon (New York: Modern Library, 2007), 4.244–45; in The John Milton Reading Room, www.dartmouth.edu/~milton/reading _room/: "See there the Olive Grove of *Academe,* / *Plato's* retirement."

19. Sarah Howe, "Others," in *Loop of Jade* (London: Chatto & Windus, 2015), 46.

20. Greene, *Five Words*, 3.

21. For a linguist's attack on the tendency of nonlinguists to treat language as a "fixed stock of words," see Geoffrey K. Pullum and Barbara C. Scholz, "Language: More Than Words," *Nature* 413.6854 (27 September 2001): 367.

22. I am hardly the first to template this passage, which appears, with some variation according to translation, in Deuteronomy 8:3, Matthew 4:4, and Luke 4:4. A Google search for *"live by * alone"* reveals a wealth of examples, including "Man cannot live by math alone," "We cannot live by skepticism alone," "we live by faith alone," "did man once live by beer alone?," and "man does not live by politics alone," the last of which is attributed to Leon Trotsky in Slavoj Žižek and Boris Gunjević, *God in Pain: Inversions of Apocalypse* (New York: Seven Stories, 2012), n.p.

23. Donald Davie, "Syntax and Music in *Paradise Lost*," in *The Living Milton*, ed. Frank Kermode (London: Routledge, 1960), 73.

24. Frank Bidart, "Borges and I," in *Desire* (New York: Farrar, Straus & Giroux, 1997), 9.

25. On the root *cyber-* and its history, see N. Katherine Hayles, *How We Became Post-human: Virtual Bodies in Cybernetics, Literature, and Informatics* (Chicago: U of Chicago P, 1999); Peter Galison, "The Ontology of the Enemy: Norbert Weiner and the Cybernetic Vision," *Critical Inquiry* 21 (1994): 228–66; Norbert Weiner, *Cybernetics or Control and Communication in the Animal and the Machine*, 2nd ed. (Cambridge, MA: MIT P, 1961); Weiner, *The Human Use of Human Beings: Cybernetics and Society* (New York: Hearst, 1967); and, most recently, Steven E. Jones, *The Emergence of the Digital Humanities* (New York: Routledge, 2014), 18, 28.

26. Donna Haraway, "A Cyborg Manifesto: Science, Technology, and Socialist-Feminism in the Late Twentieth Century," in *Simians, Cyborgs, and Women: The Reinvention of Nature* (New York: Routledge, 1991), 149–81, 163.

27. Franco Moretti, *Distant Reading* (New York: Verso, 2013), 123.

28. De Man, "Return," 23.

29. Noam Chomsky, *Cartesian Linguistics: A Chapter in the History of Rationalist Thought*, 3rd ed. (New York: Cambridge UP, 2009), 59–71.

30. James R. Hurford, *The Origins of Grammar: Language in the Light of Evolution*, 2 vols. (New York: Oxford UP, 2012), 2:267.

31. Roland Barthes, *Mythologies*, trans. Annette Lavers (New York: Farrar, Straus & Giroux, 2001), 111.

32. Milton, *Paradise Lost*, 7.567–78, in The John Milton Reading Room.

33. Ann M. Blair, *Too Much to Know: Managing Scholarly Information before the Modern Age* (New Haven, CT: Yale UP, 2010).

## Chapter 1. Linguistic Forms

1. For a smart preliminary attempt to trace the origins of this form, see Benjamin Zimmer, "On the Trail of 'the New Black' (and 'the Navy Blue')," *Language Log* (blog), 28 December 2006, itre.cis.upenn.edu/myl/languagelog/archives/003981.html. As long as the *Y* value remained fixed as *black* or *navy*, the form appeared to signify that *X* had become standard or normal. For a general account of the developmental stages of snowclones, see Arnold Zwicky, "Snowclone Mountain," *Language Log* (blog), 13 March 2009, itre.cis.upenn.edu/~myl/languagelog/archives/002924.html.

2. I adopt the phrase "turn against the linguistic turn," which describes approaches such as posthumanism, digital humanities, object-oriented criticism, speculative realism, thing theory, and actor-network theory, from Julie Orlemanski, "Scales of Reading," *Exemplaria* 26.2–3 (2014): 215–33, 215; and Nancy Partner, "Narrative Persistence: The Post-Postmodern Life of Narrative Theory," in *Re-Figuring Hayden White*, ed. Frank Ankersmit, Ewa Domanska, and Hans Kellner (Stanford, CA: Stanford UP, 2009), 81–94, 82.

3. Ferdinand de Saussure, *Course in General Linguistics*, trans. Roy Harris (Chicago: Open Court, 2002), 16.

4. See, e.g., Vincent B. Leitch et al., eds., *The Norton Anthology of Theory and Criticism*, 2nd ed. (New York: Norton, 2010); and Julie Rivkin and Michael Ryan, eds., *Literary Theory: An Anthology*, 2nd ed. (Malden, MA: Blackwell, 2005).

5. For a detailed history of structuralism, see François Dosse, *History of Structuralism*, trans. Deborah Glassman, 2 vols. (Minneapolis: U of Minnesota P, 1998). For a longer history of the concept of the sign, see Umberto Eco, *Semiotics and the Philosophy of Language* (Bloomington: Indiana UP, 1986). On the afterlife of Saussure, see Roy Harris, *Saussure and his Interpreters*, 2nd ed. (Edinburgh: Edinburgh UP, 2003). For the rise of semiotics in literary and cultural studies, see Jonathan Culler, *The Pursuit of Signs: Semiotics, Literature, Deconstruction* (Oxon, UK: Routledge, 1981); Benjamin Lee, *Talking Heads: Language, Metalanguage, and the Semiotics of Subjectivity* (Durham, NC: Duke UP, 1997); and Jeffrey Galt Harpham, *Language Alone: The Critical Fetish of Modernity* (New York: Routledge, 2002).

6. See Roland Barthes, *Elements of Semiology*, trans. Annette Lavers and Colin Smith (New York: Hill & Wang, 1999), which acknowledges fixed sequences of words as sign units. In chapter 6 I discuss the rather oblique way Barthes, in a discussion of style, begins to theorize the existence of abstract and variable linguistic signs, which he refers to as "stereotypes."

7. Saussure, *Course*, explicitly rules out the possibility of abstract linguistic signs: "The signs comprising a language are not abstractions, but real objects" (101). This does not mean that Saussure disregards the role of syntactic categories and relations, but in the *Course* these include only categories of and relations between phonetically concrete sign units.

8. Jacques Derrida, "Signature, Event, Context," in Derrida, *Limited, Inc.*, ed. Gerald Graff (Evanston, IL: Northwestern UP, 1988), 8–10, describes the presence of the mark as an "essential [predicate] . . . in a minimal determination of the classical concept of the sign"; see also Derrida, *Of Grammatology*, trans. Gayatri Spivak, corrected ed.

(Baltimore: Johns Hopkins UP, 1997), 13–14, for a discussion of the exteriority of the sign. The identification of the linguistic sign with the word in Derrida and poststructuralism more generally is derived from Edmund Husserl and, to a lesser extent, Charles Peirce, as well as Saussure. See Jacques Derrida, *Edmund Husserl's* Origin of Geometry: *An Introduction*, trans. John P. Leavey Jr. (Lincoln: U of Nebraska P, 1989), 103–4. Though it seems to me that Derrida does not, as a matter of practice, admit linguistic forms to the semiotic field, there is nothing in his writings that excludes them. In fact, I return to Derrida's writings more than once in the following pages for their account of the general conditions of the possibility of signification, which are also the conditions of the possibility of linguistic forms.

9. Derrida, *Of Grammatology*, 21. Derrida's focus on the word as the linguistic sign unit stretches across the whole of his career, right up to *The Animal That Therefore I Am*, ed. Marie-Louise Mallet, trans. David Wills (New York: Fordham UP, 2008), which challenges the linguistic distinction between human and animal through a treatment of the word *word*.

10. The term *linguistic form* risks a potential confusion. Though *form* has a long and complex history in the discipline of linguistics, current linguists use it almost exclusively to refer to phonology, morphology, and syntax (or sometimes just morphosyntax), independent of meaning and use, whereas I employ it to describe the conventional union of the two. Saussure risked an analogous confusion when he named his significant units signs (*signes*), which could be mistakenly identified with the signifier alone. A linguistic form is formal not in the sense that it is opposed to signified meaning but in the sense that it is at least partly abstracted from concrete lexical constituents and must be filled to produced an utterance. Likewise, *linguistic form* and *logical form* are both formal in the same sense: they are abstracted from concrete terms.

11. I employ the term *linguistic form* as an equivalent to what William Croft, in *Radical Construction Grammar* (Oxford: Oxford UP, 2001), 25, terms a partially or wholly "schematic construction," a construction unfilled, to various degrees, by substantive, lexical constituents. For the foundational early work in cognitive and constructional linguistics, see George Lakoff, *Women, Fire, and Dangerous Things: What Categories Reveal about the Mind* (Chicago: U of Chicago P, 1987), 462–585; Charles J. Fillmore, Paul Kay, and Mary Catherine O'Connor, "Regularity and Idiomaticity in Grammatical Constructions: The Case of *Let Alone*," *Language* 64.3 (1988): 501–38; and Ronald Langacker, *Foundations of Cognitive Grammar*, 2 vols. (Stanford, CA: Stanford UP, 1980), esp. 1:56–96. Scholars can find the seminal essays collected in Adele E. Goldberg, ed., *Cognitive Linguistics* (New York: Taylor & Francis, 2011); a clear overview presented in William Croft and Alan D. Cruise, *Cognitive Linguistics* (Cambridge: Cambridge UP, 2004), 225–90; and the leading recent account in Adele E. Goldberg, *Constructions at Work: The Nature of Generalization in Language* (New York: Oxford UP, 2006) and Goldberg, *Constructions: A Construction Grammar Approach to Argument Structure* (Chicago: U of Chicago P, 1995). See also M. A. K. Halliday, *Halliday's Introduction to Functional Grammar*, rev. Christian M. I. M. Matthiessen, 4th ed. (New York: Routledge, 2014), 64–69, for an account of the lexicogrammatical cline. I have chosen not to employ the term *construction*, partly because it covers fixed words as well as abstract schema and partly because

the term has a rather different meaning in the social constructionist theories prominent in the humanities.

12. Geoffrey K. Pullum, "Phrases for Lazy Writers in Kit Form," *Language Log* (blog),
27 October 2003, itre.cis.upenn.edu/myl/languagelog/archives/000061.html, offers a
more detailed definition of the snowclone as "a multi-use, customizable, instantly
recognizable, time-worn, quoted or misquoted phrase or sentence that can be used in
an entirely open array of different jokey variants by lazy journalists and writers." For
an index of *Language Lab* posts on snowclones, see itre.cis.upenn.edu/~myl/languagelog
/archives/000350.html; for the coinage of the term *snowclone*, see Glen Whitman's
post on *Agoraphilia*: agoraphilia.blogspot.com/2004/01/phrases-for-lazy-writers-in
-kit-form.html. For a treatment of snowclones and *X [be] the new Y*, see Elizabeth
Closs Traugott and Graeme Trousdale, *Constructionalization and Constructional Changes*
(Oxford: Oxford UP, 2013), 183–84.

13. For an early and influential argument that grammar is inherently semantic, see
Anna Wierzbicka, *The Semantics of Grammar* (Philadelphia: John Benjamins, 1988).

14. See Geoffrey K. Pullum, *The Great Eskimo Vocabulary Hoax* (Chicago: U of
Chicago P, 1991), 159–73; and Laura Martin, " 'Eskimo Words for Snow': A Case Study in
the Genesis and Decay of an Anthropological Example," *American Anthropologist*, n.s.,
88.2 (1986): 418–23, in which Martin observes that the "structure of Eskimo Grammar
means that the number of 'words' for snow is literally incalculable, a conclusion that is
inescapable for any other root as well" (419). The aboriginal peoples of the Arctic, it
should be noted, regard the term *Eskimo* as pejorative.

15. This example is from the anonymous limerick that begins "There once was a
man from Nantucket," *Bulletin: A Monthly Journal Devoted to Hoo-Hoo* 87.7 (1903): 11.
The *X* and *Y* of the limerick's opening lines also follow rather complicated prosodic rules
that I do not aim to elaborate here.

16. For a synthetic account of prototype theories of categorization that builds on
earlier work by Wittgenstein and Elena Rausch, see Lakoff, *Women, Fire, and Dangerous
Things*.

17. See Pullum, "Phrases for Lazy Writers."

18. Donald Davidson, "A Nice Derangement of Epitaphs," in *The Essential Davidson*
(Oxford: Oxford UP, 2006), 253–65, 259.

19. Jacques Derrida, in *Voice and Phenomenon: Introduction to the Problem of the Sign
in Husserl's Phenomenology*, trans. Leonard Lawlor (Evanston, IL: Northwestern UP,
2011), 6, describes the opposition between form and content as "the inaugural opposition
of metaphysics."

20. On the ditransitive, see Goldberg, *Constructions*, 3–23.

21. A note on notation: regard for this book's cultural and historical rather than
linguistic aims, the patience of my humanist readers, and the limits of my own expertise
has led me to keep formal linguistic notation simple, minimal, and relatively infrequent,
even in cases where this means forgoing potential generalizations. For a foundational
treatment of notation in construction grammar, see Paul Kay and Charles J. Fillmore,
"Grammatical Constructions and Linguistic Generalizations: The What's X Doing Y?
Construction," *Language* 75.1 (1999): 1–33.

22. Linguists distinguish between degrees of productivity. Some forms are more conservative than others. See Adele E. Goldberg and Ray Jackendoff, "The English Resultative as a Family of Constructions," *Language* 80 (2004): 532–68, for a consideration of the productivity of resultative constructions.

23. Steven Pinker, *Words and Rules* (New York: Basic Books, 1987), 7–9.

24. As Adele Goldberg writes in "Constructionist Approaches," in *The Oxford Handbook of Construction Grammar*, ed. Thomas Hoffman and Graeme Trousdale (New York: Oxford UP, 2013), 28, "When a construction of type Y contains a slot of the same type Y, the construction is recursive."

25. Though Stein's line, as it appears in the 1922 poem "Sacred Emily," in *Geography and Plays* (Boston: Four Seas, 1922), 178–88, 187, is finite, she also had it printed in a circle on the cover of *The Autobiography of Alice B. Toklas* and even on her dishware. Natalia Cecire, "Ways of Not Reading Gertrude Stein," *ELH* 82 (2015): 281–312, 285.

26. On frozen words and the linguistics of the syntagm, see Judith H. Anderson, *Words That Matter: Linguistic Perception in Renaissance English* (Stanford, CA: Stanford UP, 1996).

27. Michel Foucault writes in *The Order of Things: An Archaeology of the Human Sciences* (New York: Vintage Books, 1994), 330, that man "composes into sentences . . . words that are older than all memory."

28. William Shakespeare, *The Tragedy of Hamlet, Prince of Denmark*, ed. Barbara Mowat, Paul Werstine, Michael Poston, and Rebecca Niles (Washington, DC: Folger Shakespeare Library, n.d.), 3.4.12–15, www.folgerdigitaltexts.org.

29. Linguistic forms replicate themselves almost entirely in and through utterances. See William Croft's utterance-based theory of language change in *Explaining Language Change: An Evolutionary Approach* (London: Pearson Education, 2000), 8: "Normal replication is in essence conformity to convention in language use. Altered replication results from the violation of convention in language use." So far as I can see, there are only two other mechanisms for their reproduction. First, they can be presented, as in this book, in formal notations using variables, category descriptions, brackets, parse trees, etc. Grammar textbook often teach students linguistic forms through such notations. Second, and most recently, they can be generated through the algorithmic procedures of natural language processing, of the kind used in twitter bots. With computers we witness the advent of replication and innovation in language that does not need to pass through a biological nervous system, from eyes or ears to hand or tongue.

30. See Paul Hopper, "Emergent Grammar," *Proceedings of the Thirteenth Annual Meeting of the Berkeley Linguistics Society*, 1987, 139–57, which argues that the forms of grammar are not "fixed templates, but are negotiable in face-to-face interaction," which means that "the linguist's task" is to study "the whole range of repetition in discourse" and to "seek out those regularities that promise interest as incipient subsystems" (142).

31. Jacques Derrida, "The Law of Genre," trans. Avital Ronell, *Critical Inquiry* 7.1 (1980): 55–81, 63. Just as there is no "genreless text" (65), so too is there no formless utterance, no utterance that does not participate in one or more linguistic forms.

32. Ronald W. Langacker, "Cognitive Grammar," in *The Oxford Handbook of Linguistic Analysis*, ed. Bernd Heine and Heiko Narrog (New York: Oxford UP, 2010), 87–109, 88.

33. David Foster Wallace, *Brief Interviews with Hideous Men* (New York: Back Bay Books, 2007), 92.

34. Lee Edelman, *No Future* (Durham, NC: Duke UP, 2004). Edelman's treatment of the antisociality thesis obviously concerns more than verb tenses, but it would be surprising if the kinds of queer relationships for which he advocates did not manifest in different uses of verb tense.

35. Akhil Reed Amar, *America's Constitution: A Biography* (New York: Random House, 2005), 5.

36. Garrett Epps, *American Epic: Reading the US Constitution* (New York: Oxford UP, 2013), 4–5.

37. Michael Warner, *Letters of the Republic* (Cambridge, MA: Harvard UP, 1990), 103.

38. For brilliant treatments of the performative role of the constitutional "We," see Lee, *Talking Heads*, 321–45; and Jacques Derrida, "Declarations of Independence," trans. T. Keenan and T. Pepper, *New Political Science* 7.1 (1986): 7–15.

39. Amar, *America's Constitution*, 25.

40. Preamble to the Constitution of the Republic of South Africa, 8 May 1996.

41. E. L. Doctorow, "A Citizen Reads the Constitution," in *Jack London, Hemingway, and the Constitution* (New York: Random House, 1993), 117–38, 119.

42. G. E. Devenish, *The South African Constitution* (Durban, South Africa: LexisNexis Butterworths, 2005), 26. Devenish observes that South Africa was in an "extraordinary position to benefit from the political and constitutional successes and failures of other countries" (vi).

43. M. M. Bakhtin, "The Problem of Speech Genres," in *Speech Genres and Other Late Essays* (Austin: U of Texas P, 1986), 66–71.

44. Raymond Williams, *Culture and Society, 1780–1950*, 2nd ed. (New York: Columbia UP, 1983), xiii.

45. Claude Lévi-Strauss, "The Structural Study of Myth," *Journal of American Folklore* 68.270 (1955): 428–44. It should be noted that Lévi-Strauss regards the unit of the analysis of a myth as an open question, whereas structuralist linguistics and its successors adopted the word as the sign unit.

46. Jacques Derrida, *Positions*, trans. Alan Bass (Chicago: U of Chicago P, 1981), 41–43.

47. Martin Jay, *Cultural Semantics: Keywords of Our Time* (Amherst: U of Massachusetts P, 1998), 3. One might also offer a practical or deflationary explanation for the proliferation of keyword volumes by prominent literary intellectual and literary historians, namely, that these volumes provide a way for distinguished practitioners to gather essays on disparate topics between a single set of covers. But this explanation merely defers the initial question: Why are these essays all subsumable under the category of keywords or lexical concepts to begin with?

48. The notion of latent structure is built into latent Dirichlet allocation, a probabilistic model for topic discovery developed by David Blei, Andrew Ng, and Michael Jordan in 2003 and widely used by digital humanists. See Ted Underwood's blog *The Stone and*

*the Shell*, tedunderwood.com/2012/04/07/topic-modeling-made-just-simple-enough/, for the notion "latent structure"; and see www.cs.princeton.edu/~blei/papers/Blei2011 .pdf for "hidden structure." For a different depth metaphor, see Andrew Piper, "Reading's Refrain: From Bibliography to Topology," *ELH* 80 (2013): 373–99, which argues that the kind of digital analysis Piper calls "topology" brings into view "history's 'lexical unconscious'" or its "lexical infrastructure" (395).

49. See Ian Hacking, *Historical Ontology* (Cambridge, MA: Harvard UP, 2002), 68: "Philosophical analysis is the analysis of concepts. Concepts are words in their sites. Sites include sentences, uttered or transcribed, always in a larger site of neighborhood, institution, authority, language." For a recent, lexically based approach to intellectual history that makes use of digital tools to count words and their collocates, see Peter de Bolla, *The Architecture of Concepts: The Historical Formation of Human Rights* (New York: Fordham UP, 2013).

50. Roland Greene, *Five Words: Critical Semantics in the Age of Shakespeare and Cervantes* (Chicago: U of Chicago P, 2013), 1.

51. Annabel M. Patterson, *Milton's Words* (New York: Oxford UP, 2009), 3. For an example of Patterson's syntactic acuity, see "'How to Load and Bend': Syntax and Interpretation in Keats's *To Autumn*," *PMLA* 94.3 (1979): 449–58, which offers a brilliant critique of transformational grammar and arguments for contextual reading. It is tempting to regard Patterson's intellectual trajectory as an emblem of the trajectory of cultural and historicist scholarship more generally: following her rejection of Chomskyan linguistics on account of its universalism and ahistorical positing of "deep structures," her work turns ever more to the study of keywords, as in "Keywords: Raymond Williams and Others," *English Studies in Canada* 30.4 (2005): 66–80, part of a projected book titled *Rusty Keywords*, and "Pandora's Boxes: How We Store Our Values" (Tanner Lectures on Human Values, Berkeley, CA, 8–10 April 2008), 159–98, in which she argues for "the abstract noun as, in English at least, the form of speech that does the most work in the world. Abstract nouns, I shall try to show, are the power words in our society today, the keywords, the mega-words" (160).

52. Daniel T. Rodgers, *Contested Truths: Keywords in American Politics since Independence* (Cambridge, MA: Harvard UP, 1998), 4.

53. This synecdoche is part of our ordinary way of talking about language in English. German, by contrast, draws a useful distinction between two separate plurals of the noun *das Wort*: *die Wörter* refers to the individual, countable words that appear in lexicons, while *die Worte* refers to utterances, things said in language.

54. Ludwig Wittgenstein, *Philosophical Investigations*, trans. G. E. M. Anscombe (Oxford: Blackwell, 2001), 3–7.

55. Wittgenstein, *Philosophical Investigations*, 7e, italics original.

56. See Michael Tomasello, *Origins of Human Communication* (Cambridge, MA: MIT P, 2008), 224–25, on single word "holophrases," and 246–70, on the "grammar of requesting."

57. On the use of nouns in the imperative mood in early childhood, see Michael Tomasello, *Constructing a Language: A Usage Based Theory of Language Acquisition* (Cambridge, MA: Harvard UP, 2003), 44–93.

58. For a survey of digital methods based on counting words, see David L. Hoover, "Textual Analysis," in *Literary Studies in the Digital Age: An Evolving Anthology*, ed. Kenneth M. Price and Ray Siemens (Modern Language Association, 2013), dlsanthology .mla.hcommons.org/textual-analysis/.

59. For an example of inquiry that relies entirely on charting the relative frequency of words and sequences of words over time, see Erez Aidan and Jean-Baptiste Michel, *Uncharted: Big Data as a Lens on Culture* (New York: Penguin, 2013).

60. Although the work has not, so far as I have seen, had an impact on the quantitative digital humanities, constructional and usage-based approaches to linguistics have begun to perform complex statistical analyses of linguistic forms. See Florent Perek, *Argument Structure in Usage-Based Construction Grammar: Experimental and Corpus-Based Perspectives* (Philadelphia: John Benjamins, 2015); Joan Bybee, *Frequency of Use and the Organization of Language* (Oxford: Oxford UP, 2007); and Anatol Stefanowitsch and Stefan Th. Gries, "Collostructions: Investigating the Interaction between Words and Constructions," *International Journal of Corpus Linguistics* 8.2 (2003): 209–43.

61. See, e.g., Andrew Goldstone and Ted Underwood, "The Quiet Transformations of Literary Studies: What Thirteen Thousand Scholars Could Tell Us," *New Literary History* 45.3 (2014): 359–84, whose authors acknowledge that their "algorithm completely ignores the syntax of the articles it processes: it looks only for groups of words that tend to occur in the same articles" (361).

62. For the term *language action types*, see Jonathan Hope and Michael Witmore, "'The Hundredth Psalm to the Tune of "Green Sleeves"': Digital Approaches to Shakespeare's Language of Genre," *Shakespeare Quarterly* 61.3 (2010): 357–90, mcpress .media-commons.org/ShakespeareQuarterly_NewMedia/hope-witmore-the-hundredth -psalm/. For the notion *small words*, see Sylvia Adamson, "Understanding Shakespeare's Grammar: Studies in Small Words," in *Reading Shakespeare's Dramatic Language: A Guide*, ed. Sylvia Adamson, Lynette Hunter, Lynne Magnusson, Ann Thompson, and Katie Wales (London: Arden Shakespeare, 2001), 210–36. See Ann Banfield, "Beckett's Tattered Syntax," *Representations*, 84.1 (2003): 6–29, in the generative tradition, for a treatment of the semantically "light" function words in the "syntacticon" (17) and the role they play in Samuel Beckett's *oeuvre*.

63. Richard Rorty, *Contingency, Irony, and Solidarity* (New York: Cambridge UP, 1989), 75, 86, 73.

64. Eve Kosofsky Sedgwick, *Epistemology of the Closet* (Berkeley: U of California P, 1990), 9–10.

65. Eugene R. White, "A Song of Good Fighting," in *Songs of Good Fighting* (Boston: Lamson, Wolffe, 1898), 13.

66. Jack Kerouac, *Visions of Cody*, quoted in John Lardas, *The Bop Apocalypse: The Religious Visions of Kerouac, Ginsberg, and Burroughs* (Urbana: U of Illinois P, 2001), 185.

67. Emerson Hough, "Going Back Home," *Saturday Evening Post*, 9 July 1921, 88.

68. Harriet Burton Laidlaw, "Woman's Suffrage," S. Doc. 1035, 62nd Cong., 2nd sess., in *Senate Documents*, vol. 25 (Washington, DC: GPO, 1913), 76.

69. Corey Ford, ed., *Cold Noses and Warm Hearts* (Englewood Cliffs, NJ: Prentice-Hall, 1958), 261.

70. Louise Betts Edwards, "The Eclipse of Poetry," *East & West* 1.1 (1899): 11–17, 12, Blue Mountain Project, library.princeton.edu/projects/bluemountain/.

71. When searching a corpus using an interface that allows regular expressions with backreferencing, the search string for finding tautologous forms is (\w+) (was|were) \1. See chapter 2 on regular expressions. For an account of the broader family of tautologous constructions notated as *NP^i be NP^i* (but without past-tense instances such as *when men were men*), see Anna Wierzbicka, "Boys Will Be Boys: 'Radical Semantics' vs. 'Radical Pragmatics,'" *Language* 63.1 (1987): 95–114.

72. Judith Butler, in *Gender Trouble*, 2nd ed. (New York: Routledge, 1999), places herself in "the tradition of immanent critique that seeks to provoke critical examination of the basic vocabulary of the movement of thought to which it belongs" (vii). See, however, her claim (drawing on Friedrich Nietzsche and Monique Wittig) that "the alteration of gender at the most fundamental level will be conducted, in part, through contesting the grammar in which gender is given" (xx). My hope is that the identification and study of linguistic forms will bring grammar into the view of critique at a more culturally specific and contingent level than, in Butler's words, "the subject-verb requirement of propositional sense" (xx) or the substantivization of subjects and predicates and nouns more generally (28). Butler sometimes analyzes forms like *feel like a X*, as in Aretha Franklin's "You make me feel like a natural woman" (30), but her analysis is oriented toward the gender terms that fill the form rather than toward the cognitive work performed by the form itself.

73. Langston Hughes, *The Collected Works of Langston Hughes: The Poems, 1921–1940*, ed. Arnold Rampersad (Colombia: U of Missouri P, 2001), 131. The function of a form, like a word or phrase, can also be effectively challenged or subverted by parody. Henry Louis Gates Jr., in "Whose Canon Is It, Anyway?," *New York Times*, 26 February 1989, www.nytimes.com/1989/02/26/books/whose-canon-is-it-anyway.html, writes of the "antebellum esthetic position" that desires a nostalgic return to a time "when men were men and men were white, when scholar-critics were white men and when women and people of color were voiceless, faceless servants and laborers, pouring tea and filling brandy snifters in the boardrooms of old boys' clubs." It is unsurprising that Gates's parodic attempt and Hughes's poetic attempt to reappropriate tautologous form precede its explicit critical theorization.

74. In 2004, John Kerry adopted "Let America be America again" as his campaign slogan and even wrote the preface to a slim volume of Hughes's poetry, *Let America Be America Again; and Other Poems* (New York: Knopf Doubleday, 2004). "Fighting to make America *America* again" briefly served as Rick Santorum's campaign slogan before he disowned it upon learning its origins. See Alex Pareene, "Rick Santorum disowns campaign slogan when told a gay liberal poet came up with it," *Salon*, 15 April 2011, www.salon.com/2011/04/15/santorum_hughes_slogan/.

75. Reinhart Koselleck, "A Response to Comments on the *Geschichtliche Grundbegriffe*," trans. Melvin Richter and Sally E. Robertson, in *The Meaning of Historical Terms and Concepts: New Studies on Begriffsgeschichte*, ed. Hartmut

Lehmann and Melvin Richter (Washington, DC: German Historical Institute, 1996), 59–70, 64.

76. Hugh Kenner, "Joyce and Modernism," in *James Joyce*, ed. Harold Bloom (Philadelphia: Chelsea House, 2003), 97, quoted in Eric Bulson, "Ulysses by Numbers," *Representations* 127.1 (2014): 1–32, 1.

77. W. V. O. Quine, *Word and Object*, 2nd ed. (Cambridge, MA: MIT P, 2013), 251.

78. Cf. Saussure, *Course*, 103–4.

79. Raymond Williams, *Keywords: A Vocabulary of Culture and Society*, rev. ed. (New York: Oxford UP, 1983), 18; Thomas Kabdebó and Neil Armstrong, eds., *Dictionary of Dictionaries*, 2nd ed. (Munich: K. G. Saur Verlag, 1997).

80. For a definition of these semantic terms, see wordnet.princeton.edu/wordnet /man/wngloss.7WN.html.

81. Thomas Kuhn, *The Structure of Scientific Revolutions* (Chicago: U of Chicago P, 1962), 5.

82. See William Riley Parker, "Where Do English Departments Come From?," *College English* 28.5 (1967): 339–51, which attributes the split of English from linguistics to the "hostility of literary scholars to non-prescriptive grammar, new terminology, and the rigors of language study" (340).

83. Another somewhat less useful predecessor is the notion *construction* as it has been used in the discipline of grammar since the Modistae of the twelfth century. See Louis G. Kelly, *The Mirror of Grammar: Theology, Philosophy, and the Modistae* (Amsterdam: John Benjamins, 2002), 165–98.

84. Quintilian, *The Institutio Oratoria of Quintilian*, trans. Harold Edgeworth, 4 vols., Loeb Classical Library (Cambridge, MA: Harvard UP, 1958), 9.1.11–14.

85. For a discussion of the limitation of rhetorical figures to deviations from the norm, see Noam Chomsky, *Cartesian Linguistics: A Chapter in the History of Rationalist Thought*, 3rd ed. (New York: Cambridge UP, 2009), 75–76. Schemes, as conceived of in classical rhetoric, include only unfilled forms, not partially filled forms like *X [be] the new Y*. The Latin *forma* was, in any event, a frequent translation of the Greek *schema*.

86. Noam Chomsky, *Syntactic Structures* (Berlin: de Gruyter, 1957), 17.

87. On the notion of *perfection* in the Minimalist Program see Noam Chomsky, "Minimalist Inquiries: The Framework," in *Step by Step: Essays in Minimalist Syntax in Honor of Howard Lasnik*, ed. Roger Martin, David Michaels, and Juan Uriagereka (Cambridge, MA: MIT P, 2000), 89–155, esp. 97–121.

88. Davidson, "Nice Derangement of Epitaphs," 255–56.

89. For the goal of eliminating constructions from grammar, see Noam Chomsky, "A Minimalist Program for Linguistic Theory," in *The View from Building 20: Essays in Linguistics in Honor of Sylvain Bromberger*, ed. Kenneth Hale and Samuel Jay Keyser (Cambridge, MA: MIT P, 1993), 1–52, esp. 4. For claims regarding the "periphery" and "historical residues," see Chomsky's *Lectures on Government and Binding: The Pisa Lectures* (Berlin: Mouton de Gruyter, 1981), 8.

90. In Adele E. Goldberg's formulation, "The network of constructions captures our knowledge of language *in toto*, i.e. it's constructions all the way down." *Constructions at Work*, 18, boldface removed. For a clear, if not impartial, account of the debate

between cognitive and generative accounts of language, see Croft and Cruise, *Cognitive Linguistics*, 752–58.

91. For an example of the historical linguist's aim of defining processes of linguistic change, see Elizabeth Close Traugott and James Hopper, *Grammaticalization* (Cambridge: Cambridge UP, 2003). For a more recent, constructional approach to language change that encompasses the kinds of forms under consideration here, see Traugott and Trousdale, *Constructionalization*.

92. On the connection between genre and discourse, see Tzvetan Todorov, "The Origin of Genres," trans. Richard M. Berrong, *New Literary History* 8.1 (1976): 159–70. Todorov argues that genres emerge out of the speech acts of a pregeneric discourse, whereas my comparison of linguistic forms to genres suggests that discourse, even at the level of the sentence or phrase, is always already generic. Though I do not intend to pursue this claim here, I suppose that there is no point at which we can draw a clear distinction between linguistic and generic forms: language is genred all the way down.

93. John Rupert Firth, *Papers in Linguistics, 1934–1951* (London: Oxford UP, 1957), 11.

### Chapter 2. Search

1. See Catherine Gallagher and Stephen Greenblatt, *Practicing New Historicism* (Chicago: U of Chicago P, 2000), 16: "new historicism invokes the vastness of the textual archive."

2. The distinguishing feature of *the many* is not a threshold number of words, sentences, or documents. The roughly forty-four thousand–odd full texts in EEBO-TCP I and II is a tiny fraction of the more than thirty million full texts in Google Books, but both archives pose the same challenge to methods of literary study.

3. See, e.g., Matthew Wilkens, who writes in "Canons, Close Reading, and the Evolution of Method," in *Debates in the Digital Humanities*, ed. Matthew K. Gold (Minneapolis: U of Minnesota P, 2012), dhdebates.gc.cuny.edu/debates/text/17, that digital humanities can offer solutions to the problem of the canon "only if we are willing to reconsider our priorities for digital work in ways that emphasize quantitative methods and the large corpora on which they depend"; or Stephen Ramsay, in "Algorithmic Criticism," in *A Companion to Digital Literary Studies*, ed. Ray Siemens and Susan Schreibman (Oxford: Blackwell, 2008), www.digitalhumanities.org/companionDLS/, who writes of "the irreducible tendency of the computer toward enumeration, measurement, and verification."

4. I use the term *search* to refer to digital tools that on the basis of user specifications (usually a search string) retrieve matches from texts or other kinds of structured textual data. In this usage the term covers popular search engines like Google and Google Books, the search function of word processors, text editors, and individual websites, as well as advanced corpus and database query tools.

5. Franco Moretti, *Distant Reading* (New York: Verso, 2013); Ramsay, "Algorithmic Criticism"; Jonathan Hope and Michael Witmore, "'The Hundredth Psalm to the Tune of "Green Sleeves"': Digital Approaches to Shakespeare's Language of Genre,"

*Shakespeare Quarterly* 61.3 (2010): 357–90, mcpress.media-commons.org/Shakes peareQuarterly_NewMedia/hope-witmore-the-hundredth-psalm/. For an insight -generating example of quantitative stylistics, see Hugh Craig, "*A* and *an* in English Plays, 1580–1639," *Texas Studies in Literature and Language* 53.3 (2011): 273–93.

6. Julie Orlemanski, "Scales of Reading," *Exemplaria* 26.2–3 (2014): 215–33, 215.

7. Franco Moretti, *Graphs, Maps, Trees* (London: Verso, 2005).

8. Marshall McLuhan, *The Medium Is the Massage* (New York: Random House, 1967), 63.

9. Peter Stallybrass, "Books and Scrolls," in *Books and Readers in Early Modern England*, ed. Jennifer Anderson and Elizabeth Sauer (Philadelphia: U of Pennsylvania P, 2002), 42–79; search engines are only the latest in a long line of technologies that support discontinuous reading, including book wheels and the codex itself.

10. Susan Hockey, "The History of Humanities Computing," in *Companion to Digital Humanities*, ed. Susan Schreibman, Ray Siemens, and John Unsworth (Oxford: Blackwell, 2004), www.digitalhumanities.org/companion/.

11. Nicholas Carr, "Is Google Making Us Stupid?," *Atlantic*, July/August 2008, www.theatlantic.com/magazine/archive/2008/07/is-google-making-us-stupid /306868/; Carr, *The Shallows: What the Internet Is Doing to Our Brains* (New York: Norton, 2010); Mark Bauerlein, *The Dumbest Generation: How the Digital Age Stupefies Young Americans and Jeopardizes Our Future* (New York: Penguin, 2008).

12. Jonathan Culler, "The Closeness of Close Reading," *ADE Bulletin* 149 (2010): 20–25, 24.

13. Gayatri Spivak, "Interview with Gayatri Spivak," by Cathy Caruth, *PMLA* 125.4 (2010): 2010–25, 2010. See also Spivak's introduction to *An Aesthetic Education in the Era of Globalization* (Cambridge, MA: Harvard UP, 2012), which expresses a similar set of attitudes toward digital methods. On pastoral as a perspective, see Raymond Williams, *The Country and the City* (New York: Oxford UP, 1973), 9–45.

14. In his *Adages* Erasmus describes a "friend" who refuses to let him include passages from his copy of Suidas on the grounds that "everything is now becoming public property from which scholars hitherto had been able to secure the admiration of the common people." Desiderius Erasmus, *Adages*, in *Collected Works of Erasmus*, trans. Margaret Mann Phillips et al., ed. R. A. B. Mynors et al., vols. 31–36 (Toronto: U of Toronto P, 1982), 2.1.1. On the way early modern reference works change the conditions of scholarly research and knowledge, see Ann Blair, "Reading Strategies for Coping with Information Overload, ca. 1550–1700," *Journal of the History of Ideas* 64.1 (2003): 11–28; and Blair, *Too Much to Know: Managing Scholarly Information before the Modern Age* (New Haven, CT: Yale UP, 2010).

15. Matthew L. Jockers, *Macroanalysis: Digital Methods and Literary History* (Urbana: U of Illinois P, 2013), 8–9.

16. Alan Liu, "Where Is Cultural Criticism in the Digital Humanities?," in Gold, *Debates in the Digital Humanities*, dhdebates.gc.cuny.edu/debates/text/20.

17. Stephen Ramsay, "The Hermeneutics of Screwing Around; or What You Do with a Million Books," in *Pastplay: Teaching and Learning History with Technology*, ed. Kevin Lee (Ann Arbor: U of Michigan P, 2014), 111–20, 118. For another version of the

same founding gesture, see David L. Hoover, "Textual Analysis," in *Literary Studies in the Digital Age: An Evolving Anthology*, ed. Kenneth M. Price and Ray Siemens (Modern Language Association, 2013), dlsanthology.commons.mla.org/textual-analysis/, which acknowledges that computers are good for "searching for a vaguely remembered passage that is important for an argument or for locating every significant example of a word or phrase" before arguing that a computer's strengths are in the "statistical analysis" of vocabulary.

18. Ted Underwood, "Theorizing Research Practices We Forgot to Theorize Twenty Years Ago," *Representations* 127.1 (2014): 64–72, 66. See also Hoyt Long and Richard Jean So, "Literary Pattern Recognition: Modernism between Close Reading and Machine Learning," *Critical Inquiry* 42.2 (2016): 235–67, which builds on Underwood's critique of search in advocating for pattern recognition and machine learning.

19. Underwood, "Theorizing," 66. Underwood's critique is strongest when he notes that search tools like Google Search introduce black boxes into our research, retrieving and ordering search results according to opaque criteria like "relevance." This is not, however, an argument against search so much as it is an argument for using and designing transparent scholarly search tools and understanding their limitations. Scholars interested in topic modeling should consult Scott Weingart, "Topic Modeling for Humanists: A Guided Tour," *The Scottbott Irregular* (blog), 25 July 2012, www .scottbot.net/HIAL/?p=19113, which serves as a compendium of other introductions to topic modeling.

20. Lisa Gitelman, "Welcome to the Bubble Chamber: Online in the Humanities Today," *Communication Review* 13 (2010): 27–36, 33.

21. On the concept *reference genre*, see Blair, "Reading Strategies," 12.

22. See *Oxford English Dictionary Online*, s.v. "keyword," for its historical usage. The term is sometimes traced back to Michel Bréal, *Semantics: Studies in the Science of Meaning*, trans. Mrs. Henry Cust (New York: Dover, 1964), originally published in 1900; the phrase *keyword-in-context*, by contrast, does appear to be an invention of the digital age.

23. Michael Witmore, "Adjacencies, Virtuous and Vicious, and the Forking Paths of Library Research," *Wine Dark Sea* (blog), 8 July 2014, winedarksea.org/?p=1942. Witmore rightly speaks not of pure or unconditioned discoveries but of "manufactured serendipity," acknowledging the deliberate and principled but nonetheless limiting role of library organization in conditioning research.

24. I do not argue that print finding schemes for objects like linguistic forms could not exist, only that they historically have not existed. I suppose that any search procedure can, in principle, be supported by a possible organizational schema of print or manuscript documents as well, albeit at the practical cost of approaching the relational complexity of Leibniz's imagined encyclopedia, on which see Dan Selcer, "The Uninterrupted Ocean: Leibniz and the Encyclopedic Imagination," *Representations* 98.1 (2007): 25–50.

25. Jockers, *Macroanalysis*, 9.

26. Search methods can involve a great deal of computational complexity. See Andrew Piper, "Novel Devotions: Conversional Reading, Computational Modeling, and

the Modern Novel," *New Literary History* 46.1 (2015): 63–98, which in my reading (though perhaps not in Piper's) examines the results of a computational search tool that retrieves lexically bipartite novels, some but not all of which may turn out to be "conversional."

27. Because I'm concerned with the history of natural languages, I do not treat database and information query languages like Xquery or Xpath. With the growth of Text Encoding Initiative (TEI) document collections, query languages based on markup languages like XML (Extensible Markup Language) will likely become more central to humanities inquiry, and philological inquiry into linguistic forms is no exception. On TEI, see Syd Bauman, Paul Caton, Mavis Cournane, and Julia Flanders, "Names Proper and Improper: Applying the TEI to the Classification of Proper Nouns," *Computers and the Humanities* 31.4 (1997): 285–300; and Julia Flanders and Carole Mah, "Some Problems of TEI Markup and Early Printed Books," *Computers and the Humanities* 31.1 (1997): 31–46. On the role of XML in digital media, see Alan Liu, "Transcendental Data: Toward a Cultural History and Aesthetics of the New Encoded Discourse," *Critical Inquiry* 31.1 (2004): 49–81.

28. I quote Ernst Curtius's abbreviation of the passage from *European Literature and the Latin Middle Ages* (New York: Pantheon, 1953), 58. Curtius prefaces the description of the contest with the claim that its participants had memorized alphabetized lists of thousands of *sententiae*, but this overlooks the extent to which they recall lines of poetry according to criteria that are not alphabetic. For the full version of the anecdote, which adduces many lines of poetry that answer the respective challenges, see Athenaeus, *The Deipnosophistae*, vol. 4, trans. S. Douglas Olson, Loeb Classical Library (Cambridge, MA: Harvard UP, 2006), 10.457.

29. Ann Blair, "Note Taking as an Art of Transmission," *Critical Inquiry* 31.1 (2004): 85–107, 85.

30. Jakob Werner, *Lateinische Sprichwörter und Sinnsprüche des Mittelalters* (Heidelberg: C. Winter, 1912).

31. Athenaeus, *Deipnosophistae*, 10.458. The line can be found in *Comicorum Atticorum Fragmenta*, ed. Theodorus Kock, 3 vols. (Leipzig: B. G. Teubner, 1888), 3:452.

32. The CMU Pronouncing Dictionary is available at speech.cs.cmu.edu/cgi-bin /cmudict. The twitter feed @pentametron, created by Ranjit Bhatnagar, uses the CMU dictionary to identify iambic pentameter lines, which it then arranges into rhyming couplets, collected at pentametron.com. See also Elizabeth Scott-Baumann and B. Burton, "Encoding Form: A Proposed Database of Poetic Form," *Appositions* 3 (2010), appositions.blogspot.com/2010/05/ben-burton-elizabeth-scott-baumann.html, which proposes a database of English verse that would be searchable by a wide range of formal features like rhyme scheme, stanza form, prosodic and metrical patterns.

33. See Jerome McGann, "Database, Interface, and Archival Fever," *PMLA* 122.5 (2007).

34. Lev Manovich, *The Language of New Media* (Cambridge, MA: MIT P, 2001), 228. For a response to Manovich's claim that database and narrative are "natural enemies," see N. Katherine Hayles, "Narrative and Database: Natural Symbionts," *PMLA* 122.5 (2007): 1603–8: "Because database can construct relational juxtapositions but is helpless to

interpret or explain them, it needs narrative to make its results meaningful. Narrative, for its part, needs database" in order to "test the generality of its insights" (1603).

35. Neil Stephenson, *Snow Crash* (New York: Bantam, 1993), 107. For a semiotic reading of the novel, see Walter Benn Michaels, *The Shape of the Signifier: 1967 to the End of History* (Princeton, NJ: Princeton UP, 2004), 19–66.

36. In what follows I limit my account of search languages to "regular languages," the most restrictive level of the Chomsky hierarchy. In the future, humanists might investigate the search capacities of context-free, context-sensitive, and recursively enumerable languages, which theoretically would allow for the retrieval of a natural language sentence under any formal specification. For the seminal article on what came to be known as the Chomsky hierarchy, see Noam Chomsky, "On Certain Formal Properties of Grammars," *Information and Control* 2.2 (1959): 137–67.

37. Daniel Rosenberg, "Stop, Words," *Representations* 127.1 (2014): 83–92, 91.

38. For an online tutorial on the uses of regex in digital humanities research, see Shawn Graham, Ian Milligan, and Scott Weingart, *The Historian's Macroscope: Big Digital History*, www.themacroscope.org/?page_id=521, which also offers a useful tutorial. Regular expressions can use strings of characters to perform most or all of the "advanced" search functions found in search engines: proximity search, Boolean operators, collocations, "fuzzy searching," and so on.

39. On the accuracy of POS-tagging methods, see chapter 9 of Daniel Jurafsky and James H. Martin, *Speech and Language Processing*, 3rd ed., web.stanford.edu/~jurafsky /slp3/.

40. William Shakespeare, *The Tragedy of Hamlet, Prince of Denmark*, ed. Barbara Mowat, Paul Werstine, Michael Poston, and Rebecca Niles (Washington, DC: Folger Shakespeare Library, n.d.), 3.1.66, www.folgerdigitaltexts.org.

41. Zora Neale Hurston, *Their Eyes Were Watching God* (Urbana: U of Illinois P, 1991), 1. Tagged and parsed sentences produced by the Stanford Parser and the Stanford POS Tagger at nlp.stanford.edu:8080/corenlp/.

42. Stanford NLP has developed a version of regex for searching parse trees. See nlp .stanford.edu/software/tregex.html; and Roger Levy and Galen Andrew, "Tregex and Tsurgeon: Tools for Querying and Manipulating Tree Data Structures" (paper, 5th International Conference on Language Resources and Evaluation, January 2006), https://nlp .stanford.edu/pubs/levy_andrew_lrec2006.pdf.

43. Regex web tutorials and guides abound, but I have found regexone.com particularly helpful. See Martin Mueller, "BlackLab: Searching a TCP Corpus by Linguistic and Structural Criteria," *Scalable Reading* (blog), 23 July 2013, scalablereading .northwestern.edu/?p=296, for a discussion of learning pattern-matching languages for humanities research.

44. On the role of the hermeneutic circle in digital humanities, and specifically in quantitative contexts, see D. Sculley and Brad Passaneck, "Meaning and Mining: The Impact of Implicit Assumptions in Data Mining for the Humanities," *Literary and Linguistic Computing* 23.4 (2008): 409–24.

45. Andrew Pickering, "The Mangle of Practice: Agency and Emergence in the Sociology of Science," *American Journal of Sociology* 99.3 (1993): 559–89.

46. The most useful method of altering search strings might be termed *despecifica-tion*, which involves replacing a constraining pattern—a particular POS tag, a string of fixed characters—with one or more wildcards, completely open "blanks." Despecification can retrieve valid results mistakenly excluded from earlier searches.

47. John Guillory, "How Scholars Read," *ADE Bulletin* 146 (2008): 8–17, 13.

48. See Sean Latham, "New Age Scholarship: The Work of Criticism in the Age of Digital Reproduction," *New Literary History* 35.3 (2004): 411–26. Latham writes that "the results produced by search engines thus constitute not simply a new kind of index, but a new kind of textuality" (416).

49. Mark Davies, *The Corpus of Historical American English* (2010–) 400 Million Words, 1810–2009, corpus.byu.edu/coha/.

50. Roman Jakobson, "Two Aspects of Language and Two Types of Aphasic Distur-bances," in *Language in Literature*, ed. Krystyna Pomorska and Stephen Rudy (Cam-bridge, MA: Belknap-Harvard UP, 1987), 95–114, 99.

51. The idiom *give the lie* is used with the female object *her* only nine times. See *As You Like It* 5.4.93–101, where Touchstone describes "the lie direct" as the seventh and final stage of social engagement preceding a duel. *[Give] X the lie* is best construed as an idiomatic use of the ditransitive, since the same idiom can also take an indirect object, as in *Give the lie to X*. Other idioms, such as *She gave him what for*, work only in the ditransitive and are unacceptable with an indirect object, as with *She gave what for to him*.

52. For purposes of illustration, I describe the structuralist mechanism as a slot machine, but as Roy Harris suggests in *The Language Machine* (Ithaca, NY: Cornell UP, 1987), 9–21, the conceit of language as a selection-and-combination machine is already present in Jonathan Swift, *Gulliver's Travels* (New York: Rand McNally, 1912), 204–26. Visiting the grand academy at Lagado, Swift witnesses a machine in which "die" covered with "all the words" of the Balnibarbian language "in their several moods, tenses, and declensions" rotate on wires to form "broken sentences" (205).

53. Roman Jakobson, "Linguistics and Poetics," in Pomorska and Rudy, *Language in Literature*, 62–94, 71.

54. These and other Google poems can be found at www.googlepoetics.com. See also gutenberg-poetry.decontextualize.com/ and the poems in Ara Shirinyan, *Your Country Is Great: Afghanistan–Guyana* (New York: Futurepoem, 2008), which were created by searching Google for *X is great*, where *X* is filled by an alphabetical list of country names.

55. Gerard Manley Hopkins, "Poetic Diction," in *The Journals and Papers of Gerard Manley Hopkins*, ed. Humphry House and Graham Storey (London: Oxford UP, 1959), 84.

56. For the distinction between primary and secondary epic see C. S. Lewis, *A Preface to Paradise Lost* (New York: Oxford UP, 1961), 13.

57. On centos, see Scott McGill, *Virgil Recomposed: The Mythological and Secular Centos in Antiquity* (New York: Oxford UP, 2005).

58. Percy Bysshe Shelley, "A Defense of Poetry," in *Essays, Letters from Abroad, Translations and Fragments* (London: Edward Moxon, 1852), 28. See also K. W. F. Schlegel's "ever-becoming, self-transforming, unending poem of the entire human race," quoted

in Noam Chomsky, *Cartesian Linguistics: A Chapter in the History of Rationalist Thought*, 3rd ed. (New York: Cambridge UP, 2009), 68.

59. Latham, "New Age Scholarship," 416. In Latham's Benjaminian reading, search results disenchant the auratic linearity of traditional reading practices.

60. N. Katherine Hayles, *How We Think: Digital Media and Contemporary Technogenesis* (Chicago: U of Chicago P, 2012), 12. See also James Sosnoski, "Hyper-Readings and Their Reading Engines," in *Passions, Pedagogies, and Twenty-First Century Technologies*, ed. Gail E. Hawisher and Cynthia L. Selfe (Logan: Utah State UP, 1999).

61. Reuben A. Brower, "Reading in Slow Motion," in *In Defense of Reading: A Reader's Approach to Literary Criticism*, ed. Brower and Richard Poirier (New York: Dutton, 1962), 3–21, 9.

62. Samuel Taylor Coleridge, *Biographia Literaria*, vol. 1 (London: Rest Fenner, 1817), 8. Brower, in "Reading in Slow Motion," 7, quotes this passage and remarks that "the Reverend James Bowyer and not Coleridge, it appears, was the original new critic."

63. Matthew L. Jockers, Matthew Sag, and Jason Schultz, *Brief of Digital Humanities and Law Scholars as Amici Curiae in Authors Guild v. Google*, 3 August 2012, dx.doi.org/10. 2139/ssrn.2102542. For a discussion of how texts are used in quantitative research, see Mark Sample, "The Poetics of Non-Consumptive Research," *SampleReality* (blog), 22 May 2013, www.samplereality.com/2013/05/22/the-poetics-of-non-consumptive-reading. On the legal background of nonconsumptive research, see John Unsworth, "Computational Work with Very Large Text Collections: Interoperability, Sustainability, and the TEI," *Journal of the Text Encoding Initiative* 1 (2011), http://jtei.revues.org/215.

64. Francis Bacon, *Essayes* (London, 1597), sig. B1v.

65. Maurice S. Lee, "Searching the Archives with Dickens and Hawthorne: Databases and Aesthetic Judgment after the New Historicism," *ELH* 79.3 (2012): 747–71, 752. Lee puts the focus not on search tools themselves but on the disciplinary norms and presuppositions that guide what we search for, in particular the way "historical databases in nineteenth-century literary studies are conditioned for better and for worse by what was once called the New Historicism" (750).

66. Lee, "Searching," 766.

67. Michel Foucault, *The Archaeology of Knowledge and the Discourse on Language*, trans. A. M. Sheridan Smith (New York: Pantheon, 1972), 118–19. I employ Foucault's notion of rarity without observing his prohibitions on exegesis or on reference to particular speaking subjects. I also suppose that the rarity of linguistic forms can be more readily accessed than that of Foucault's "statements" (*énoncé*), which rely on an insupportable notion of synonymity.

68. Foucault, *Archaeology of Knowledge*, 119.

69. Compare the results of searching EEBO-TCP corpus version 3 in the CQPweb, cqpweb.lancs.ac.uk, *outrageous _N\**, with the results of searching the BYU Corpus COHA, *outrageous [n\*]*. The obvious exception to the restriction of *outrageous* to the personal domain is Hamlet's phrase "outrageous fortune," which is quoted frequently in twentieth-century texts. The claim only applies to *outrageous* when it is used as an attributive adjective; further investigation would be needed to establish its role as a

predicative, postpositive, depictive, resultative, and so on. This method of distributional analysis, which takes into account lexical categorization and function rather than
simply assessing proximity of words, has its roots in Zellig Harris, "Distributional
Structure," in *The Structure of Language: Readings in the Philosophy of Language*, ed.
Jerry A. Fodor and Jerrold J. Katz (Englewood Cliffs, NJ: Prentice-Hall, 1964), 33–49,
43–44.

70. The history of EEBO is far more complicated and fascinating than I can fully
explore here; see Erica Zimmer and Meaghan Brown, "History of Early English Books
Online," *Folgerpedia* (blog), 26 May 2017, folgerpedia.folger.edu/History_of_Early
_English_Books_Online; Ian Gadd, "The Use and Misuse of *Early English Books Online*,"
*Literature Compass* 6.3 (2009): 1–13; Bonnie Mak, "Archaeology of a Digitization," *Journal
of the American Society for Information Science and Technology* 65.8 (August 2014): 1515–26,
doi: 10.1002/asi.23061; and Diana Kichuk, "Metamorphosis: Remediation in Early
English Books Online (EEBO)," *Literary and Linguistic Computing* 22.3 (2007): 291–303.

71. As Gadd, "Use and Misuse," 4, observes, these selection criteria are based on
the selection criteria for A. W. Pollard and G. R. Redgrave, *A Short-Title Catalogue of Books
Printed in England, Scotland, and Ireland, and of English Books Printed Abroad, 1475–1640*,
rev. ed. (London: Bibliographical Society, 1976–91).

72. On the term *archive* as it has been employed in the digital context, see Katherine D. Harris, "Archive," in *Digital Keywords: A Vocabulary of Information Society and
Culture*, ed. Benjamin Peters (Princeton, NJ: Princeton UP, 2016), 45–53; and Kenneth M. Price, "Edition, Project, Database, Archive, Thematic Research Collection:
What's in a Name?," *Digital Humanities Quarterly* 3.3 (2009), www.digitalhumanities.org
/dhq/vol/3/3/000053/000053.html. For a survey of theories of archives and the way
they have been shaped by power, see Marlene Manoff, "Theories of the Archive from
across the Disciplines," *portal: Libraries and the Academy* 4.1 (2004): 9–5. For a seminal
article on the colonial construction of the archive, see Gayatri Chakravorty Spivak, "The
Rani of Sirmur: An Essay in Reading the Archives," *History and Theory* 24.3 (1985):
247–72. And for strong critiques, from an archivist's perspective, of the way the term
*archive* has been employed to describe collections of digital texts, see Kate Theimer,
"Archives in Context and as Context," *Journal of Digital Humanities* 1.2 (2012), journalof-
digitalhumanities.org/1-2/archives-in-context-and-as-context-by-kate-theimer/; and
Theimer, "A Distinction Worth Exploring: 'Archives' and 'Digital Historical Representations,'" *Journal of Digital Humanities* 3.2 (2014), journalofdigitalhumanities.org/3-2/a
-distinction-worth-exploring-archives-and-digital-historical-representations/.

73. See Matthew L. Jockers, *Macroanalysis: Digital Methods and Literary History*
(Urbana: U of Illinois P, 2013), 67–81; Ted Underwood, "Understanding Genre in a
Collection of a Million Volumes," Figshare (2014), dx.doi.org/10.6084/m9.figshare
.1281251; and Underwood, "The Life Cycles of Genres," *Journal of Cultural Analytics*,
23 May 2016, culturalanalytics.org/2016/05/the-life-cycles-of-genres.

74. Further examples include African American Newspapers, www.accessible
-archives.com/2011/02/african-american-newspapers; and The Poetess Archive,
idhmcmain.tamu.edu/poetess/. Also important in this regard are organizations like
the Advanced Research Consortium (ARC), the Networked Infrastructure for

Nineteenth-Century Electronic Scholarship (NINES), the Medieval Scholarly Alliance (MESA), 18thConnect, and others that seek to aggregate and make scholarship and archival documents available for centralized search and cataloging.

75. Cited from the "History" page of the Women Writers Project, www.wwp .northeastern.edu/about/history/, now relocated to Northeastern University. See Julia Flanders, "The Women Writers Project: A Digital Anthology," in *Electronic Textual Editing*, ed. Lou Burnard, Katherine O'Brien O'Keeffe, and John Unsworth (New York: Modern Language Association, 2006), 138–49; and Georgianna Ziegler, "Women Writers Online: An Evaluation and Annotated Bibliography of Web Resources," *Early Modern Literary Studies* 6.3 (2001), extra.shu.ac.uk/emls/06-3/ziegbib.htm.

76. Andrew Cole, *The Birth of Theory* (Chicago: U of Chicago P, 2014), 24–25; David Aers, "A Whisper in the Ear of Early Modernists; or, Reflections on Literary Critics Writing the 'History of the Subject,'" in *Culture and History, 1350–1600: Essays on English Communities, Identities and Writing*, ed. Aers (Detroit: Wayne State UP, 1992), 177–202, 179. On the ongoing omission of the medieval from histories of materialism, see Kellie Robertson, "Medieval Materialism: A Manifesto," *Exemplaria* 22.2 (2010): 99–118.

77. On the effects of copyright on the shape of digital history, see Benjamin Schmidt, "Digital History and the Copyright Black Hole," *Sapping Attention* (blog), 21 January 2011, sappingattention.blogspot.com/2011/01/digital-history-and-copyright -black.html.

78. On the semiotic challenges facing the remediation of medieval manuscripts, see Elaine Treharne, "Fleshing Out the Text: The Transcendent Manuscript in the Digital Age," *Postmedieval* 4.4 (2013): 465–78. As I write this, the Digitized Medieval Manuscripts project (digitizedmedievalmanuscripts.org/) links to image files of more than twenty thousand medieval manuscripts in more than three hundred digital libraries. But only a fraction of these have been transcribed as full text, and the transcribed texts are not searchable using a centralized interface. The Folger Shakespeare Library has begun the arduous task of producing semidiplomatic translations of its collection of early modern manuscript documents. See folgerpedia.folger.edu/Early_Modern _Manuscripts_Online_%28EMMO%29; and collation.folger.edu/2013/11/emmo-early -modern-manuscripts-online.

79. Existing resources, like the *Middle English Dictionary*, quod.lib.umich.edu/m /med/, which provides variant spellings for each head word, will make the problem of standardization and search more tractable.

80. See Theodore E. Mommsen, "Petrarch's Conception of 'The Dark Ages,'" *Speculum* 17.2 (1942): 226–42. Mommsen shows that Petrarch's description of the epoch "stretching from the fall of the Roman Empire down to his own age" (237) as *tenebrae*, "dark" (234), was not a response to the lack of documents but an interested judgment on the worth of the culture.

81. Ferdinand de Saussure, *Course in General Linguistics*, trans. Roy Harris (Chicago: Open Court, 2002), 8.

82. Franco Moretti, "Style, Inc. Reflections on Seven Thousand Titles (British Novels, 1740–1850)," *Critical Inquiry* 36.1 (2009): 134–58.

83. Jonathan Hope and Michael Witmore, "'The Hundredth Psalm to the Tune of "Green Sleeves"': Digital Approaches to Shakespeare's Language of Genre," *Shakespeare Quarterly* 61.3 (Fall 2010): 357–90, mcpress.media-commons.org/ShakespeareQuarterly _NewMedia/hope-witmore-the-hundredth-psalm/. For statistical characterizations of early English print and early modern drama, see the Visualizing English Print Project, vep.cs.wisc.edu.

84. There is a substantial literature on corpus design. For an overview, see Douglas Biber, "Representativeness in Corpus Design," *Literary and Linguistic Computing* 8.4 (1993): 243–57. For corpus methods more generally, see Tony McEnery and Andrew Hardie, *Corpus Linguistics: Method, Theory and Practice* (Cambridge: Cambridge UP, 2012).

85. See, e.g., Lev Manovich, "Trending: The Promises and the Challenges of Big Social Data," in Gold, *Debates in the Digital Humanities*, 460–75, dhdebates.gc.cuny.edu /debates/text/15. For a probing treatment of the relation between the methodology of digital humanities and that of the social sciences, see Tanya E. Clement, "Where Is Methodology in Digital Humanities?," in Gold, *Debates in the Digital Humanities*, dhde-bates.gc.cuny.edu/debates/text/65.

### Chapter 3. *Was It for This?* and the Study of Influence

1. For big data approaches to literary influence, see David Bamman and Gregory Crane, *Discovering Multilingual Text Reuse in Literary Texts*, white paper, Perseus Digital Library, www.perseus.tufts.edu/publications/2009-Bamman.pdf; Bamman and Crane, "The Logic and Discovery of Textual Allusion" (paper, LaTeCH [Language Technology for Cultural Heritage Data], Marrakech, Morocco: LREC, 2008), dl.tufts.edu/catalog/tufts: PB.001.002.00004; David A. Smith, Ryan Cordell, and Elizabeth Maddock Dillon, "Infectious Texts: Modeling Text Reuse in Nineteenth-Century Newspapers," *Proceedings of the Workshop on Big Humanities* (Silicon Valley, CA: IEEE Computer Society Press, 2013), www.ccs.neu.edu/home/dasmith/infect-bighum-2013.pdf; and Matthew L. Jockers, *Macroanalysis: Digital Methods and Literary History* (Urbana: U of Illinois P, 2013), whose chapter titled "Influence" (154–68) says much about measuring similarity but virtually nothing about influence as such.

2. See Bruno Latour, *Reassembling the Social: An Introduction to Actor-Network Theory* (New York: Oxford UP, 2005). Much recent work in digital humanities has sought to reconstruct and analyze networks. See Franco Moretti, "Network Theory, Plot Analysis," in *Distant Reading* (New York: Verso, 2013), 211–40; David K. Elson, Nicholas Dames, and Kathleen R. McKeown, "Extracting Social Networks from Literary Fiction," in *Proceedings of the 48th Annual Meeting of the Association for Computational Linguistics* (Stroudsburg, PA: Association for Computational Linguistics, 2010), 138–47, www1.cs.columbia.edu/~delson/pubs/ACL2010-ElsonDamesMcKeown.pdf; and Ed Finn, *Becoming Yourself: The Afterlife of Reception*, Stanford Literary Lab Pamphlet 3 (Stanford, CA: Stanford Literary Lab, 2011), litlab.stanford.edu/LiteraryLabPamphlet3.pdf. Finn builds "networks of recommendations based on consumer purchases drawn from Amazon" and from co-occurrences of book titles in "professional and consumer reviews" (3).

3. On the complicated relationship between "materiality" and actor-network theory, see Bruno Latour, in "Can We Get Our Materialism Back Please?," *Isis* 98.1 (2007): 138–42, who wants to rehabilitate the term; and Graham Harman, in *Prince of Networks: Bruno Latour and Metaphysics* (Melbourne, Australia: re.press, 2009), 107–12, who argues for disposing of it. I follow Latour in reclaiming *materialism* not as the idealist doctrine that all things can be reduced to some brute *res extensa* but rather as an investment in attending to the heterogeneity of things and the agency they exercise.

4. William Wordsworth, *The Prelude: The Four Texts (1798, 1799, 1805, 1850)*, ed. Jonathan Wordsworth (New York: Penguin, 1995), 3. The draft fragment is transcribed from "MS JJ." Parenthetical references to poetry are to line numbers.

5. Jonathan Wordsworth, letter to the editor, *TLS*, 18 April 1975, 428.

6. Walter Kaiser, letter to the editor, *TLS*, 9 May 1975, 512.

7. John Woolford, letter to the editor, *TLS*, 6 June 1975, 627.

8. Jonathan Wordsworth, letter to the editor, *TLS*, 6 June 1975, 627; Henry Woudhuysen, email correspondence with author, 4 June 2012.

9. Jonathan Wordsworth, letter to the editor, *TLS*, 11 July 1975, 778.

10. Paul Haeffner, letter to the editor, *TLS*, 25 July 1975, 840.

11. Howard Erskine-Hill, letter to the editor, *TLS*, 26 September 1975, 1094.

12. Jonathan Wordsworth, "Fructifying Spots of Time," *TLS*, 11 November 1977, 1330.

13. When he reprinted this portion of the review in chapter 2 of *The Borders of Vision* (Oxford: Clarendon, 1982), 420, Jonathan Wordsworth reaffirmed his continuing desire for a "striking classical source" and dismissed the *Aeneid* yet again.

14. For a discussion of the role of source study and influence hunting in the disciplinary history of literary studies, see Ted Underwood, *Why Literary Periods Mattered* (Stanford, CA: Stanford UP, 2013), 119–21, 124–27.

15. See, e.g., *The Prelude, 1798–1799, by William Wordsworth*, ed. Stephen Parrish (Ithaca, NY: Cornell UP, 1977), 6; John T. Ogden, "Was It for This?," *Wordsworth Circle* 9.4 (1978): 371–72; Leslie Brisman, *Romantic Origins* (Ithaca, NY: Cornell UP, 1978), 312–13; Susan Wolfson, *The Questioning Presence: Wordsworth, Keats, and the Interrogative Mode in Romantic Poetry* (Ithaca, NY: Cornell UP, 1986), 146–50, 156–57; Geoffrey Hartman, "'Was it for this . . . ?': Wordsworth and the Birth of the Gods," in *Romantic Revolutions: Criticism and Theory*, ed. Kenneth R. Johnston, Gilbert D. Chaitin, Karen Hansen, and Herbert Marks (Bloomington: Indiana UP, 1990), 8–25; John A. Hodgson, "'Was It for This . . . ?': Wordsworth's Virgilian Questionings," *Texas Studies in Literature and Language* 33.2 (1991): 125–36; Robert J. Griffin, *Wordsworth's Pope* (New York: Cambridge UP, 1995), 102–7; and Simon Bainbridge, "'Was it for this[ . . . ]?': The Poetic Histories of Southey and Wordsworth," *Romanticism on the Net* 32–33 (2003–4).

16. Google books can be found at books.google.com; EEBO at eebo.chadwyck.com; EEBO-TCP at eebo.odl.ox.ac.uk/e/eebo/; Literature Online at literature.proquest.com.

17. Joseph Glanvill, *Lux Orientalis* (London, 1662), 51.

18. Duncan Wu proposes Wrangham in *Wordsworth: An Inner Life* (Oxford: Blackwell, 2002), 120.

19. For the indispensable work on Wordsworth's reading see Duncan Wu, *Words-worth's Reading, 1770–1799* (Cambridge: Cambridge UP, 1993). The phrase appears in Vicesimus Knox, ed., *Extracts, Elegant, Instructive, and Entertaining, in Poetry* (London, 1791), 23, 146, 159, 191. See also Bruce Graver, "Duncan Wu's *Wordsworth's Reading: 1770–1790*: A Supplementary List with Corrections," *Romanticism on the Net* 1 (1996), www.erudit.org/en/journals/ron/1996-n1-ron413/005711ar/, which contains further suggestions regarding Wordsworth's reading of Virgil.

20. Ezra Pound, *Guide to Kulchur* (New York: New Directions, 1938), 134.

21. Bloom, *Anxiety of Influence*, 96.

22. On the Renaissance use of the term *commonplace*, see Kathy Eden, *Friends Hold All Things in Common: Tradition, Intellectual Property, and the Adages of Erasmus* (New Haven, CT: Yale UP, 2001). On Aristotle's *koinoi topoi*, see *On Rhetoric*, trans. George A. Kennedy (New York: Oxford UP, 1991), 45–47. Present-day uses of the term *commonplace* are, as it were, commonplace, cutting across critical approaches, including historicisms both new and old. See, e.g., David Norbrook, *Writing the English Republic* (Cambridge: Cambridge UP, 2000), 177: "The caterpillar analogy was commonplace"; Stephen Greenblatt, *Shakespearean Negotiations: The Circulation of Social Energy in Renaissance England* (Berkeley: U of California P, 1988), 33: "the role of religion in preserving the social order was a commonplace"; Stephen Orgel, *Impersonations: The Performance of Gender in Shakespeare's England* (Cambridge: Cambridge UP, 1996), 119: "the association of cross-dressing with prostitution was commonplace"; and Stanley Wells, *Shakespeare, Sex, and Love* (Oxford: Oxford UP, 2010), 166: "The image of orgasm as a 'little death' was commonplace."

23. On black boxes and black-boxing, see Bruno Latour, *Science in Action: How to Follow Scientists and Engineers through Society* (Cambridge, MA: Harvard UP, 1987), 1–20, 1.

24. See, however, Paul Strohm, "Historicity without Historicism?," *postmedieval: a journal of medieval cultural studies* 1.3 (2010): 380–91, which argues that the New Historicism has been particularly susceptible to accepting pervasiveness without transmission: "Although nobody believes in the 'spirit of an age' anymore, new historicism was no less reliant than old upon an unacknowledged belief in some kind of spirit-medium or ether in which unexpected cultural affinities might emerge and repetitions and replications occur, by an unexplained process of effortless transmission" (381). On the astrological link between influence and a phrase or idea being "in the air," see C. S. Lewis, *The Discarded Image* (Cambridge: Cambridge UP, 1964), 110.

25. Because the method of tracing influence demonstrated here takes syntax into account, it diverges from other digital approaches, like topic modeling, word-frequency analysis, and semantic cohort methods, that discard syntax in order to measure the relative frequency or co-occurrence of words in a document. For a sophisticated demonstration and theorization of topic modeling, see Andrew Goldstone and Ted Underwood, "The Quiet Transformations of Literary Studies: What Thirteen Thousand Scholars Could Tell Us," *New Literary History* 45.3 (2014): 359–84; for an extended discussion of relative-frequency analysis, see Stephen Ramsay, *Reading Machines: Towards an Algorithmic Criticism* (Urbana: U of Illinois P, 2011), 32–82; for an application of the semantic cohort method, see Ryan Heuser and Long Le-Khac, *A Quantitative Literary History of 2,958*

*Nineteenth-Century British Novels: The Semantic Cohort Method*, Stanford Literary Lab Pamphlet 4 (Stanford, CA: Stanford Literary Lab, 2012), litlab.stanford.edu /LiteraryLabPamphlet4.pdf.

26. Roman Jakobson, "Shifters, Verbal Categories, and the Russian Verb," in *Russian and Slavic Grammar: Studies, 1931–1981*, ed. Linda R. Waugh and Morris Halle (New York: Mouton, 1984), 42–44.

27. Mary Leapor, "Upon her Play Being Returned to her Stain'd with Claret," in *Poems by Eminent Ladies*, [comp. George Coleman and Bonnell Thornton], 2 vols. (London, 1755), 2:133.

28. On the history of stop words, see Daniel Rosenberg, "Stop, Words," *Representations* 127.1 (2014): 83–92.

29. Latin text and English translation from Virgil, *Aeneid*, in *Eclogues, Georgics, Aeneid 1–6*, trans. H. Rushton Fairclough, rev. ed., Loeb Classical Library (Cambridge, MA: Harvard UP, 1935), 338–39.

30. I have altered the Fairclough *Aeneid* translation, 440–41, to make evident the parallel with Aeneas's earlier lament.

31. For a study of Wordsworth's classical education, see Richard W. Clancey, *Wordsworth's Classical Undersong* (New York: St. Martin's, 1999), esp. 1–51. For extensive treatment of his education more generally, see T. W. Thompson, *Wordsworth's Hawkshead*, ed. Robert Woof (London: Oxford UP, 1970); and Ben Ross Schneiderman, *Wordsworth's Cambridge Education* (New York: Cambridge UP, 1957).

32. See M. L. Clark, *Classical Education in Britain, 1500–1900* (Cambridge: Cambridge UP, 1959). Clancey, *Wordsworth's Classical Undersong*, 26, notes that Hawkshead had an unusually intense focus on learning Greek as well as Latin.

33. On Wordsworth's early reading of Virgil, see Duncan Wu, "Three Translations of Virgil Read by Wordsworth in 1788," *Notes and Queries* 37.4 (1990): 407–9.

34. Early English translators of the *Aeneid*, like Surrey and Stanyhurst, often translate only books 2 and 4 or only the first four books.

35. Virgil, *Virgil's Aeneid*, trans. Christopher Pitt, vol. 1 (London, 1736). Wordsworth's copy of Pitt's Virgil is now in the collection of Paul F. Betz, who generously allowed me to view it.

36. Wu, *Wordsworth's Reading*, 140–41.

37. Virgil, *Virgil's Aeneid* (Pitt), 4.971–72. See also Duncan Wu, "Three Sources for Wordsworth's *Prelude* Cave," *Notes and Queries* 38.3 (1991): 298–99, 298.

38. Though it is now more common to use these terms to refer to facing-page translations, they have been used since the nineteenth century to refer as well to highly literal translations. See *Oxford English Dictionary Online*, s.vv. "trot," "crib," and "pony."

39. William Wordsworth, *Translations of Chaucer and Virgil*, ed. Bruce Graver (Ithaca, NY: Cornell UP, 1998), 155–63, 273.

40. Hodgson, "Was It for This . . . ?," 129.

41. For the strict definition of an epic formula, see Albert B. Lord, *The Singer of Tales*, ed. Stephen Mitchell and Gregory Nagy, 2nd ed. (Cambridge, MA: Harvard UP, 2000). Even under a more relaxed definition, Virgil is not using a classical formula.

42. Hodgson, "Was It for This . . . ?," 132. In order to argue that *Was it for this* is the "straightforward" translation of Aeneas's (and presumably Anna's) line, Hodgson must denigrate other translations. Of Dryden's he writes, "Here the initial simplicity, and even the very spirit of these questions, is obscured" (133). He describes Ogilby's 1650 *Aeneid* as "unidiomatic" and Wordsworth's own 1823–24 translation as "sadly stilted" (135n19).

43. Virgil, *Aeneid* (Graver), 2.892–93, in Wordsworth, *Translations*.

44. Virgil, *Virgil's Aeneid* (Pitt), 2.893–94.

45. Charles Anthon, *The Æneid of Virgil* (New York: Harper & Bros., 1843), 428, follows the "standard" translation before adding that the Latin is "more literally" translated as "was it this on account of which." See also the annotation to line 2.664 in Virgil, *The Bucolics, Georgics, and Aeneid of Virgil*, ed. Edward Moore (Boston: Bazin & Ellsworth, 1849), 447; Virgil, *P. Vergili Maronis Opera: The First Six Books of the Aeneid*, ed. John Conington and Henry Nettleship (London: Whittaker, 1863), 176; and Virgil, *Virgil's Aeneid Books 1–6*, ed. H. R. Fairclough and Seldon L. Brown (New York: B. H. Sanborn, 1920), 306.

46. Henry Howard, Earl of Surrey, "Second Book of Virgil's Aeneid," in *The Works of Henry Howard, Earl of Surrey, and of Sir Thomas Wyatt the Elder*, ed. George Frederick Nott, 2 vols. (London, 1815), 1:119. Gavin Douglas's 1513 Scots *Aeneid*, the first to translate the whole poem into a modern Germanic language, renders the lines thus: "Is this the way, my haly moder, that thou/Suld keip me fais and firis passyng throw?" Virgil, *Virgil's Aeneis, Translated into Scottish Verse*, trans. Gavin Douglas (Edinburgh, 1710), 61.

47. Virgil, *The First Foure Bookes of Virgils Aeneis*, trans. Richard Stanyhurst (London, 1583), 39.

48. Bruno Latour illustrates how standards are extended through networks using the example of metrology, the standardization of measure. See Latour, *We Have Never Been Modern*, trans. Catherine Porter (Cambridge, MA: Harvard UP, 1993), 119–20; and Latour, *Reassembling the Social: An Introduction to Actor-Network Theory* (New York: Oxford UP, 2005), 227–29. The connection between metrology and translation is elaborated in Michael Wintroub, "Translations: Words, Things, Going Native, and Staying True," *American Historical Review* 120.4 (2015): 1185–1227.

49. *Oxford English Dictionary Online*, s.v. "source." For a brilliant study of the topos of the source and its liquid metaphors, see David Quint, *Origin and Originality in Renaissance Literature* (New Haven, CT: Yale UP, 1983).

50. Because it rejects the notion of a single, ultimate origin, the network has no difficulty accounting for multiple points of origins, even apparently independent ones such as, for example, the discovery of the calculus by Newton and Leibniz.

51. Latour, *Reassembling the Social*, 52–53.

52. Erskine-Hill, "Prelude."

53. John Harington, "Apologie of Poetry," preface to Lodovico Ariosto, *Orlando furioso in English heroical verse, by Iohn Haringto[n]* (London, 1591), viii.

54. Robert Southey, "History," in *The Annual Anthology*, [ed. Samuel Coleridge and Charles Lamb], vol. 2 (Bristol: Biggs, 1800), 88–89. The poem was republished at least sixteen times before Southey's death in 1843.

55. The letter is quoted in Jonathan Wordsworth, introduction to William Wordsworth, *The Prelude*, xxv.

56. Jacques Derrida, *Limited Inc.*, ed. Gerald Graff (Evanston, IL: Northwestern UP, 1988).

57. Thomas Collins, *The Tears of Love* (London, 1615), 42.

58. Samuel Brandon, *The tragicomoedi of the vertuous Octauia* (London, 1598), G1r.

59. Thomas Heywood, *Troia Britannica, or Great Britain's Troy* (London, 1609), canto 10, p. 216. Heywood also uses the formula in his tragedy *The Rape of Lucrece* (London, 1608): "Was it for this you plac'd my regiment / Vpon a hill, to be the sad spectator / Of such a generall cowardise?" (sig. 1v).

60. Ovid, *Ovid's Metamorphoses in Fifteen Books, Translated by the Most Eminent Hands* (London, 1717), 304; these lines are listed as having been translated by the poet John Gay. Nineteenth- and twentieth-century translators also widely render these lines as "Was it for this."

61. The classical back formation of the phrase made its way into translations of Latin prose as well. See, e.g., Cicero's *Pro Caelio* in William Duncan's *Cicero's Select Orations* (London, 1792), 332–33, where "was it for this" is used to translate "ob hanc causam."

62. The dictum that agents must *do* something to show up in a network is helpfully captured in the bibliographer Randall McLeod's term *transformission*, which refers to the way texts are transformed as they are transmitted. See Randall McLeod, "Information on Information," *Text* 5 (1991): 240–81.

63. Mark S. Granovetter, "The Strength of Weak Ties," *American Journal of Sociology* 78.6 (1973): 1360–80. Granovetter observes that "whatever is to be diffused can reach a large number of people, and traverse greater social distance . . . when passed through weak ties rather than strong" (1366).

64. For a different account of network as metaphor, see Christopher D. Kilgore, "Rhetoric of the Network: Toward a New Metaphor," *Mosaic: A Journal for the Interdisciplinary Study of Literature* 46.4 (2013): 37–58.

65. Robert Southey, *Letters Written During a Short Residence in Spain and Portugal* (London, 1797), 279–80; Francis Quarles, "Hieroglyph VIII," in *Hieroglyphikes of the Life of Man* (London, 1638), 31.

66. William Cowper, *The Poetical Works of William Cowper*, ed. Robert Southey, vol. 1 (London: Bohn, 1854), 84.

67. Johann Wolfgang von Goethe, *Wilhelm Meister's Journeyman Years, or the Renunciants*, trans. Krishna Winston, ed. Jane K. Brown, vol. 10 of *Goethe's Collected Works* (New York: Suhrkamp, 1989), 302; Franco Moretti, "Style, Inc. Reflections on Seven Thousand Titles (British Novels, 1740–1850)," *Critical Inquiry* 36.1 (2009): 134–58.

68. For a vivid depiction of how a schoolmaster should correct the translations of his students, see Roger Ascham, *The Scholemaster*, in *English Works of Roger Ascham*, ed. William Aldis Wright (Cambridge: Cambridge UP, 1970), 183–84.

69. See Wu, *Wordsworth*.

70. Arthur F. Marotti, *John Donne, Coterie Poet* (Madison: U of Wisconsin P, 1986).

71. F. R. Leavis, *The Great Tradition* (New York: G. W. Stewart, 1948).

72. John Law, "Notes on the Theory of the Actor-Network: Ordering, Strategy and Heterogeneity," *Systems Practice* 5 (1992): 379–93, 380.

73. On Wordsworth's access to various libraries and book collections, see appendixes 4–7 in Wu, *Wordsworth's Reading*, 171–86. On the issue of material networks, see Robert Darnton, "What is the History of Books?," *Daedalus* 111.3 (1982): 65–83. There is no question, for example, that Darnton's "communication circuit," or one of the many subsequent revisions of it, describes a necessary causal part of the network that led to the diffusion of *Was it for this*. In his more recent work Darnton has shifted from discussing circuits to discussing networks; see Darnton, *Poetry and the Police: Communication Networks in Eighteenth-Century Paris* (Cambridge, MA: Belknap-Harvard UP, 2010). See also Alan Liu, "From Reading to Social Computing," *Literary Studies in the Digital Age: An Evolving Anthology* (MLA Commons), dlsanthology.commons.mla.org/from-reading-to-social-computing; Liu writes that book history has moved inquiry beyond the triad of author, text, and reader to restore to view "other vital nodes in the circuit" of literary production, including the "editor, publisher, bookseller, shipper, balladmonger or peddler, annotator, and so on" (para. 17).

74. Karl Marx, *Grundrisse*, trans. Martin Nicolaus (New York: Penguin, 1993), 110.

75. Bruno Latour, "On Using ANT for Studying Information Systems: A (Somewhat) Socratic Dialogue," in *The Social Study of Communication and Information Technology: Innovation, Actors, and Contexts*, ed. Chrisanthi Avgerou, Claudio Ciborra, and Frank Land (New York: Oxford UP, 2004), 62–76, 68. See also Rita Felski, "Context Stinks!," *New Literary History* 42.4 (2011): 573–91.

76. From the preface to Harold Bloom, *The Anxiety of Influence*, 2nd ed. (Oxford: Oxford UP, 1997), xiii.

77. Harold Bloom, *A Map of Misreading* (New York: Oxford UP, 1975), 71.

78. Bloom, *Map*, 18–19.

79. Bloom, *Map*, 19.

80. On Bloom's reduction of the plurality of intertexts to that of the predecessor, see Graham Allen, *Intertextuality*, 2nd ed. (New York: Routledge, 2011), 137.

81. See Michel Foucault, "The Discourse on Language," in *The Archaeology of Knowledge and the Discourse on Language*, trans. A. M. Sheridan Smith (New York: Pantheon, 1972), 221: "This principle [the author] is not constant at all times. All around us, there are sayings and texts whose meaning or effectiveness has nothing to do with any author to whom they might be attributed: mundane remarks, quickly forgotten; orders and contacts that are signed, but have no recognizable author; technical prescriptions anonymously transmitted."

82. T. S. Eliot, "Tradition and the Individual Talent," in *The Sacred Wood: Essays on Poetry and Criticism* (New York: Knopf, 1930), 52–58.

83. On the development of the concept of intertextuality out of the writings of M. M. Bakhtin, see Julia Kristeva, *Desire in Language* (New York: Columbia UP, 1980), 64–91.

84. Roland Barthes, "The Death of the Author," in *Image—Music—Text*, trans. Stephen Heath (New York: Hill & Wang, 1977), 142–48, 146.

85. Bruno Latour, *The Pasteurization of France*, trans. Alan Sheridan and John Law (Cambridge, MA: Harvard UP, 1988), 212–38; John Milton, *Areopagitica*, in *The Complete Prose Works of John Milton*, vol. 2, ed. Ernest Sirluck (New Haven, CT: Yale UP, 1959), 492.

86. M. H. Abrams, *Natural Supernaturalism: Tradition and Revolution in Romantic Literature* (New York: Norton, 1971), 96. Wordsworth references the Aeolian harp in the 1850 *Prelude* 1.96; the "Aeolian lyre," or wind harp, also serves as a central figure for poetic influence in Percy Shelley's *Defense of Poetry*, in *Shelley's Poetry and Prose*, ed. Donald H. Reiman and Neil Fraistat (New York: Norton, 2002), 511. See M. H. Abrams, *The Mirror and the Lamp: Romantic Theory and the Critical Tradition* (Oxford: Oxford UP, 1953), 51–52, for the classic account; Timothy Morton, "An Object-Oriented Defense of Poetry," *New Literary History* 43.2 (2012): 205–24, for a treatment that seeks to "transcend anthropocentrism" (1); and Thomas L. Hankins and Robert J. Silverman, "The Aeolian Harp and the Romantic Quest of Nature," in *Instruments and the Imagination* (Princeton, NJ: Princeton UP, 2014), 101–27, for a study of the harp's role as an actual scientific and musical instrument.

87. On actor-network theory as an attempt to overcome "the agency/structure debate," see Bruno Latour, "On Recalling ANT," in *Actor Network Theory and After*, ed. John Law and John Hassard (Oxford: Blackwell, 1999), 15–25, 16.

88. Critics have invariably noticed, for example, that Wordsworth leaves ambiguous the reference of the phrase's second pronoun, *this*. In earlier uses of the phrase the demonstrative *this* often refers not to a specific fact (like the failure to write a poem) but to a vague though all-encompassing situation. The indeterminacy of the pronoun in *The Prelude*, in other words, differs only in degree, not kind, from the indeterminacy of many of its predecessors.

89. In the terms of network science, this is the problem of multimodal or multipartite networks, which become increasingly resistant to analysis, and especially quantitative characterization, as the number of node types increases. On multimodal networks in humanities research, see Scott Weingart, "Networks Demystified 9: Bimodal Networks," *The Scottbot Irregular* (blog), 21 January 2015, www.scottbot.net /HIAL/?p=41158.

### Chapter 4. *Act as If* and Useful Fictions

1. Letter to the editor, *Weekly Louisianian*, 8 November 1879, 2, retrieved from the African American Newspapers Series 1, 1827–1998, through NewsBank /Readex.

2. See the direct-advertisement section in *Popular Science*, July 2007, 109; and Rev. Gary Brodsky, *Act as If . . . And Get Whatever You Want* (GSL Media, 2010), books .google.com/books?id=aBQe8rXcrgYC&pg=RA1-PA119&lpg=RA1-PA119&dq=Rev .+Gary+Brodsky,+Act+as+If+.+.+.+And+Get+Whatever+You+Want&source=bl&ots =LHFvuBsk6K&sig=2KW77nddPVa6gIZcwtUW-ALINEQ&hl=en&sa=X&ved=0ahUKEwj Z7ZOphdDWAhXhiFQKHVyCCGMQ6AEILTAB#v=onepage&q=Rev.%20Gary%20Brodsky %2C%20Act%20as%20If%20.%20.%20.%20And%20Get%20Whatever%20You%20Want &f=false.

3. Holly Boyd, *Act as If* (Barnesville, OH: A1 Organizing, 2007), books.google.com /books?id=hEZyBAAACAAJ&dq. See also Joe Lavelle, *Act As If It Were Impossible To Fail: The Employee Handbook That Your Employer Hasn't Given You* (Charleston, SC: BookSurge, 2009).

4. Farrah Gray, *Reallionaire: Nine Steps to Becoming Rich from the Inside Out*, with Fran Harris (Deerfield Beach, FL: Health Communications, 2004), 235, 258. See also Lorin Woolfe, *The Bible on Leadership: From Moses to Matthew—Management Lessons for Contemporary Leaders* (New York: American Management Association, 2002), 23: "Act as if someone else with more power than you is watching"; and Richard Carlson, *Don't Sweat the Small Stuff with Your Family* (New York: Hyperion, 1998), which instructs readers to "imagine that someone else is in the room watching you" (175).

5. B. J. Gallagher, *Why Don't I Do the Things I Know Are Good for Me? Taking Small Steps toward Improving the Big Picture* (New York: Berkley, 2009), 75. Elizabeth Wurtzel, *More, Now, Again: A Memoir of Addiction* (New York: Simon & Schuster, 2002), 181, recounts being advised to "act as if you believe you will remain sober" even when she knew another drink awaited her.

6. The lines are usually attributed to the educational psychologist William W. Purkey (as in en.wikipedia.org/wiki/William_Watson_Purkey), though they have since entered the public domain. Susannah Clark and Richard Leigh include some of the lines in the country song "Come From the Heart," published in 1987 and performed by Kathy Mattea on the album *Willow in the Wind* (Mercury, 1989).

7. Michel Foucault, *Technologies of the Self: A Seminar with Michel Foucault*, ed. Luther H. Martin, Huck Gutman, and Patrick H. Hutton (Amherst: U of Massachusetts P, 1988), 16–49.

8. I write of imperatives, but for the purposes of my argument it makes no difference whether an author tells us to act, recommends that we must or should act, or writes, "Let us act." Exhortations and statements of necessity, obligation, or norms are, for the purposes of the intellectual tradition explored here, functionally equivalent.

9. Charles Taylor, *A Secular Age* (Cambridge, MA: Harvard UP, 2007), 3.

10. Cicero, *Pro Plancio*, trans. N. H. Watts, Loeb Classical Library (Cambridge, MA: Harvard UP, 1979), 38.93. He also quotes a principle that he attributes to Scipio Africanus: "We must always live as if we expected to have to give an account of what we have been doing" (Semper ita vivamus ut rationem reddendam nobis arbitremur). Cicero, *The Verrine Orations*, 2 vols., trans. L. H. G. Greenwood, Loeb Classical Library (Cambridge, MA: Harvard UP, 1935), 2.2.28.

11. English text from *Epictetus his Morals, with Simplicius his Comment*, trans. George Stanhope, 2nd ed. (London, 1700), 423. For Simplicius's Greek and a Latin translation by Hieronymo Wolfio, see Epictetus, *Epicteti Stoici Philosophi Enchiridion . . . Quibus adjiciuntur hac Editione Simplicii Commentarius in Enchiridion Epicteti* (London, 1670), 291.

12. Seneca, *Ad Lucilium Epistulae Morales*, trans. Richard M. Gummere, 3 vols., Loeb Classical Library (Cambridge, MA: Harvard UP, 1917–25), 1:25.5.

13. Thomas Browne, *Religio Medici*, in *The Major Works*, ed. C. A. Patrides (New York: Penguin, 1977), 119.

14. John Tillotson, sermon 81, in *The Works of the Most Reverend Dr. John Tillotson*, 2nd ed., 2 vols. (London, 1717), 1:612.

15. Quoted from the Douay-Rheims translation, with Greek New Testament original inserted. The King James Version uses "act as though" for verses 29–30 but breaks the pattern for verse 31: "And they that use this world, as not abusing *it*."

16. Ignatius of Loyola, *The Spiritual Exercises of St. Ignatius*, trans. George A. Ganss (Chicago: Loyola UP, 1992), 129, translation slightly modified.

17. Jonathan Edwards, "The Sin and Folly of Depending on Future Time," in *The Works of President Edwards* (1808–29; reprint, 10 vols. in 4, New York: Leavitt & Allen, 1856), 4:359. See also Richard Baxter, *A Call to the Unconverted* (Glasgow: Chalmers & Collins, 1825), 320.

18. Legal fictions, which are frequently expressed using the *X as if Y* syntax, are a related phenomenon, although such fictions function as procedural accommodations rather than technologies of the self.

19. Desiderius Erasmus, *The Education of a Christian Prince*, ed. Lisa Jardine (Cambridge: Cambridge UP, 1997), 6. See also p. 134: "It is a splendid thing, when the situation demands it, to defeat a foe by valor. Who denies that? But how much more splendid to act as if no one were your enemy. However outstanding it may be to beat back an enemy, it is surely a finer form of victory to stand aloof from him."

20. Blaise Pascal, *Pascal's Pensées*, intro. T. S. Eliot (New York: Dutton, 1958). Citations are to Leo Brunschvicg's 1897 edition.

21. On the difference between evidential and practical reasons for belief, see Nicholas Rescher, *Pascal's Wager: A Study of Practical Reasoning in Philosophical Theology* (Notre Dame, IN: U of Notre Dame P, 1985), 7–23, 44–70. Rescher seeks to join Pascal's practical justification of belief to those of Kant and James, but without fully acknowledging the differences (39–42).

22. Louis Althusser, "Ideology and Ideological State Apparatuses (Notes towards an Investigation)," in *Lenin and Philosophy and Other Essays*, trans. Ben Brewster (London: New Left Books, 1971), 158. See also Slavoj Žižek, "How Did Marx Invent the Symptom?," in *The Sublime Object of Ideology* (London: Verso, 1989), 33–39.

23. See Ian Hacking, "The Logic of Pascal's Wager," in *Gambling on God: Essays on Pascal's Wager*, ed. Jeff Jordan (Lanham, MD: Rowman & Littlefield, 1994), 21–29, 25: "There is no cant to Pascal. He accepts as a piece of human nature that belief is catching: if you go along with pious people, give up bad habits, follow a life of 'holy water and sacraments,' intend to 'stupefy one' into belief, you will become a believer. . . . One cannot decide to believe in God. One can decide to act so that one will very probably come to believe in God."

24. William Shakespeare, *The Tragedy of Hamlet, Prince of Denmark*, ed. Barbara Mowat, Paul Werstine, Michael Poston, and Rebecca Niles (Washington, DC: Folger Shakespeare Library, n.d.), 3.4.181, www.folgerdigitaltexts.org. On habit as a cause of belief in the early modern period, see Ramie Targoff, *Common Prayer: The Language of Public Devotion in Early Modern England* (Chicago: U of Chicago P, 2001).

25. Aristotle, *Nichomachean Ethics*, trans. Terence Irwin (Indianapolis: Hackett, 1985), 1103b–1105b.

26. See Aristotle, *On Interpretation*, trans. Harold P. Cooke, Loeb Classical Library (Cambridge, MA: Harvard UP, 1973), 16a3.

27. Thomas Traherne, *Christian Ethicks* (London, 1675), 344. For a critical text with introduction and commentary, see Thomas Traherne, *Christian Ethicks*, ed. Carol L. Marks and George Robert Guffey (Ithaca, NY: Cornell UP, 1968).

28. Traherne, *Christian Ethicks* (1675), 333.

29. Traherne, *Christian Ethicks* (1675), 345.

30. Immanuel Kant, *Critique of Pure Reason*, ed. Paul Guyer and Allen Wood (New York: Cambridge UP, 1998). I cite the *Critique of Pure Reason* using the standard A and B pagination of the first (1781) and second (1787) editions, respectively.

31. See Henry E. Allison, *Kant's Transcendental Idealism: An Interpretation and Defense* (New Haven, CT: Yale UP, 1986), 437–48.

32. "Si Dieu n'existait pas, il faudrait l'inventer," in Voltaire, "Epître à l'auteur du livre des Trois imposteurs," in *Oeuvres complètes de Voltaire*, ed. Louis Moland, vol. 10 (Paris: Garnier, 1877), 403.

33. In English texts this emphasis is usually marked by bold font; in German texts by both bold font and spacing between the letters: "**a l s   o b**."

34. Immanuel Kant, *Groundwork of The metaphysics of morals*, in *Practical Philosophy*, ed. and trans. Mary J. Gregor, vol. 4 (Cambridge: Cambridge UP, 1996), 421. With the exception of the *Critique of Pure Reason*, Kant's works are quoted from the English translations noted and cited by the volume and page numbers of the Akademie edition of *Kant's gesammelte Schriften* (Berlin, 1902–). The FLN is usually treated as a subvariation of the first major formulation, the Formula of Universal Law (FUL). On the different formulations of the categorical imperative, see Stephen Philip Engstrom, *The Form of Practical Knowledge: A Study of the Categorical Imperative* (Cambridge, MA: Harvard UP, 2009), 160–64. Kant restates the FLN in *Critique of Practical Reason* 5:44.

35. Allen W. Wood, *Kant's Ethical Thought* (Cambridge: Cambridge UP, 1999), 80.

36. See D. D. Raphael and A. L. Macfie's introduction to Adam Smith, *The Theory of Moral Sentiments* (Oxford: Clarendon, 1976), 31. Citations are to Adam Smith, *The Theory of Moral Sentiments*, ed. Ryan Patrick Hanley, intro. Amartya Sen (New York: Penguin, 2009).

37. Smith, *Theory of Moral Sentiments*, 186.

38. Smith, *Theory of Moral Sentiments*, 187.

39. Smith, *Theory of Moral Sentiments*, 187.

40. Smith, *Theory of Moral Sentiments*, 187–88.

41. For distortions of the Kantian imperative, see Hannah Arendt, *Eichmann in Jerusalem: A Report on the Banality of Evil* (New York: Penguin, 1994), 136–37; and Jean-Paul Sartre, *Saint Genet: Actor and Martyr* (London: Heinemann, 1988), 67. See also Sartre, *The Emotions: Outline of a Theory*, trans. Bernard Frechtman (New York: Citadel, 1993), 58; and Sartre, *The Family Idiot: Gustave Flaubert, 1821–1857* (Chicago: U of CP, 1994), 142.

42. Hans Vaihinger, *The Philosophy of 'As if,'* trans. C. K. Ogden (Mansfield Centre, CT: Martino, 2009), viii. Vaihinger's fictionalism, introduced to literary studies by Frank Kermode, *The Sense of an Ending: Studies in the Theory of Fiction* (New York: Oxford UP,

1967), has generated a small but spirited debate among critics. See, e.g., Wolfgang Iser, *The Fictive and the Imaginary: Charting Literary Anthropology* (Baltimore: Johns Hopkins UP, 1993); David Wayne Thomas, "Gödel's Theorem and Postmodern Theory," *PMLA* 110 (1995): 248–61; Nelson Goodman, *Ways of Worldmaking* (Indianapolis: Hackett, 1978); and Barry Stampfel, "Hans Vaihinger's Ghostly Presence in Contemporary Literary Studies," *Criticism* 40.3 (1998): 437–54. As Stampfel notes, contemporary criticism has faulted Vaihinger primarily for his positivist, idealist, and metaphysical assumptions.

43. Although Vaihinger briefly mentions American Pragmatism in the preface to the English edition of *The Philosophy of 'As If'* (vii), which he composed in 1924, he does not fully elaborate the differences between that philosophy and his own. See Heinrich Scholz, *Die Religionsphilosophie des Als-ob* (Leipzig: Felix Meiner, 1921), 95–123, which compares the philosophies of Vaihinger and William James.

44. William James, *The Principles of Psychology*, vol. 2 (New York: Holt, 1918), 321–22, italics original.

45. William James, "Philosophical Conceptions and Practical Results," in *The Writings of William James*, ed. John J. McDermott (Chicago: U of Chicago P, 1977), 348.

46. William James, *The Will to Believe, and Other Essays in Popular Philosophy*, ed. Frederick Burkhardt, Fredson Bowers, and Ignas K. Skrupskelis (Cambridge, MA: Harvard UP, 1979), 16.

47. James, *Will to Believe*, 17.

48. James, *Will to Believe*, 20.

49. James, *Will to Believe*, 52.

50. William James, *The Varieties of Religious Experience* (New York: Barnes & Noble, 2004), 58–59.

51. William James, "The Gospel of Relaxation," *Scribner's Magazine* 25 (January–June 1899): 499–507. "The Gospel of Relaxation" was widely reproduced in other magazines and popular publications.

52. Theodore Roosevelt, *Theodore Roosevelt, An Autobiography* (New York: Charles Scribner & Sons, 1922), 52. Roosevelt writes that he learned this "theory" from the novelist Frederick Marryat but notes that he retells the theory in his own language.

53. Walter Lippmann, *A Preface to Politics* (1914; reprint, Ann Arbor: U of Michigan P, 1962), 83–84.

54. Dale Carnegie, *How to Win Friends and Influence People* (New York: Simon & Schuster, 2009), 73–74, in a chapter titled "Smile."

55. See, e.g., James Lloyd, *I'm on Fire, Watch me Burn: Secrets to Captivating Presentations* (Newbury Park, CA: 9 Screens International, 2003), 44; Robert K. Throop and Marion Castellucci, *Reaching Your Potential: Personal and Professional Development* (Boston: Cengage Learning, 2003), 19; and Julie A. Ross, *How to Hug a Porcupine: Negotiating the Prickly Points of the Tween Years* ([New York]: McGraw-Hill Professional, 2008), 103.

56. See Kant, *Groundwork*, 4:415–16.

57. Vaihinger, *Philosophy of 'As if,'* 125.

58. Kermode, *Sense of an Ending*, 41.

59. Steve Chandler, *100 Ways to Motivate Yourself* (n.p.: Maurice Bassett, 2001), 75.

60. *Boiler Room*, written and directed by Ben Young, New Line Cinema, released 18 February 2000, www.youtube.com/watch?v=x8JkSEvyFhM&NR=1.

61. Rainer Maria Rilke, *"Archaïscher Torso Apollos,"* in *Rilke: Selected Poems*, trans. C. F. MacIntyre (Berkeley: U of California P, 1940), 92.

62. Taylor, *Secular Age*, 3.

63. Charles Taylor, *Varieties of Religion Today: William James Revisited* (Cambridge, MA: Harvard UP, 2002), 59.

64. Peter E. Gordon, "The Place of the Sacred in the Absence of God: Charles Taylor's *A Secular Age*," *Journal of the History of Ideas* 69.4 (2008): 647–73, 655.

65. Taylor, *Secular Age*, 312: "In spite of the continuing place of God and immortality in his scheme, [Kant] is a crucial figure also in the development of exclusive humanism, just because he articulates so strongly the power of inner sources of morality." On the vexed question of Kant's role in secularization, see Peter Byrne, *Kant on God* (Burlington, VT: Ashgate, 2007); and Gordon E. Michalson, *Kant and the Problem of God* (Oxford: Wiley-Blackwell, 1999).

66. Sigmund Freud, *The Future of an Illusion*, ed. and trans. James Strachey (New York: Norton, 1961), 36.

67. Freud, *Future of an Illusion*, 36n6.

68. Freud, *Future of an Illusion*, 37.

69. Freud, *Future of an Illusion*, 36. Freud's rejection of Vaihinger's *as if* proves useful to later psychoanalytical and feminist thinkers. See, e.g., Joan Riviere, "Womanliness as a Masquerade," in *The Inner World and Joan Riviere: Collected Papers, 1929–1958*, ed. Athol Hughes (New York: Karnac, 1991), which describes a woman who, to hide her wish for masculinity, has internalized a "compulsion to hide all her technical knowledge . . . making her suggestions in an innocent and artless manner, as if they were 'lucky guesses'" (95). Although Freud unambiguously rejects the *as if* with regard to religion, he appears to be more accepting of useful fictions in other cases, as with the fantasies of fetishists. Octave Mannoni, "Je sais bien, mais quand-même . . . ," in *Clefs pour l'imaginaire ou l'autre scène* (Paris: Editions du Seuil, 1969), 9–33, offers *I know very well, but all the same* as the logical (and linguistic) form of the Freudian fetish. See also Julia Kristeva's account of Helen Deutch's "as-if personalities" in *New Maladies of the Soul*, trans. Ross Guberman (New York: Columbia UP, 1995), 195–96. While it is impossible to make categorical judgments about such a diverse discourse, psychoanalysis and its successors tend to treat the *as if* as a diagnosis rather than a practical imperative.

70. See J. B. Schneewind, *The Invention of Autonomy: A History of Modern Moral Philosophy* (New York: Cambridge UP, 1998); Francis Oakley, *Natural Law, Laws of Nature, Natural Rights: Continuity and Discontinuity in the History of Ideas* (New York: Continuum, 2005); Samuel Moyn, *The Last Utopia: Human Rights in History* (Cambridge, MA: Belknap-Harvard UP, 2010); Lynn Hunt, *Inventing Human Rights: A History* (New York: Norton, 2008); and David Johnston, *A Brief History of Justice* (Chichester, UK: Wiley-Blackwell, 2011).

71. Quentin Skinner, "Meaning and Understanding in the History of Ideas," in *Meaning and Context: Quentin Skinner and His Critics*, ed. James Tully (Princeton, NJ: Princeton UP, 1988), 29–67.

72. Quentin Skinner, "Language and Social Change," in Tully, *Meaning and Context*, 119–32. In posing the vast question of how we should understand "social innovation and legitimation" by means of studying keywords, Skinner writes that he plans to use Williams as a "stalking horse" for a larger class of approaches (119).

73. Tully, *Meaning and Context*, collects many valuable critical essays. See also Lotte Mulligan, Judith Richards, and John Graham, "Intentions and Conventions: A Critique of Quentin Skinner's Method for the Study of the History of Ideas," *Political Studies* 27.1 (1979): 84–98; and, more recently, Martin Jay, "Historical Explanation and the Event: Reflections on the Limits of Contextualization," *New Literary History* 42 (2011): 557–71. Although I have focused on Skinner's influence on intellectual history, Michel Foucault's Nietzschean insistence that meaning does not survive changes in regimes of power has similarly discouraged transhistorical inquiry. See Michel Foucault, *The Archaeology of Knowledge and the Discourse on Language*, trans. A. M. Sheridan Smith (New York: Pantheon, 1972), 166–77.

74. Skinner, "Meaning and Understanding," 55.

75. Skinner, "Meaning and Understanding," 56.

76. Skinner, "Meaning and Understanding," 55.

77. Skinner, "Meaning and Understanding," 55.

78. Skinner, "Meaning and Understanding," 39.

79. Lorenzo Valla, *On the Donation of Constantine*, trans. G. W. Bowersock (Cambridge, MA: Harvard UP, 2007), sec. 42. Valla's awareness of linguistic anachronism extended to grammar as well as words, as in section 44.

80. Erich Auerbach, "Vico's Contribution to Literary Criticism," in *Studia Philologica et Litteraria in Honorem L. Spitzer*, ed. A. G. Hatcher and K. L. Selig (Bern: Franke Verl, 1958), 34.

### Chapter 5. *WWJD?* and the History of *Imitatio Christi*

1. Darrel L. Bock, *How Would Jesus Vote? Do Your Political Positions Really Align with the Bible?* (New York: Howard Books, 2016).

2. From the publisher's description for Don Colbert, *What Would Jesus Eat?* (Nashville: Thomas Nelson, 2002), at www.amazon.com/Ultimate-Program-Eating -Feeling-Living/dp/product-description/0785265678.

3. See Jay W. Richards, "What Would Jesus Drive?," *National Review*, 25 September 2007, energy.nationalreview.com/articles/222272/what-would-jesus-drive/jay-w -richards.

4. See, however, Brendan Vaughan, *What Would MacGyver Do? True Stories of Improvised Genius in Everyday Life* (New York: Hudson Street, 2006); E. N. Berthrong, *What Would Confucius Do? Wisdom and Advice on Achieving Success and Getting Along with Others* (New York: Marlowe, 2005); and Jim McBride, "Team Blessed to Have Damon," *Boston Globe*, 31 October 2004, archive.boston.com/sports/baseball/redsox/articles/2004/10 /31/team_blessed_to_have_damon/.

5. See John D. Caputo, *What Would Jesus Deconstruct? The Good News of Postmodernity for the Church* (Grand Rapids, MI: Baker Academic, 2007).

6. See esp. Gregory S. Jackson, "'What Would Jesus Do?': Practical Christianity, Social Gospel Realism, and the Homiletic Novel," *PMLA* 121.3 (2006): 641–61; and Jackson, *The Word and Its Witness: The Spiritualization of American Realism* (Chicago: U of Chicago P, 2009), 157–214. On Sheldon and his novel, see also Timothy Miller, *Following "In His Steps": A Biography of Charles M. Sheldon* (Knoxville: U of Tennessee P, 1987); Paul S. Boyer, "*In His Steps*: A Reappraisal," *American Quarterly* 23 (Spring 1971): 60–78; and James H. Smylie, "Sheldon's *In His Steps*: Conscience and Disciple-ship," *Theology Today* 32 (April 1974): 32–45. Journalistic accounts of the WWJD? phenomenon also usually trace it back to Sheldon. See also Damien Cave, "What Would Jesus Do—About Copyright?," Salon.com, 25 October 2000, salon.com /business/feature/2000/10/25/wwjd; and Emily Nussbaum, "Status Is . . . for Evangelical Teen-Agers; Jewelry for Jesus," *New York Times*, 15 November 1998, www .nytimes.com/1998/11/15/magazine/status-is-for-evangelical-teen-agers-jewelry-for -jesus.html.

7. The passages from Origen, Cyprian, Ambrose, and Jerome are quoted in Giles Constable, "The Ideal of the Imitation of Christ," in *Three Studies in Medieval Religious and Social Thought* (New York: Cambridge UP, 1995), 151, 154, 155, and are meant to be representative rather than exhaustive. Extensive searching in the *Patrologia Latina* and the *Acta sanctorum* has yielded only further instances of indicative imitation. For technological reasons I discuss later, these searches are not wholly conclusive.

8. Augustine, *The City of God against the Pagans*, trans. and ed. R. W. Dyson (New York: Cambridge UP, 1998), 8.17.338.

9. Quoted in Constable, "Ideal," 184.

10. Thomas Aquinas, *Summa Theologiae*, trans. Samuel Parsons and Albert Pinheiro, 61 vols. (New York: Cambridge UP, 2006), 53:71.

11. Quoted in Constable, "Ideal," 189.

12. Thomas à Kempis, *The Earliest English Translation of the First Three Books of the "De Imitatione Christi,"* ed. John K. Ingram (London: Early English Text Society, 1893), 1.1.1–8, 1.1.2.

13. On the diversity of medieval imitative practices, see Constable, "Ideal"; Caroline Walker Bynum, *Holy Feast and Holy Fast: The Religious Significance of Food to Medieval Women* (Berkeley: U of California P, 1987); David Aers and Lynn Staley, *The Powers of the Holy: Religion, Politics, and Gender in Late Medieval English Culture* (University Park: Pennsylvania State UP, 1996); and Sarah McNamer, *Affective Meditation and the Invention of Medieval Compassion* (Philadelphia: U of Pennsylvania P, 2010).

14. Nicholas Love, *The Mirror of the Blessed Life of Jesus Christ*, ed. Michael G. Sargent (Exeter, UK: U of Exeter P, 2005), 10–11.

15. Martin Luther, *Lectures on Galatians* and *Lectures on Genesis*, in *Luther's Works on CD-ROM*, trans. and ed. Jaroslav Pelikan and Helmut T. Lehmann, 55 vols. (St. Louis: Concordia, 1963), 26:352, 4:192.

16. Henry Smith, *The Wedding Garment* (London, 1590), 5 (sig. A3r). On Smith's life and fame as a preacher, see Gary W. Jenkins, "Smith, Henry (*c.* 1560–1591)," *Oxford Dictionary of National Biography* (Oxford: Oxford UP, 2004), www.oxforddnb.com/view /article/25811. In an earlier, article version of this chapter, "WWJD? The Genealogy of

a Syntactic Form," the first instance identified was in 1631. Locating an earlier instance was the product of both a larger archive of texts (including EEBO-TCP II as well as TCP I) and a more capacious and flexible search using the string *((jesus|lord|savior|christ) (\*){0,10} (would|wold|wolde|vvould|vvold|vvolde) (not)? (have)? \_V\*|(would|wold|wolde |vvould|vvold|vvolde) (\*){0,10} (jesus|lord|savior|christ) (not)? (have)? \_V\*)* in the cqpweb.lancs.ac.uk interface.

17. Smith, *Wedding Garment*, 8–9 (sigs. A4v–A5r).

18. Smith, *Wedding Garment*, 10 (sig. A5v).

19. Edward Reynolds, "The Life of Christ," in *Three Treatises of "The Vanity of the Creature," "The Sinfulnesse of Sinne," and "The Life of Christ": Being the Substance of Severall Sermons Preached at Lincolns Innes* (London, 1631), 427.

20. Jeremy Taylor, *Holy Living* (London, 1656), 378.

21. Jeremy Taylor, *The Great Exemplar of Sanctity and Holy Life According to the Christian Institution* (London, 1649), 9.

22. Thomas White, *A Method and Instructions for the Art of Divine Meditation* (London, 1672), 304.

23. John Everard, *The Gospel Treasury Opened* (London, 1657), 132, 179, 206, italics mine.

24. Richard Steele, *A Plain Discourse upon Uprightness Shewing the Properties and Priviledges of an Upright Man* (London, 1672), 137.

25. John Carter, *The tomb-stone, and A rare sight* (London, 1653), 163, italics original.

26. Joseph Hall, *Holy Raptures; or, Pathetical Meditations of the Love of Christ* (London, 1652), 52–53.

27. On early modern changes in the affective identification with Christ's suffering, see Jan Frans van Dijkhuizen, *Pain and Compassion in Early Modern English Literature and Culture* (Cambridge: D. S. Brewer, 2012).

28. For eighteenth-century instances of conditional imitation, see Jacques Saurin, *Sermons on the Attributes of God*, 4 vols. (Cambridge, 1775–82), 2:133–34; and Thomas Robinson, *Scripture Characters: or, a Practical Improvement of the Principal Histories in the Old and New Testament*, 4 vols. (London, 1800), 3:79. Many instances appear in the collected works of seventeenth-century divines, such as Edmund Calamy, *The Nonconformist's Memorial: Being an Account of the Ministers, Who Were Ejected or Silenced after the Restoration*, 2 vols. (London, 1778), 2:614.

29. Richard Cecil, *Remains of the Reverend Richard Cecil*, ed. Josiah Pratt (Philadelphia, 1843), 267.

30. D. L. Moody, *Glad Tidings: Comprising Sermons and Prayer-Talks* (New York, 1876), 315.

31. "The Christian Master's Present to His Household," *Church of England Magazine*, 22 July 1848, 62.

32. A. Marryat, *Friendly Words for Our Girls: A Series of Readings for Daily Use* (London, 1875), 76.

33. E. H. Bickersworth, "What Would Jesus Do?," in *Home Words for Heart and Hearth*, ed. Charles Bullock (London: Hand and Heart, June 1880), 177.

34. "What Would Jesus Do?," *Home Missionary* 61 (January 1889): 430.

35. Nancy Fix Anderson, "Linton, Elizabeth Lynn (1822–1898)," *Oxford Dictionary of National Biography* (Oxford: Oxford UP, 2004), www.oxforddnb.com/view/article /16742.

36. Elizabeth Lynne Linton, *The True History of Joshua Davidson* (London, 1872), 80–81.

37. Jackson, "What Would Jesus Do?," 642. As I did in the article version of this chapter, Jackson mistakes the grammatical category of the subjunctive mood, which designates the inflection of verbs, for the notional or semantic category of the conditional. In the phrase *if it be now*, *be* is the subjunctive inflection of the verb *to be*; the use of subjunctive verbs in English has declined over centuries. Some linguists, like Rodney Huddleston, in *Introduction to the Grammar of English* (New York: Cambridge UP, 1984), distinguish between "'mood' as a category of grammar and 'modality' as a category of meaning" (166), but I do not observe this distinction rigorously here; see Huddleston, *Introduction*, 164–76, for a treatment of auxiliaries and modality in English.

38. See Charles Sheldon, *In His Steps (What Would Jesus Do?)* (1897; reprint, Uhrichsville, OH: Barbour, 1985), one of countless editions published in the twentieth century. See Erin Smith, "'What Would Jesus Do?': The Social Gospel and the Literary Marketplace," *Book History* 10 (2007): 193–221; and Miller, *Following "In His Steps,"* 66–102, for a discussion of sales. Because of the peculiar publication history of *In His Steps* (lack of copyright protection meant it was widely pirated), exact sales estimates are impossible.

39. Sheldon, *In His Steps*, 15.

40. Sheldon, *In His Steps*, 9.

41. Sheldon, *In His Steps*, 132.

42. Sheldon, *In His Steps*, 17–18.

43. Charles Sheldon, *"Jesus Is Here!": Continuing the Narrative of "In His Steps (What Would Jesus Do?)"* (New York: Hodder, 1914), ii.

44. Sheldon, *In His Steps*, 131.

45. Charles Sheldon, preface to *In His Steps To-Day: What Would Jesus Do in Solving the Problems of Present Political, Economic, and Social Life?* (New York: Fleming H. Revell, 1921), 11.

46. John White Chadwick, *In His Steps: A Sermon* (Boston: George H. Ellis, 1899), 38–39.

47. Thomas M. Greene, *The Light in Troy: Imitation and Discovery in Renaissance Poetry* (New Haven, CT: Yale UP, 1982), 17, 9.

48. Galileo Galilei, *Dialogue Concerning the Two Chief World Systems*, trans. Stillman Drake (Berkeley: U of California P, 1953), 119–20; for the Italian text, see Galilei, *Dialogo sopra i massimi sistemi*, ed. Ottavio Besomi and Mario Helbing (Padua: Editrice Antenore, 1998), 136.18.2–3.

49. Though it is beyond the scope of this chapter, the history of the conditionalization of Aristotle in early modern scientific discourse awaits investigation. Hieronymus Cardano, writing of discoveries regarding the relative effects of the sun and moon on the flow of the air in his *Commentarii in Hippocratis De Aere* (Basel, 1570), supposes that "if Aristotle had known this [*si igitur haec nouisset Aristotles*], he would have believed

[*credidisset*] that the air moved rather than remaining still" (7, sig. A4r). Like Galileo, Pierre Gassendi, in *Epicuiri Meteorologia*, 2 vols. (n.p., 1649), imagines Aristotle's response to subsequent advances in instrumentation, writing that "if Aristotle had known [*si cognovisset Aristotles*] about the thermometer [*Thermometrum*], this wonder would have delighted him [*mirificè eum delectasset*]" (2:986, sig. HHHhhh3r–v). My thanks to Craig Martin for bringing these passages to my attention.

50. Commenting on the earlier, article version of this chapter, Michael Witmore and Jonathan Hope write in "'Après le déluge, More Criticism': Philology, Literary History, and Ancestral Reading in the Coming Posttranscription World," *Renaissance Drama* 40 (2012): 135–50, that the conditional indicates that "a *certain way* of understanding the distance of the present from the past becomes possible at a given moment: we move from an occurrence to a state of mind or a perceptual possibility. But of course we cannot know whether a cognate discourse—casuistry, for example—introduces another idiom for counterfactual thinking that produces the same deliberative effect with different syntactic units. We cannot know, that is, that a variant or cognate form of a particular word or discourse unit exists *until we know what it is* (and so can search for it)" (146). This is precisely right. Philological inquiry into words entails the same difficulty: because words are signs, we cannot rule out the possibility that a concept, mode of deliberation, or kind of understanding is not elsewhere signified by a different word or combination of words. In suggesting that the conditional may complement or displace the tropological sense of scripture as a strategy for connecting with Christ as exemplar, I aim to extend Witmore and Hope's point a step further: the sign of a particular kind of historical awareness or counterfactual deliberation may not be an idiom—"a variant or cognate form of a particular word or discourse unit"—at all, but rather a hermeneutic procedure.

51. Thomas Aquinas, *Summa Theologica* (online ed., 2008), pt. 1, question 1, art. 10, www.newadvent.org/summa/1001.htm#article10. On the continuing role of figurative interpretation in Protestant reading practices, see Barbara Lewalski, *Protestant Poetics* (Princeton, NJ: Princeton UP, 1979), 75–76.

52. Dante Allegheri, letter to Cangrande della Scala, in *Dante: The Critical Heritage*, ed. Michael Caesar (New York: Routledge, 1999), 94.

53. On Protestant literalism and renewed attention to figurative and rhetorical language, see Lewalski, *Protestant Poetics*, 72–110; on the reversal or deconstruction of the meaning of the terms *literal* and *figurative*, see Thomas Luxon, *Literal Figures: Puritan Allegory and the Reformation Crisis in Representation* (Chicago: U of Chicago P, 1995), 33–76.

54. Jackson, "What Would Jesus Do?," interprets the Social Gospel movement as a way of collapsing secular into sacred time through allegory, allowing readers to "see through the veil of history to the recurring patterns underneath," to "universal truths" (653). Conditional imitation, however, operates entirely within the secular, immanent plane of existence, without making reference to an eternal, sacred, or underlying reality. Where allegory refers to the present in its secondary signification, the counterfactual modality of *What would Jesus do?* refers, in its primary signification, to a nonexistent or nonactual world. Allegorical and modal strategies of bridging

historical difference are historically as well as conceptually distinct, though both are at work in the literature of the Social Gospel movement.

55. See, e.g., John Selden, *The Historie of Tithes* (London, 1618), 44; Degory Wheare, *The Method and Order of Reading Both Civil and Ecclesiastical Histories* (London, 1685), 182; and John Milton, "Prolusion 7," in *The Complete Prose and Essential Poetry of John Milton*, ed. William Kerrigan, John Rumrich, and Stephen M. Fallon (New York: Modern Library, 2007), 796: "Throughout this continent a few hundred years ago all the noble arts had perished and the Muses had deserted all the universities of the day, over which they had long presided; blind illiteracy had penetrated and entrenched itself everywhere, nothing was heard in the schools but the absurd doctrines of driveling monks, and that profane and hideous monster, Ignorance, assumed the gown and lorded it on our empty platforms and pulpits and in our deserted professorial chairs."

56. As Anthony Grafton writes in "Future Reading," *New Yorker*, 5 November 2007, www.newyorker.com/reporting/2007/11/05/071105fa_fact_grafton, "The supposed universal library, then, will be not a seamless mass of books, easily linked and studied together, but a patchwork of interfaces and databases, some open to anyone with a computer and WiFi, others closed to those without access or money."

57. See quod.lib.umich.edu/c/cme/. Because the status of this archive, assembled by University of Michigan faculty and last updated in 2006, is uncertain, I place little weight on evidence derived from it.

58. See Christopher Sutton, *Disce Viuere: Learne to Liue: A Briefe Forme of Learning to Liue, Wherein Is Shewed, That the Life of Christ Is the Most Perfect Patterne of Direction to the Life of a Christian* (London, 1602).

59. Digital archives will also likely change the way we cite textual and bibliographic claims. Take the claim I made earlier, that conditional *imitatio Christi* becomes widespread around the middle of the nineteenth century. Rather than citing the bibliographic information for potentially hundreds of works to justify this claim, one might instead direct readers to a specific digital archive (e.g., Google Book Search) and a search string (e.g., *would AROUND (10) "jesus do" date:1825–1875*).

60. Searching archives of earlier periods is made considerably more challenging by spelling variation. Before *would* became the dominant spelling around 1550, the word was also spelled *wold, wolde, wald, wholde*, and a wide variety of other ways, listed in the entry for *willen*, in the *Middle English Dictionary*, quod.lib.umich.edu/m/med/. See earlyprint.wustl.edu for the frequency of various spellings of the word from 1473 to 1700. In modern as in earlier stages of English, *would* is also shortened to an enclitic, as in *he'd*.

61. Sir Thomas Malory, *Le morte Darthur*, ed. William Caxton (London: David Nutt, 1889), 20.7.809; *Oxford English Dictionary Online*, s.v. "will."

62. *Articles to be enquired of in the generall visitation of Edmonde Bisshoppe* (London, 1554), sig. C1v.

63. See *Oxford English Dictionary Online*, s.v. "will."

64. Quoted with emphasis in Terttu Nevalainen, *An Introduction to Early Modern English* (New York: Oxford UP, 2006), 112, which describes the disappearance of

multiple negation, especially in the upper social strata, by the seventeenth century (111–13). For seminal early work in the study of syntactic change, see Elizabeth C. Traugott, "Diachronic Syntax and Generative Grammar," in *A Reader in Historical and Comparative Linguistics*, ed. Alan R. Kieler (New York: Holt, Rinehart, & Winston, 1972), 201–16; and David Lightfoot, *Principles of Diachronic Syntax* (New York: Cambridge UP, 1979).

65. Michel Foucault, *The Archaeology of Knowledge and the Discourse on Language*, trans. A. M. Sheridan Smith (New York: Pantheon, 1972), 118–19.

66. Thomas Starkey, *A Dialogue between Pole and Lupset*, ed. Thomas Frederick Mayer (London: Royal Historical Society, 1989), 49, from *Oxford English Dictionary Online*, s.v. "will"; the earliest instance of the conditional *would* listed in the *OED* is 888 CE.

67. It is beyond my purpose here to enumerate all the lexicogrammatical resources necessary for producing statements about the conditional imitation of Christ, but see Adele E. Goldberg, *Constructions at Work: The Nature of Generalization in Language* (New York: Oxford UP, 2006), 166–82, on subject-auxiliary inversion, including its role in counterfactual conditionals.

68. Desiderius Erasmus, *Desiderius Enchiridion Militis Christiani: An English Version*, trans. and ed. Anne M. O'Donnell (Oxford: Early English Text Society, 1981), 11, 136, 139.

69. Desiderius Erasmus, *Ciceronianus, or, A Dialogue on the Best Style of Speaking*, trans. Izora Scott (New York: Columbia UP, 1908), 70–71.

70. Epictetus, *Enchiridion*, in *The Discourses as Reported by Arrian*, trans. W. A. Oldfather, 2 vols. (Cambridge, MA: Harvard UP, 1952), 2:78. Asking what a classical author would do was usual enough among humanists of the sixteenth and seventeenth centuries. The pedagogue Roger Ascham, for example, instructs schoolmasters to correct their students by pointing out that "*Tullie* would have used such a worde, not this: *Tullie* would have placed this word here, not there: would have used this case, this number, this person, this degree, this gender," and so on. Roger Ascham, *The Scholemaster*, in *English Works of Roger Ascham*, ed. William Aldis Wright (Cambridge: Cambridge UP, 1970), 184. In the introduction to his 1697 translation of the *Aeneid*, John Dryden writes, "I have endeavored to make Virgil speak such English as he would himself have spoken, if he had been born in England, and in this present age." Quoted in Robert Fitzgerald, introduction to Virgil, *The Aeneid*, trans. John Dryden, ed. Fitzgerald (New York: Macmillan, 1964), 17.

71. Erasmus, *Ciceronianus*, 78.

72. This is to say, in the terms of Charles J. Fillmore's brilliant lecture on idiomaticity, www1.icsi.berkeley.edu/~kay/bcg/leco2.html, that "What would Jesus do?" was an encoding idiom that was not also a decoding idiom.

73. So-called clones of *What Would Jesus Do?* usually vary only in one category rather than two: *What would Jesus Deconstruct?* varies the verb while "What Would Edith Wharton Do?" varies the subject. The question word, usually *what*, matches the verb, as in *How Would Jesus Vote?* or *Who Would Jesus Bomb?*

74. On *do so* anaphora as the general test for verb phrase constituency, see Peter W. Cullicover and Ray Jackendoff, *Simpler Syntax* (New York: Oxford UP, 2005), 125–31.

75. George Lakoff, *Women, Fire, and Dangerous Things: What Categories Reveal about the Mind* (Chicago: U of Chicago P, 1987), 12–117.

76. See www.zazzle.com/what_would_cthulhu_do_t_shirt-235382686557900013.

77. It is not my concern here either to distinguish what Paul Grice, in *Studies in the Way of Words* (Cambridge, MA: Harvard UP, 1991), 21–24, calls saying and implicating or to challenge this distinction, though accepting linguistic forms as conventional sign units will presumably require a revised account of the relation between coded meaning and implied meaning. On the sorts of semantic and pragmatic meaning associated with variously "formal idioms," see Paul Kay and Laura A. Michaelis, "Constructional Meaning and Compositionality," in *Semantics: An International Handbook of Natural Language Meaning*, ed. Claudia Maienborn, Klaus von Heusinger, and Paul Portner, vol. 3 (Berlin: de Gruyter, 2012), 2271–96.

78. See William Grimes, "In an Age of Strife, What Would Buddha Do?," *New York Times*, 27 December 2004, www.nytimes.com/2004/12/27/books/in-an-age-of-strife -what-would-buddha-do.html; and Jamil Momand, "What Would Muhammad Do?," *Los Angeles Times*, 9 February 2006, articles.latimes.com/2006/feb/09/opinion/oe-momand9, for examples of how other imitative traditions have taken up the linguistic form abstracted from *What would Jesus do?*

79. This prediction supposes that new language learners, lacking knowledge of diachronic change, will not continue to infer the prototypicality of Jesus through frequency or other cues. Though Saussure supposed that language is learned as a purely synchronic system, historical linguists have long observed that speakers understand their language as temporally stratified, composed of residual, dominant, and emergent elements. The changes in *[Wh-Word] would X Y?*, including the loss of a prototype, are instances of the general operation that Jacques Derrida, in *Of Grammatology*, trans. Gayatri Spivak, corrected ed. (Baltimore: Johns Hopkins UP, 1997), 48, calls the "becoming-unmotivated" of the sign.

80. Franco Moretti, "Conjectures on World Literature," *New Left Review* 1 (2000): 54–68, 64.

### Chapter 6. Milton's Depictives and the History of Style

1. See Eva Schultze-Berndt and Nikolaus P. Himmelmann, "Depictive Secondary Predicates in Crosslinguistic Perspective," *Linguistic Typology* 8 (2004): 59–131, for a comprehensive treatment and definition of depictives. In earlier work these constructions were referred to, variously, as *predicative adjuncts*, *quasi-predicates*, *predicate appositives*, and *pseudo-complements*. See F. Th. Visser, *An Historical Syntax of the English Language*, vol. 1 (Leiden: E. J. Brill, 1963), 214–15. For a brief literary treatment of adjuncts, see Leo Knuth, "How Stately Was Plump Buck Mulligan?," *James Joyce Quarterly* 7.3 (1970): 204–9.

2. All citations of *Paradise Lost* are to the online edition in The John Milton Reading Room, ed. Thomas H. Luxon, www.dartmouth.edu/~milton.

3. See G. L. Hendrickson, "The Origin and Meaning of the Ancient Characters of Style," *American Journal of Philology* 26.3 (1905): 249–90; Morris W. Croll, *Style, Rhetoric and Rhythm: Essays*, ed. J. Max Patrick (Princeton, NJ: Princeton UP, 1966); Annabel M.

Patterson, *Hermogenes and the Renaissance* (Princeton, NJ: Princeton UP, 1970); and Debora K. Shuger, *The Christian Grand Style in the English Renaissance* (Princeton, NJ: Princeton UP, 1988). Patterson follows the same sorts of protagonists even as she argues for the influence of Hermogenes's seven Ideas of style rather than Cicero's three types. She acknowledges that "an 'Idea of style' is very different from 'a style'" (xiii).

4. Frederick Mosteller and David L. Wallace, *The Federalist: Inference and Disputed Authorship* (New York: Addison-Wesley, 1964).

5. The literature on authorship attribution is too voluminous to cite fully or summarize here. For an extensive survey, see Patrick Juola, "Authorship Attribution," *Foundations and Trends in Information Retrieval* 1.3 (2006): 233–34.

6. See Hugh Craig, "Stylistic Analysis and Authorship Studies," in *A Companion to Digital Humanities*, ed. Susan Schreibman, Ray Siemens, and John Unsworth (Oxford: Blackwell, 2004), http://www.digitalhumanities.org/companion/. On the relative neglect of style in New Historicism and cultural studies (particularly in treatments of Renaissance literature), see Marshall Brown, "Le Style est l'homme même: The Action of Literature," *College English* 59.7 (1997): 801–9.

7. For the most revealing measurement of trends that I have seen, see Ted Underwood and Jordan Sellers, "The Emergence of Literary Diction," *Journal of Digital Humanities* 1.2 (2012), journalofdigitalhumanities.org/1-2/the-emergence-of-literary-diction-by-ted-underwood-and-jordan-sellers/.

8. Georges-Louis Leclerc, Comte de Buffon, *Discours sur le style*, ed. Adolphe Hatzfield (Paris: Lecoffre, 1872), 24.

9. See, e.g., Isaac D'Israeli, "Of Style," in *Miscellanies* (London, 1796). On the difference between chronicle and history, see Hayden White, *Metahistory: The Historical Imagination in Nineteenth-Century Europe* (Baltimore: Johns Hopkins UP, 1975).

10. Quoted from Carlo Ginzburg, "Style as Inclusion, Style as Exclusion," in *Picturing Science, Producing Art*, ed. Caroline Jones and Peter Galison (New York: Routledge, 1998), 27–54, 38.

11. Leo Spitzer, *Linguistics and Literary History: Essays in Stylistics* (Princeton, NJ: Princeton UP, 1948), 19.

12. Jeff Dolven, "Reading Wyatt for the Style," *Modern Philology* 105.1 (2007): 65–86, 79–80.

13. Dolven, "Reading Wyatt," 74.

14. Paul Valéry, *Oeuvres*, ed. Jean Hytier, 2 vols. (Paris: Bibliothèque de la Pléiade, 1957 60), 2:629, 1:439 41.

15. Jorge Luis Borges, "Pierre Menard, Author of the *Quixote*," in *Collected Fictions*, trans. Andrew Hurley (New York: Penguin, 1998), 88–95, 91, 92, 94.

16. Arthur Schopenhauer, "Uber Schriftstelleri und Stil," in *Parerga und Paralipomena: Kleine philosophische Schriften* (Berlin: Hahn, 1851), 429: "Dieser zeigt nämlich die formelle Beschaffenheit aller Gedanken eines Menschen, welche sich stets gleich bleiben muß; was und worüber er auch denken möge. Man hat daran gleichsam den Teig, aus dem er alle seine Gestalten knetet, so verschieden sie auch seyn mögen."

17. Nelson Goodman, "The Status of Style," *Critical Inquiry* 1.4 (1975): 799–811.

18. See Jacques Derrida, *Voice and Phenomenon: Introduction to the Problem of the Sign in Husserl's Phenomenology*, trans. Leonard Lawlor (Evanston, IL: Northwestern UP, 2011), 42–43, for an especially clear account of repetition through difference as the condition of signification.

19. For an argument that the term *style* is too confused to be worth preserving, see Bennison Gray, *Style: The Problem and its Solution* (The Hauge: Mouton, 1969).

20. Cf. Goodman, "Status of Style," 807, which takes *in the style of* to indicate only the propriety of style, its association of a work "with one rather than another artist, period, region, school," while passing over its apropriability.

21. Erich Auerbach, *Mimesis: The Representation of Reality in Western Literature*, trans. Willard Trask (Princeton, NJ: Princeton UP, 2003).

22. Auerbach says in his later "Epilegomena to *Mimesis*" that his work "arose from the themes and methods of German intellectual history and philology; it would be conceivable in no other tradition than in that of German romanticism and Hegel." Auerbach, *Mimesis*, 571.

23. Seneca, *Ad Lucilium Epistulae Morales*, trans. Richard M. Gummere, 3 vols., Loeb Classical Library (Cambridge, MA: Harvard UP, 1917–25), 2:84.5. Like Cicero, Seneca sought to classify style into basic or opposed kinds or levels; see epistles 114 and 115, which opposed the vitiated style of Cicero and others. Appropriately enough, Seneca's metaphors for imitation are themselves culled from other texts. For the metaphor of the bee, see esp. Plutarch, *De audiendis poetis* 30c–d, 32e–f; *De audiendo* 41e–42b; and *De profectibus in virtute* 79b–d.

24. Roland Barthes, "Style and its Image," in *Style: A Literary Symposium*, ed. Seymour Chatman (New York: Oxford UP, 1971), 3–10; for discussion and responses, see 11–15.

25. See Norbert Wiener, *Cybernetics: Or Control and Communication in the Animal and the Machine* (Cambridge, MA: MIT P, 1948), which defines cybernetics as "the scientific study of control and communication in the animal and the machine." The term soon came to designate the broader study of organic and mechanical systems.

26. For an explicitly transformational approach to Milton's style, see Seymour Chatman, "Milton's Participial Style," *PMLA* 83.5 (1968): 1386–99.

27. See Richard Ohmann, "Generative Grammars and the Concept of Literary Style," in *Contemporary Essays on Style*, ed. Glen A. Love and Michael Payne (Glenview, IL: Scott, Foresman, 1969), 133–48; Donald Freeman, "Keats's 'To Autumn': Poetry as Process and Pattern," *Language and Style* 11 (1978): 3–17; and E. D. Hirsch Jr., "Stylistics and Synonymity," *Critical Inquiry* 1 (1975): 559–79.

28. Auerbach's Ciceronianism does not prevent him from attending to markers of style and their histories. In his virtuoso reading of Dante, for example, he quotes the words of Farinata, "O Tosco, che per la città . . . ," observing that "the construction, 'O thou who' is extremely solemn and comes from the elevated style of the antique epic. Dante's ear remembers its cadence as it remembers so many other things in Virgil, Lucan, and Statius. I do not think the construction occurs before this in any medieval vernacular." While "the master" Virgil's "own relative clauses after a vocative are perfectly beautiful" (two examples, from the first two books of the *Aeneid*, are adduced), they are "never so concise and arresting" (179). Such analyses, which have historical

value only as a result of Auerbach's immense learning and authority, are brought in as evidence of conceptual synthesis rather than as the proper substance of style's history.

29. Ginzburg, "Style as Inclusion."

30. For a persuasive attempt to match the markers of Spenser's style to the doctrinal concept of the middle, or "flowery," style, see David Scott Wilson-Okamura, *Spenser's International Style* (New York: Cambridge UP, 2013), 70–137.

31. Stanley Fish, *Is There a Text in This Class? The Authority of Interpretive Communities* (Cambridge, MA: Harvard UP, 1982), 253–54.

32. "Wer teilt die fließend immer gleiche Reihe." Johann Wolfgang von Goethe, *Faust*, trans. Walter Kaufmann (New York: Random House, 1990), 74, line 146.

33. Spitzer, *Linguistics and Literary History*, 2.

34. For an introduction to the fundamentals of commonplace books and commonplacing, see Adam G. Hooks, "Commonplace Books," in *The Encyclopedia of English Renaissance Literature*, 3 vols., ed. Garrett Sullivan Jr. and Alan Stewart (London: Wiley Blackwell, 2012), 1:206–9. For a detailed study, see Ann Moss, *Printed Commonplace Books and the Structuring of Renaissance Thought* (New York: Oxford UP, 1996).

35. Roger Ascham, *The scholemaster or plaine and perfite way of teachyng children, to vnderstand, write, and speake, the Latin tong* (London, 1570), 57.

36. Henry Peacham, *The Garden of Eloquence* (London, 1577), sig. E3v.

37. John Milton, *Accedence commenc't grammar* (London, 1669), 11–14.

38. For a more detailed version of this argument, one that also begins with Fish, see Eugene R. Kintgen, "Reconstructing the Interpretive Conventions of Elizabethan Readers," in *Language, Text and Context: Essays in Stylistics*, ed. Michael Toolan (New York: Routledge, 1992), 93–107.

39. It is beyond the scope of this chapter to discuss the imitative practices and conventions of various periods, but two texts can, perhaps, suggest both their range and their persistence. For the practice of oral composition in preliterate societies, see Albert B. Lord, *The Singer of Tales*, ed. Stephen Mitchell and Gregory Nagy, 2nd ed. (Cambridge, MA: Harvard UP, 2000). For an account of how Ralph Ellison studied, marked, and imitated the sentences of Ernest Hemingway, see Brian Hochman, "Ellison's Hemingways," *African American Review* 42.3–4 (2008): 513–32.

40. Ronald David Emma, "Grammar and Milton's English Style," in *Language and Style in Milton*, ed. Ronald David Emma and John Shawcross (New York: Frederick Ungar, 1967), 73.

41. William Blake was apparently taken with the split form of this phrase. He alters it to "human form divine," a trigram that appears in *Songs of Innocence*, *Milton: a Poem*, and *Jerusalem: The Emanation of the Giant Albion*.

42. Hilda M. Hume, "On the Language of Paradise Lost," in Emma and Shawcross, *Language and Style in Milton*, 70.

43. *Oxford English Dictionary Online*, s.v. "luxuriant."

44. By asserting that vines "creep," I take Milton to be punning subtly on the use of the word *creeper* to refer to vines. The *Oxford English Dictionary Online*, s.v. "creeper," lists Francis Bacon's *Sylva Sylvarum* (London, 1626) as the first instance of this use: "They are Winders and Creepers; as Ivy, Briony, Hops, Woodbine."

45. For a brief historical account of the relationship between adverbs and adjectives, see N. F. Blake, *A Grammar of Shakespeare's Language* (New York: Palgrave, 2002), 73–74, 151–52.

46. Janette Richardson, "Virgil and Milton Once Again," *Comparative Literature* 14.4 (1962): 321–31, 325, boldface mine.

47. Emma, "Grammar and Milton's English Style," 73. William Shakespeare, *The Tragedy of Richard II*, ed. Barbara Mowat, Paul Werstine, Michael Poston, Rebecca Niles (Washington: Folger Shakespeare Library, n.d.), 2.1.181, www.folgerdigitaltexts.org.

48. *Oxford English Dictionary Online*, s.v. "orbicular."

49. On the mobility of adverbs within the sentence, see Thomas Boyden Ernst, *The Syntax of Adjuncts*, Cambridge Studies in Linguistics 96 (New York: Cambridge UP, 2002), 1–3. On the complicated relationship between depictive adjectives and adverbials, see Schultze-Berndt and Himmelmann, "Depictive Secondary Predicates," 60–62, 119–23.

50. Noam Chomsky, *Syntactic Structures* (The Hague: Mouton, 1957), 15. On further permutations of Chomsky's sentence, see, e.g., Denis Bouchard, *The Semantics of Syntax: A Minimalist Approach to Grammar* (Chicago: U of Chicago P, 1995).

51. For attempts to characterize the rules governing depictives, see Jane Simpson, "Depictives in English and Walpiri," in *Secondary Predication and Adverbial Modification: The Typology of Depictives*, ed. Nikolaus Himmelmann and Eva Schultze-Berndt (New York: Oxford UP, 2005); Edwin Williams, "Predication," *Linguistic Inquiry* 4 (1981): 31–69; Tova R. Rapoport, "Adjunct-Predicate Licensing and D-Structure," in *Perspectives on Phrase Structure: Heads and Licensing*, ed. Susan D. Rothstein, Syntax and Semantics 25 (New York: Academic, 1991), 159–87; Rapoport, "Structure, Aspect, and the Predicate," *Language* 75.4 (December 1999): 653–77; and Schultze-Berndt and Himmelmann, "Depictive Secondary Predicates," 59–131.

52. T. S. Eliot, "Milton II," in *On Poetry and Poets* (New York: Farrar, Straus & Giroux, 1957), 175.

53. See Milton's note on "The Verse," in The John Milton Reading Room, www .dartmouth.edu/~milton/reading_room/pl/note/text.shtml.

54. Stanley Fish, *Surprised by Sin: The Reader in Paradise Lost*, 2nd ed. (Cambridge, MA: Harvard UP, 1994).

55. Christopher Ricks, "Over-Emphasis in *Paradise Regained*," *Modern Language Notes* 76.8 (1961): 701–4; Ricks, *Milton's Grand Style* (Oxford: Clarendon, 1963), 17–19.

56. *Oxford English Dictionary Online*, s.v. "Hesperian"; Patrick Hume, *Annotations on Milton's Paradise Lost* (London, 1695), 123. See also Earl Miner, William Moeck, and Stephen Jablonski, eds., *Paradise Lost, 1668–1968: Three Centuries of Commentary* (Lewisburg, PA: Bucknell UP, 2004), 304.

57. For a list of common quasi-copulas, see Visser, *Historical Syntax*, 215–19.

58. See also Visser, *Historical Syntax*, 214.

59. Spitzer, *Linguistics and Literary History*, 19; Ricks, *Milton's Grand Style*, 78.

60. As part of the research for this chapter, I worked with Chris Curtis, a computational linguist, to develop a depictive search: a machine learning classifier that uses a support vector machine to identify depictives in a corpus of parsed sentences. At the time

of writing, the classifier was not performing with anything approaching sufficient recall or precision.

61. See Virgil, *Aeneid* 6.706, "hunc circum innumerae gentes populique volabant," which describes the souls waiting to be reborn as innumerable but does not delay the adjective or place it at the start of a line, as Homer does.

62. We could also construe Homer's *murioi* as a substantive noun—much in the way we speak of "the rich" or "the poor"—and subject of the verb: "The countless stood."

63. Helen Darbyshire, ed., *The Early Lives of Milton* (London: Constable, 1932), 179, 343.

64. Gregory Machacek, *Milton and Homer: Written to Aftertimes* (Pittsburgh: Duquesne UP, 2011), 32.

65. Citations to the 1850 text of *The Prelude* are to William Wordsworth, *The Prelude: The Four Texts (1798, 1799, 1805, 1850)*, ed. Jonathan Wordsworth (New York: Penguin, 1995).

66. Wallace Stevens, "Sunday Morning," in *The Collected Poems of Wallace Stevens* (New York: Vintage, 1990), 66–71.

67. Miles Coverdale, *Biblia the Bible* ([Southwark, UK?], 1535), Psalms 104:25.

68. John Milton, *Paradise Regained*, 4.335–38, in The John Milton Reading Room, www.dartmouth.edu/~milton/reading_room/pr/book_4/text.shtml; Mary Ann Radzinowicz, *Milton's Epics and the Book of Psalms* (Princeton, NJ: Princeton UP, 1989), 9.

69. John Dryden, *Essays of John Dryden*, ed. W. P. Ker, 2 vols. (Oxford: Clarendon, 1926), 1:268, 2:29; Virgil, *Aeneis*, in *The Works of Virgil*, trans. John Dryden (London, 1697), 560, lines 744–49.

70. See, e.g., M. Robert Anton, *The philosophers satyrs* (London, 1616), sig. B3v: "This glorious globe . . . Is whirld from East to West orbicular." Because CQPweb accepts regular expressions, it is possible to search for all instances of a word like *orbicular* that follows a verb by four words or less: _VV* (_*){0,4} {orbicular}.

71. The prayer is from a letter published in *A tender visitation of heavenly love*, by Richard Farnsworth, John Whitehead, and Thomas Greene (London, 1666).

72. Franco Moretti, *Distant Reading* (New York: Verso, 2013), 162.

73. Thomas N. Corns, *Milton's Language* (Oxford: Blackwell, 1990).

74. For an example of how automated classification of sentence structures can be submitted to quantitative analysis, see Sarah Allison, Marissa Gemma, Ryan Heuser, Franco Moretti, Amir Tevel, and Irena Yamboliev, *Style at the Scale of the Sentence*, Stanford Literary Lab Pamphlet 5 (Stanford, CA: Stanford Literary Lab, 2013). There is no discussion in the pamphlet of the accuracy of their automated sentence classification procedures.

75. Milton's note on "The Verse."

76. Obviously the conventions of earlier periods addressed some kinds of quantitative measures, such as the number of stresses and syllables in a line or the number of lines in a sonnet. At issue here are aggregate quantitative measures that only become visible through counting and computing.

77. See J. P. Kincaid, R. P. Fishburne, R. L. Rogers, and B. S. Chissom, *Derivation of New Readability Formulas (Automated Readability Index, Fog Count, and Flesch Reading Ease*

*formula) for Navy Enlisted Personnel*, Research Branch Report 8–75 (Memphis: Chief of Naval Technical Training, Naval Air Station, 1975). For a history of readability statistics, see George R. Klare, "The Formative Years," in *Readability: Its Past, Present, and Future*, ed. Beverley L. Zakaluk and S. Jay Samuels (Newark, NJ: International Reading Association, 1988), 14–34; and Klare, "Readability," in *Handbook of Reading Research*, ed. P. David Pearson, Rebecca Barr, Michael L. Kamil, and Peter Mosenthal (New York: Longman, 1984), 681–744. I recall with some embarrassment that in middle school I used to revise my essays based on the Flesch-Kinkaid Grade Level test, lengthening my sentences and using bigger words in order to achieve a higher grade-level score.

78. Craig, "Stylistic Analysis and Authorship Studies."

79. See Michael Witmore, "The Ancestral Text," *Wine Dark Sea* (blog), 9 May 2011, winedarksea.org/?p=979.

80. For the claim that we "have never been human," see Donna Haraway, *When Species Meet* (Minneapolis: U of Minnesota P, 2008), 1–133. Haraway borrows the formulation of her posthumanist argument from Bruno Latour, *We Have Never Been Modern*, trans. Catherine Porter (Cambridge, MA: Harvard UP, 1993).

81. Stephen Ramsay, *Reading Machines: Towards an Algorithmic Criticism* (Urbana: U of Illinois P, 2011), 32–57. For the concept *deformance*, see Jerome McGann, "Deformance and Interpretation," with Lisa Samuels, in McGann, *Radiant Textuality: Literature after the World Wide Web* (New York: Palgrave, 2001), chap. 4.

82. Ramsay, *Reading Machines*, 32.

83. On the translation into quantitative measures, see Franco Moretti, *"Operationalizing": Or the Function of Measurement in Modern Literary Theory*, Stanford Literary Lab Pamphlet 6 (Stanford, CA: Stanford Literary Lab, 2013), 1–13.

84. See Timothy Williamson, "On the Structure of Higher-Order Vagueness," *Mind* 108.429 (1999): 127–43; and Williamson, *Vagueness* (London: Routledge, 1994). Williamson's epistemicism, though it argues for precise boundaries for vague concepts, is not useful for translating quantitative measures, since it also holds that those precise boundaries are unknowable.

85. Allison et al. observe in "Style at the Scale," 26, that "there are concepts—like "blue", "bald", or "tadpole"—that signify through a certain amount of vagueness, rather than despite it, and style is probably one of them."

86. Underwood and Sellers, "Emergence of Literary Diction."

87. See Matthew L. Jockers, *Macroanalysis: Digital Methods and Literary History* (Urbana: U of Illinois P, 2013), 108; Jockers briefly considers, and wisely rejects, two numinous worlds that have their own causal order: Jung's "collective unconscious" and Rupert Sheldrake's account of an occult, magical, or "telepathy-like interconnection between organisms."

88. See Martin Mueller, "The Great Digital Migration," *Scalable Reading* (blog), 7 May 2014, scalablereading.northwestern.edu/2012/08/13/the-great-digital-migration/, on the "algorithmic amenability" of digital texts.

89. Corns, *Milton's Language*, 32–33.

90. Corns, *Milton's Language*, 32.

91. *Latinity* appears in English as early as the mid-seventeenth century as a term of praise meaning, as Edward Phillips later defined it, "an incorrupt speaking or pronouncing of the Latin tongue." *The new world of English words* (London, 1658). See Gulielmus Gnaphaeus, *The Tragedy of Ascolatus*, trans. John Palsgrave (London, 1640), sigs. A4v–B1r, for an early use.

92. Ezra Pound, *ABC of Reading* (Boston: Faber, 1991), 51; Pound is rendering judgment on *Paradise Lost* 5.611–12.

93. I take no side here in the Latinity debate, a debate that materialist inquiry, because it works through the comparative study of markers that appear in texts of both languages, will tend to dissolve in any case. For the most sensitive account of this debate, see John Hale, *Milton's Languages: The Impact of Multilingualism on Style* (Cambridge: Cambridge UP, 1997), 105–30, which argues that the syntax and diction of Latin and English are largely overlapping categories.

94. Graham Harman, *Tool-Being: Heidegger and the Metaphysics of Objects* (Chicago: Open Court, 2002), 21.

95. Allison et al., "Style at the Scale."

### Chapter 7. Shakespeare's Constructicon

1. David Crystal and Ben Crystal, *Shakespeare's Words: A Glossary and Language Companion* (New York: Penguin, 2002); Thomas Dolby, *The Shakespearian Dictionary: Forming a General Index to All the Popular Expressions, and Most Striking Passages in the Works of Shakespeare* (London, 1832).

2. On the concept of reference genres, see Ann Blair, "Reading Strategies for Coping with Information Overload, ca. 1550–1700," *Journal of the History of Ideas* 64.1 (2003): 11–28, 12.

3. See Andrew Becket, *A Concordance to Shakespeare* (London, 1787); Samuel Ayscough, *An Index to the Remarkable Passages and Words Made Use of by Shakspeare* (London, 1790); and Arthur Sherbo, "Ayscough, Samuel (1745–1804)," *Oxford Dictionary of National Biography* (Oxford: Oxford UP, 2004), www.oxforddnb.com/view/article/953. For automatic concordancing, see AntConc (www.laurenceanthony.net/software/antconc/) or the concordance function of Open Source Shakespeare (www.opensourceshakespeare .org/concordance/).

4. Eric Partridge, *Shakespeare's Bawdy: A Literary and Psychological Essay, and a Comprehensive Glossary* (London: Routledge, 1947).

5. R. Chris Hassel, *Shakespeare's Religious Language: A Dictionary* (New York: Continuum, 2005); Marion Gibson and Jo Ann Esra, *Shakespeare's Demonology: A Dictionary* (London: Arden Bloomsbury, 2014); Nicki Faircloth and Vivian Thomas, *Shakespeare's Plants and Gardens: A Dictionary* (London: Arden Bloomsbury, 2014). For further titles in the Arden Shakespeare Dictionary series, see www.bloomsbury.com /uk/series/arden-shakespeare-dictionaries.

6. The coinage of *constructicon* is usually attributed to Dan Jurafsky, "A Cognitive Model of Sentence Interpretation: The Construction Grammar Approach," International Computer Science Institute Technical Report (Berkeley: International Computer Science Institute, 1993), 6, www.icsi.berkeley.edu/ftp/global/pub/techreports/1993/tr-93-077.pdf.

7. Except in cases where they appear as the result of a corpus search or are cited in specific editions, passages from Shakespeare's works are quoted from *Shakespeare's Plays from Folger Digital Texts*, ed. Barbara Mowat, Paul Werstine, Michael Poston, and Rebecca Niles (Washington, DC: Folger Shakespeare Library, n.d.), www .folgerdigitaltexts.org. For the classic discussion of idioms, see Geoffrey Nunberg, Ivan A. Sag, and Thomas Wasow, "Idioms," *Language* 70 (1994): 491–538, which defines an idiom as an expression for which "meaning and use can't be predicted, or at least entirely predicted, on the basis of a knowledge of the independent conventions that determine the use of their constituents when they appear in isolation from one another" (492).

8. On the *way*-construction *[NPj [V NPj's way OBL]]*, see Elizabeth Closs Traugott and Graeme Trousdale, *Constructionalization and Constructional Changes* (Oxford: Oxford UP, 2013), 76–93; Adele E. Goldberg, *Constructions: A Construction Grammar Approach to Argument Structure* (Chicago: U of Chicago P, 1995), 199–218; and Michael Israel, "The *Way* Constructions Grow," in *Conceptual Structure, Discourse, and Language*, ed. Adele E. Goldberg (Stanford, CA: Center for the Study of Language and Information, 1996), 217–30.

9. For an extended treatment of the ditransitive construction, see Adele E. Goldberg, *Constructions at Work: The Nature of Generalization in Language* (New York: Oxford UP, 2006), 26–33; I have adapted the continuum of constructions for inclusion in a constructicon from p. 5.

10. See Andrew Hardie, "CQPweb—Combining Power, Flexibility and Usability in a Corpus Analysis Tool," *International Journal of Corpus Linguistics* 17.3 (2012): 380–409.

11. Stephen Greenblatt, *Shakespearean Negotiations: The Circulation of Social Energy in Renaissance England* (Berkeley: U of California P, 1988), 4.

12. Paul Innes, *Class and Society in Shakespeare: A Dictionary* (London: Continuum, 2007).

13. Seneca, *Hercules Oetaeus*, in *Seneca his tenne tragedies, translated into Englysh*, trans. John Studley (London, 1581), 214.

14. See George T. Wright, "Hendiadys and *Hamlet*," *PMLA* 96 (1981): 168–93. For the classic treatment of Shakespeare's "schemes of grammar," see Sister Miriam Joseph, *Shakespeare's Use of the Arts of Language* (New York: Columbia UP, 1947), 43–89. One might alternatively parse "rogue and peasant slave" as two attributive adjectives modifying a single noun head.

15. My rehearsal of transformational analysis is obviously, and necessarily, both cursory and reductive. For a landmark treatment of *wh-movement*, see Noam Chomsky, "On wh-movement," in *Formal Syntax*, ed. Peter W. Culicover, Thomas Wasow, and Adrian Akmajian (New York: Academic, 1977). For leading examples of transformational approaches to literature, see Richard Ohmann, "Literature as Sentences," *College English* 27.4 (1966): 261–67; Donald Freeman, "Keats's 'To Autumn': Poetry as Process and Pattern," *Language and Style* 11 (1978): 3–17; and Seymour Chatman, "Milton's Participial Style," *PMLA* 83.5 (1968): 1386–99.

16. I have omitted pattern matches that have an obviously different structure, as in the epilogue to *As You Like It*, where Rosalind complains: "What a case am I in then

that am neither a good epilogue nor cannot insinuate with you in the behalf of a good play!" (lines 7–9).

17. For a facsimile of the Q1 page, sig. E4v, see Internet Shakespeare Editions, internetshakespeare.uvic.ca/Library/facsimile/book/BL_Q1_Ham/32.

18. For an influentially skeptical view of the concept of memorial reconstruction, see Laurie E. Maguire, *Shakespearean Suspect Texts: The "Bad" Quartos and Their Context* (New York: Cambridge UP, 1996). For the history of the reception and scholarly treatment of Q1, see Zachary Lesser, *Hamlet after Q1: An Uncanny History of the Shakespearean Text* (Philadelphia: U of Pennsylvania P, 2014).

19. Retrieved using the same search string in the CQPweb corpus of Shakespeare's First Folio, also available (for free) at CQPweb, cqpweb.lancs.ac.uk.

20. See article 9 in Church of England, *Articles, whereupon it was agreed by the archbishoppes and bishoppes* (London, 1571), 7.

21. William Shakespeare, *Hamlet*, ed. Ann Thompson and Neil Taylor, Arden Shakespeare, 3rd ser. (London: Arden, 2006), 217.

22. Searching for negated past participles is also possible using relatively simple regular expressions and POS tags: *(un\*_VVN\*|dis\*_VVN\*|in\*_VVN\*) \* (un\*_VVN\*| dis\*_VVN\*|in\*_VVN\*) \* (un\*_VVN\*|dis\*_VVN\*|in\*_VVN\*).*

23. In contrast to the first list of search results, the list in table 7.2 contains false hits, some of which, like "revealed and made known" and "supposed and taken for granted," have clearly different syntactic structures, albeit similar discursive functions.

24. M. M. Bakhtin, "Discourse in the Novel," in *The Dialogic Imagination: Four Essays*, ed. Michael Holquist, trans. Caryl Emerson and Michael Holquist (Austin: U of Texas P, 1981), 294. For the seminal treatment of how Bakhtin's notion of dialogism can inform the study of Shakespeare's language, see Lynne Magnusson, *Shakespeare and Social Dialogue* (Cambridge: Cambridge UP, 1999).

25. I hasten to acknowledge that the best of Shakespeare's close readers are frequently able to hear the provenance even of abstract and empty linguistic forms. To my mind, no critic has been more talented in this regard than Stephen Booth. See his *Shakespeare's Sonnets: Edited With Analytic Commentary* (New Haven, CT: Yale UP, 1977); and Booth, *An Essay on Shakespeare's Sonnets* (New Haven, CT: Yale UP, 1969). I understand corpus query tools in part as hearing aids, prosthetic extensions of and partial replacements for the acuity of Booth's ear, which allow us to turn that acuity to the interpretive, historicist, and sociological aims his own research has largely abjured.

26. Alexander Schmidt, *Shakespeare-Lexicon: A Complete Dictionary of All the English Words, Phrases and Constructions in the Works of the Poet*, 2 vols. (Berlin: G. Reimer, 1874–75).

27. The literature on the comparative correlative is extensive, but two articles have been especially influential: Charles J. Fillmore, "Varieties of Conditional Sentences," in *Proceedings of the Third Eastern States Conference on Linguistics: The University of Pittsburgh, Pittsburgh, Pennsylvania, October 10–11, 1986*, ed. Fred Marshall (Columbus: Ohio State University, 1987): 163–82; and Peter Culicover and Ray Jackendoff, "The View from the Periphery: The English Comparative Correlative," *Linguistic Inquiry* 30 (1999): 543–71.

28. See Charles J. Fillmore, Russell R. Lee-Goldman, and Russell Rhodes, "The FrameNet Constructicon," in *Sign-Based Construction Grammar*, ed. Hans C. Boas and Ivan A. Sag (Chicago: Center for the Study of Language and Information, 2011), 309–72, for a treatment of how abstract and variable constructions can be cataloged and represented in a constructicon. For an account of the cognitive organization of constructions, see Goldberg, *Constructions*, 67–100. The FrameNet lexicon is available at framenet.icsi.berkeley.edu. See also Hiroaki Sato, "A Search Tool for FrameNet Constructicon," *Proceedings of the Eighth International Conference on Language Resources and Evaluation* (2012), www.lrec-conf.org/proceedings/lrec2012/pdf/563_Paper.pdf.

29. Peter Stallybrass, "Against Thinking," *PMLA* 122.5 (2007): 1580–87, 1581–82.

30. Stallybrass, "Against Thinking," 1581.

31. Stallybrass, "Against Thinking," 1583.

32. I say "presumably" because this is not always the case: one might, for example, know that the variable idiom *hoist with [Possessive Pronoun] own petard* (as in *Hamlet* 3.4.230) roughly means "hurt by [his, her, its, their, our] own plan" without also knowing the meaning of the words *hoist* (lifted, launched) and *petard* (bomb).

33. Robert Rollock, *A treatise of Gods effectual calling*, trans. Henry Holland (London, 1603), 177, sig. X3; Abraham Fraunce, *The lavviers logike* (London, 1588), 87, sig. A.iii.r.

34. As in the earlier lists of search results, not all results are genuine matches.

35. George Gifford, *A short reply* (London, 1591), 86, sig. M2v, boldface mine.

36. The chief sources of the Protestant doctrine of Christian liberty were Martin Luther's *On the Freedom of A Christian* and book 3, chapter 19, of John Calvin's *Institutes*. For a brief survey of the doctrine and its history in England, see Arthur Barker, "Christian Liberty in Milton's Divorce Pamphlets," *Modern Language Review* 35.2 (1940): 153–61, esp. 153–56.

37. Thomas Bell, *The survey of popery* (London, 1596), 260, sig. S3v, boldface mine.

38. Bakhtin, "Discourse in the Novel," 259–422, 259, 279–80, 348.

39. M. M. Bakhtin, *Problems of Dostoevsky's Poetics*, ed. Caryl Emerson (Minneapolis: U of Minnesota P, 1984), 143. Bakhtin comes closest to discussing the dialogic character of linguistic forms in the discussion of grammar in his essay "The Problem of Speech Genres," in *Speech Genres and Other Late Essays* (Austin: U of Texas P, 1986), 66–71, before he moves on to define what he calls "the *real unit* of speech communication: the utterance" (71). Following Bakhtin, Julia Kristeva also locates dialogism within the word; see "Word, Dialogism, and Novel," in *Desire in Language* (New York: Columbia UP, 1980), 64–90.

40. Bakhtin, "Discourse in the Novel," 262–63.

41. Bakhtin, "Discourse in the Novel," 294.

42. Shakespeare scholars have led cultural and historicist approaches to the study of grammar and syntax. See Magnusson, *Shakespeare and Social Dialogue*; Magnusson, "A Play of Modals: Grammar and Potential Action in Early Shakespeare," *Shakespeare Survey* 62 (2009): 69–80; Sylvia Adamson, "Questions of Identity in Renaissance Drama: New Historicism Meets Old Philology," *Shakespeare Quarterly* 61.1 (2010): 56–77; and Brian Cummings, *The Literary Culture of the Reformation: Grammar and Grace* (Oxford: Oxford UP, 2002).

43. Edwin Abbott Abbott, *A Shakespearian Grammar* (London: Macmillan, 1869); Wilhelm Franz, *Shakespeare-Grammatik* (Cöthen, Germany: O. Schulze, 1897); N. F. Blake, *A Grammar of Shakespeare's Language* (London: Palgrave, 2001); Jonathan Hope, *Shakespeare's Grammar* (London: Arden, 2003).

44. Raymond Williams, *Keywords: A Vocabulary of Culture and Society*, rev. ed. (Oxford: Oxford UP, 1983).

### Chapter 8. God Is Dead, Long Live Philology

1. For one prominent example, see Jacques Derrida, *Of Grammatology*, trans. Gayatri Chakravorty Spivak, corrected ed. (Baltimore: Johns Hopkins UP, 1997), which seeks to recover the Nietzschean conception of a radicalized "interpretation" that liberates "the signifier from its dependence or derivation with respect to the logos and the related concept of truth or the primary signified" (19).

2. Martin Heidegger, *Being and Time*, trans. John Macquarrie and Edward Robinson (New York: Harper, 1962), 189. Heidegger's thinking often unfolds explicitly through the analysis of linguistic forms as well as words; this is the case with what he calls the as-structure, which he describes as interpreting *something as something, X as Y*.

3. In challenging the linearity of the linguistic signal asserted by Saussure in *Course in General Linguistics*, trans. Roy Harris (Chicago: Open Court, 2002), 69–70, I am merely following the lead of virtually all linguistics after Chomsky, though in a decidedly anti-Chomskyan tradition.

4. Quantitative digital humanities work has generally supposed that digital tools reveal large patterns and longer trends but do not contribute to the interpretation of individual works of literature. For an early argument to this effect, see Mark Olsen, "Signs, Symbols and Discourses: A New Direction for Computer-Aided Literature Studies," *Computers and the Humanities* 27.5/6 (1993/94): 309–14.

5. See Eric Von Der Luft, "Sources of Nietzsche's 'God is Dead!' and its Meaning for Heidegger," *Journal of the History of Ideas* 45.2 (1984): 263–76; and Olaf Pluta, "'Deus est mortuus': Roots of Nietzsche's 'Gott ist todt!' in the Later Middle Ages," *Bochumer philosophisches Jahrbuch fur Antike und Mittelalter* 5.1 (2000): 129–45.

6. Martin Heidegger, "The Word of Nietzsche," in *The Question Concerning Technology, and Other Essays*, trans. William Lovitt (New York: Garland, 1977), 61.

7. Alain Badiou, *Briefings on Existence*, trans. Norman Madarasz (Albany: State U of New York P, 2006), 21. I distinguish interpretations of Nietzsche's dictum from attempts to rewrite or displace it, as in Jacques Lacan, *The Four Fundamental Concepts of Psychoanalysis*, ed. Jacques-Alain Miller, trans. Alan Sheridan, Seminar of Jacques Lacan Book XI (New York: Norton, 1998), 59: "For the true formula of atheism is not *God is dead* . . . the true formula of atheism is *God is unconscious*."

8. Badiou, *Briefings on Existence*, 23.

9. See, e.g., Martin Heidegger, *An Introduction to Metaphysics*, trans. Ralph Manheim (New Haven, CT: Yale UP, 1959), 52–70.

10. The quantifiability of syntactic ambiguity is essential to the computational parsing and construal of natural language. Most natural language processors attempt

to resolve syntactic ambiguity by assigning relative probabilities to a finite number of alternative syntaxes on the basis of the frequency of their occurrence in a reference corpus. For a more detailed account of syntactic ambiguity and its role in computational processing of language, see Daniel Jurafsky, "A Probabilistic Model of Lexical and Syntactic Access and Disambiguation," *Cognitive Science* 20 (1996): 137–94. I don't propose to take account of all forms of ambiguity here; my account excludes, for example, ambiguities of quantification and scope, though these are also finite and therefore quantifiable.

11. On the speculative grammar of the *modistae*, see Rens Bod, *A New History of the Humanities: The Search for Principles and Patterns* (Oxford: Oxford UP, 2013), 78–81. Noam Chomsky, *Cartesian Linguistics: A Chapter in the History of Rationalist Thought*, 3rd ed. (New York: Cambridge UP, 2009), 78–92, claims that the *Port-Royal Grammar* maintains the necessity of simple judgments employing the copula *est* as the deep structure of which all surface structures are transformations. The version of this claim in generative grammar's X-bar theory is that sentences have an inflectional head, expressing properties like tense or aspect, even if this head is not realized in the sentence's surface representation.

12. [Antoine Arnauld and Claude Lancelot], *Grammaire générale et raisonnée* (Paris, 1660), 91.

13. Michel Foucault, *The Order of Things: An Archaeology of the Human Sciences* (New York: Vintage Books, 1994), 93.

14. Heidegger, *Introduction to Metaphysics*, 92.

15. Derrida, *Of Grammatology*, 23. See also Derrida, "Letter to a Japanese Friend," in *A Derrida Reader: Between the Blinds*, trans. Peggy Kamuf (New York: Columbia UP, 1991), 275, where Derrida writes that "'deconstruction' is precisely the delimiting of ontology and above all of the third person present indicative: S is P"; Derrida, "Form and Meaning: A Note on the Phenomenology of Language," in *Margins of Philosophy*, trans. Alan Bass (Chicago: U of Chicago P, 1982), 155–74, where he writes of "the privilege of the *is* or the predicative statement" (170); and the entirety of Derrida, "The Supplement of Copula: Philosophy before Linguistics," in *Margins of Philosophy*, 175–205. Following the texts of Husserl, Heidegger, and (implicitly) Foucault before him, Derrida inquires into the copula *to be* (*etre*) as the transcategorial word or mark whose effect, even in its absence, is "to open language onto its exterior, to articulate the linguistic with the nonlinguistic" (196). I suppose here, contrary to the traditions assessed by these thinkers, that the transcategorial condition of possibility of assertion is not the verb *to be*, any other equivalent word or distribution of words, or even a supplementary absence of the word (as, for example, in a pause), but the abstract form of predication as such, including mere juxtaposition. In Derrida's terms, being is capable of signifying itself, of opening language to nonlanguage, in the absence of a name for "Being" (183). This would mean that *to be* is only one overt, lexical means of marking copulation, the joining of subject and predicate, albeit a mark privileged in some, but not all, languages by virtue of being, as Ronald W. Langacker puts it in "Cognitive Grammar," in *The Oxford Handbook of Linguistic Analysis*, ed. Berne Heine and Heiko Narrog (New York: Oxford UP, 2010), 87–109, the "maximally schematic member of its class" of "imperfective verbs" (104). The exceptionality and "privilege" of the

verb *to be* dissipates when we accept that abstract linguistic forms like *SP*, no less than overt lexical marks, are signs in their own right. While Derrida is right about the priority of philosophy to linguistics, Benveniste is nevertheless correct that it is ethnocentric to suppose that the verb *to be*, rather than predication as such, is the universal condition of the possibility of affirmation in language, as Heidegger does when he writes, in *An Introduction to Metaphysics*, that "assuming that the word 'being' did not even have its vaporous meaning, there would not be a single word" (82). See Emile Benveniste, "The Nominal Sentence" and "The Linguistic Function of 'To Be' and 'To Have,'" in *Problems in General Linguistics*, trans. Mary Elizabeth Meek (Coral Gables, FL: U of Miami P, 1971), 131–44 and 163–80, esp. 165–66.

16. Nietzsche does write "Gott starb," as in *Also Sprach Zarathustra* (Berlin: de Gruyter, 1988), 15, but neither he nor his interpreters elevate this into a pronouncement or formula on par with "Gott ist todt."

17. On the notion of expressions instantiating a hierarchy of variously abstract or schematic sign units, or symbolic assemblies, see Ronald W. Langacker, *Cognitive Grammar: A Basic Introduction* (Oxford: Oxford UP, 2008), 3–26.

18. Peter Abelard, *Epitome Theologiae Christianiae*, in *Patrologia Latina*, ed. J. P. Migne, 221 vols. (Berlin, 1835) 178:1715, col. B; Martin Luther, *Haußpostilla* (Nürnberg, 1584), sig. diii v; Martin Luther, *Biblia* (Wittemberg, 1583), 185; Friedrich Nietzsche, *The Gay Science*, trans. Josefine Nauckhoff (Cambridge: Cambridge UP, 2001), 58. Nietzsche could easily have looked up multiple German instantiations of *Gott ist P* in Karl Friedrich Wilhelm Wander, *Deutsches Sprichworter-Lexicon*, 5 vols. (Leipzig: F. A. Brockhaus, 1870), 2:31–35.

19. Immanuel Kant, *Der einzig mögliche Beweisgrund zu einer Demonstration des Daseyns Gottes* (Königsberg, 1763), 9–10, sigs. A4r–v.

20. Georg Wilhelm Friedrich Hegel, *Phänomenologie des Geistes* (Berlin: Duncker und Humblot, 1832), 50; Hegel, *Phenomenology of Spirit*, trans. A. V. Miller, rev. ed. (New York: Oxford UP, 1978), 38.

21. Ernst H. Kantorowicz, *The King's Two Bodies: A Study in Mediaeval Political Theology* (Princeton, NJ: Princeton UP, 1957), 410–11.

22. Karl Baumbach, *Staats-Lexicon* (Leipzig, 1882), 495, s.v. "Rex non moritur."

23. Nietzsche, *Gay Science*, 109.

24. See, e.g., Pluta, "Deus est mortuus."

25. That various forms may accommodate "Gott ist todt" can be treated as an extension of the lexical concept of homonymy, since all of these forms, in their instantiation, sound the same.

26. Absent either a set of a priori formal constraints (parsimony, economy, simplicity, perfection, etc.) or the check of historical inquiry and interpretation (comparative evidence of signifying conventions retrieved from the archive), the potential number of forms instantiated by even the simplest of utterances is nonfinite. See Saul Kripke, *Wittgenstein on Rules and Private Language*, rev. ed. (Cambridge, MA: Harvard UP, 1992), 7–54.

27. Since Nietzsche wrote and published "Gott ist todt" in multiple texts, it is possible that the same sequence of words instantiates a different form or set of forms in each of its appearances.

28. On the limits of truth-conditional approaches to semantics and specifically to synonymy, see Adele E. Goldberg, *Constructions: A Construction Grammar Approach to Argument Structure* (Chicago: U of Chicago P, 1995), 103; and Charles Fillmore, "An Alternative to Checklist Theories of Meaning," *Berkeley Linguistics Society* 1 (1973): 123–31.

29. See Aristotle, *Categories. On Interpretation. Prior Analytics*, trans. H. P. Cooke and Hugh Trennedick, Loeb Classical Library (Cambridge, MA: Harvard UP, 1938), 16.

30. See Richard Gaskin, *On the Unity of the Proposition* (New York: Oxford UP, 2008), for a compelling account of the (infinitely regressing) glue that holds the proposition together.

31. On Husserl's concept of "free ideality," see Jacques Derrida, *Edmund Husserl's Origin of Geometry: An Introduction*, trans. John P. Leavey Jr. (Lincoln: U of Nebraska P, 1989), 70–72. Even if we choose to understand *SP* as the limit case of abstraction from empirical utterances, we are still confronted with the transcendental question of this limit's origin. Is the *SP* that is an element of the speaker's linguistic competence a fully abstract or empty form, identical to this transcendental limit, or does it retain a structure derived from the predicative utterances from which it was abstracted, only approaching the empty, transcendental limit asymptotically?

32. I adopt my examples of signifying systems from Roland Barthes, *Elements of Semiology*, trans. Anette Lavers and Colin Smith (New York: Hill & Wang, 1999), 25–31.

33. Roland Barthes, *The Language of Fashion*, trans. Andy Stafford (New York: Bloomsbury, 2013), 27. Because the signifying units of dress are precisely what is at issue in his treatment, Barthes goes on to compare them with both syntax and phonology. Though he suggests that fashion, as presented in newspapers and magazines, "brings the semiologist back towards a lexical state of the vestimentary signs" (28), he later concludes that the "univocal lexicon" (44) posited by fashion journalism is a mythology, an ideological "distortion" (39).

34. For an excellent primer on musical form that has much to teach us about linguistic form, see William E. Caplin, *Classical Form: A Theory of Formal Functions for the Instrumental Music of Hayden, Mozart, and Beethoven* (New York: Oxford UP, 1998).

35. Michel Foucault, *The Order of Things: An Archaeology of the Human Sciences* (New York: Vintage Books, 1994), 382.

36. Foucault, *Order of Things*, 379.

37. Foucault, *Order of Things*, 380.

38. Michel Foucault, "Maurice Blanchot: The Thought from Outside," trans. Brian Massumi, in *Foucault/Blanchot*, by Michel Foucault and Maurice Blanchot (New York: Zone Books, 1987), 54.

39. Foucault, to be sure, historicizes grammar as a disciplinary formation and as an object in the field of linguistic knowledge, as in *The Order of Things*, 81–92, and in his 1969 introduction to Arnauld and Lancelot's *Grammaire générale et raisonnée*, in Michel Foucault, *Dits et écrits*, ed. Daniel Defert and François Ewald, 4 vols. (Paris: Gallimard, 1994), 1:733–52. But a historical account of grammar itself (as one might offer an account of a historical vocabulary) is a different enterprise from the history of the study of grammar. See also *The Archaeology of Knowledge and the Discourse on Language*, trans.

A. M. Sheridan Smith (New York: Pantheon, 1972), 207, where Foucault vaguely describes generative grammar as a different but "related analysis."

40. Foucault, *Order of Things*, 382. Following the path established by Jacques Derrida, *The Animal That Therefore I Am*, ed. Marie-Louise Mallet, trans. David Wills (New York: Fordham UP, 2008), animal studies scholars, most prominently Cary Wolfe in *What Is Posthumanism?* (Minneapolis: U of Minnesota P, 2010), 31–48, have contested language as the property that distinguishes human from animal. Yet the deconstructive work of Derrida and Wolfe, at least, has remained firmly lexicocentric, operating within a treatment of the word (what Derrida calls *l'animot*, "the animal word") that leaves the concept of grammar unchallenged as the innate power proper solely to man.

41. Foucault, *Order of Things*, 381. Though Foucault aims, as he says to Giulio Preti in "The Question of Culture," in *Michel Foucault Live: Collected Interviews, 1961–1984*, ed. Sylvère Lotringer (1972; reprint, New York: Semiotext[e], 1996), to "historicize . . . the transcendental," he cannot dismiss the possibility of the transcendental as an "irreducible *residuum*." Similarly, my formulation here does not rule out the possibility of grammar as an innate or transcendental capacity, even if that capacity were to be reconceived as the condition of the possibility of any constructicon whatsoever.

42. Geoffrey Galt Harpham, *Language Alone: The Critical Fetish of Modernity* (New York: Routledge, 2002), ix, 45.

43. See Michael Tomasello, *Constructing a Language: A Usage Based Theory of Language Acquisition* (Cambridge, MA: Harvard UP, 2003), for an extensive account of the species-specific cognitive abilities that allow humans, but not other primates, to learn and employ language.

44. Harpham, *Language Alone*, 26.

45. Foucault, *Order of Things*, 386.

46. For a recent account of grammar as the answer to the anthropological question—as the differentiating inheritance of humankind—see Noam Chomsky, *What Kind of Creatures Are We?* (New York: Columbia UP, 2016), 1–26. To the extent that Chomsky allies his account of grammar with Descartes, as in *Cartesian Linguistics: A Chapter in the History of Rationalist Thought*, 3rd ed. (Cambridge, MA: Cambridge UP, 2009), the assimilation of grammar to the sign system offers an anti-Cartesian linguistics as the continuation of the anti-Cartesian account of the subject. The historical validity of Chomsky's claims for a Cartesian linguistics tradition has been powerfully challenged by Hans Aarsleff in "The History of Linguistics and Professor Chomsky," *Language* 46.3 (1970): 570–85.

47. For seminal works on subject formation, see Lacan, *Écrits*; Louis Althusser, *On the Reproduction of Capitalism: Ideology and Ideological State Apparatuses*, trans. G. M. Goshgarian (New York: Verso, 2014); Judith Butler, *Gender Trouble*, 2nd ed. (New York: Routledge, 1999); Gayatri Chakravorty Spivak, "Can the Subaltern Speak?," in *Marxism and the Interpretation of Culture*, ed. Cary Nelson and Lawrence Grossberg (Urbana: U of Illinois P, 1988), 271–313; Spivak, *A Critique of Postcolonial Reason* (Cambridge, MA: Harvard UP, 1999); and bell hooks, *Yearning: Race, Gender, and Politics* (Cambridge, MA: South End, 1990), 20. Much of the last few decades of thinking on subject formation is

gathered and eloquently synthesized in the essays collected in Butler's *Senses of the Subject* (New York: Fordham UP, 2015).

48. Althusser, *On the Reproduction of Capitalism*, 190.

49. In popular venues, essays claiming that the digital humanities will remove the humanities from its traditional concerns and methods have constituted a minor genre in their own right. See, e.g., Stephen Marche, "Literature Is Not Data: Against Digital Humanities," *Los Angeles Review of Books*, 28 October 2012, lareviewofbooks.org/article /literature-is-not-data-against-digital-humanities; Steven Pinker, "Science is Not Your Enemy," *New Republic*, 6 August 2013; Leon Wieselthier, "Crimes against Humanities," *New Republic*, 3 September 2013, www.newrepublic.com/article/114548/leon-wieseltier -responds-steven-pinkers-scientism; and Adam Kirsch, "Technology Is Taking Over English Departments," *New Republic*, 2 May 2014, www.newrepublic.com/article /117428/limits-digital-humanities-adam-kirsch. Though Marche, Kirsch, and Wieselth- ier are opposed to Pinker's call for the assimilation of the humanities to the sciences, they share with him the belief that the digital humanities is by its nature opposed to humanistic inquiry. Such claims are less frequent in academic writing, though see David L. Hoover, "The End of the Irrelevant Text: Electronic Texts, Linguistics, and Literary Theory," *Digital Humanities Quarterly* 1.2 (2007), www.digitalhumanities.org /dhq/vol/1/2/000012/000012.html.

# Index

Abbott, Edwin Abbott, 210
Abelard, Peter, 133, 216
Abrams, M.H., 94
abstraction, xvii, xix, 6, 8, 11, 18, 22, 26, 87, 129, 151, 159, 194, 196, 204, 210, 213, 217, 220, 223, 230n7, 282n31
*act as if*: Brodsky's books on, 99; Dale Carnegie and, 124–25; as counterpart to *WWJD*, 113; Erasmus and, 257n19; form of, 100; heuristic tradition of, 104; history of, xvi, 126; William James and, 116, 118, 122–23; Immanuel Kant and, 109–13, 123; Walter Lippmann and, 117; and manipulability of the real, 120; Blaise Pascal and, xiv, 104–8, 114–15; Pauline, 103; as a positive imperative, 101; pragmatic, 119, 129; Seneca's, 102; seventeenth-century divines and, 108; Thomas Traherne and, 107
adjectives, depictive. *See* depictives
Aers, David, 56
Affleck, Ben, 120
Alcoholics Anonymous, 99
algorithms, 29, 58, 184, 236n61
*Aliens*, 8
allatonceness, 32
AltaVista, 33
Althusser, Louis, 5, 105, 224
Amar, Akhil Reed, 14, 16
Andrews, Lancelot, x
Anthony, Susan B., 14
Aquinas, Thomas, 133, 145
archives, 3; digital, xii–xiii, xv–xvi, xviii, 19, 22, 31, 37, 45, 52, 54, 56–57, 64, 72, 85, 88, 97, 146, 152, 162, 199, 209, 225, 246n72; inclusive, 30; as inegalitarian, 59; nature of the, 33; versus corpora, 58. *See also* search
Arden Shakespeare Dictionary, 194, 199
Ariosto, 67, 68, 71, 80–82
Aristotle, 72, 106, 131, 143–44, 219, 264–65n49
Articles of Confederation, 15–17

articulation, 52, 102, 125
Ascham, Roger, 167, 267n70
associations, 86–91, 95–96
Athenaeus of Naucratis, 38–39
attachments, 170–73, 177–78, 214, 218. *See also* categorization
Auerbach, Erich, xvii, 129, 155, 159–60, 162–63, 178, 270–71n28
Augustine, 133, 146
Austen, Jane, xiii, 89, 131
Ayscough, Samuel, 193

Bacon, Francis, 29, 52, 112
Badiou, Alain, 213–14, 219
Bakhtin, Mikhail, 201, 209–10
Balzac, Honoré de, 9
Bamman, David, 64
Banks, John, 70
Barthes, Roland, xv, 5, 93, 161, 162, 205–6, 209, 221
Baudelaire, Charles, 157
Baxter, Richard, 152
Beaumont, Sir George, 81
Becket, Andrew, 193
Behn, Aphra, 70
Berkeley FrameNet, 204
Bernard of Clairvaux, 133
Bhabha, Homi, 6
Bible, 5, 134, 159, 162, 164; Coverdale, 179; King James, 216
Bidart, Frank, xii
Blair, Ann, xx, 38
Blake, N.F., 210
Blake, William, 271n41
blogs, 3, 8, 90
Bloom, Harold, 63–64, 68, 70, 72, 92, 97
*Boiler Room*, 120
Borges, Jorge Luis, 158
Bourdieu, Pierre, 90
Bowyer, James, 51
Boyd, Holly, 99
Brandon, Samuel, 70, 83
Brassier, Ray, 183